CALIFORNIA

A Study of American Character

A CALIFORNIA LEGACY BOOK

Santa Clara University and Heyday Books are pleased to publish the California Legacy series, vibrant and relevant writings drawn from California's past and present.

Santa Clara University—founded in 1851 on the site of the eighth of California's original 21 missions—is the oldest institution of higher learning in the state. A Jesuit institution, it is particularly aware of its contribution to California's cultural heritage and its responsibility to preserve and celebrate that heritage.

Heyday Books, founded in 1974, specializes in critically acclaimed books on California literature, history, natural history, and ethnic studies.

Books in the California Legacy series appear as anthologies, single-author collections, reprints of important books, and original works. Taken together, these volumes bring readers a new perspective on California's cultural life, a perspective that honors diversity and finds great pleasure in the eloquence of human expression.

Series editor: Terry Beers
Publisher: Malcolm Margolin
Advisory committee: Stephen Becker, William Deverell, Peter Facione, Charles Faulhaber, David Fine, Steven Gilbar, Dana Gioia, Ron Hansen, Gerald Haslam, Robert Hass, Jack Hicks, Timothy Hodson, James Houston, Jeanne Wakatsuki Houston, Maxine Hong Kingston, Frank LaPena, Ursula K. Le Guin, Jeff Lustig, Tillie Olsen, Ishmael Reed, Alan Rosenus, Robert Senkewicz, Gary Snyder, Kevin Starr, Richard Walker, Alice Waters, Jennifer Watts, Al Young.

Thanks to the English Department at Santa Clara University and to Regis McKenna for their support of the California Legacy series.

CALIFORNIA

A Study of American Character

**FROM THE CONQUEST IN 1846
TO THE SECOND VIGILANCE COMMITTEE
IN SAN FRANCISCO**

BY

JOSIAH ROYCE

Introduction by Ronald A. Wells

Santa Clara University, Santa Clara
Heyday Books, Berkeley

Library of Congress Cataloging-in-Publication Data

Royce, Josiah, 1855-1916.
  California : a study of American character / Josiah Royce ; introduction by Ronald A. Wells.
     p. cm.
Originally published: Boston : Houghton, Mifflin, 1886.
  ISBN 1-890771-52-X (pbk. : alk. paper)
  1. California--History. 2. National characteristics, American. 3. San Francisco Committee of Vigilance of 1856. I. Wells, Ronald, 1941- II. Title.
  F865 .R83 2002
  979.4--dc21
                                        2002010510

Cover Design: Rebecca LeGates. Image of California State Constitution courtesy of the California State Archives.
Printing and Binding: Banta Book Group, Menasha, WI

Orders, inquiries, and correspondence should be addressed to:
       Heyday Books
       P. O. Box 9145, Berkeley, CA 94709
       (510) 549-3564, Fax (510) 549-1889
       www.heydaybooks.com

Printed in the United States of America

10 9 8 7 6 5 4 3 2 1

Contents

Acknowledgments

This work could not have been undertaken and accomplished without help. I wish to thank: Dirk and JoAnn Mellema of Walnut Creek, California, whose inspiration and generosity made possible the study of California and the West at their alma mater; James Bratt and William Katerberg, successive directors of the Mellema Program in Western American Studies at Calvin College; C. Stephen Evans, former Dean for Research and Scholarship at Calvin, for a Calvin Faculty Research Fellowship and for pointing me toward a grant from the MacGregor Foundation; Allan Waddilove, the brilliant and indefatigable research assistant provided by the MacGregor grant; the archival staffs at Harvard, UC Berkeley, and UCLA, who were unfailingly helpful; and, finally, Barbara, my wife and intellectual partner, a scholar in her own right, who supports me and improves my ideas and writing.

Foreword

In 1886, Josiah Royce, a young instructor at Harvard University, published a book that was among the first serious histories of California. It has a long nineteenth-century title: *California, From the Conquest in 1846 to the Second Vigilance Committee in San Francisco: A Study of American Character* (hereafter we will simply call it *California*). It has been mostly forgotten by those who would interpret the meaning of the American phase of California history, with the notable exception of Kevin Starr. As we seek to sort out the various meanings for us of California's founding, we do well to listen again to Josiah Royce, a writer who both admired and criticized what was to become "the California dream" in the American mind.[1]

Royce had not set out to be a historian of California. When the intended author for the California volume in the American Commonwealth series died suddenly, the editor at Houghton Mifflin, Horace Scudder, moved to fill the gap by asking friends in the academic and business communities of Cambridge and Boston for suggestions. He soon came upon Royce, who had come to Harvard as a one-year replacement for William James.

James later said in a letter to a friend that he enjoyed the company of Royce "who is just thirty years old and a perfect little Socrates for wisdom and humor."[2] This "little Socrates" was chosen for the state history series not because he was an academically trained historian of California but because he was available through Harvard connections and because he was a native Californian. Later, he would make a name for himself as a moral philosopher, teaching at Harvard for thirty years and writing more than a score of books and many articles on philosophy.[3] While it is his role as historian that interests us here, we cannot take Royce's historical work out of the context of his larger efforts in philosophy.[4]

Though not trained in history, Royce did his research and writing with the concerns of a scholar, with meticulous attention to detail and documentation. In fact, he later told a friend that writing history was much more difficult than writing philosophy, because in history one had to stick to empirical reality.[5] Not only did he think and write like a scholar, he had the good fortune to have nearly unlimited access to the library of publisher and historian Hubert Howe Bancroft.[6] Moreover, he was unique in being the first scholar, lucky or otherwise, to write on California who was himself a native of the state. He brought an intuitive feel to the subject, and a passion born out of his desire to see the moral significance of the "new land" of his birth. Royce was also unique in another respect: in researching California, he asked his mother to write her memoirs of being a forty-niner. As a result, Royce wrote a better book than he might otherwise have done, and we have a superb account of pioneer life from a woman's perspective. A generation later, Yale historian Ralph Henry Gabriel edited and introduced what Sarah Bayliss Royce had called her "Pilgrimage Journey," publishing it as *A Frontier Lady*.[7]

Royce's native town, Grass Valley, was only about a half-dozen years older than he was, and it aroused in him a great curiosity about the nature of society:

> My earliest recollections include a very frequent wonder as to what my elders meant when they said this was a new community. I frequently looked at the vestiges left by the former diggings of miners, saw that many pine logs were rotten, and that a miner's grave was to be found in a lonely place not far from my own house. Plainly men had lived and died thereabouts....The logs and graves looked old. The sunsets were beautiful. The wide prospects when one looked across the Sacramento Valley were impressive and had long interested the people of whose love for my country I heard much. What was there then in this place that ought to be called new, or for that matter, crude?[8]

It was from an early age, he later recalled, that his ideas about the nature of persons and society in community were formed:

> I strongly feel that my deepest motives and problems have centered about the Idea of the Community, although this idea has only gradually come into my consciousness. This was what I was intensely feeling, in the days when my sisters and I looked across the Sacramento Valley, and wondered about the great world beyond our mountains.[9]

Royce's interest in the history of California was lifelong. Although he did not write professionally about California after 1891, the whole of his philosophical work was framed by his preoccupation with the failure of, and the need for, community in his native state. Although Royce was, as a philosopher, concerned with the abstract, ideas came to life for him only in the realities of life as lived. As he developed philosophical positions on loyalty, provincialism, and the great community, California was never far from his mind. If there is one single point to be distilled from Royce's *California,* and from his other work, it is that humans cannot escape social duties. As Patricia Nelson Limerick would later write in *The Legacy of Conquest,* "The cruel but common lesson of western history: postponements and evasions catch up with people."[10]

I have read all of Royce's writings on California, and I have also read his personal letters in the archives at Harvard University and at the University of California, Berkeley, some of which were later collected and published in an excellent edition by John Clendenning. Taken together, they reveal a man who began work on California in a relatively lighthearted spirit, possibly unaware of the enormity of the task ahead; but they also reveal a person who matured as a scholar and as a moral observer of society in the process. In the story of California, he saw the triumph that others had seen, but saw tragedy too; he saw the heroism that other writers saw, but treachery too; he joined with others in celebrating the best in American character as shown in early California, but he also saw the worst, and was not afraid to say so.

What strikes one in reading Royce's *California,* as well as his many journalistic pieces in the battle of words that followed the book's publication, is his responsible, careful, and nuanced tone, especially as compared to what his letters indicate of how he really felt. His letters reveal a person who is shocked, even appalled at times, by California history, but even more shocked by the attempts of participants and their descendants to cover up the odious aspects of that history.

Some scholars attribute Royce's disinclination to accept a heroic narrative grounded in the concept of manifest destiny to his own unhappy childhood and school days. It is alleged that, somewhere down deep in Royce's soul, he thoroughly disliked those who caused social exclusion or who bullied weaker people.[11] One doesn't know what to make of psychological explanations for Royce's work, other than that they seem plausible; whether or not they are persuasive is another matter. In any event, Royce was a moral social analyst who decried injustice and became downright angry with those who lied about and tried to cover up the injustices they had perpetrated.

Many scholars, even those sympathetic to Royce, believe he overdid it, both in terms of his verbosity and of his seemingly relentless (some would say obsessive) pursuit of the legend of John C. Frémont. As to the first point, any modern reader would question Royce on his verbiage; where one word would do, he used two. Several of his editors at the time asked him to delete parts of his works, and it seems he was the same way in person. If Royce was asked a question, all the available space was filled by the answer, leaving some questioners sorry they had asked.[12] Royce was nothing if not thorough, but he seems not to have mastered the difference between thoroughness and overstatement. The other charge, that Royce went way over the top in his pursuit of Frémont, for example, is not so easy to concede. In the end, I think we must sympathize with Royce;

even if he wrote too much on the Frémont legend, perhaps that was because the legend, as he lamented, would not go down. This foreword, then, may appear to join Royce in overemphasizing the Frémont affair, but since that affair is crucial—both to California and to Royce's credibility in our eyes—we must follow the documents on this matter.

In 1846, Captain John C. Frémont, already a well-known explorer, associated himself with a group of Americans along the Sacramento River who were restive under Mexican control. They declared themselves a republic, raised a flag, and the Bear Flag revolt had begun. The question, in 1846 and when Royce wrote about it forty years later, was this: on what orders did Frémont act? The Frémont legend was, and is, vital to California history. If Frémont was, as he claimed, acting on orders from the U.S. government, then Californians must rightly regard him as their hero; if he had no orders, his arrogant actions and their poisonous effect on ethnic relations make him the villain in the piece. Frémont was, after all, the first Republican candidate for president, and he had a considerable reputation, based on his early California career.

In the summer of 1884, as Royce began his research in Bancroft's unique library of documents, memoirs, and newspapers, it soon became obvious that things did not look good for Frémont. But, cautious and scholarly, Royce wondered if there were an alternative interpretation. As it turned out, a friend from his Berkeley undergraduate days, William Carey Jones (later to be a founder of legal studies at Berkeley), was also a nephew of Frémont on his mother's side. Jones agreed to set up an interview between Royce and Frémont, and Royce sent Jones examples of the sorts of questions he wanted to ask (by then, General) Frémont. Royce was deferential, saying that he had no need to bother the aged hero if documentary evidence could be produced to satisfy his questions.[13] The Frémonts—the general and his wife, Jessie, the daughter of Senator Thomas Hart Benton—preferred an interview. It took place in December 1884 at the Frémont home in New York.

Royce had obtained a copy of an 1846 dispatch from Secretary of State James Buchanan to Thomas Larkin, the American consul at Monterey in the 1840s. The document was vitally important because it disclosed the American policy in California and revealed who had been meant to execute it. It was clear that the Polk administration had intended to bring California into the Union, and Larkin was using peaceful persuasion—not conquest—to ensure that the Californios would agree to this transition. Larkin, then, was the government's secret agent in California, not Frémont.

During the interview, Royce kept quiet about having a copy of the Larkin dispatch in his pocket. The Frémonts insisted that no such dispatch existed and that Larkin could never have been trusted by Polk for such a delicate assignment. They insisted that Frémont was the government's man in California.[14] "Royce perversely did not reveal that he had copied such a telltale document," writes a recent biographer of Frémont.[15] Royce's written account of the interview leaves little room for doubt that he enjoyed catching the great pathfinder lying, but his silence may have revealed more caution than perversity: he realized that a young scholar attempting to deconstruct the Frémont legend would meet stiff opposition, and at that point he had not verified the copy he carried in his pocket (one of Bancroft's copies) against the original dispatch.

In the early spring of 1885, Royce made a quick trip to Washington, D.C. He went to the department of state, and after some negotiations over what today we would call national security issues, he was allowed to see the original Larkin dispatch. By mid-April 1885, Royce knew what he had to do. On April 14, he wrote to his editor, Horace Scudder, and to a key assistant in the Bancroft enterprise, Henry L. Oak, to tell them the news: the archives in Washington finally and fully confirmed their belief that the documents in Bancroft's possession were not only true and accurate, but all that there was on the subject.[16] Frémont was now doubly damned: not only was Larkin surely the only agent of the policy—one of peace—toward the

Californios, but there were no instructions to Frémont at all.
Royce now believed, as he told Oak, that he could apply "the
thumb-screw" to the Frémonts in a way he could not have done
when he had seen only Bancroft's copy. Even so, Royce was a
cautious scholar, and he wanted to give the Frémonts another
chance to exonerate themselves. On the same day, April 14,
1885, he wrote Jessie Benton Frémont, disclosing what he had
found in Washington and saying that the documentary evidence
did not seem to support the general's view of the events of
1846. Royce repeated that he wanted to do justice to the
Frémonts, and he urgently requested them to reveal their secrets,
just as the government in Washington had done.[17]

In the summer of 1885, Royce made another visit to the
Frémonts. He later reported what had transpired to Henry L.
Oak in Berkeley. Royce pleaded with the Frémonts to reveal
something that would shed a different light on the Bear Flag
affair, now that the government's secrets were out. The conversation was cordial, Royce wrote, with the general "dignified and
charming," and Mrs. Frémont "calm, sunny, and benevolent."
But in the face of the facts, Royce told Oak, Frémont "lied, lied
unmistakably, unmitigatedly, hopelessly. And that was his only
defence [sic]."[18] Still, Royce considered another possibility. He
had suggested to Oak that the problem might not be so much
with events as with the general's memory of them, that "his
memory and not his design is now the deceiver."[19] Now, with
his book nearly finished, Royce wrote again to Jessie Frémont,
asking, "How shall I explain these facts consistently with
General Frémont's present memory?"[20] Significantly for our
story, Jessie Benton Frémont never replied to Royce's letter.

Royce's *California* was published in 1886, causing quite a
stir among those interested and involved in the early history of
American California and in the reputations made in those
years. Royce was surprised by the virulence of the attacks on
him and his book, and by the friendships it would cost him;
he was equally surprised at the lengths he would have to go to
defend what he had written. It is not so much that he was

naive, as one historian has recently charged,[21] but that the issues he raised were—and are—genuinely troublesome. Royce's book, in the end, allows us to begin to see an alternative narrative for the history of California.

A Brief Summary of *California*

Royce wanted his history to be more than a factual recounting of early days; he was interested in the events of history for themselves, but even more for "their value as illustrating American life and character."[22] That paradoxical "character" was displayed, as Royce saw it, on the one hand as careless, hasty, and blind to social duties; on the other hand as "cheerful, energetic, courageous, and teachable" (2).

Royce did not really doubt the inevitability of the American conquest; nor, in his view, did the Californios. What the latter feared was the coming of bad Americans. The good American, to Mexicans and to Royce, was represented by Thomas Larkin, "the only American official who can receive nearly unmixed praise" for his work in California (38). The bad American was, of course, represented by John C. Frémont. Those attitudes, Royce insists, that the American "national character made us assume towards the Californians at the moment of our appearance among them as conquerors, we have ever since kept, with disaster to them, and not without disgrace and degradation to ourselves" (49).

Royce then proceeds to the lengthy and detailed analysis of Frémont's various escapades. Royce is particularly hard on the leaders of the Bear Flag uprising, especially Robert Semple and William B. Ide. He mounts the evidence against Frémont and finds his actions wanting in moral character, at one point saying they amounted to atrocity (135). Nevertheless, Royce ends the Frémont section with magnanimity and grace, admitting that he cannot fully fathom "what inner motives" drove Frémont.

The lines from *California* most quoted by scholars and journalists are these: "The American as conqueror is unwilling to appear in public as a pure aggressor....The American wants to persuade not only the world, but himself, that he is doing God service in a peaceable spirit, even when he violently takes what he has determined to get" (151). While Royce would have no part in such hypocrisy, he would not judge all Californians, preferring to note that while the Mexican War had come to be regarded with "shame and contempt," the acquisition of California continued, ironically, to be regarded as "a God-fearing act...[and part of] our devotion to the cause of freedom" (156). For Royce, history was not to be a happy patriotic story. Rather, he wrote the book "to serve the true patriot's interest in a clear self-knowledge, and in the formation of sensible ideals of national greatness" (49). California, therefore, is the true parent of Limerick's *Legacy of Conquest,* for in it Royce sees that "conquest" is indeed the right word for what happened in California, and that the attitudes of conquest continued after 1846. In this respect, he hoped his book would be a reminder, and a guide for the future:

> So that when our nation is another time about to serve the devil, it will do so with more frankness, and will deceive itself less by half-conscious cant. For the rest, our mission in the cause of liberty is to be accomplished through a steadfast devotion to the cultivation of our own inner life, and not by going abroad as missionaries, as conquerors, or as marauders among weaker peoples. (156)

The singular injustice perpetrated by Frémont and Commander John D. Sloat was the second conquest of the Californios in 1847, which sealed the division between Anglo and Mexican Californians ineradicably. When the Californios resented, and sometimes resisted, the Americans, they were seen as rebels and traitors, which Royce thought forged "one more link in the fatal chain of injustice" (194).

Royce examines the Gold Rush within his overall thesis of order and disorder. Drawing from his own family's difficult trek to California in 1849, he notes the "religious" aura often associated with arrival in California, and the consequent sense of entitlement among the new settlers. They hoped for—even expected—a great deal from California, and when "foreigners" got in their way, there was often a violent reaction. Royce regards such actions as a disgrace to American ideals of liberty and fairness. And so-called miner's justice was more than disgraceful: it retarded social maturity in the Anglo-American community by instilling a sense that quick, unambiguous justice could be had cheaply. Royce's passion shows clearly as he imagines the racist state of mind that allowed lynching juries to convict their victims on little evidence: "One could see his guilt, so plainly, we know, in his ugly, swarthy face, before the trial began....And if he was a native Californian, a born 'greaser,' then so much the worse for him" (363-4). Yet despite his passion, or perhaps because of it, Royce could marvel at the way in which mining communities had been able to learn from this "inner social disease" and begin the process of renewal within a generation. They were, in the end, able to found real communities, to move, in his terms, "from social foolishness to social steadfastness" (375).

In Royce's discussion of San Francisco's first ten years, we find "dramatic incidents that belong to the painful side of the struggle for order" (378). Here, he contradicts early pioneer mythology that reveled in the "wicked" history of the city. To the contrary, the legendary gambling men and easy women were "but the froth on the turbid current" (398). The transient quality of early San Francisco life did indeed leave the stain of individuality that forsook solidarity, but that was overcome by institutions of a conservative character, especially churches and families, that showed people their social duty. The committees of vigilance were, of course, central to the early history of San Francisco, as were the crime and corruption of the early 1850s. Royce once again goes to the heart of the matter, blaming the obviously guilty malefactors (e.g. the fraud Henry Meiggs), but placing more blame on a complacent society with little apparent respect for social responsibility. In the famous case of the murder of the reform-minded editor James King of William, Royce was the first scholar to see the significance of the social composition of the vigilance committee that convicted and executed the murderers: it seems this committee of "the best men" of San Francisco asserted their own social and economic power in order to thwart total mob rule. It was, as Royce noted, "a businessman's revolution" (440).

Royce's final subject is the emotionally charged dispute over land titles. Because of what Royce called "the rapacity" of "predatory disregard" on the part of the Americans (467), few of the guarantees given the Californios at the time of the conquest were upheld. The Land Act of 1851, according to Royce, only slightly dignified the wholesale movement of land from Californian to American hands. Worse yet, the titles thus manipulated did not end up in the hands of ordinary Americans, but with greedy speculators and lawyers. This was, Royce says, to cause "lasting injury" to the whole state of California.

In his conclusion, Royce restates his belief that California history is more than a local or regional concern. California in the 1850s was an immature society characterized by social irresponsibility—by people who "love mere fullness of life and lack reverence for the relations of life" (500). By the time Royce wrote *California*, the community had found a kind of social "salvation," but only because it learned the lessons it had heretofore "despised and forgotten." For Royce, it was only by "confessing" that past to each other that Californians would find the way forward.

The Aftermath of *California*

Following the publication of *California*, Royce's life entered a strange phase. Never one to be coy about his thinking, nor shy about telling all who would listen what he was working on, he became unusually secretive in the summer of 1886. He concealed from his friends the fact that he was writing, of all things, a novel. Several of his correspondents asked what he was writing now that his two books—*The Religious Aspect of Philosophy* and *California*—were out. He wrote to Millicent Shinn at *Overland Monthly* that he was writing things "of a light sort, but such as make my pen swing a trifle."[23]

The swinging of Royce's pen did not bring forth a trifle in a literal sense. It was a huge book, and Royce nearly apologized to publisher Horace Scudder for its "portentous" length. He gave it a title too melodramatic for even a Victorian publisher to use; so Royce's "Just Before Nightfall" was duly published by Houghton Mifflin as *The Feud of Oakfield Creek*.

Some scholars of Royce's life and work are genuinely puzzled about why Royce wrote this novel and where it fits into his larger work. Perhaps Kevin Starr is right to suggest that *Oakfield Creek* is a reprise of what Royce had tried to do in *California:* to show that social duty and loyalty were the stuff of the moral life, and that they were often sorely lacking in early California history.[24] The novel deals with archetypal characters in California history, such as the noble populist and the greedy capitalist, the latter probably patterned after Leland Stanford. But it is not a very good novel. It drew little positive criticism and few sales.

What was Royce thinking? A person with a great future ahead of him in philosophy, a secure position at Harvard, and the ability to write credible history did not need to wear himself out writing a poor novel. Moreover, Royce dedicated the novel to William James. Of the twenty books that Royce was to write, this was the least likely to be associated with that august name.

There is no doubt Royce was worn out. He suffered a nervous breakdown during the academic year 1887-88. He couldn't write. He felt listless. His chronic insomnia worsened. Showing his well-honed skill of denial, he said he was physically fit but mentally spent. While he looked well enough, he confessed that "the little devil in the brain is there all the time." Like many late-Victorian intellectuals who suffered breakdowns—William James, Max Weber, Abraham Kuyper—Royce left his wife and children behind and took a curative holiday alone. Others preferred the baths of Switzerland and Germany, but Royce took passage on a ship out of Boston in February 1888, traveled around the Cape of Good Hope, and was in Australia by May. Somewhere along the way his "head-weariness" disappeared. After some time in Australia and New Zealand, Royce took another ship to Oakland to visit family in California. He arrived back in Cambridge in September 1888, just in time for the new academic year,[25] and wrote to his old mentor, Daniel Coit Gilman, that he felt "like a bent bow, all ready to thwang."[26]

These few details about Royce's breakdown and recovery are meant to highlight a question about his judgment. Over the next three years, Royce was to engage in two public controversies in which he criticized his opponents relentlessly. One was about a mediocre philosopher in Cambridge, Francis Abbot, whom Royce had belittled in print. It became noteworthy because of Abbot's highly placed family connections. The other was a renewal of the long-standing feud with General John C. and Mrs. Jessie Frémont. "Thwang" he did, and if "the little devil" was no longer in his brain, Royce himself may have appeared to be the devil to the family and friends of John C. Frémont. Perhaps the two public rows are connected, for they both concerned men who, in Royce's opinion, did not possess the stuff of greatness but whose egos demanded public acclaim and honor. One of Royce's colleagues, George Herbert Palmer, later wrote of Royce: "Perhaps overconsiderate in dealing with students of middling powers, he was exacting with men of capacity, impatient with pretenders, and scornful in exposing careless ignorance."[27] I wonder if we see Royce at his best during 1888 to 1891, when he was just back from recuperative leave. While Royce himself was silent on the subject, readers of, for example, *The Nation* must have wondered about it when they saw Royce tilting at both Abbot and Frémont. Even if Royce was correct in his positions, one is bound to note that he seems not to have possessed the ability to know when he had won an argument and when he should let it go. When Royce had finished, the

reputation of Abbot was ruined; if Frémont's was not fully
ruined, it was not because Royce had backed off.

Four national magazines were to be drawn into the controversy between Royce and the Frémonts and their friends.
During 1890 and 1891, *The Nation, Overland Monthly, Century,*
and *Atlantic Monthly* would receive pieces from Royce. An
examination of letters from Royce's editors reveals that they
were eager at first to get Royce's work but then began to ask
him to cut back on the length of previously assigned articles,
and finally to curtail them.

Royce's sense of mission, and the passion behind it, can be
seen in a letter to Robert Underwood Johnson, editor of
Century, who had engaged him as an ad hoc editor for the publication of some documents relating to early California history.
Royce laid out an elaborate plan for publishing documents in
Century that would, once and for all, destroy the credibility of
the Frémonts and of those who supported their version of history.[28] Royce was aware of and vexed by the attempts of the
descendants and friends of the Frémonts to construct a history
of heroism and progress: "Beware, I should say to any fellow
student of those days, beware old Frémont's withered branch,
beware the awful avalanche of yarns that the Sloat family, the
children of the settlers and the like, have in store."[29] Royce was
especially saddened by the fact that William Carey Jones, the old
college friend who had introduced him to Frémont, was not
only lost as a friend but was working with his aunt to portray a
version of the story contrary to Royce's. Royce later wrote that
he had only done his duty as a scholar in regard to Frémont;
and that his only fault was being "prolix" on the subject.[30] No
one would quarrel with Royce about his prolixity; one might,
however, wonder about his judgment in not having controlled it.

Written only a few months after Frémont's death in 1890,
Royce's article for *Atlantic Monthly* laid out again the case
against the general.[31] Royce later wrote that the article was "the
most cold-bloodedly cussed thing that I ever attempted."[32] In
the article, Royce uses as a foil an article published in France

proclaiming Frémont "the conqueror of California." With droll wit and cutting irony, Royce disputes the claim. But while he says he would like to lay the legend to rest, Royce observes that Frémont's life is such a mixture of fact and fiction that a mere rendition of the facts might not deal finally with the fictive part. Once again, Royce rehearses the whole story of the Larkin dispatch, the lack of any credible evidence that Frémont had any instructions from the U.S. government, and the loss of hope for good relations between Americans and native Californians. The tone of Royce's piece can be sensed from a small excerpt:

> The seizure of California in 1846 was one of the least credible affairs in the highly discreditable Mexican War.…The whole criminal enterprise [was]…not so much against Mexico, who the whole war robbed, as against the native Californians. It was surely by no means good policy for our government to harass them in advance of the outbreak of the intended war with Mexico.[33]

Royce states flatly that Frémont not only acted contrarily to American policy but disobeyed orders, all for his own glory.

There were two other matters of documentary concern to be settled in order for Royce to put the lid finally on the coffin of Frémont's ill-deserved reputation. First was the assertion of the Frémont faction that Frémont had acted to thwart British designs on California. Second, there was the assertion by Royce's former friend William Carey Jones and others that Frémont knew that hostilities with Mexico had already begun when he acted. If true, this would clearly exculpate Frémont from charges of disobeying the Polk and Buchanan policy of peaceful persuasion. Acting as ad hoc editor for *Century,* Royce produced the relevant documents, along with two pages of contextualizing commentary. The documents indicated that there had been no real British threat to California[34] and that Frémont could not have known about war prior to the Bear Flag affair. In any case, Frémont had written to

Commodore J. B. Montgomery that he would not initiate hostilities even if war did break out with Mexico.[35]

One would think that no more could be said on the subject, but *Century* editor Robert Underwood Johnson had already promised the Frémonts a final chance to rebut Royce. Disappointed by the article Mrs. Frémont sent under the signature of her late husband, Johnson enlisted the support of William Carey Jones to rewrite it.[36] Two interesting points emerge from the Frémont-Jones article: the admission that Frémont knew about the Larkin dispatch all along; and the assertion, in a letter by George Bancroft, secretary of the navy during the Mexican War, that Lt. Archibald H. Gillespie, the envoy who had delivered the Larkin dispatch, had communicated orders to Frémont that he was to exercise a relatively free hand in securing California for the United States.[37] If it were true that Frémont actually had instructions from Washington to engage in hostilities if he deemed the policy of peaceful persuasion to be no longer viable, then Frémont's actions and reputation would be home free.

Royce appealed to his old friends in publishing, but both Johnson at *Century* and Shinn at *Overland Monthly* turned him down, saying that enough had already been said on the subject, and all sides had been heard. Royce appealed then to Scudder, editor of his *California* and now editor of *Atlantic Monthly*. Scudder also declined, but he asked Royce to consider, in the light of all the new evidence, writing a new edition of *California*. That did not appeal to Royce, who wanted to make a single, short, final statement "to set the thing at rest for all future students." He especially did not want to let this apparent refutation from the Frémont side stand "at the very moment when my own view is so near its final confirmation for all who are well-informed."[38]

The Nation published Royce's final piece. He showed that George Bancroft's statement to Frémont could not have been accurate. It was written, Royce said, by a friend trying to help a friend—moreover, a friend whose memory, forty years later, was faulty. Royce also expressed his indignation at the admission that

Frémont had indeed known of the Larkin dispatch all along, five years after Frémont had "insisted upon his denial to me, as a historical student, for publication in my book." Royce did not directly call Frémont a liar (he had promised the editor he'd go easy this time) but said the general's life was a "romance." The final paragraph sees Royce's real passion rise again. He restates, one more time, the policy of the United States toward the native Californians. Writing with obvious bitterness, Royce notes that Frémont knew about that policy but "thwarted [it] for his own glory, whereof he got a great deal":

> I should myself never think of attacking the Frémont legend so often were it not so unsubstantially immortal. I shall rejoice, indeed, if ever the pale ghost ceases to walk in the broad daylight. The twilight regions of our historical consciousness in this country will probably never be rid of it.[39]

This historian notes, perhaps ruefully, that Royce's prediction more than a century ago was more correct than not. Despite the facts of the case against the Frémont myth, serious academic biographers in the twentieth century continued to write books with titles like *The West's Greatest Adventurer*.[40] Frémont's most recent biographer still holds out hope that Frémont had secret instructions, though "we shall probably never know their full content."[41] Perhaps some historians of California and the West cannot give up on Frémont because to do so would require a full-scale revision of the main narrative of the state in which the Bear Flag still flies above the capitol.

Royce's *California* and the New Western History

From the vast body of literature about historical study, one recent book emerges as a singularly useful demonstration of the ways in which our approach to history has changed: *Telling the Truth About History,* by Joyce Appleby, Lynn Hunt, and Margaret Jacob.[42] By "telling the truth," Appleby and her colleagues do not mean to imply that other, prior historians were telling lies. Rather, they mean that there was once a single narrative about American history accepted by most Americans as part of their heritage. It was a story of achievement, of how a nation of immigrants made the first liberal democracy, and of how that nation became the economic success story of modern world history. Now, Appleby et al. suggest, when the vision of American history is made to expand beyond dominant groups, the historical picture changes. As the Appleby team writes, "We routinely, even angrily, ask: Whose history? Whose science? Whose interests are being served by these ideas and stories? The challenge is out to all claims of universality."[43]

This idea—what we call the social construction of knowledge—has transformed the way we think about the American West in general and California history in particular. American history, in its academic, professional setting, grew up with the history of the West. In a pathbreaking essay in 1893, "The Significance of the Frontier in American History," Frederick Jackson Turner articulated a vision for American history that has been hard to shake.[44] While many important points can be drawn from Turner, two are vital: that American interaction with the frontier provides an essential window for understanding the development of democracy in America; and that the frontier "closed" about 1890, thus ending forever the most "American" phase of our history.

Generations of historians have reacted to Turner in a variety of ways. But most importantly for our purposes, the newer historians ask different questions than did Turner and his followers. Today we want to know the experience of women, Native Americans, and other "outsiders"; we want to know a total history of the West. Moreover, the practitioners of this newer mode of historical discourse question the whole notion of "conquest" in moral terms. Instead of how the West was "won," we look at the historic treatment of natives and other non-whites, women, and even the land itself; we might ask how the West was abused, oppressed, and some might even say raped. This, in short, is a discussion of a different order.

Novelist Larry McMurtry is mistaken when he says that these new inquiries amount to the "failure studies" of American Western history, in that they debunk the stories of heroism and vision among the conquerors.[45] The intense work of, for example, Patricia Nelson Limerick, Donald Worster, Clyde Milner, William Cronon, Richard White, and Lillian Schlissel does indeed ask searching—even searing—questions, challenging the triumphalist viewpoint that was prominent in American history texts until fairly recently. McMurty is correct when he reminds us that some of the uncomfortable truths emerging in the new Western history have long been known, but he vitiates his own point and unintentionally vindicates Limerick and others when he notes that Americans typically have not wanted "to receive bad news from out West."[47] In his autobiographical reflection *Walter Benjamin at the Dairy Queen,* McMurtry expresses his frustration, having tried to subvert the core myths of the West through irony and parody in *Lonesome Dove,* about ever deconstructing them:

> Readers don't want to know and can't be made to see how difficult and destructive life in the Old West really was. Lies about the West are more important to them than truths, which is why the popularity of the pulpers—Louis L'Amour particularly—has never dimmed."[48]

In the end, McMurtry is doleful, asking, "Are our myths safe for a few more years, or must we westerners face up to living with nothing more stirring than our suburbs now that John Wayne is dead?"[49]

What is lost in the new way of history is not the real American West, which was always, as Woody Guthrie observed, "hard, ain't it hard" for the people and the land. What is lost is the West of the imagination. McMurtry recalls noting a sadness in his aged father's eyes, a sadness begotten of having known the newness of the West and now knowing that his children would never see it. It does not belittle McMurtry's poignant memory to include the sadness in other aged eyes—those of Indians on marginal reservations and of the migrant farmworkers in the fields of California. The "conquest" was about them and their ancestors, and Patricia Nelson Limerick is surely right to call our attention to the unbroken links between the past and the present. In *The Legacy of Conquest,* she collapses the intellectual world given us by Frederick Jackson Turner. Where Turner saw no continuity between the culture-shaping time of the "frontier" and our own time, Limerick insists that there are fundamental continuities of race, ethnicity, gender, and economics between that time and the present.

We need not give up all the stories of the past, even as we acknowledge the more recently discovered stories of other actors in the California drama. We need not give up the stories of hardship, bravery, courage, and generosity now that we also know that there were at least equal measures of cowardice, treachery, greed, and ill-gotten luxury. Historian Richard Etulain has recently described—with great care and sensitivity—the sorts of morally nuanced, socially complex, and self-reflective stories that are needed for the new history to unite past and future generations.[50] The goal is not to subvert one major story in order to raise up another, but to disclose the multiple nature of realities in the West.

Conceding that the Gold Rush was not worth the cost of one Indian child's life, the eminent historian Kevin Starr praises recent historians while, with great insight and feeling, asking us not to lose sight of what he calls the founding time of (American) California:

> Would it be better that the Gold Rush never happened? Is that what we are saying? Is that what we are saying when we contemplate the tragic dimensions of

experience? Would it be better that there were no
California? That we not be here? Which is to say that
America not be here?[51]

Starr approvingly quotes Patricia Nelson Limerick's comment,
made at a symposium during the *Gold Rush!* exhibition at the
Oakland Museum of California, that "human beings regularly
do bad things." Starr invokes the Judeo-Christian tradition by
calling these bad things "sins" which, when taken together,
"constitute a grave burden on the present because these sins are
now a part of our living history."[52] Starr wants to affirm the
good and socially useful aspects of early California history, but
for him, that affirmation must always be in tandem with an
acknowledgment of "the sins of the fathers" and a determination "that these sins are not being recommitted in our own
time." He sees California's experience as a "prophetic probe, for
better or for worse, of the larger American experience."[53] At the
end of the article in which these words are written, one finds a
reproduction of a cartoon drawing of Josiah Royce, reading
from a very large text!

As Robert Hine has suggested, Royce saw the history of the
American West as metaphysics, with society moving from the
willfulness of individualism to the social cohesion of genuine
community.[54] The glue that holds the community together (and
at the same time prevents collectivist statism) is what Royce calls
"loyalty," a word probably better defined in our time as "solidarity." Some Roycean interpreters think this to be an essentially
religious insight that has much to say about American values.
Whether or not readers of *California* will agree with Royce's
religious insistence will, of course, depend upon how they construct the moral life. But Kevin Starr presses us further: "The
moment we mention sin, we must also mention repentance,
atonement, healing, and forgiveness....But for all the tangled
burden of the past...[California] is struggling toward redemption
and the light."[55]

There is one element missing from Starr's litany of "religious" actions: confession. It is precisely here that Royce's California is so compelling. Royce thought the early history of California to be of "divinely moral significance," and he wrote his history for "any fellow Californian who may perchance note the faults of which I make confession."[56] There is neither suggestion of a sectarian viewpoint nor recommendation of any particular theological tradition or religious expression here. For Royce, the only saving grace, the only path to social salvation, was solidarity within a community. Whether or not Kevin Starr is right—that with redemption the "Pacific City on the Hill"[57] can still flourish—is for future generations of Californians to determine. For Royce's part, he neither condemned nor condoned the behavior of all Californians. He too sought the balance that many of the new Western historians seek, trying not to overemphasize what Starr calls the dark side of California history while trying, as McMurtry advocates, to retain the West of the imagination. Royce's *California*—a study of American character, as the subtitle proclaims—may help us to develop the more fully orbed historical consciousness that any healthy society needs.

Ronald A. Wells
Calvin College
Grand Rapids, Michigan
Summer, 2002

Notes

1. Kevin Starr, *America and the California Dream* (New York: Oxford University Press, 1973).
2. *The Letters of William James,* ed., Henry James (London: Longmans, Green, 1920), 1:249.
3. Royce's best-known works include *The Religious Aspect of Philosophy* (1885), *The Spirit of Modern Philosophy* (1892), *The World and the Individual* (1900-01), *The Philosophy of Loyalty* (1908), and *Lectures on Modern Idealism* (1919).
4. For biographies of Royce, see especially John Clendenning, *The Life and Thought of Josiah Royce* (Madison: University of Wisconsin Press, 1985; rev. ed., Nashville: Vanderbilt University Press, 1999); Robert V. Hine, *Josiah Royce:*

Foreword

From Grass Valley to Harvard (Norman: University of Oklahoma Press, 1992).
5. Letter, Royce to Henry L. Oak, September 17, 1885, *The Letters of Josiah Royce*, ed., John Clendenning (Chicago: University of Chicago Press, 1970), 178.
6. Bancroft is credited with having written, along with his assistants, the monumental thirty-nine-volume history of the American West, Mexico, and Central America now known as *The Works of Hubert Howe Bancroft*.
7. *A Frontier Lady: Recollections of the Gold Rush and Early California*, ed., Ralph Henry Gabriel (New Haven: Yale University Press, 1932).
8. Royce, *The Hope of the Great Community* (New York: Macmillan, 1916), 5.
9. Ibid.
10. Patricia Nelson Limerick, *The Legacy of Conquest: The Unbroken Past of the American West* (New York: Norton, 1987), 95.
11. Clendenning, *Life and Thought*, 32-38; Robert Glass Cleland, "Introduction," Royce, *California* (New York: Alfred A. Knopf, 1948), xiii.
12. Clendenning, *Life and Thought*, 330-331.
13. Letter, Royce to William Carey Jones, September 23, 1884, Jones papers, Bancroft Library, Berkeley.
14. Letter, Royce to Oak, December 9, 1884, *Letters,* 141-145.
15. Andrew Rolle, *John Charles Frémont: Character as Destiny* (Norman: University of Oklahoma Press, 1991), 260.
16. Letter, Royce to Horace Scudder, April 14, 1885, Scudder papers, Berkeley; Letter, Royce to Oak, April 14, 1885, Oak papers, Berkeley.
17. Letter, Royce to Jessie Frémont, April 14, 1885, Oak papers, Berkeley.
18. Letter, Royce to Oak, August 8, 1885, Oak papers, Berkeley.
19. Ibid.
20. Letter, Royce to Jessie Frémont, August 20, 1885, Oak papers, Berkeley.
21. Rolle, *Frémont,* 260.
22. Royce, *California,* vii (hereafter all references to the book will appear parenthetically in the text, with the pages listed referring to the original 1886 edition and this edition).
23. Letter, Royce to Millicent Shinn, August 7, 1886, Shinn papers, Berkeley.
24. Starr, *California Dream,* 164-166.
25. Clendenning, *Life and Thought,* 144-158.
26. Letter, Royce to Daniel Coit Gilman, September 6, 1888, in Clendenning, *Letters of Josiah Royce,* 225.
27. George Herbert Palmer, "Philosophy," in *The Development of Harvard University, 1869-1929,* ed., Samuel Eliot Morison (Cambridge: Harvard University Press, 1930), 13.
28. Letter, Royce to Robert Underwood Johnson, August 29, 1890, Johnson papers, Berkeley.
29. Letter, Royce to Johnson, June 4, 1890, Johnson papers, Berkeley.
30. Letter, Royce to Shinn, August 7, 1886, Shinn papers, Berkeley.
31. Royce, "Frémont," *Atlantic Monthly,* 66 (October, 1890): 548-557
32. Quoted in Clendenning, *Life and Thought,* 169.
33. Royce, "Frémont," 553.
34. "Light on the Seizure of California," *Century,* n.s., 18 (September, 1890): 792-795.

35. The letter, dated June 16, 1846, is reproduced in Royce's article "Montgomery and Frémont: New Documents on the Bear Flag Affair," *Century,* n.s., 19 (March, 1891): 780-788.

36. Letter, Robert U. Johnson to William C. Jones, October 13, 1890, Jones papers, Berkeley; Letter, Royce to Johnson, October 19, 1890, Johnson papers, Berkeley; Letter, Jessie Benton Frémont to William C. Jones, October 28, 1890, reprinted in Pamela Herr and Mary Lee Spence, "By the Sundown Sea: The Los Angeles Letters of Jessie Benton Frémont, 1888-1902," *California History,* 71 (Winter, 1992/93): 479-480.

37. John C. Frémont, "The Conquest of California," *Century,* n.s., 19 (April, 1891):917-928.

38. Letter, Royce to Scudder, April 7, 1891, Scudder papers, Berkeley; Letter, Scudder to Royce, April 13, 1891, Royce papers, Harvard.

39. Royce, "The Frémont Legend," *The Nation,* 52 (May 21, 1891): 425.

40. Allan Nevins, *Frémont: The West's Greatest Adventurer* (New York: Harper, 1928).

41. Rolle, *Frémont,* 76.

42. Joyce Appleby, Lynn Hunt, and Margaret Jacob, *Telling the Truth About History* (New York: Norton, 1997).

43. Ibid., 9.

44. This famous essay is most conveniently found as the first chapter in Turner's *The Frontier in American History* (New York: Henry Holt, 1920).

45. Larry McMurtry, "How the West Was Won or Lost," *The New Republic* (October 22, 1999): 32-38.

46. Ibid., 33.

47. McMurtry, *Walter Benjamin at the Dairy Queen: Reflections at Sixty and Beyond* (New York: Simon and Schuster, 1999), 55.

48. McMurtry "How the West Was Won or Lost," 32.

49. Forrest G. Robinson, *The New Western History* (Tucson: University of Arizona Press, 1997), 80.

50. Richard Etulain, "Western Stories for the Next Generation," *Western Historical Quarterly,* 31 (Spring, 2000): 5-23.

51. Starr, "The Gold Rush and the California Dream," *California History,* 77 (Spring, 1998): 58. In a recent, brilliant review of Starr's "Dream series," Forrest G. Robinson suggests the essentially "religious" nature of Starr's work: "Spiritual Radiance, Expressive Delight: The Baroque Historiography of Kevin Starr," *California History,* 78 (Winter, 1999/2000): 274-285, 304.

52. Ibid., 61.

53. Ibid., 66.

54. Hine, *From Grass Valley to Harvard,* 166-185.

55. Starr, "The Gold Rush," 67.

56. Royce, *California,* 501.

57. Starr, "The Gold Rush," 67.

TO
MY MOTHER
A California Pioneer of 1849

Josiah Royce, n.d. Photo courtesy of UCLA Photographic Services.

Author's Preface

MORE elaborate and learned volumes than the present one have recently been devoted in large part to the history of Spanish and Mexican California before 1846. This book is concerned, in the main, only with American California, and with that only during the early and exciting formative years, from 1846 to 1856. This history of the beginnings of a great American commonwealth has seemed to me sufficient and worthy to occupy the whole of such a volume as the present one, in view both of the interest of the events and of their value as illustrating American life and character.

The purpose has been throughout to write from the sources. For the history of the conquest in 1846 official and private documents of original value have been used in so far as was possible, while, as the reader will at once see, the interregnum, the early mining life, and the history of San Francisco affairs have in general been described directly from such early newspapers as I have been able to read, the later testimony of pioneers and the views of subsequent historical writers being used here mainly to check, to complete, or to explain what the early newspapers tell us. As to the method of study employed, the social condition has been throughout of more interest to me than the individual men, and the men themselves of more interest than their fortunes, while the purpose to study the national character has never been lost sight of in the midst of even the most minute examination of certain obscure events. Nor has a certain unity in the whole narrative been absent from my mind as I have written. Through all the complex facts that are here set down in their somewhat confused order, I have felt running the one thread of the process whereby a new and great community first came to a true consciousness of itself. The story begins with the seemingly accidental doings of detached but in the sequel vastly influential individuals, and ends just where the individual ceases to have any very great historical significance for California life, and where the community begins to be what it ought to be: namely, all-important as against individual doings and interests.

As to the originality of the various parts of this book, the later chapters are written with relatively the most complete independence of fellow workers. In the first and second chapters and in part in the third chapter I have, on the other hand, to make my most important acknowledgments for help received. To Mr. Hubert Howe Bancroft I owe the very great privilege of a free use of his immense collection of original documents on the early history, especially of the conquest — a privilege of which I took advantage during the whole of the summer vacation of 1884. And from both Mr. Bancroft and his able collaborators I received, during all this time, frequent and most friendly oral advice about the use of the collection itself. As Mr. Bancroft's library contains the material for his own great work, now in process of publication, on the history of the Pacific states of North America, I feel especially indebted to the generosity that so freely placed this original material at my disposal in advance of the publication of the results obtained by Mr. Bancroft and his collaborators themselves. Where I have referred to these original documents, I have used in my notes the abbreviation B.MS. as a general name for all of them. My own freedom of judgment I have, of course, sought to retain throughout, although for the formation of many of my opinions and arguments I am much indebted to the suggestions gained through conversation and correspondence with Mr. Bancroft and his collaborators concerning some such disputed points as the Gillespie mission of 1845–6, the English designs on California, and other matters of conquest history. But the results that I have here written down are, as they stand, always my own final judgment upon all the evidence that I could obtain. Where they are mistaken, I therefore am alone to blame, and not Mr. Bancroft's documents. Much of the evidence presented has been, moreover, in every case the result of my own independent research, carried on in Eastern libraries; and in so far I have been absolutely my own guide. Of the able and exhaustive volumes that have already appeared in Mr. Bancroft's series on the history of California, I have freely used in my preliminary sketch the portions that deal with colonial California down to 1840. Beyond this I have had no access to Mr. Bancroft's book, and anticipate, of course, correction of some of my facts and opinions when that most elaborate investigation shall appear. I feel it greatly to my disadvantage, in fact, to publish my own volume in advance of so well-equipped and important a research as the work of Mr. Bancroft and his collaborators is sure to prove. I regret to have been unable to make any use whatever of the just issued *History of California* by Mr. Theodore H. Hittell, which appeared too late to help me.

Among general libraries, I owe most to the Library of Harvard College. The librarian, Mr. Winsor, has in particular constantly and very patiently aided me with suggestions and criticisms, and the library authorities have kindly provided, during the course of the work, for the purchase of much material without which the book, especially in the later chapters, would have been almost impossible. The American Antiquarian Society at Worcester, the Massachusetts State Library in Boston, the Boston Athenæum Library, the Mercantile Library of San Francisco, and the Library of the California Pioneers have all generously answered my various requests for permission to use material in their possession, and to most of them I also owe much for free opportunities to search in their collections after material not previously known or catalogued.

I have further to acknowledge the courtesy of the present Secretary of State in giving me the use of important official documents in the Department Archives at Washington; and also the kindness of the present Secretaries of War and of the Navy, as shown by their prompt and explicit answers to my questions concerning historical documents in their possession. Mr. R. S. Watson of Milton, Massachusetts, and Mr. E. S. Osgood of Cambridge, have very kindly helped me with their valuable reminiscences of vigilance-committee times. Mr. T. G. Carey of Cambridge has put at my disposal important MS. material of his own. President D. C. Gilman of Baltimore, Mr. Arthur Rogers of San Francisco, and Mr. William Carey Jones of Berkeley, California, have also supplied me with advice and with valuable printed matter. My obligations to the patience and courtesy of General and Mrs. Frémont for the free use of their time in discussing matters connected with the conquest in 1846 will, I hope, appear amidst all the very plain criticism of General Frémont's views and conduct to which I have found myself driven by indubitable historical evidence. To Mr. Charles Shinn, finally, I am indebted for the gift of advance sheets of his book on *Mining Camps*, whereby I was much furthered in my work on that subject.

A word in conclusion as to the limitations of this book. For the sake of preserving as far as possible the unity of the story, I have had to omit almost all reference to such matters as, belonging to the history of California before 1856, still became of importance only in view of the events of later years. Such matters are the beginnings of literary activity in the San Francisco community in 1854, the first movements towards establishing university education in the state, or, again, the first phases of the long and exciting Chinese agitation. Even in speaking of the partisan political life I have had to pass over, with a mere mention, events and persons that in a history of the next ten years would become so important as to make them seem, by reflected light, much more significant even before 1856 than I have had room to cause them to appear. I trust that these defects will be pardoned by a generous reader, who may also find my doubtless too numerous mistakes of detail not altogether inexcusable in a book that deals with so complex, exciting, and ill-recorded a period as this, and that is written, after all, by a student whose professional business is one not commonly regarded as duly conversant with this actual world of picks, pans, cradles, and vigilance committees. What I could do in a labor of love I have done, both to attain accuracy of detail and to make clear the meaning of a truly wonderful historical process.

CAMBRIDGE, MASS., *March* 9, 1886

California

"Von Sonn' und Welten weiss ich nichts zu sagen,
Ich sehe nur, wie sich die Menschen plagen."

MEPHISTOPHELES, IN THE PROLOGUE TO *Faust*

Chapter I

INTRODUCTION: THE TERRITORY AND THE STRANGERS

Tᴴɪs book is meant to help the reader toward an understanding of two things: namely, the modern American state of California, and our national character as displayed in that land.

For both purposes the period of California history between 1846 and 1856, between the beginnings of our national occupation of the territory and the close of the Second Vigilance Committee of San Francisco, is especially instructive. This is the period of excitement, of trial, and of rapid transformation. Everything that has since happened in California, or that ever will happen there so long as men dwell in the land, must be deeply affected by the forces of local life and society that then took their origin. And, for the understanding of our American national character in some of its most significant qualities, this life of surprise and of searching moral ordeals has a still too little appreciated value.

The American community in early California fairly represented, as we shall see, the average national culture and character. But no other part of our land was ever so rapidly peopled as was California in the first golden days. Nowhere else were we Americans more affected than here, in our lives and conduct, by the feeling that we stood in the position of conquerors in a new land. Nowhere else, again, were we ever before so long forced by circumstances to live at the mercy of a very wayward chance, and to give to even our most legitimate business a dangerously speculative character. Nowhere else were we driven so hastily to improvise a government for a large body of strangers; and nowhere else did fortune so nearly deprive us for a little time of our natural devotion to the duties of citizenship. We Americans therefore showed in early California new failings and new strength. We exhibited a novel degree of carelessness and overhastiness, an extravagant trust in luck, a previously unknown

3

blindness to our social duties, and an indifference to the rights of foreigners, whereof we cannot be proud. But we also showed our best national traits — traits that went far to atone for our faults. As a body, our pioneer community in California was persistently cheerful, energetic, courageous, and teachable. In a few years it had repented of its graver faults, it had endured with charming good humor their severest penalties, and it was ready to begin with fresh devotion the work whose true importance it had now at length learned — the work of building a well-organized, permanent, and progressive state on the Pacific coast. In this work it has been engaged ever since, with fortunes that always, amid the most remarkable changes, have preserved a curious likeness to the fortunes of the early days, and that, in numerous and recent instances, have led to a more or less noteworthy and complete repetition of certain early trials, blunders, sins, penalties, virtues, and triumphs.

This introductory chapter will aim to supply the chief facts necessary for an understanding of the ten years of busy life whose social aspects we are hereafter to examine. In the later chapters I shall endeavor to dwell with especial detail upon such facts, external, social, or individual, as illustrate and explain the history of American civilization in the state of California.

I. *The Land*

THE GENERAL topographical outlines of California are shown at once by the map. If one excludes the earliest settled and now very richly productive coast region south of Santa Barbara, the barren interior regions of San Bernardino County and of the adjoining territory to the southward, the other barren strip of land in Mono and Inyo counties, east of the Sierras and south of Mono Lake, and, finally, the great mountainous coast and interior lands of the extreme north, one has still left the main body of the state: namely, the central Coast Range, the great valley of the two rivers (the Sacramento and San Joaquin), and the main chain of the Sierra Nevada Mountains. This chief and central portion of the state shows to the Pacific Ocean a generally bold and rugged coast-line, with successive ranges of hills, nearly parallel to the coast, rising in some places to the height of three or four thousand feet. North of the latitude of Monterey this coast is often daily obscured in summer by cold and persistent fogs, which, climbing the Coast Range, or projecting in long gray tongues through the gaps of the range, finally disappear, as one goes inward, in the dry and cloudless summer air of the great interior valley. In this level and fertile valley the two rivers — the one rising far to the north, near Mount Shasta, the other in the Sierras of Fresno County — flow through their opposing courses and, meeting at last, discharge their waters by the two intermediate bays into the main body of the great San Francisco Bay, and so, through the Golden Gate, into the ocean. The two rivers, as they flow, receive from numerous tributaries the waters of the Sierra Nevada Range, which bounds the great valley on the east. The mountains of this range rise very gradually, at first in gently sloping and irregularly disposed lines of foothills, to the rugged and snowy highest ridges, which vary in elevation from nine or ten thousand to twelve or even fourteen thousand feet above sea level. Through the foothills the westward-flowing rivers have worn vast deep canyons, whose scenery has a character peculiar to this range. East of the summit there is a rapid descent, through steep and glacier-worn, but now often nearly dry and always very wild gorges, to the broken plateaus of the desert region. Not a drop of the water that flows down this eastern slope of the great chain reaches the sea, all being lost in "sinks" or in salt lakes. The largest of the eastward-flowing rivers are but great mountain torrents.

The great central valley and mountain region of California, thus roughly outlined, is a country full of telltale landscapes that show at a glance to the traveler the general topographical structure of the whole land. In the gently mountainous regions of even the more rugged of our Eastern states one may wander for many days, and see many picturesque or imposing landscapes, without getting any clear notion of the complex water system of the country through which he journeys. In most such hilly regions, if he climbs to some promising summit, hoping to command therefrom a general view of the land about him, he often sees in the end nothing but a collection of gracefully curving hills similar to the one that he has chosen. Winding valleys divide these hills with their endlessly complex and often broken lines. He gets no sense of the ground plan of the region. It seems a mass of hills, and that is all. Painfully, with the aid of his map, he identifies this or that landmark and so at last comprehends his surroundings, which, after all, he never really sees. But in the typical central Californian landscape, as viewed from any commanding summit, the noble frankness of nature shows one at a glance the vast plan of the country. From hills only eighteen hundred or two thousand feet high, on the Contra Costa side of San Francisco Bay, you may on any clear day see, to the westward, the blue line of the ocean, the narrow Golden Gate, the bay itself at your feet, the rugged hills of Marin County beyond, and the smoky outlines of San Francisco south of the Gate; you may follow with the eye, to the southward, the far-reaching lower arm of the great bay, and may easily find the distant range of the Santa Cruz Mountains; while to the eastward and northward you may look over the vast plains of the interior valley and dwell upon the great blue masses of the Sierra Nevada rising far beyond them and culminating in the snowy summits that all summer long would gleam across to you through the hot valley haze. From the Sierras themselves you might see the reverse of the picture. In the upper foothills, where I spent my childhood, we used to live in what seemed a very open country, with not many rugged hills near us, with the frowning higher mountains far to the eastward, and with a pleasant succession of grassy meadows and of gentle wooded slopes close about us. But just beyond the western horizon that the darkly wooded hills bounded, there loomed up from a great distance two or three sharp-pointed summits that were always of a deep blue color. These we knew to belong to the Coast Range; and the far-off ocean was, we fancied, rolling just at the western base of these peaks. If now we walked a mile or two to some higher hilltop, the whole immense river valley itself seemed at the end of our walk to flash of a sudden into existence before our eyes, with all its wealth of shining and winding streams, with the "Three Buttes," near Marysville, springing up like young giants from the midst of the plain, and with the beautiful, long, and endlessly varied blue line of the Coast Range bounding the noble scene on the west. Of course, what we could actually see of the great valley was but a very little part if compared to the whole; but the system upon which this interior region of the state was planned we as children could not fail to comprehend both very early and very easily.

The Coast Range is broken down at one point to give an entrance from the ocean through the Golden Gate into the Bay of San Francisco, upon the west shore of which, as we have just seen, lies San Francisco itself. North of the Gate the Coast Range forms a bolder and more rugged coast-line than towards the south. Almost directly east of San Francisco rises beyond the Contra Costa hills the blue summit of Monte Diablo, the most noteworthy landmark of the Coast Range for all the central portion of the state. From the summit of this peak, at an elevation of some 3,800 feet, one can best of all view the portion of the state with which the early American life had most to do.

The climate of California is too generally known now to need special description here. In the dry season, from June to September or October, there is a local climate close along the coast itself, from about the latitude of Santa Cruz northward, which, by reason of daily northwest winds and fogs, is as invigorating to all healthy people as it is disagreeable. One leaves San Francisco in summer, if at all, not to enjoy a cool holiday away from the city's oppressive heat, but to get into a warmer air. All the southern half of the state and all the interior valleys enjoy during the dry season clear and hot days, with cool and very restful nights. The rainy season is everywhere somewhat tedious, by reason of its two or three, or perchance more, very long and heavy southwest rain-storms; but in the intervals of these long rains, if, as commonly chances, no noticeable "cold wave" weather follows them (and so no example of the occasional bitter northers), then indeed one has the true chance to enjoy nature. Then one sees, perhaps in January or February, the clearest of skies and feels the most perfect of airs. The new grass springs on every hill, the song-birds are countless, and, by April and May, the vast fields of wildflowers are in full bloom. But April and May are the spendthrift months of wealthy nature. A few golden weeks of absolute freedom from winds and rains, of warmth and of sunshine, give place at last to the long sleep of the dry season, rainless also, and, in the interior, as windless and as dreamy as the climate of Lotus Island.

The first effect of the California climate is to improve the general health of nearly all newcomers, unless, indeed, being afflicted with pulmonary troubles, they should find the windy northern and central coast climate in the dry season too severe for them. Then, however, the interior valleys or the southern coast are still open to them and are very healthful. But one secondary effect of the climate is indeed not so favorable for anyone, in that the comparative evenness of the successive seasons prompts active people to work too steadily, to skip their holidays, and, by reason of their very enjoyment of life, to wear out their constitutions with overwork. Here is a fact of considerable importance for the understanding of California civilization. In early days, moreover, by reason of the utter carelessness of the mining population, fevers and dysentery were very prevalent in the Sacramento Valley and in the foothills of the Sierra. But people who so ate, drank, and lived as many of the miners chose to do hardly deserve commiseration for their well-earned diseases, even as the climate deserves but little blame therefor. On the whole, save in these careless early years, the country has been remarkably free from epidemics. Of the great present material resources of the land there is no need to speak here. We deal with the men.

II. *Outlines of Older California History*

THE SETTLEMENTS of Spanish missionaries within the present limits of the state of California date from the first foundation of San Diego in 1769. The missions that were later founded north of San Diego were, with the original establishment itself, for a time known merely by some collective name, such as the Northern Missions.[1] But later the name California, already long since applied to the country of the peninsular missions to the southward, was extended to the new land, with various prefixes or qualifying phrases; and out of these the definitive name Alta California at last came, being applied to our present country during the whole period of the Mexican republican ownership. As to the origin of the name California, no serious question remains that this name, as first applied, between 1535 and 1539, to a portion of Lower California, was derived from an old printed romance, the one that Mr. Edward Everett Hale rediscovered in 1862, and from which he drew this now accepted conclusion. For in this romance the name California was already before 1520 applied to a fabulous island, described as near the Indies and also "very near the Terrestrial Paradise." Colonists whom Cortes brought to the newly discovered peninsula in 1535, and who returned the next year, may have been the first to apply the name to this supposed island, on which they had been for a time resident.[2]

The coast of Upper California was first visited during the voyage of the explorer Juan Cabrillo in 1542-3. Several landings were then made on the coast and on the islands, in the Santa Barbara region. Cabrillo himself died during the expedition (on January 3, 1543), and the voyage was continued by his successor, Ferralo, who sailed as far north as 42°. The whole undertaking resulted in some examination of the coast-line as far as Cape Mendocino and in a glimpse of the native population that lived along the southern shores of the present state.[3]

In 1579 Drake's famous visit took place. During the latter half of June and nearly the whole of July, he remained in what *The World Encompassed* calls a "convenient and fit harbor" (about 38° 30'), where the ship was grounded for repairs, and where the expedition had considerable intercourse with the natives.

---

[1] H. H. Bancroft: *History of California*, Vol. I, p. 67.

[2] Ibid., Vol. I, p. 66; E. E. Hale, in *American Antiquarian Soc. Proceedings* for 1862; *Atlantic Monthly*, Vol. XIII, p. 265.

[3] Bancroft, op. cit., Vol. I, pp. 69–81.

One of the accounts complains, in extravagant fashion, of the chilly air and of the fogs of the region, and, in general, we get information from the accounts about the "white banks and cliffs, which lie toward the sea," and hear about what we now know as the Farallones, the rocky islets that lie just outside what we call the Golden Gate. While the other details of the stories, as given, are obviously in large part imaginary, there can be no doubt that Drake did land near this point on the coast and did find a passable harbor, where he stayed some time. It is almost perfectly sure, however, that he did *not* enter or observe the Golden Gate, and that he got no sort of idea of the existence of the great bay; while, for the rest, it is and must remain quite uncertain what anchorage he discovered, although the chances are in favor of what is now called Drake's Bay, under Point Reyes. This result of the examination of the evidence about Drake's voyage is now fairly well accepted, although some people will always try to insist that Drake discovered our Bay of San Francisco.[4]

The name San Francisco was probably applied to a port on this coast for the first time by Cermeñon, who in a voyage from the Philippines in 1595 ran ashore, while exploring the coast near Point Reyes. It is now, however, perfectly sure that neither he nor any other Spanish navigator before 1769 applied this name to our present bay, which remained utterly unknown to Europeans during all this period. The name Port of San Francisco was given by Vizcaino, and by later navigators and geographers, to the bay under Point Reyes, characterized by the whitish cliffs and by the rocky islets in the ocean in front of it. The coincidence of the name San Francisco with the name of Sir Francis Drake is remarkable, but doubtless means nothing. Christian names are, after all, limited in number; and those who applied this name to the new port were Spaniards and Catholics, while Drake was a freebooter and an Englishman.[5]

In 1602–3 Sebastian Vizcaino conducted a Spanish exploring

---

[4] On this voluminous controversy I pretend to no sort of independent opinion. See Bancroft, op. cit., Vol. I, pp. 81–94, for both result and references.

[5] Ibid., p. 97.

expedition along the California coast. He visited San Diego and Monterey bays, saw during his various visits on shore a good deal of the natives, and in January 1603 anchored in the old Port of San Francisco, under Point Reyes. From this voyage a little more knowledge of the character of the coast was gained; and thenceforth geographical researches in the region of California ceased for over a century and a half.[6]

With only this meager result we reach the era of the first settlement of Upper California. The missions of the peninsula of Lower California passed in 1767, by the expulsion of the Jesuits, into the hands of the Franciscans; and the Spanish government, whose attention was attracted in this direction by the changed conditions, ordered the immediate prosecution of a long-cherished plan to provide the Manila ships, on their return voyage, with good ports of supply and repairs, and to occupy the northwest land as a safeguard against Russian or other aggressions. For the accomplishment of this end the occupation of the still but vaguely known harbors of San Diego and Monterey was planned. The zeal of the Franciscans for the conversion of the gentiles of the north seconded the official purposes, and in 1768 the Visitador General of New Spain, José de Gálvez, took personal charge at La Paz of the preparation of an expedition intended to begin the new settlements in the north. The official purpose here, as in older mission undertakings, was a union of physical and spiritual conquest, soldiers under a military governor co-operating to this end with missionaries and mission establishments. The natives were to be overcome by arms in so far as they might resist the conquerors, were to be attracted to the missions by peaceable measures in so far as might prove possible, were to be instructed in the faith, and were to be kept for the present under the paternal rule of the clergy, until such time as they might be ready for a free life as Christian subjects. Meanwhile, Spanish colonists were to be brought to the new land as circumstances might determine, and, to these, allotments of land were in some fashion to be made. No grants of land in a legal sense were made or promised to the

---

[6] *Ibid.* Vizcaino's voyage attracted much more general attention than the earlier explorations of Cabrillo had received.

mission establishments, whose position was to be merely that of spiritual institutions, entrusted temporarily with the education of neophytes and with the care of the property that should be given or hereafter produced for this purpose. On the other hand, if the government tended to regard the missions as purely subsidiary to its purposes, the outgoing missionaries to this strange land were so much the more certain to be quite uncorrupted by worldly ambitions, by a hope of acquiring wealth, or by any intention to found a powerful ecclesiastical government in the new colony. They went to save souls, and their motive was as single as it was worthy of reverence. In the sequel the more successful missions in Upper California became, for a time, very wealthy; but this was only by virtue of the gifts of nature and of the devoted labors of the padres.

In January of 1769 the first of four expeditions, all intended for San Diego Harbor, set sail. Of the four expeditions, two were to go by land and two by sea; the last land expedition including Governor Portolá, and the famous head of the missionaries, Father Junípero Serra. The water expeditions suffered seriously from scurvy. About eighty Spanish friars and soldiers were at last united at San Diego, the first ship arriving April 11, 1769, and the first mission being founded, after the arrival of all four parties, on the 16th of July. An expedition that set out forthwith overland under Portolá to explore the northern coast and to find the harbor of Monterey actually passed the real port without recognizing it in the beginning of October. They marched still northward along the coast, until, on October 31, they came in sight of the Farallones, and of Point Reyes, which they saw from a place near the present Point San Pedro, on the southern part of the ocean coast of San Francisco Peninsula. Still, of course, ignorant of the existence of our present bay, they were not ignorant of the existence and current description of the old Port of San Francisco, with its cliffs and its little islands, and they at once recognized the place. A detachment was sent forward to reach this port at Point Reyes, and during the absence of this detachment some of the soldiers of the main party, while hunting, climbed the hills and first saw the great bay itself. The detach-

ment soon returned, having been unable to pass the Golden
Gate. After some days of further wandering on the peninsula,
the expedition returned towards Monterey.[7]

Thus began the career of Spanish discovery and settlement
in California. The early years show a generally rapid progress,
only one great disaster occurring — the destruction of San
Diego Mission in 1775, by assailing Indians. But this loss was
quickly repaired. In 1770 the Mission of San Carlos was
founded at Monterey. In 1772 a land expedition, under Fages
and Crespi, first explored the eastern shore of our San Francisco Bay, in an effort to reach by land the old Port of San
Francisco. This expedition discovered the San Joaquin River,
and, unable to cross it, returned without attaining the object
of the exploration. After 1775 the old name began to be generally applied to the new bay, and so, thenceforth, the name
Port of San Francisco means what we now mean thereby. In
1775 Lieutenant Ayala entered the new harbor by water. In
the following year the Mission at San Francisco was founded,
and in October its church was dedicated.

Not only missions, however, but pueblos, inhabited by Spanish colonists, lay in the official plan of the new undertakings.
The first of these to be established was San Jose, founded in
November 1777. The next was Los Angeles, founded in September 1781. The pueblos were intended, among other things,
to supply the new missions with the needed grain; but for a
good while they were not very prosperous.

The missions, on the other hand, had an organization and a
devout earnestness of superintendence that secured their swift
progress. They multiplied quickly in number, nine existing already in 1787 within the limits of California. In 1780, the sixteen missionary priests then present in the land were the spiritual rulers of some three thousand native converts. By the end
of the century there were eighteen missions, with forty padres,
and with a neophyte population of 13,500. Crops of from
30,000 to 75,000 bushels per year were by this time produced in

---

[7] For the account in full of this discovery of our San Francisco
Bay, collated from the sources, whereof the principal is Father
Crespi's diary of this expedition, see chap. vi of Bancroft's Vol. I.

the territory; and there were 70,000 horses and cattle, while the mission buildings and other properties were together valued at about a million pesos.[8] Such, then, was the material progress of the missionary work. The personal enthusiasm of Father Junípero, who from 1769 until his death in 1784 was at the head of mission affairs, has earned for him since a great popular reputation for ability and saintliness, a reputation made permanent by the biography that came from the pen of his friend Palou. And about Serra's high worth as a man and a Christian there is indeed no controversy among those who know his career. As to the value of these mission methods themselves opinions will no doubt always differ, although the matter seems to me a fairly plain one. The charges of systematic cruelty brought against the fathers were, to be sure, founded on a very superficial knowledge of their work. But these charges are not the real ones to be made against their efficiency. They had a poor understanding of sanitary precautions, and it was partly because of this that the death-rate at their missions was always very high. Their method of training, moreover (and this is the main consideration), did not really civilize their converts, but only made these hopelessly dependent upon them. The final outcome of their work, therefore, as we must conclude, was, for the cause of true spiritual progress in California, simply nothing; for, with their power, nearly every trace of their labors vanished from the world. But no one can question their motives; nor may one doubt that their intentions were not only formally pious, but truly humane. For the more fatal diseases that so-called civilization introduced among these Indians only the soldiers and colonists of the presidios and pueblos were to blame; and the fathers, well knowing the evil results of a mixed population, did their best to prevent these consequences, but in vain, since the neighborhood of a presidio was frequently necessary for the safety of a mission, and the introduction of white colonists was an important part of the intentions of the home government. But, after all, upon this whole toil of the missions, considered in itself, one looks back

---

[8] See the brief summary in Bancroft's *North Mexican States*, Vol. I, p. 749, as well as the fuller statements in Vol. I of the *California*.

with respectful regret, as upon one of the most devout and praiseworthy of mortal efforts and, in view of its avowed intentions, one of the most complete and fruitless of human failures. The missions have meant, for modern American California, little more than a memory, which now indeed is lightened up by poetical legends of many sorts. But the chief significance of the missions is simply that they first began the colonization of California.

Although commercial intercourse with foreigners was forbidden in the land, still, towards the close of the old century and the opening of the new, one finds some foreign attention attracted to California. The first foreign visitor had been the Frenchman, La Pérouse, in 1786. In 1792 Vancouver had visited the coast. In 1796 the first American ship, the *Otter*, of Boston, had appeared at Monterey and had obtained wood and water for her voyage. Both La Pérouse and Vancouver had described the land and the missions, the latter with some animadversions on the defenseless state of the country, and with expressions of surprise that so very small a force of soldiers could keep in awe so many thousands of natives. In 1806 the first Russian ship came to the port of San Francisco, from Sitka, under the direction of Rezanov, an official of high position, who had gone to Sitka as inspector of the establishments there. His purpose at the moment was to purchase supplies for the now nearly starving colony of Sitka. Although such transactions with foreigners were forbidden to the Californians, still, after long and vain negotiations with Governor Arrillaga, and with the commandant of the presidio, Argüello, Rezanov at last gained his commercial purpose by dint of making successful love to the beautiful daughter of Argüello, the Doña Concepción of the well-known and highly romantic tale that has since grown up out of this incident. Rezanov was actually betrothed, in the end, to the fair young daughter; and when he set out, with his purchases made, it was under the solemn promise to return and marry his new beloved as soon as possible. He died, however, while on the way across Siberia during his return to St. Petersburg. The story, told in several versions, and immortalized in Mr. Bret Harte's best poem, has won many tears. Rezanov him-

self describes the affair, in his reports, as a purely business-like
stroke of diplomacy, whereby he gained the decisive official
help of the Argüello family. Whether he was sincere in his love
or not, Doña Concepción undoubtedly was in hers. She died,
as nun, at Benicia, in 1857.[9]

This first Russian visit was followed, in 1812, by the founding
of a Russian colony under the auspices of the Fur Company
at "Ross," as the newcomers named their own settlement, which
was on the coast, about eighteen miles above Bodega Bay, and
a little north of the mouth of Russian River. Here the company
built a fort, negotiated and traded with the natives, secured
from the latter what the Russians later affected to consider a
title to the land, and remained in the place for some thirty
years, until 1841. The colony was especially useful as a trading
and supply station for the Fur Company. Its inhabitants numbered, as time went on, from 150 to 400, of mixed Russians,
Aleutian, and, later, California Indian blood; the force was always under the control of military officers and was kept in strict
discipline. Notwithstanding the numerous official obstacles in
their way, the Russians managed to get a good deal of grain
and provisions, by trade, from the Spaniards, and later raised
some grain themselves. These supplies were sent to various
Russian northern stations. But in the end the settlement
proved a failure for its purposes and was abandoned. A colony,
in the strict sense, this establishment never became, and such
plans of territorial acquisition as originally had to do with its
foundation were never developed to any noteworthy result.[10]
The establishment excited, from the first, just indignation and
considerable apprehension on the part of the Spanish authorities, and, later, of the Mexican authorities; but there was never
an open collision.

With the political events of the Spanish rule, and with the
life of the missions during their remaining years of prosperity

---

[9] The complete account from the sources is in Bancroft: *California*, Vol. II, pp. 64 ff.

[10] See in particular, on the life and industries of this settlement,
Bancroft: *California*, Vol. II, pp. 629 ff.

in the early part of our century, we have no further need to deal. The situation of the whole country was of course much altered when the independence of Mexico was proclaimed in California, at the beginning of 1822. There was, indeed, no active resistance thought of. In March arrived the news of the success of Iturbide's imperial regency. On the 9th of April a junta met at Monterey, composed of the last Spanish Governor, Sola, and of the principal officers present in the territory. This body passed resolutions of acquiescence in the new government and took the prescribed oath.[11] A commissioner, sent from Mexico to see that the new order of things was properly introduced into California, brought into existence the first provincial *diputación* or legislature in November of that year. This body was called upon by the commissioner to elect a governor, and in November chose Don Luis Argüello as the first of the series of Mexican governors.

The history of California under Mexican rule falls into two unequal periods: the one of comparative quiet, extending to 1831, the second being characterized by the rapid growth of a local California patriotism and by political feuds. Throughout both these periods the little province had to a great extent the management of its own affairs, and its subjection to Mexico proved at most times and in most respects a very imperfect subjection. Foreign trade was now permitted, under rather harassing restrictions, of which the most significant was an enormously high tariff. The population grew somewhat slowly. Mr. Bancroft's list of inhabitants at the close of the first volume of his *California* includes some 1,700 names of male settlers, soldiers, etc., of Spanish blood, who are actually on record as having lived in the province at some time between 1769 and 1800. The recorded and estimated aggregate white population was, in the year 1790, 990; in the year 1800, 1,800; and in the year 1810, 2,130.[12] Under the Mexican rule the white population had increased by 1830 to 4,250; and by 1840 to 5,780. Between this period and the conquest, as I suppose, the white

---

[11] Ibid., Vol. II, p. 451.
[12] Ibid., Vol. II, p. 158.

population may have been further increased by some 1,500 or 2,000 souls. It was popularly estimated at the moment as somewhere between 8,000 and 12,000 in 1846.

As for the general course of events during the Mexican period, one has first to note the very early change from the imperial to the republican form of government in Mexico — a change that the friars in California regarded with great displeasure and foreboding,[13] and which they opposed by word of mouth to an extent to which they had not opposed the change from Spanish sovereignty that was introduced by the imperial regency. Their leaders refused, in 1825, to take the prescribed oath to the republic and caused thereby some trouble to the civil authorities; but the only effect was slightly to increase the difficulties of local government, and, in the sequel, to widen the breach between the old clerical order of things and the new order that must inevitably spring up under Mexican dominion. From 1826 to 1830 the province quietly and gradually grew "toward the Mexican ideal of republicanism and the secularization of the missions," to quote Mr. Bancroft's words.[14] The Governor first sent, in the Mexican republican interest, to take charge of California was Echeandía, who came in October 1825; but the home government undertook little further, in those years, for the good of California, unless sending a few convicts to the land, in February 1830, be considered such an undertaking. In 1829 a revolt of some unpaid soldiers at Monterey, assisted by some native Californians, undertook to put the country into native Californian hands, while professing, for form's sake, firm allegiance to the central Mexican government, and alleging, as justification of the rising, abuse of authority on the part of Echeandía, whose headquarters were in the south. The leader of the revolt was a convict ranchero, Solís by name; but the movement gained no foothold in the south, and, after a bloodless pretense at a conflict near Santa Barbara, the rebels under Solís fled back again northwards to Monterey, only to find that town already turned against them.

---

[13] Ibid., Vol. II, p. 517; Vol. III, pp. 16 ff.

[14] Ibid., Vol. III, p. 31. On Governor Echeandía's career in California, see chaps. ii–vi of the same volume.

The movement now, of course, entirely collapsed, and Echeandía remained for the time in undisputed power. His work as Governor was partly devoted to the beginnings of the Mexican plan for the secularization of the missions of California. The original intention of Spain had been, as we know, to use the missions as stepping-stones, over which to pass to the true civilization of the new land. The entire failure of the missions effectively to civilize their neophytes or to prepare them for citizenship could not prevent, in republican Mexico, the effort to bring to an end the experiment that had failed so completely. In 1826 Echeandía issued a decree for the partial emancipation of the neophytes of San Diego, Santa Barbara, and Monterey — a decree whereby he freed them to some extent from the authority of the friars; and in 1830 he brought before the California legislative body a secularization plan, providing for the gradual transformation of the missions into pueblos and for giving each neophyte a share of property. The plan was approved by the legislature, and then forwarded to the supreme government for confirmation before it should be put into operation.

But in 1830 Echeandía was succeeded by Manuel Victoria, who had for some time been military commandant in Lower California, and who was appointed in March and arrived in December to assume the governorship of Alta California. There was some willful delay in the transfer of the office, and Victoria received the command in January 1831, just after his predecessor had rather hastily and vainly attempted to put into immediate effect his own plan of secularization before retiring. Victoria was welcomed by the friars as an opponent of secularization; but his rule, conducted after the fashion of a soldier, was with the non-clerical Californians unpopular and was brief. He did not convene the legislature, he seemed throughout arbitrary, and in criminal matters he sometimes transgressed his legal authority. Thus dissatisfaction grew general, both in the north and in the south, and quickly culminated in a successful revolt. Victoria was wounded in a fight with the insurgents near Los Angeles — a fight in which but two men in all were killed; and, deserted by his followers, the fallen Gov-

ernor consented to accept a chance to return to Mexico from
California, in December 1831.[15]

An interregnum followed, during 1832, with many domestic
quarrels over the governorship in the early part of that year;
but these were brought to an end by the expectation of a new
governor from Mexico. This new Governor proved to be José
Figueroa, an able man and a good official, whose services in
California, coupled as they were with an engaging personal
behavior, gained for him in the end the admiration of all the
Californians. His administration was interrupted by the vexatious and abortive Mexican colonization scheme that the Hijar
and Padrés party were commissioned to carry out, in 1834,
under official sanction. Part of the leader's (Hijar's) commission having been countermanded by fresh orders from Mexico,
which came to hand after the arrival of the colony in California, a quarrel sprang up between the Governor and Hijar as to
matters both of policy and of authority — a quarrel that led to
some rather serious difficulties. The whole colonization scheme
finally came to an end in 1835, although it had by that time
been the means of adding some two hundred to the population
of California. As for secularization, that approached slowly and
surely under Figueroa's administration, although he himself
was too moderate to aim for the moment at more than a gradual emancipation of the neophytes. But the same influences that
had led to the colonization scheme had acted in Mexico to
cause immediate secularization to be ordered, in a decree of
the Mexican Congress of August 17, 1833; and Hijar, with his
colony, in 1834, prepared to take part in the execution of this
decree. The failure of Hijar's plans did not prevent the secularization decree from having a certain effect. The padres began,
at certain missions, to slaughter the mission cattle and to sell
their produce as rapidly as possible. They also neglected their
unsalable properties very considerably, and in the meanwhile
the number of neophytes present at the missions began to show
a rapid decrease. Figueroa died in September 1835.[16]

---

[15] On Victoria's career, see ibid., Vol. III, chap. vii.

[16] See, for the events of his career, ibid., Vol. II, chaps. ix–xii,
pp. 240 ff.

With Figueroa's death begins a time of extremely complex political intrigue and conflict in California. The jealousy that Californians now more and more felt against all Mexican interference was henceforth joined with a rapidly growing jealousy between the northern and southern parts of the territory of California itself, to the disturbance of all political relations. Figueroa at his death left the governorship to José Castro, and the military commandancy to the ranking officer of the territory, Gutiérrez. The former gave over his civil office to Gutiérrez in January 1836; and the latter ruled for four quiet months, until the coming of Mariano Chico, who had been appointed by the central government to succeed Figueroa. Chico was the best hated, and, as to personal reputation, the most unfortunate of all the Mexican governors in California, although his rule was very brief. He had to encounter the growing jealousy aforesaid, and his personal bearing was such as to inflame rather than to conciliate it, insomuch that the Californians joined thenceforth in circulating exaggerated stories against him,[17] denouncing him as "tyrant, rascal, and fool." Furious personal quarrels, threatened rebellion, and lack of support from the central government forced him to retire in July of the same year; and Gutiérrez was once more left at the head of affairs. But the jealousy of everything Mexican was still growing. The mass of the Californians, although of the republican party, had found that Mexican republicanism brought no good to the land; while the padres, looking back regretfully to the old Spanish days, used their influence also to bring Mexican authority into discredit. The better Californian families felt themselves superior in blood to the most of the Mexicans; and the foreigners present in the land, numerous enough at this time to be influential, were equally opposed to Mexico.[18] The result of all this was the Alvarado revolution, in November 1836. With a force that included some American hunters and some foreign sailors, the revolutionists got possession of Monterey and sent Gutiérrez to Mexico; all of which was accomplished,

---

[17] Ibid., Vol. III, p. 427.
[18] This summary of the situation is founded on Bancroft's, in Vol. III, p. 449.

after the Californian fashion of civil warfare, without the shedding of blood and by the mere show of force. The country was declared a sovereign state, which was thenceforth to have, if possible, only a federal union with Mexico; the legislature elected Alvarado Governor ad interim, and the new administration began with seemingly good prospects. But the south, the Los Angeles and San Diego country, was still to be conciliated before California could be united in the new movement.[19] Though the Mexican flag still waved at Monterey, the reports carried to the south attributed to the revolutionists extravagant designs, such as the defiance of Mexico, the delivery of the province into American hands, and the subversion of the Catholic faith.[20] A patriotic reaction was therefore threatened from Los Angeles, and Alvarado had to go south with a force, to meet in person the influences arrayed against him. He was successful in winning general support at Santa Barbara, and he entered Los Angeles itself, without serious resistance, in January 1837. Further complications ensued; but in May the political success of Alvarado's cause in the south seemed already complete, and in a proclamation the new Governor declared the country free and united, although he never gave up the union with Mexico. But such complete practical freedom as he had thus far planned was indeed to be given up; for in June 1837 Andrés Castillero arrived as Mexican commissioner to California. He at first joined the opponents of Alvarado at San Diego and, with an armed force of southerners, under the leadership of partisan opponents of Alvarado, once more threatened to restore Mexican supremacy and to overthrow the northern leader. Castillero had been commissioned in Mexico to bring to California the constitutional laws of December 1836, which represented the new order in Mexico, and to receive the oaths of allegiance to this new order from Californian officials. Alvarado, before any collision of forces could take place, now resolved to dispose of the southern opposition by removing its chief ostensible cause; that is, by coming to terms with Castillero, by giving up his idea of

---

[19] For the revolution, see ibid., Vol. III, pp. 452–76.
[20] Ibid., Vol. III, p. 480.

mere federation, and by thus consenting to submit himself to constitutional Mexican authority. He hoped, not wrongly, as the sequel proved, that he could in this way get confirmation of himself as Mexican Governor, and at the same time, so to speak, "dish" his southern enemies. This "triumph in defeat" [21] Alvarado gained by coming into friendly relations with Castillero, and by persuading him to go back to Mexico in Alvarado's own interest, so as to get what Castillero had not yet, authority to receive Alvarado's submission, and further authority to make the latter, who still stood in the position of rebel, the constitutional governor of California. The southern opposition was thus for the time overcome.

In October 1837 the news of the appointment of a new Governor, Carlos Carrillo, reached the land. The appointment had been made before Alvarado's submission was heard of. The opponents of Alvarado were now once more delighted; Carrillo was himself a well-known Californian and commanded sympathy in the south. But, as turned out, he was politically incapable, and Alvarado forthwith determined to resist him, and did so successfully. In the subsequent warfare one little "battle" took place at San Buenaventura, which resulted in the death of one man and in the flight of the forces that represented Carrillo's party. In April 1838 Carrillo himself capitulated at Las Flores, some fifty or sixty miles north of San Diego; and Alvarado was again left, after this once more nearly bloodless conflict, in actual command of the country.

The successful rebel and able political leader was now erelong confirmed by the central government as constitutional governor of what was henceforth to be called the "Department of California," and thus the northern party triumphed over the south and over the Mexicans also. The rest of the rule of Alvarado was indeed not perfectly peaceful. In 1840 he quarreled somewhat bitterly with General Vallejo, his relative, his *comandante general*, and his former partisan. In the same year a much more serious and important event took place: namely, the expulsion to Mexico of above forty foreigners, a company largely made up of Americans and Englishmen, sail-

---

[21] Ibid., Vol. III, p. 527.

ors, hunters, and vagabonds. Among them was one Isaac Graham, who had taken part with Alvarado himself in the revolution of 1836, and whom the expulsion, as it was represented to our public, converted into a great hero. He was, however, a rascal, and, as the documents show, even such were nearly all his fellows in exile. But the American and English governments were led to look upon the affair as an outrage, and eighteen of the expelled returned in freedom next year. The charge made against the exiles was that of plotting against the government, and this charge was not entirely unfounded; but as it was not legally proved, the expulsion was not in form justifiable, although far too much has since been made of the so-called outrage, for which Mexico had later to pay.[22]

In 1842 Mexico made one more effort to give California a Mexican Governor, in the person of General Micheltorena. His well-meaning rule was embittered by the unfortunate character of the Mexican recruits that he brought with him when he came, since some of them were convicts, and all were disliked. In the end the Californians, of nearly all parties, joined in a revolt against Micheltorena, at the end of 1844. In January 1845 the united insurgents, having retreated to the south, were followed nearly to Los Angeles by the little regular army of Micheltorena, which had been joined by a force from the Sacramento Valley, consisting of American riflemen and of Indian servants of Captain Sutter. On the insurgent side, also, there were some Americans, residents in the south, who had a horror of the bad repute of Micheltorena's soldiers and who were determined to see all these "convicts" expelled from California. The Americans, however, from the two sides, met in a parley before the battle and resolved to remain neutral. The "battle" itself was as bloodless as most Californian encounters. Tremendous cannonading is sometimes said, in the accounts, to have taken place. Two or three horses and mules were hurt; but the armies on both sides kept well out of range. The result was the capitulation of Micheltorena, the success of a new revolutionary government, and, towards the close of the year, a new

---

[22] Bancroft's account, as far as yet published, is in his "Pioneer Register," Vol. III, p. 763, of the *California*.

mission of pacification from Mexico, and a new recognition of the existing order of things as the legal one. The Governor of the department was now Pio Pico, who was of the south and was the senior legislator of the *diputación*, while the *comandante general* was José Castro, who had formerly been prominent as a partisan of Alvarado and who lived at Monterey. The old quarrel of north and south quickly reappeared between these two, and the rest of the political history of California until the time of our conquest is one of intrigue and petty quarrel, which might have led to another bloodless civil war in 1846, had we not intervened with our own fashion of fighting. Civilized warfare was, in fact, introduced into California through the undertakings of our own gallant Captain Frémont. For in civilized warfare, as is well known, somebody always gets badly hurt.

III. *The Californians as a People*

AFTER this hasty glance at the past history of our province, we must describe in brief the character of the people, the condition of the country at the moment of our conquest, and the doings of our own countrymen in the land in the times before the conquest.

California, as we see, was in 1846 an outlying and neglected Mexican province. Its missions, once properous, had had their estates in large part secularized during the later years, had fallen into decay, and were now helpless and sometimes in ruins. The mission Indians had in large part disappeared. The church was no longer a power. The white population was made up principally of Spanish and Mexican colonists, whose chief industry was raising cattle for the hides and tallow, and whose private lives were free, careless, and on the whole, as this world goes, moderately charming and innocent. So at least those who really knew them always tell us. These people were gay and jovial, full of good fellowship and hospitality. Nearly all the better families of the community were superior to the average Mexicans, having generally a purer Castilian blood, since in many cases the colonists had come almost directly from Spain.

Crime was confined in general to the lower sorts of people in the towns. The rancheros lived much as comparatively well-to-do countrymen of happy and unprogressive type always live when in a mild climate. They rode a great deal, dressed in gay colors, visited one another frequently, had very pleasant social gatherings, enjoyed many sports together, drank at times, gambled a little, lived to a good old age, and had very large families. In the towns the life was a trifle more complex and there was a sharper distinction of social classes. But the heartiest hospitality, especially to strangers, was here, as in the country, almost universal. The rancheros paid their debts to the Yankee traders in the towns on the coast a little slowly; but they were still on the whole a very honest folk, and generally paid in the end, in the currency of the country — that is, in hides, which the traders received at the uniform value of two dollars apiece and sent to the United States by the Boston-bound ships. These ships, on their outward voyages, brought many-colored calicoes, together with boots, shoes, and nearly all the manufactured goods consumed in the country; and the natives paid enormous prices for these things, of course without ever dreaming of home manufactures.

The political feuds of the later years must not be interpreted as meaning that the Californians were revengeful and cruel, or that the whole thoughts of the people were devoted to quarrels and bitterness. On the contrary, the bloodless playfulness of these civil wars themselves, with their furious proclamations, their mock battles — noisy but harmless — and their peaceful endings, sufficiently characterizes the geniality, the simple-mindedness, the childish love of display, and the really humane tenderheartedness of this proud, gay, unprogressive, not very courageous, but surely comparatively guiltless people. Their private vices were of a youthful and sensuous but not of a deeply corrupt type. Their domestic life itself was generally pure and devoted. Their wives and daughters were in almost all cases above reproach, and were models of their own sort of womanhood. Sailor-boys, such as the young Dana's associates, might indulge in characteristic gossip about the supposed frailties of all Californian women — gossip such as was repeated in some passages of the *Two Years Before the Mast* — but those who knew the Californians well and lived among them have no such flippant remarks to make. Domestic fidelity is a very frequent virtue among at least the women of peoples that are at once Catholic and pastoral; and these Californian women were too remote from the world, and too decently trained, to hear of the vices of city life. The men, indeed — and especially the younger men — in such life as lay outside of domestic relations, lacked moral fiber; and some of the ablest of them early fell a prey to drunkenness or to worse vices. But their vices indicated, as I have said, rather a foolish youth than the developed brutality that our own Anglo-Saxon frontiersmen of the worst sort are accustomed to show. However worthy our American merchants and immigrant families often were in those days, our trappers and other like homeless wanderers in California in the years before 1846 were commonly a very far worse set than the Californians; a fact that these vagabonds themselves were not slow to realize, and one that inspired them individually with the most violent hatred and disgust towards all the rightful dwellers in the land.

The Californians had, of course, little opportunity for cultivation, and they had generally few intellectual ambitions. But, like the southern peoples of European blood generally, they had a great deal of natural quickness of wit, and in their written work often expressed themselves with ease and force. Their women were fascinating conversers, even when not at all educated. Their more noteworthy men, such as Alvarado, Vallejo, and others, were often persons of very marked intelligence and even of considerable reading. The curiously unequal æsthetic sense of the people always puzzled the American observer. They spoke and gestured with what seemed to our dull eyes wonderful grace. They appeared to be born musicians, and, quite without training, they sang finely and played their guitars skillfully and spiritedly. They dressed with true southern taste. All their movements on foot or on horseback were easy and picturesque; and their keen perception of beauty was in some ways marvelous. But, on the other hand, their houses were often very dirty and were seldom in the least attractive; and if one attributes this to their simplicity and to their total lack of power to buy better things for their houses, one has still to mention that curiously disgusting practice of many rancheros who were accustomed to slaughter animals and to strip and clean the carcasses almost, as it were, in their dooryards and so to make the ground not far from their houses look like Golgotha. Hospitality to a stranger sometimes included slaughtering before his eyes the bullock that he was to eat and preparing the carcass on the spot. And early travelers are never weary of complaining of the fleas found in nearly all the houses.

That the Californian was uninventive and was content in his way with atrociously awkward mechanical devices follows, of course, very easily from his national character and habits. His wagons had four sections of a log for wheels. He had hardly any good firearms and could not use what he had to advantage against any American frontiersman, being himself no marksman. He took care of his cattle and horses well enough for his very simple purposes, but cared little for further agricultural progress, and seldom even thought of using milch-cows. He was patriotic in his devotion to what he often called his country — namely, California itself. He was a fairly good citizen, submissive to his alcaldes, or local judges, and he was reasonably loyal to the political faction that he had for the time espoused. But in politics, as in morals and in material wealth, he was unprogressive. When his time of trial should arrive he would show no great power of endurance. The coming temptations and excitements, the injustice and the unkindness of a conquering and often wickedly progressive race, would often find him morally weak, and would rapidly degrade him, too often losing for him his manhood and his soul altogether, to his own bitter shame, and often to the still greater shame of his stronger brother, the carelessly brutal American settler or miner.

IV. *The Americans in California before the Conquest*

Somewhat early in the century there appeared on the California coast American trading-vessels and whalers. By the voyage of the trading-vessel *Sachem* in 1822 the trade between

Boston and California was opened, and a cargo of tallow and hides was obtained at Monterey.[23] Hereafter the American trade rapidly increased and in the end became the chief trade in existence on the coast during the Mexican period. From the East, meanwhile, trappers and hunters began to come overland to California as early as 1826, which was the year of a trapping party led by Jedediah S. Smith.[24] From both of these sources of communication California received in the sequel additions to her population. The first Americans who were led to take up their residence in the land were, for the most part, men of character and ability, who were concerned in the Boston trading enterprises. Some of those who thus came, even before 1830, have since been, in their own callings, prominent in California affairs down nearly to the present moment. When the newcomers had business in the land and were well-disposed persons, they were, during the early Mexican period, very welcome among the hospitable Californians. Many applied for naturalization as Mexican citizens and obtained it. A considerable number, in the sequel, married into California families; some acquired land grants and became very prosperous. Mexican law, meanwhile, was always in form very strict about requiring passports of foreigners and about subjecting them to a good deal of official watching. Such restrictions proved, however, of little practical inconvenience to men of good behavior and of responsible position in California.

Before 1835 about thirty of the hunters who had entered California in the various overland parties are said to have taken up a more or less permanent abode in the land.[25] The popular feeling towards foreigners was in 1835 still tolerant and in many cases very cordial, and little fear of foreign aggression existed. In all, perhaps three hundred, according to Mr. Bancroft's estimate, would express the number of the foreign male population in 1835.[26] It was in this year that the young Dana's

---

[23] Ibid., Vol. II, p. 475.

[24] Ibid., Vol. III, p. 152.

[25] Ibid., Vol. III, p. 393.

[26] Ibid., Vol. III, p. 402. This includes "sons of pioneers by native wives."

visit fell. In 1836 the American hunters near Monterey, together with some other foreigners, took part, as we have seen, in the Alvarado revolution. By 1840, as we have also seen, some of these very men had rendered themselves so obnoxious as to bring about the expulsion of the less welcome foreigners in that year — an expulsion that did not affect Americans of any position in the land, and that was probably not very seriously disapproved by the American merchants themselves, or by the American landowners. Yet with the time of this occurrence the era of greater or less trouble with foreigners may be said to have begun. But no general hatred or oppression of foreigners, such as has often been attributed to the Californians of this period, ever existed before 1846. The troubles, such as they were, were caused, during these last few years, almost altogether by the lawless, or at best suspicious, acts of a few foreign vagabonds. Such persons — escaped sailors, wandering hunters, adventurous rascals of various sorts — were from time to time a source of trouble and anxiety to Californian alcaldes and governors. Such Americans as these were of course the loudest in their protests when they were arrested or expelled, and such freely threatened that American citizens would take the first opportunity that offered to free this land from what these law-breakers naturally regarded as Mexican oppression. No wonder that all Californians came to dislike such people as these, and that some prominent men of the country extended this personal dislike to our whole nation. But, before the era of the conquest itself, we cannot say that the Californians as a people were enemies of the American nation, or that we by rights need have feared any very violent opposition from them to our own national schemes of commerce and of possession in the Pacific regions. In 1842, just as Micheltorena was on his way from Mexico to California, about to enter on his duties as Governor, our naval commander in the Pacific, Commodore Thomas Ap Catesby Jones, hearing at Callao an unfounded report that our national difficulties with Mexico about Texas had already culminated in war, formed a hasty resolution to seize upon the ports of California, in advance of further orders from his government. Accordingly he sailed to Monterey, entered the harbor, and seized the port, without meeting any resistance to his raising of the flag. The act produced no small momentary consternation in Monterey, but nobody there seems to have planned any serious measures of further defense. Hearing, however, that the report upon which he had acted was unfounded, Jones took down the flag the next day, apologized, and retired, stopping, on his voyage, at San Pedro, and visiting at Los Angeles the new Governor Micheltorena himself. Jones's apologies were accepted with goodwill by the Californians, and, while the central Mexican government took every possible diplomatic advantage of the outrage, in the correspondence that ensued with our government, the Californian people themselves, in their benighted state of semi-independence, showed a very imperfect sense of how much they had been injured by this insult offered to Mexico. The American merchants on the coast felt their intercourse with the Californians no less cordial than before, and the incident passed by without further evil consequences.[27]

Most prominent, in the later years, among the American merchants on the coast was Thomas O. Larkin, a native of Massachusetts, a shrewd and able trader, who had come to California already in 1832 and who in the end acquired a considerable fortune as owner of a wholesale and retail store in Monterey. It was he who, in 1844, was made by our government the first,

[27] For the correspondence between the Mexican and American governments about this affair see House Ex. Doc., 3rd Sess., 27th Congr., Vol. V, Doc. 166. For the views of the Californians, see Mr. Alfred Robinson's *Life in California* (New York, 1846), pp. 210 ff.; also Consul Larkin's letters to the State Department as later cited. Mr. Robinson's whole book is one of the best of the early American accounts of the people and of American life in the land. The author is, in 1885, still living in San Francisco, certainly the oldest surviving American pioneer, and a man of very fine ability and judgment. Much of the foregoing view of the Californian life and of the intercourse with Americans I have derived from unpublished statements now in Mr. Bancroft's library. Of these one of the most interesting descriptions of the people is that by Mr. W. H. Davis, a MS. entitled "Glimpses of the Past." Mr. Bancroft's invaluable treasures, the Larkin Papers, throw a great deal of indirect light on the same topic.

and, as it proved, the last, American consul. It was also he who, during the years between 1840 and 1846, most wisely and cautiously brought to bear his not inconsiderable personal influence to increase the goodwill of the native Californians towards the American government and people, and who, by occasional letters to newspapers at home, labored to make his countrymen understand the importance of California. As we shall hereafter see, Larkin is the only American official who can receive nearly unmixed praise in connection with the measures that led to our acquisition of California. His actual effectiveness was indeed greatly hindered by the unwarranted doings of other people; but he occupies the happy position of having done his official duty in the matter so far as he knew his duty.

Larkin, though a clever servant in this one position, was no educated man. In his dispatches to the State Department he often writes rather uncouthly; but he always writes sensibly. In his business relations he was enterprising, fully possessed of his provincial shrewdness, and sometimes overbearing; but his hospitality is always highly praised by the Americans of the time before the conquest, while his influential position as merchant at Monterey, together with his later official rank, made his house for some years before 1846 the social headquarters of the Americans in California. After the gold-discovery he became for a while quite wealthy and lived for some years in the East. He is said to have expressed chagrin (not, to be sure, without good cause) in view of the lack of appreciation that prominent people always showed for his past services in helping to win California. This imperfectly educated California trader no doubt appeared, in his later years, to poor advantage in New York and Washington, where he had no influential friends to sound his praises in political circles; but history will give him the credit of having been his country's most efficient instrument in California at the period of the conquest.

His correspondence, both with his mercantile friends in California and with the State Department at Washington, has been preserved among his family papers and is now in Mr. H. H. Bancroft's hands. It is the best source extant concerning the moods, the hopes, the fears, the murmurings, the petty personal quarrels, the private gossip, and the whole social life of the American traders in California before the conquest; and, as we shall see, it is the only source, save the Washington archives, whence can be derived a knowledge of the true official story of the conquest itself.

Between 1839 and 1846 there grew up in the Sacramento Valley a settlement of Americans, composed partly of most worthy and conservative men and partly of such wanderers as I before have mentioned. Of all the early American undertakings in the land, this was naturally the one that aroused most seriously and justly the suspicions of the Californians. Most of these newcomers reached California overland. Many of them were persons but little known to the natives, while some of them were, unfortunately, too well known. Only a few of them appeared very frequently, or were well and favorably regarded, on the coast. The others were understood, after 1844, to be occasionally plotting a rising against the authorities of the department; and some of them were certainly men of bad character. Therefore, although the settlement, whose nucleus was Captain J. A. Sutter's Fort, near the junction of the American and Sacramento rivers, was an officially recognized thing, and although Sutter himself was a regular officer of the government, and had received in 1841 a land grant of the maximum legal amount (eleven square leagues) from Governor Alvarado, still the Californians suspected Sutter's settlers more than they did any other large company of Americans, and feared very often the consequences that might ensue if many more immigrants came over the Sierras. It was never so much any official American aggression as the coming of bad Americans that the Californians of those days seriously and justly dreaded. There was indeed never any thought of actually expelling these newcomers, because everyone saw the impossibility, after 1843, of any such attempt. And if the new settlers should prove peaceable men, the Californians were never disposed to maltreat them. But the settlers themselves were frequently the most willing to give a boastful and bad account of the great things that they would yet do in the land.

John A. Sutter himself was of Swiss family and of German

birth. He long (to say the least of it) permitted the story to be circulated that he had been in the service of Charles X in France; but in later years he admitted the falsity of the report. After living some years in our country and becoming a citizen, he came to California in 1839, by the way of the overland route to Oregon, and by a sea passage from Oregon via the Sandwich Islands. He at once founded, with official permission, his settlement in the Sacramento Valley, and two years later got his grant of land. In 1841 he was joined by some of the American immigrants who came overland that year, and the subsequent years saw a rapid increase of his prosperity and of the numbers of those who either assisted him or took up land under his grant or used his fort as their rendezvous. He employed many Indians, raised large crops of grain, aimed to make his little colony the producer of nearly all its own supplies, showed much hospitality to newcomers, and in 1845 undertook to assist Governor Micheltorena in the latter's troubles. In consequence of this last blunder he was on poor terms with the successful revolutionary authorities during the brief remainder of the Mexican period. In character Sutter was an affable and hospitable visionary, of hazy ideas, with a great liking for popularity, and with a mania for undertaking too much. A heroic figure he was not, although his romantic position as pioneer in the great valley made him seem so to many travelers and historians. When the gold-seekers later came, the ambitious Sutter utterly lost his head and threw away all his truly wonderful opportunities. He, however, also suffered many things from the injustice of the newcomers. He died a few years since in poverty, complaining bitterly of American ingratitude. He should undoubtedly have been better treated by most of our countrymen, but, if he was often wronged, he was also often in the wrong, and his fate was the ordinary one of the persistent and unteachable dreamer. He remained to the end a figure more picturesque than manly in our California life.

The settlers at and near Sutter's Fort included some families and a number of very able young men. In January 1844 the fort was visited by the first exploring expedition that the young officer of engineers, then Lieutenant Frémont, conducted to the land. The expedition had crossed the Sierras in midwinter; and now, greatly exhausted and nearly starved, the men were over-joyed to meet with the delights of Sutter's hospitality. This expedition it was that the young leader so finely described in his great Report, a work that soon became almost universally known and that will always remain a monument of literary skill in its kind. While the exploring expedition had really visited little country that was not already more or less known to settlers or to trappers, this description first let the public hear of the places that had been seen. I fancy that this Report will be, in future generations, General Frémont's only title, and a very good one, to lasting and genuine fame.

Just at the very moment of the conquest the greatest of the overland immigrations, so far, was taking place, that to California and Oregon in 1846. Although this company reached the land after the conquest, their journey should be treated of before the conquest, because when they set out they knew nothing of the change. The importance of their movement, which brought to California directly several hundred new settlers, and by way of Oregon many more, cannot well be overestimated. The men of 1846 afterwards joined the other Americans, during the interregnum, in building up for themselves the strong conservative sentiment that proved so useful in the constitutional convention of 1849. The newcomers arrived in time, also, to join in suppressing the revolt of the winter of 1846-7; and their journey overland was marked by numerous interesting incidents, of which we have good accounts. Two of the best books ever written on emigrant life were produced by men of this company; [28] and the latest of all the immigrants of this year formed the famous and unhappy Donner party, whose sufferings will always remain prominent among the tales of human sorrow. Their story belongs to the winter of 1846-7; but, as I have said, all these events are in effect prior to the conquest, of which the people concerned knew nothing until they reached California.

---

[28] J. Q. Thornton's *Oregon and California* (New York, 1849, 2 vols.) and Edwin Bryant's *What I Saw in California* (New York, 1848).

The Donner party, to speak very briefly of this affair, consisted of some eighty men, women, and children. On the way they were belated by the difficulties of the new route that they had taken, by the south side of Salt Lake. On the Humboldt River provisions ran low, their forebodings increased, and their gloom was deepened by an affray in which one of the best men in the train struck down and killed a young companion during a quarrel caused by the delay of a wagon. The homicide was tried, and condemned to exile from the train, in which his own family was traveling. He actually made his way to California on foot, in advance of the train, and later helped to relieve his family and his comrades.

This affray was a characteristic result of the nervous strain incident to the old-fashioned sort of emigrant life among people who are not well accustomed to such life; but it was only a prophecy of the demoralization that was to follow. Crossing the Humboldt Desert, the party reached the Truckee Canyon, where they were met by a couple of Sutter's Indians, who had been sent, with mule-loads of beef, to meet and temporarily to supply them. After this, when they had gone up a little beyond the present town of Truckee, they came in view of the summit range, already covered with snow. The sight destroyed for a time all their good sense. In wild and irregular efforts to cross the steep range in this snow, they lost two or three days, and at last, when they had begun to make up their minds to the horrible thought of wintering in the mountains, upon such provision as they had and upon such as they could yet make by slaughtering their animals, they lost still some hours in brooding over their fate. At this crisis a great storm arose, and in one fatal night their cattle were buried in the snows beyond hope of recovery, and they were left to live as they might in the poor huts that must now be their only refuge. Sutter's two Indians remained with them, as helpless as themselves.

The subsequent tale of starvation, of the "Forlorn Hope," and of its great effort to reach the settlements in the Sacramento Valley — an effort in which seven out of the twenty-two in the "Forlorn Hope" succeeded — of the successive relief expeditions from the valley, of the great loss of life in the whole Don-

ner party, of the resort to human flesh, and of the final rescue
in the late winter and in the spring of 1847, all this is too long
for us to tell here.[29] The story is a very instructive one, however, as an illustration of just the strength and the weakness
that men and women of our century and race show under such
trials; and it well deserves the elaborate treatment that it has
in later times received.

In closing our account of California as the conquest found
it, I have yet two things to mention that proved in the sequel
to be of vast importance to all concerned. One is the system of
land grants that, in the later years, had more and more developed itself. Most of the ranches in California in 1846 were
held under grants made by the various governors of California
— grants legally subject to a confirmation from the general government, although this confirmation was not usually considered
of sufficient importance to be actually obtained. The governors
made their grants under colonization laws and were therefore
limited somewhat as to the number of square leagues that
could be granted to one person and as to the places and conditions of the grants. No exact survey was ever made of the tracts
granted, which usually were defined, each as so and so many
square leagues, to be taken within given outside boundaries,
the boundaries themselves being generally natural ones, or else
parallels of latitude. Another fashion of land grants existed,
however, within the limits of legally recognized pueblos, or
towns. Each of these had, namely, in theory, a tract of four
square leagues, within which its authorities might grant lots of
land to actual settlers. This tract was of course actually ill defined, and the nature of the town's title to the land was, to our
American minds, somewhat obscure. Upon individual land-
titles, whether derived from ranch grants or pueblo rights,

---

[29] The best authority is McGlashan's *History of the Donner Party*
(San Francisco, 1880). Thornton's account in his *Oregon and California* is also good. Sutter's two Indians were killed and eaten by the
starving members of the "Forlorn Hope"; and the hospitable Sutter,
in his latest statements, complained bitterly of this ungrateful act,
whereby, as he says, he lost not only his beef but his two good
Indians.

there frequently were imposed, by the terms of the grant, special conditions, whose nature also often seemed obscure, since in many cases they were left unobserved, although the grant might still receive, in all later years, every practical official recognition. On the whole, then, this system of Mexican grants, simple, vague, and useful enough for the purposes of a pastoral people widely scattered over a vast territory, was sure to cause doubt, vexation, and sorrow whenever a new and numerous population should appear and whenever the land should grow valuable.

The other important fact to be mentioned is that, between 1836 and 1846, on the shores of San Francisco Bay, at a considerable distance from the old mission in one direction and from the presidio of San Francisco in another, there had grown up the beginnings of the modern city in the village of Yerba Buena, named from the cove in front of it. This little village was from the first a trading-place, whose dwellers were mostly Americans, Englishmen, and other foreigners. The Hudson's Bay Company maintained an establishment here for some years, but withdrew it in 1845. The most prominent men there at the beginning of 1846 were a few American merchants. Grants of lots of land had been made at Yerba Buena, and this portion of the already legally existent pueblo of San Francisco (whose boundaries, had they been then defined, would have extended far to the south on the peninsula) occupied in many minds the place of the promising nucleus of a future great city.

With this preliminary sketch of the country, of its inhabitants, and of its strangers, in the days before our conquest, we must pass to the proper subject of our discourse, to the coming, to the deeds, and to the fortunes of our people in California between 1846 and 1856.

Chapter II

THE AMERICAN AS CONQUEROR: THE SECRET
MISSION AND THE BEAR FLAG

IN the strict sense, we Americans have seldom been conquerors, and early California shows us our nation in this somewhat rare character. A few men did the work for us, but their acts were in some cases directly representative of the national qualities, and in others of far-reaching influence on the life and character of our people in California in the subsequent days. For both reasons these acts concern us deeply here and are very instructive for our purposes.

Moreover, the story of the conquest belongs, for yet other reasons, even more to national than to local annals. Our plans for getting the coveted land, and the actual execution of these plans, are a part of the drama of the Mexican War, and our national honor is deeply concerned in the interpretation given to the facts. As for the treatment of these facts here, a bare summary would be, in the present day, more vexatious than a detailed study; for a bare summary would either leave all the mysteries unsolved or else seem to fill all the gaps with mere dogmas. The whole story of the conquest is turbid with popular legends. We cannot follow the narrative in a simple way and tell incident after incident. The condition of our knowledge of the subject forbids such a purely narrative procedure save in fragments. What can be given might indeed be suggestively entitled "Commentaries on the Conquest" in a very literal sense of the word *commentary*. We have to employ numerous sources of information and to use our best historical intelligence. Yet I beseech the reader not to despair of finding in this chapter the interest that properly belongs to a dramatic series of events. These very problems of the conquest, the mysteries that have hung over parts of the story, are, as I have just hinted, themselves dramatic, and the investigation seems to me to present many elements of exciting interest, even apart from the original fascination of the incidents.

The subsequent history of the American people in California

turns, I have suggested, in large measure upon the occurrences
of the conquest. The prejudices, the enmities, and the mistakes
of that unhappy time bore rich fruit in the sequel, determining
to a great extent the future relations of the newcomers and the
natives; and these relations in their turn determined, in no
small degree, both the happiness and the moral welfare of the
newcomers themselves. We must understand the conquest if
we are to understand what followed. The attitude that chance,
the choice of one or two representative men, and our national
character made us assume towards the Californians at the moment of our appearance among them as conquerors we have
ever since kept, with disaster to them and not without disgrace
and degradation to ourselves. The story is no happy one; but
this book is written, not to extol our transient national glories,
but to serve the true patriot's interest in a clear self-knowledge
and in the formation of sensible ideals of national greatness.

From the point of view of the study of historical fact as such,
this history of the conquest is one of the strangest examples of
the vitality of the truth. Never were the real motives and methods of a somewhat complex undertaking more carefully or, by
the help of luck, more successfully hidden from the public than
the methods and motives of certain of our national agents in
California at the time of the conquest have for a generation
been hidden. And never has accident more unmercifully turned
at last upon its own creations.

I. *The Confidential Agent, and the Beginnings of War*

As the reader knows from the foregoing, our hearts were set
upon California as one prize that made the Mexican War
most worth fighting. The Bay of San Francisco, the future commerce of the Pacific, the fair and sunny land beyond the Sierras, the full and even boundary westward, the possible new
field for the extension of slavery — such motives were powerful
with some or all of our leaders. The hasty seizure of Monterey
in 1842, although wholly disavowed by our government, was a
betrayal of our national feeling, to say the least, if not of our
national plans, which no apology could withdraw from plain

history. Meanwhile, with more or less good foundation, we had strong fears of both England and France as dangerous rivals in the acquisition of this Western land. In short, to use the phrase so often repeated by opponents of the Mexican War, California formed a great part of the "Naboth's vineyard" that we coveted and that for years we had expected some day to get by the fairest convenient means.

Nor was our desire for California in itself an evil. However difficult the righteous satisfaction of the desire might prove, this desire was inevitable. Our national duty doubtless forbade our cheerful surrender of the Pacific coast to any European power. And by sloth, neglect, and misgovernment Mexico had done all she could do to make her California vineyard bring forth wild grapes and to forfeit her proprietary rights in its soil. Not "Naboth" in this case was the one whom we were most in danger of wronging, although indeed we did wrong him fearfully. He, poor fellow, was distracted in his own house, tilled not his own fields, and often was stained with blood. It was the true proprietor of California that, when we coveted the land, we were most apt to injure; it was the disorganized but not wholly unpromising young nation of a few thousand cheerful, hospitable, and proud souls on the Pacific coast that we were especially bound to respect. With their goodwill if possible, and at all events with the strictest possible regard for their rights, we were bound in honor to proceed in our plans and undertakings on the Pacific coast. The Mexican War, if deliberately schemed, and forced into life through our aggressive policy, would be indeed a crime; but it would be adding another great crime if we wronged these nearly independent Californians while assailing their unkind but helpless mother.

The slow and steady growth of the American settlements in California was not the result of any definite plot on the part of our government. Yet, as the correspondence of the State Department with Consul Larkin shows, the government was curious concerning this very matter; and the American colonization was looked upon as a fortunate occurrence for us, and as a process that, if let alone by the course of events and particularly by European aggressors, might of itself suffice, here as in Texas, to secure to us the country. Yet nobody intended to leave the decision of the matter to so slow a process as this. Natural colonization would need to be assisted.

During 1845, and after the accession of the Polk administration, our government was busily preparing for the expected Mexican War; and of course California had a large place in the cabinet policy. Buchanan was then Secretary of State, Marcy of War, and Mr. George Bancroft of the Navy. To Buchanan naturally fell much of the work of dealing directly with Naboth; while Mr. Bancroft prepared repeated instructions to our naval squadron in the Pacific and strengthened it gradually for its work. Just how California entered into these administration plans, this there was good reason at the time for keeping profoundly secret. It is helpful, however, to remind ourselves that there were, on the surface of things, three definable and not unnatural ways of undertaking the task. Possibly no one was chosen; possibly one was decidedly preferred; possibly they were in some way combined. But, stated in a merely formal way, and for our own purposes sharply distinguished, they were: (1) to wait until war had been forced upon Mexico and actually begun, and thereupon to seize the department of California as an act of war; (2) to undertake, with semiofficial support of some sort, the colonization of the country by an unnaturally rapid immigration of Americans into it; and (3) to take advantage of the strained relations already existing between California and the mother country and, by means of intrigue, to get the land through the act of its own native inhabitants.

The question as to the use made of these possible plans is, however, at once complicated for us by the fact that the conquest, as it actually occurred in 1846, seems to express on the face of events a plan that at least in part differs from all the foregoing, and that for boldness, both physical and moral, would surpass them altogether. This plan is the one usually supposed to have found expression in the singular operations of the gallant young Captain Frémont with his surveying party, in the spring of 1846. I must beg the reader to approach this very curious historical problem with a mind quite free from all presuppositions, since, as we shall soon see, the historians of California have always been not only much perplexed about the matter, but also in some respects misled. The whole truth about Captain Frémont's operations in California in 1846 has never so far been told. But, at all events, whatever the truth, the appearances, as they have been interpreted, have certainly been made to indicate a fourth plan, whose independence of all moral considerations on the part of the government said to have ordered it, and whose audacious vigor, would put it on a level with that Russian Central Asian policy whereof the Penjdeh incident has recently reminded the world. The execution of this supposed plan gave Captain Frémont a national reputation, nearly made him, ten years later, president, and still remains his most popular title to distinction.

To speak of this supposed fourth plan is to plunge at once into the incidents of the conquest itself, and forces us to begin with its romantic first scene, the "Bear Flag affair." We shall indeed have to return later to the point of departure, and from the California affairs of 1846 we shall need to go back to the Washington councils of 1845; but this defect in our narrative is not ours, but belongs of necessity to the comprehension of a problematic and, in the past, partly legendary story.

The young Captain Frémont, of the topographical engineers, had, as we all know, and as the foregoing chapter has more particularly shown, acquired before 1845 a great public reputation by what most people called a kind of discovery of California, inasmuch as he had described his own journey thither and in a most excellent narrative had brought the fair land before the eyes of numberless readers. When he set out in 1845 on a new expedition, he was certain to be followed with no little interest. This time it was at least his ostensible object to explore the most direct routes to the Pacific coast, and to do topographical work in California. He was accompanied by some sixty men — surveyors, guides, and assistants. The party were well armed and had about two hundred horses. During the winter they came in two divisions through the Sierras, and when the two divisions had found each other once more, after considerable difficulty, the captain, almost alone, went, with a

passport from Sutter, to Monterey, and asked permission from
Castro "to winter" with his party "in the valley of the San
Joaquin, for refreshment and repose." So he tells us himself,[1]
and adds that leave was granted, "and also leave to continue
my explorations south to the region of the Rio Colorado." In
the last days of February, as he then says, he began his march
south, "crossing into the valley of the Salinas." The purpose of
going south from the San Joaquin Valley to the Rio Colorado
by way of the Salinas Valley, as if one should set out to survey
the region from the Mohawk Valley to the Potomac by crossing over into the Connecticut River Valley, was neither at the
time nor in the immediately following investigations made perfectly plain by the friends of Captain Frémont, although he has
since given a more definite explanation. At all events, we have
his assurance before the Kearny court-martial that "the object
of the expedition was wholly of a scientific character, without
the least view to military operations, and with the determination to avoid them as being, not only unauthorized by the government, but detrimental or fatal to the pursuit in which I
was engaged." Under these circumstances a difficulty that now
occurred with General José Castro was especially unfortunate,
both for the pursuit in which Captain Frémont was so far engaged and for other interests. In the midst of his march through
the Salinas Valley, and as a result of petty occurrences for
which his rude men were by no means blameless, Captain Frémont received a notification from Castro to depart, accompanied with threats of violence in case he should not obey. The
consequence is well known. The young captain "took a position on the Sierra," on the Gavilan peak, overlooking the Salinas
Valley, "intrenched it, raised the flag of the United States, and
awaited the approach of the assailants." But Castro's anxiety to
assail such a position, guarded by American riflemen, was more
apparent than real. And, on the other hand, the gallant captain
of the topographical party desired only to bid a temporary defiance and was not anxious to begin an aggressive war. After
a few days he retired, aiming for the San Joaquin Valley and

[1] In his defense before the Kearny-Frémont court-martial, Sen.
Ex. Doc. 33, 30th Congr., 1st Sess., p. 372.

retreating with leisurely stages northward. This was in March 1846. He passed through the Sacramento Valley towards Oregon, and had already reached the Oregon border, on the banks of Klamath Lake, when he was overtaken by a newcomer from Washington, Lieutenant Archibald Gillespie, who had nearly caught up with the main party, when Captain Frémont, advised of Gillespie's approach, turned back with a few men and met him.

The meeting was a romantic one, but its romance sounds very hackneyed now, since the tale has been repeated in so many books of Western adventure. It is enough to remind the reader that the night following the meeting was enlivened by an attack made by lurking Indians, who killed three of Captain Frémont's men before the wholly unguarded little company were fairly awake, and who were then promptly repulsed. But before this incautious sleep had taken possession of the camp, Gillespie had delivered to the young captain a packet of family letters from Senator Benton, a letter of introduction from the Secretary of State at Washington, and some oral information of an official nature. Gillespie had left Washington with secret personal instructions from the President, and with a secret dispatch, early in November 1845. This meeting on the shores of Klamath Lake took place on the evening of the 9th of May 1846. Gillespie, after reaching Monterey and seeing Consul Larkin there, had promptly sought out Captain Frémont, whom the government had quite certainly intended him to meet.

The nature of the information delivered to Captain Frémont has remained heretofore, for the public, a mystery; and writers have vied with one another in guesses, although they have usually inferred that, at all events, what Gillespie delivered somehow officially authorized Captain Frémont's subsequent course.

The common argument upon this topic insists especially upon the peculiar facts about Gillespie's mission — facts made public in some well-known later testimony that will concern us farther on. The lieutenant had come in haste across Mexico, had brought with him nothing written relating to his mission save his letters of introduction and the private packet from

Senator Benton, whose contents, as we shall see, are said to
have been otherwise secured against intrusion. But the really
important, directly official part of his mission — namely, his
secret dispatch — had been committed to memory by the lieutenant — and then destroyed before he landed in Mexico. In
California he repeated its contents to Captain Frémont. The
obvious inference, as people very plausibly say, is, in view of
the subsequent events, that Captain Frémont was instructed to
use his force to attempt what was possible, with the least needful compromising of his government, in the way of stirring up
the American settlers and any other available persons against
the authority of the department, so as to get for us the territory
in advance of the declaration of war. If possible, says this commonly received story, he was to avoid too great prominence as
an officer of the United States, but he was by all means to get
the territory. And so here would be the fourth plan above mentioned. If that actually was our plan, which indeed yet remains
to be tested, then we were not to trouble ourselves to get first,
in the eyes of the world, a show of belligerent authority; nor
were we, by multiplying the numbers of our countrymen settled in the land, to acquire gradually a color of right to interfere on their behalf; nor yet were we, by peaceful intrigue
with the native government of the already rebellious department, to win its leaders over to our side. These methods would
all have been morally dubious. The fourth method, if it was
truly our method, would certainly call for no doubts as to its
true nature in the light of the moral law. According to that
method, we should have used the presence of this gallant
young officer, with his armed force, to seize for ourselves without warning upon an unprotected department, and so in time
of peace to gain for our country the prize of war. Precedents
enough can indeed be found in history for such undertakings,
but this plan would be, at least in our brief annals, not a frequently adopted device, nor one precisely pleasing to the con-
sciences of the more sensitive of our countrymen. Such, then,
is one traditional understanding of the matter, and of course
this understanding throws all the responsibility on the government.

The reader must not, however, hastily conclude that Gillespie's mission is to be so readily understood; for possibly, in the absence of further light, we may fail to do justice both to the cabinet and to Captain Frémont — who, for the rest, is usually considered as merely the instrument — unless we suspend our decision a little. But, at all events, what immediately followed seems on its face to support the theory that this supposed fourth plan was the real object of Gillespie's mission. For so soon as the instructions had been delivered, Captain Frémont returned to the Sacramento Valley; and not long afterwards certain settlers who visited his camp near the "Buttes" began to hear, and to repeat, both to him and to one another, wild and alarming rumors of what Castro and the Californians were intending to do to our countrymen. Castro, they declared, had proclaimed it as his purpose to drive all Americans out of the country, to lay waste their farms, to raise the Indians against them, to destroy them altogether. The captain of the surveying party still declined to accede to the appeals of these frequenters of his camp for immediate armed interference in their behalf, but he gave them to understand that if they were assailed, he would help them. One story, and in fact the most authoritative one, also knows that in secret he spoke more plainly, and that his orders alone brought about the first hostile act of Americans against the government of the department. Of this we shall hear more soon; but in any case, whether his words or the courage of the settlers produced the first outbreak, certain it is that early in June hostilities began. A band of horses, the property of the Californian government, was just then, as it chanced, in charge of a party of men containing among its chief members Lieutenant Arce. This party were bringing the horses from Sonoma to the south, by a circuitous route — namely, by way of Sutter's Fort, fording the Sacramento River near that point. A band of American settlers, some twelve in number, led by one Merritt, a frontiersman of no great reputation for all virtues, came upon this party after it had forded the Sacramento and had passed southward some miles. The Americans seized upon the body of horses, but released the men, who, quite unprepared for such an attack, had made no resistance. The latter were now charged to take the news to Castro at their pleasure. The marauding Americans sent the horses to Captain Frémont's camp and then, quickly reinforced, as the news flew, by settlers, who now, at any rate, felt certain that hostilities with Castro must come, rapidly proceeded to Sonoma, took possession of the unguarded and sleeping town on the morning of June 14, and thereafter sent as prisoners to Sutter's Fort, under an escort, four leading men of the place, General Vallejo, his brother Salvador, Mr. Leese, and M. Prudon.

The main body of the Americans, remaining at Sonoma, were quickly strengthened by numerous additions of a very miscellaneous character. Some of the settlers who thus came were peaceable men, of high respectability, who felt that now the thing was once begun, every American man must join it in self-defense. Others, again, of good character, were seriously alarmed by the aforesaid rumors, which they had heard near Captain Frémont's camp. Others who came were just such rogues and vagabonds as might be expected under the circumstances.[2] At Sonoma they awaited in arms Castro's coming, not to mention the generally desired appearance of their expected ally, Captain Frémont; they chose officers, helped themselves in the town to whatever supplies they needed for their new military life, and also did what most of all has been remembered concerning their brief life together at Sonoma: namely, they raised their new flag, a standard of somewhat uncertain origin as regards the cotton cloth whereof it was made; and on it they painted with berry-juice something that they called a Bear.

II. *The Bear Flag Heroes*

So far we have followed the results of the acts of the young Captain Frémont, regarding the whole as his undertaking. But in the little interval that elapsed before he appeared in person at Sonoma, these Bear Flag men, more or less conscious of their independent responsibilities, lived through a very curi-

---

[2] My impressions on these matters are founded in part on MS. statements and in part on documents hereafter to be quoted.

ous episode of California history — one that seemed to some of them afterwards ineffably glorious, and that in fact was unspeakably ridiculous, as well as a little tragical, and for the country disastrous. Until Captain Frémont considered himself warranted in coming to the help of this Spartan band to save them from their not often clearly visible, but, in their glowing fancy, multitudinous hosts of enemies, the Bear Flag men had things all their own way; and the gallant captain was directly responsible, at the moment, neither for their glory nor for their misbehavior. They had, as a rule, the wildest notions of what they were there to do. The first party, left behind when the prisoners were taken to Sutter's Fort, increased rapidly, as I have said; but of course these additions were stragglers, and every man brought his private conceptions. Captain Frémont had come with the United States army to liberate the country; the wicked Spaniards were assailing the inoffensive Americans at Sonoma, who needed the help of their brave comrades; the Americans had determined to be free from Spanish misrule and had raised aloft the standard of freedom and equal rights; in a shorter form, the fun had begun — such were notions that filled some men's heads. Others, as I have suggested, well knew that they were there engaged as marauders in making quite an unprovoked assault on the Californians. One, Mr. William Baldridge, in his statement made for Mr. Bancroft's library, says, as he looks back on those days: "My own sentiments were that making war upon the Californians was an act of great injustice; but, as the deed had been done, I preferred taking the risk of being killed in battle to that of being sent to Mexico in irons." But Mr. Baldridge himself remained in doubt for some time after the beginning of the difficulties as to whether war would really result. The whole affair, to his mind, was "brought on so gradually" that, even after the motley company had spent a number of days together, few could have given any connected account of what had really brought them there. The few that could give any connected account, however, are the ones who endow the whole affair with its true humor.

Among the party who "surprised the fortress" of Sonoma, or who, in plain speech, waked up the sleeping and defenseless villagers on the morning of June 14, was the noble-hearted Dr. Semple, a man at that time not quite forty years of age, a Kentuckian, about seven feet high in the body, and in soul, of course, incomparably loftier. He was not exactly a typical frontiersman, although he liked to appear as such; [3] nor yet a typical statesman, although he was conscious of some approach in spirit to that dignity. Nor was he a typical orator, nor even a typical product of the world's higher civilization, although at times he seemed to himself to be all of these things. He was, however, a man of some natural ability, and of an especially American talent for public affairs, but he was subject to the chief characteristic follies of his time and nation. He could preside well at a public meeting, and he later made an excellent president of the constitutional convention in 1849. He was enterprising, kindly, and honest. As editor of the *Californian*, in 1846–8, he did good public service. But these excellences are as characteristic of our nation and of frontier training as are his weaknesses. In our truly American fashion he trusted in liberty, speech-making, God, and the press; he was boastful, garrulous, oratorical, evidently putting all due trust in the public discussions of great questions by wrangling fellow citizens. When American interests were concerned as against foreigners, he was as blind as the divine justice, only with a slightly different result. Those who knew him in early days never forgot his vast height, his ready flow of speech, his righteous, glowing, and empty idealism, his genial assumption of statesmanship, his often highly serviceable cleverness, his sturdy honor and uprightness, his ambition, and, after all, his ineffectiveness in accomplishing the objects of his ambition.

Now Dr. Semple became, as fortune would have it, the Thucydides of the Bear Flag War. If one objects to this assertion that in fact there was no real Bear Flag War, only some pillage and skirmishing, we should, indeed, have to admit the

---

[3] "He is in a buckskin dress," says his later partner, Walter Colton (*Three Years in California*, New York, 1852, p. 32), writing but a few months after this time, "a foxskin cap; is true with his rifle, steady with his pen, and quick at the type-case."

objection, but should, in reply, leave it to the reader to modify accordingly his conception of the Thucydides. But the history, the "Treasure Forever," appeared, at all events, for the first in Semple's *Californian*.[4] It was used by Edwin Bryant in his well-known book, and it has later passed in part into the county histories and other great authorities on California annals. Dr. Semple himself returned with the convoy of the prisoners to Sutter's Fort, but his inner consciousness was quite adequate to the lofty story of the Sonoma doings whenever his honest eyes happened to give him no information.

Dr. Semple, in his account, felt "justified in saying that the world has not hitherto manifested so high a degree of civilization." For the Bear Flag party was at first "without officers or the slightest degree of organization, and with no publicly declared object," and yet it did no wrong. This, of course, is the kind of disorganized and unconscious filibustering that is always associated with the highest civilization, and one is prepared to follow the goodhearted doctor in his further assertion that the watchword of all the party was "equal rights and equal laws." One of the number, indeed, as we learn from Dr. Semple himself, interpreted this watchword very naturally, I fancy, but a little hastily, by proposing to make a fair and equal division of the spoils found at Sonoma; "but a unanimous indignant frown made him shrink from the presence of honest men, and from that time forward no man dared to hint anything like violating the sanctity of a private house or private property." Dr. Semple is, in this assertion, doubtless right; as, after he himself left for Sutter's Fort, hints were quite superfluous. The intentions and the methods used were, of course, perfectly honest; as some have stated the case, one "borrowed supplies on the faith and credit of the Bear Flag government," a "degree of civilization" that, to be sure, was not quite unprecedented. But then, as we see, divinely authorized as their business was, the Bear Flag men could not expect to be fed by the ravens, nor to gather pots of manna on the already dry and yellow summer

---

[4] I know it in its republished form in the *Californian* for May 29, 1847 (San Francisco Pioneers' Library file). See, for Bryant's summary and quotation of it, his *What I Saw in California*, pp. 286 ff.

hills about Sonoma. The motives that prompted them were, as Dr. Semple says of Merritt's individual motives,[5] "too high, too holy," to permit them "for a moment to suffer private feelings to bias" them "in public duties." "Their children, in generations yet to come, will look back with pleasure upon the commencement of a revolution carried on by their fathers upon principles high and holy as the laws of eternal justice." But, this being so, it was morally required that fathers, for the sake of posterity, should take good care of their own health. And the "credit" of the Bear Flag government was both necessary and (in view of the absence of weapons and pugnacity among the good people of the Sonoma district) sufficient to supply what was needed for this purpose.

Dr. Semple never recovered from his admiration for the heroic civilization of the Bear Flag Republic. In later times he liked to retell the story to the innocent newcomers of the gold period; and he sincerely hoped to reach at least the governorship of California by virtue of the halo of glory in which he saw, both the great "revolution" at Sonoma, and himself as once a humble servant of the Bear Flag state. In fact, only a year later, when he was Fourth of July orator at San Francisco, the great events of this brief period inspired him to say, with becoming long-armed gestures, and to print, later, in the *Californian*, just as I here quote them, certain burning words that must not be forgotten: "If we conquer country, we have no prince to claim it, or to dictate laws for its rule; no tyrant hand is laid upon them, but the glorious American eagle spreads her balmy wings over even a conquered people, and affords them protection and freedom. . . . Tyrants trembled on their thrones, and wrong and oppression is hiding their deformed heads."[6]

---

[5] See, in Bryant, op. cit., p. 290.

[6] *Californian* for July 10, 1847. In the rival Yerba Buena paper, the *Star*, a correspondent failed not to notice the humorous side of this scene: Dr. Semple as orator, his great form half bent over his manuscript, his back turned on the ladies of the audience, and his eloquence unchecked by grammatical considerations. *Star* for July 17, Bancroft Library file.

But small states are noted for their large proportion of great men, and when Dr. Semple went back to Sutter's Fort there was left behind at Sonoma a second statesman, of equal native genius, but of less sunny temperament, to adorn the Bear Flag Republic. This was William Ide. Providence evidently meant this man to typify for us, even more than Dr. Semple could do, our national talent and mission for civilizing the benighted Spanish American peoples of this continent. His career, indeed, was short, and was happily marked by no violent atrocities of his own choosing; and, in so far, he is not typical. But he had the same characteristic and delicate appreciation of human rights and duties that promised so much success to us, at that time, in our efforts to do good to our neighbors. He had all our common national conscience; he was at heart both kindly and upright, like the great doctor; and, like the doctor again, he was an idealist of the ardent and abstract type. He differed from Dr. Semple chiefly in a curious intensity of inner life that forbade him, save on rare occasions, to speak his whole mind. His fellow men generally misunderstood him, and he resolutely bore with their misunderstandings and expressed his willingness to forgive them. But he forsook none of his fixed notions, and the plainest trait about him was his obstinacy. People called him a Mormon; but that story was false. He was at the time of this affair not very young, having been born about 1796.

His life has been sketched, and his own account of his connection with the Bear Flag affair printed, by his family, not very long since, in a privately circulated book, of which I first consulted a copy at Mr. Bancroft's library.[7] He was a native of Rutland, Massachusetts, had spent his youth in Vermont, and

---

[7] I have since bought a copy of this still uncommon book, which surely deserves a wide circulation. It has three separate titles, all long, the principal one beginning: *A Biographical Sketch of the Life of William B. Ide, with a minute and interesting account of*, etc. (the whole forming an "old-fashioned title-page, such as presents a tabular view of the volume's contents"). The copyright is dated 1880, and the book is said to be "published for the subscribers," place not mentioned. Ide's personal narrative begins with chap. ix, p. 100, and ends with chap. xvi, on p. 206.

later had lived in the West, as farmer, school-teacher, and carpenter. He had met with some adversities of fortune, which had turned him, in religion, from a transient love of Universalism back to Orthodoxy; he had been active sometimes as peacemaker in Western land disputes, but he had had no practical experience in political business. To California he went with the emigration of 1845. In the mountains he did what gained him, later, some traditional fame among the emigrants — dragging his wagons, one by one, up and over a place on the Truckee route that less obstinate men had supposed wholly inaccessible for wheeled vehicles. In 1846, after a tedious winter, he and his family went on to a farm comparatively high up in the Sacramento Valley, and that very spring the reports began to be circulated among these northern settlers that Castro was coming to drive all Americans out of the land. Ide hastily set out, "stirred to the quick," as one family account has it,[8] and joined the first party that went to Sonoma.

Yet, before setting out for Sonoma, Ide had been among those settlers who went to Captain Frémont's camp, on hearing the alarming rumors, in order to get his help. The answers of the captain had seemed to Ide's sturdy and untutored soul vague and not strictly moral. The captain seemed, he declares, to want the settlers to do some aggressive, warlike deed, and, in particular, to steal certain horses, and thus to provoke Castro to hostility. Thus, also, when the Mexican War should begin, the settlers would, according to Ide's understanding of the plan, have had some part in hastening the conquest. This whole plot, desiring the settlers to anticipate hostilities under United States instigation, but without any open and immediate violation of neutrality from Captain Frémont's own party until the thing should be under way, seemed to Ide's honest wit unintelligible, especially if, as he sincerely thought, Castro had really made this terrible threatening proclamation, and was soon coming in force. As he understood the thing, it was simple self-defense. If the settlers, then, could not be helped by Captain Frémont as an officer of the United States, the captain might at least re-

---

[8] Ibid., p. 62.

main quiet and let the settlers so do their duty as independently to earn their political freedom. With the taking of the horses Ide had no part. He heard distinctly that Captain Frémont meant to go East at once, after getting supplies; and when, later, he heard that the horses were taken, and that a party was now setting out for Sonoma, he joined it, no doubt with the full intention, in case a proper opportunity should offer, of doing his share to make it, not a part of some dark plot to get the land for the United States government, but a movement for "national independence." He hated Captain Frémont's scheme of what Ide somewhat cleverly calls "neutral conquest." This, by the way, is the only clever phrase of Ide's known to me.

But, as even Ide felt, the first blow having been struck, men must, if possible, work together and suspend their quarrels. Cheerfully he would follow any recognized leader in so far as that was necessary to secure American rights. Therefore, on the way down to Sonoma, it was generally deemed best not to broach the subject of independence. Nobody, Ide tells us, knew exactly what they were to do, save that it was to be something that would yet further anger Castro, that it was not to involve "unnecessary violence," and that it included the seizure of prominent men at Sonoma. In the early morning of the 14th General Vallejo's residence was surprised and surrounded [9] by the assailants. After some parley Merritt and Semple entered, with one Knight as interpreter. Vallejo greeted them cordially, invited them to explain the objects of the party and to draw up articles of capitulation, which he in his defenseless position as

---

[9] Baldridge, in his statement, B. MS., says of this scene: "When the general became fully aware of their presence, he went out and asked what they wanted, to which no one answered, for the good reason, I believe, that none of them knew what reply to give. He then asked them if they had taken the place, to which he was answered in the affirmative. He then returned to his room, but soon reappeared with his sword girded on, which he offered to surrender to them; but as none of the party manifested any disposition to receive it, he returned to his room again and replaced the sword." All this well fits in with Ide's narrative at this point. See Ide, op. cit., p. 124.

quiet resident on his own estate would gladly sign.[10] Meanwhile he produced something to drink, Ide tells us, and the high commissioners tarried long. The company outside, whose "high and holy" aspirations were not yet, like Semple's within the house, fortified for the day by anything comforting, became impatient and chose one Grigsby as captain, who entered and was likewise long lost to view. At last Ide's moment came, and he, the incorruptible, ventured within the enchanted dwelling, elected by acclamation to inspect the negotiations. He found all the high contracting parties moderately drunk and still poring over the written articles of capitulation that Vallejo, as he implies, must have arranged very much to suit himself. Ide indignantly seized them and rushed forth to read them to the company outside. This aroused Grigsby and the others with Vallejo, who knew, after all, well enough, no doubt, what Captain Frémont had privately instructed them to do with General Vallejo, and who, shortly afterwards, although not without a pretense of hesitation, announced their intention to go back to Sutter's Fort with the chief prisoners.[11] At this point, however, questions began to arise among the party: "By what authority are we, after all, here? and has Captain Frémont, or anybody else, authorized in writing the arrest of these men?" Merritt and Grigsby would give no satisfactory answer. Semple, we may suppose, was probably absorbed in the glorious contemplations natural to a man in his position, not to say condition. Ide gives us a fine picture of the confusion that soon began to prevail among the heroes as they considered this

---

[10] These details, otherwise known, are rather implied than expressed in Ide's narrative.

[11] Vallejo's articles of capitulation, by which, as I understand the matter, he seems to have intended to secure to himself personal liberty, on condition of his promise to engage in no hostilities against the party, were thus promptly rejected by the somewhat confused brains of the commissioners themselves as soon as they reflected; and thus some good drinks were wasted. Here again one sees a "degree of civilization" not quite unprecedented. Vallejo, in the sequel, bitterly complained of this, which he chose to consider broken faith. I gather these facts from B. MS. evidence.

topic, and found, after all, no clear answer.[12] "One swore he would not stay; another swore we would all have our throats cut; another called for fresh horses; and all were on the move, — every man for himself." The moment was Ide's, and he seized it, and henceforth he gained that consciousness of historical significance which inspires all his honest, sober, and infinitely absurd tale. He came boldly forward, speaking plainly. He would lay his bones here before he would run like a coward. What were they there for? Was it not for some truly worthy object, — namely, after all, independence? Nay, said he: "we are robbers, *or we must be conquerors.*" This remark of Ide's narrowly escaped being clever; but it was not. It was only the outburst of his honest anxiety to be and do something noble and wondrous. "The speaker, in despair, turned his back upon his receding companions." The crisis was soon past. They rallied and, as he says, elected him captain on the spot. The convoy of the prisoners returned to Sutter's Fort, and he remained with his gallant men on the conquered territory.

As for what followed, we must take the reader a little into confidence, before going with Ide's tale yet another step, by quoting again from Mr. Baldridge, who remembers the thing thus, in his B. MS.: "Ide was a strong, active, energetic man, and, in our judgment, was possessed of many visionary if not utopian ideas. . . . Consequently, within a short time he was the most unpopular man among us. . . . Finally he was seized with a fit of writing, which continued almost incessantly for several days, all the time keeping his own counsel." Mr. Baldridge does not remember that Ide was considered by his fellows as in any sense captain, until after this writing fit had borne fruit, when Ide called a meeting, read his famous proclamation, announced his plan, and was then indeed elected by acclamation, but only because everybody chose to regard the whole thing, for the moment, as a good joke, and because nobody foresaw the consequence that would follow, in the distribution of this play-captain's document broadcast through the land, as the program of the Bear Flag Republic.

Ide's memory, however, is different, being especially colored

---

[12] Op. cit., p. 127.

by his notions of what captaincy and a government were. As a born statesman, he had his views about the true ideal state. Equal rights would of course prevail in it. And to this end, in the first place, there should be in the ideal state now about to be born no taxation of the "virtuous, industrious, self-governing free men," and all compulsory taxation should therefore be inflicted upon criminals, who were not on that account, however, to be considered as receiving any license for crime. Furthermore, public servants should be paid only just enough to keep them free from the effects of the love of money; how much this salary would amount to Ide never precisely computed. And, as a still more important requisite of good government, there should be no compulsory military *or other* service to maintain the cause of liberty: "for that [namely, compulsion] would prove that its people were unworthy of its blessings, or that those blessings were no longer worth enjoying." [13] A government whose subjects were thus free to do just as they liked, save when they were guilty of actual crime, and whose criminals, meanwhile, had therefore to fear only an authority that possessed no possible means of compelling any virtuous subject to join in a legal suppression of crime — in short, a government by general good humor — was of course best represented by this Bear Flag republic itself, with its slowly increasing population of from twenty-five to fifty or sixty faithful and straggling subjects, no one of whom, save Ide, was really quite aware of the very existence of his country. And its government was indeed well represented by Ide himself, whom nobody exactly knew to be governor. As he tells us: "By the unanimous vote of the garrison, all the powers of the four departments [of government] were conferred, for the time being, upon him who was first put in command of the fort; yet Democracy was the ruling principle that settled every measure, Vox Populi our rule." [14] Of this statement we may say that the unanimous vote of the garrison undoubtedly did confer not only on Ide, but on every man alike, the powers of the four departments: namely, as concerned his own person; and there was only a general

---

[13] Ibid., p. 145.
[14] Ibid., p. 134.

agreement to drill in company, under certain chosen officers, of whom one was Lieutenant Ford, soon to be further memtioned. So far Ide was right. These "self-consecrated victims to the god of Equal Rights" dwelt thus in peace together, and furthermore, according to Ide, considered what they might do to distinguish themselves in any external way from a band of marauders. The raising of the Bear Flag was one device. Ide himself proposed also the issuing of a proclamation, but the populace of the republic, expecting Captain Frémont soon to interfere, were unwilling to authorize this; and hence Ide's democratic earnestness and candor in shutting himself up and writing (very secretly, as he supposed, and during the small hours of several successive nights) that particular Vox Populi which he afterwards undertook to circulate through California. Writing this proclamation in thirty or forty copies, nearly though not quite identical in wording, helped to wear out Ide's constitution, and, as his family declare, hastened in later years his death. Ide also wrote to the American naval commanders on the coast, not for assistance, but, as he in substance declares, to warn them to let the new republic alone in its inalienable rights. Nor was this all. The great plan of Ide's free government must be got into the minds of the benighted native Californians of the Sonoma district. And one of Ide's earliest acts was directed to this end. For reasons of prudence, and others, easily comprehensible, the Bear Flag party had seen fit, forthwith, to arrest a good many of the native citizens thereabouts, and to crowd them into what Ide calls the "calaboose." How consistent this was with the "high and holy" aims of the "revolution" Ide was fully able to show. The inhabitants having been thus collected "between four strong walls," since "they were more than twice our number," Ide entered with an interpreter, and, as he says, using the third person himself, "he went on to explain [to them] the cause of our coming together; our determination to offer equal justice to all good citizens; that we had not called them there [that is, to the 'calaboose'] to rob them of their liberty, nor to deprive them of any portion of their property, nor to disturb their social relations with one another, nor yet to desecrate their religion. He went on to explain to them the com-

mon rights of all men, and showed them that these rights had
been shamefully denied them by those heretofore in authority
. . . that we had been driven to take up arms in defense of life
and the common rights of man." "He went on further to say
that although he had for the moment deprived them of that
liberty which is the right and the privilege of all good and just
men, it was only that they might become acquainted with his
unalterable purpose." In short, he declared that he intended to
give them fair warning; to let them sign a treaty of peace if
they would; nay even, if they insisted steadfastly upon being
enemies, to let them go again and prepare themselves for the
battle, which he referred to with "all the fierce, determined
energy of manner that such an emergency was calculated to
inspire." But first he must teach them, by this stay in the calaboose and by this lecture, what the inalienable rights of man
are, and what he and his friends proposed to do. "We are few,"
he said, "but we are firm and true." [15]

The address, Ide confesses, "was not the twentieth part interpreted"; "yet the importance of success in the measure, to
persons circumstanced as we were, gave expression that would
have been understood by every nationality and tongue under
heaven; and the *Spaniard*, even, embraced the commander as
he pronounced the name of WASHINGTON. There was a glow of
feeling beaming from his [that is, from the 'Spaniard's'] eye
that defied all hypocracy [*sic*], as he said, 'Suffer my companions to remain until we complete a treaty of peace and
friendship, and then go and come as friends, only that we be
not required to take arms against our brethren.' "

The scene, in its way, is a monumental work of poor Ide's
unconscious art. The pathos of this Yankee carpenter's prematurely aged vanity, as it expresses itself, years later, in these
ardent and proud reminiscences; the obvious honesty and kind-
heartedness of his purposes; the picture of a fool's glory that
he so well paints; the impotent nonsense that, as he speaks, his
winged words convey in vain to the puzzled interpreter, and
that these sleepy, impassive, bewildered countrymen of Sonoma, with their great soft black eyes fixed upon him, helplessly

---

[15] Ibid., p. 134.

feel to mean some fearful threat of the heretic robbers from the Sacramento Valley — all this scene is so perfect in itself, and, after all, so terribly representative, that one cannot easily forget it. One can but speak for oneself, and, for my part, if ever I hear in future of our great national mission on this continent as civilizers of the Spanish American peoples, if ever I find that this mission has come once more, as it surely some day will come, to the surface of our vainglorious national consciousness, I shall be able to think of nothing but poor Ide, the self-appointed Yankee captain of a chance crowd of marauders, standing benevolently in the "calaboose," before the forty or fifty innocent and imprisoned citizens of Sonoma, and feeling in his devout kindliness that he does God service while he bellows to them an unintelligible harangue, "not a twentieth part interpreted," about man's inalienable rights to liberty and equality, and while he concludes with a reference to Washington, believing himself, meanwhile, to be the Father of the Bear Flag Republic.

The proclamation was erelong, without any distinct disavowal on the part of the Bear Flag men, sent abroad by messengers in the land south of San Francisco Bay. It has been printed frequently since, and is usually thought to be the real official expression of the movement. The movement, however, could have had no one expression, since it had no one purpose, but comprised whatever chanced to result from the original instigation of Captain Frémont and from the individual minds of the settlers concerned. The proclamation asserted that Castro had ordered the Americans out of the country and had threatened their lives and property and the lives of their families. It attributed to the past government vast wickedness and mischief, and it promised great blessings from the new government. It suggested Ide's peculiar political ideas, and it made the usual devout appeal to Heaven, which, if marauders and insurgents in their official expressions are to be believed, favors nothing so well at any time as a general scrimmage, and the side that begins the same.[16]

---

[16] See for one copy of the proclamation Ibid., p. 138. It is easy to find some one of the copies of Ide's proclamation printed in books

Ide was, on the whole, a character that can well be compared to no creation in literature that I happen to know about, save to the Bellman, in *The Hunting of the Snark.* Of the Bear Flag party, whose "high and holy" aims somewhat resemble the aims of the Snark-hunters, Ide was captain, very much in the sense in which the Bellman was captain of his resolute band. As the whole of the Bellman's notion for crossing the ocean consisted in ringing his bell, so Ide, toiling in the small hours over his proclamations, had similarly simple notions about sailing the ship of state. As the Bellman on occasion referred to maxims "tremendous but trite," so Ide's proclamation contains several such references. Ide was in fate more like the Baker, in that his Snark was undoubtedly a Boojum, and in that he accordingly, in due time, softly, if not quite silently, vanished away. But as to character, he was a perfect expression, only in Yankee form, of the Bellman; and I consider Ide's own account of himself an indirect and unconscious tribute to the poetical genius of "Lewis Carroll," who has so perfectly and undesigningly immortalized just his type of wisdom.[17]

While Ide governed, Lieutenant Ford made war. The little military incidents of these days, important not in themselves, but in their consequences, are easily to be summarized. The Californian government actually had no force north of the Bay of San Francisco at the beginning of the affair. But what could be collected farther south was promptly sent, under the com-

on California history. See Bryant's *What I Saw in California,* p. 290; *The Annals of San Francisco,* p. 92. None of the standard authorities shows any proper sense of the real significance and insignificance of this paper.

[17] I have space only to refer to yet other monumental passages of Ide's narrative: his noble efforts to get the poor alcalde of Sonoma to understand the aforesaid philosophical theory of the projected Bear Flag Constitution (p. 147), and his difficulties with those of his own garrison who "earnestly contended that a Spaniard had no right to liberty, and but very little right to the enjoyment of life" (p. 148). One of the most engaging things in the volume before us is furthermore the innocent admiration with which the editors of Ide's narrative, in their entire ignorance of the facts, regard the wildest of his honest absurdities.

mand of Joaquín de la Torre, whose approach became known at Sonoma June 23. Lieutenant Ford, the military leader of the Bears, marched out with a little force to meet him; and an encounter took place about twelve miles from San Rafael. The Californians lost two men killed and some wounded at the very first fire and, dreading the rifles of the Bear party, retired without further struggle. They were of course in no wise well armed. Thus was shed the first blood in "battle" between Americans and Californians. The Bear men received here no hurt. After this skirmish the marauding settlers at Sonoma were in comparative safety, as no force could for some time be brought against them. But Captain Frémont, who had received news of their danger, reached Sonoma with his whole force on June 25. Although his instigation had begun the insurrection, he was not to win any special military renown in this first part of the conquest; for the Californian force, which he now actively pursued, cleverly eluded him by a ruse and escaped across the bay. De la Torre, namely, sent a false message, purporting to be from Castro, and announcing an imminent attack upon Sonoma. This, sent in the hands of an Indian, fell, as was intended, into Captain Frémont's possession and led him back from his pursuit to protect the threatened town. De la Torre had time to cross to Yerba Buena before the mistake was discovered. A detachment of Captain Frémont's men later crossed the bay to Yerba Buena, took prisoner the captain of the port, spiked some guns at the presidio, and returned.

These irregular hostilities must, I have said, be judged by their effects, and, as I now yet further add, by the effects that chance later warded off, but that for the moment seemed imminent. The whole country towards the south, as far as the tale penetrated, was alarmed and exasperated at the news, which was, of course, naturally exaggerated in the telling. It was not that the physical mischief done had actually been enormous, but that the injustice of the attack seemed to the native population so obvious, and the designs indicated by it so appallingly dangerous to their happiness and their rights. The mystery of the affair made it worse. Ide's proclamation was circulated in manuscript form south of the bay, and that pretended to announce a new independent republic. But Captain Frémont's name was quickly associated by rumor and fact with the business, which was therefore believed to be the outcome of American official intrigue. An irregular guerrilla warfare appeared certain. If the Americans were treacherous enough to seize Sonoma without warning, to deliver over its inhabitants to confinement and their property to marauders, what were they not capable of doing further? The worst that unfriendly suspicion could have feared of the newcomers now seemed realized. The longing among those of the California politicians who desired English protection for an immediate English interference on their behalf waxed very strong at the news; and there can be little doubt that, if fortune had delayed the outbreak of the Mexican War, or the coming of the news of it, but a little longer, and had thus delayed the interference of the American fleet, the English commander of the *Juno,* on the California coast, or possibly Admiral Seymour himself, of the *Collingwood,* who arrived during July, and who, for all we know, *might* have arrived almost or quite as soon in any case, would have been the object of overtures from prominent men for an acceptance on the part of his government of a protectorate of California, which might then have declared its independence of Mexico. Whether these overtures would have been supported or not by the body of the distracted Californians, and whether any English commander would have been justified at that time by his government in accepting such proposals, or whether our navy would have passively permitted the thing, are matters that belong not yet to our tale. I mention them now only to suggest that, in case there was, as a well-known tradition will have it, an imminent English plot to get possession of California, the irregular revolution instigated by Captain Frémont was the best possible means that could have been chosen to frighten and to plague the Californians into the arms of England at once. Somewhat suspicious seems, therefore, this well-known tradition, when it repeats from volume to volume and from decade to decade the thoughtless assurance that the Bear Flag affair saved California from the rapacity of England. But of the tradition and the truth about this matter I shall hereafter speak further.

Meanwhile, as I must add, to explain in part the undying hatreds that grew out of this unhappy Bear outbreak, these hostilities did not pass by without some of the natural attendants of such affairs. Early in the days at Sonoma two of the Bear Flag men, Cowie and Fowler, were taken prisoners by an irregular party of Californians and then murdered. Stories, whose foundation, as it appears, cannot be tested with certainty, because the records of trustworthy eyewitnesses are lacking, are to be found, as most readers know, in the later American accounts, attributing to these irregular Californians not only the murder, but also the previous torture, of these two men. I fancy that we must regard the affair, at all events, as a sort of lynching and must judge it by remembering how our Western farmers would have treated any marauding Mexicans who had been caught after they had assailed defenseless American towns and robbed peaceful inhabitants. Our Western lynchers often torture as well as kill. But this act, surely in no sense justifiable, however natural the furious exasperation of the assailed Californians may have made it at the moment, was far outdone by men among the Americans, who, during Captain Frémont's pursuit of Torre to San Rafael, murdered in cold blood near that place three defenseless non-combatants, men of known respectability and of no connection with the hostilities. These were the Haro brothers and Bereyessa. The act was causeless and can receive no shadow of justification, and it was not done by any irregular party. As to the responsibility I have nothing to add.

Very happily this scene of the Bear Flag War was closed before further bloodshed could follow, by the coming of news of hostilities on the Rio Grande and by the consequent raising of the American flag by Commodore Sloat at Monterey. The latter had left Mazatlán on the first receipt of this news, had come in his flagship to join his vessels that were already on the coast, and, in obedience to his previously received official instructions, had prepared to seize upon Monterey and San Francisco harbors. He had indeed hesitated some days at Monterey without action, but on July 7 the deed was done. Sloat thereupon sent orders to the *Portsmouth* at San Francisco to seize that port, and dispatched a courier to convey intelligence of his acts to Captain Frémont, who, having nobody to fight on the north shore of the bay, had returned for the time with his main force to Sutter's Fort. As soon as the courier reached the captain, the latter set out for Monterey with his force. And thus the operations of the Bear Flag affair became merged in those of the conquest proper.

Yet, ere bidding farewell to the conquerors of the fortress of Sonoma, I must call attention to one document that especially illustrates their "high and holy" aims. It was written, indeed, just after the regular conquest had been proclaimed, and is the more characteristic for that. It was written by the redoubtable Grigsby, who had been left in command at Sonoma under the new order of things, and was addressed to Captain Montgomery, in San Francisco Bay.[18]

CUARTEL, SONOMA, *July* 16, 1846

To CAPTAIN MONTGOMERY, U. S. Ship *Portsmouth*

Dear Sir, — Yesterday I received Lieutenant Bartlett's letter. . . . The Spaniards appear well satisfied with the change. The most of them have come forward and signed articles of peace. Should they take up arms against us, or assist the enemy in any way, they forfeit their lives, property, etc. All things are going on very well here at present. . . . There are some foreigners [i.e., Americans or Englishmen] on this side that have never taken any part with us. I wish to know the proper plan to pursue with them: whether their property shall be used for the use of the garrison or not (they are men of property). We wish your advice in all respects, as we are a company of men not accustomed to such business. . . . There are some poor men here that are getting very short of clothing. I wish to know in what way it might be procured for them. . . .

Your obedient servant,

JOHN GRIGSBY, Captain

---

[18] Sen. Ex. Doc. 1, 2nd Sess., 29th Congr., p. 665.

III. *Sloat, the Administration, and the Mystery of the Secret Mission*

SUCH is the outer history of the "Bear Flag Revolution." But we must enter into more details before we can hope to find the true interpretation of the movement.

So much, however, is to be noted, ere we proceed, as to the relation of the movement to Sloat's action. Events seemed to bring the Bear Flag affair into close connection with the official conquest proper. But we should blunder sadly if we supposed that Sloat had been in any case instructed to co-operate with Captain Frémont or with the settlers, or that the Bear Flag affair was in any sense an official signal for the interference of our squadron. Of Sloat's instructions I shall speak in due time, but they very certainly were not framed with any apparent reference to Captain Frémont's conduct or to Gillespie's mission. Sloat was to wait until he should hear from the Atlantic of actual war between the United States and Mexico. Then he was to seize upon the Californian ports. He had no warning that his work was to be lightened by previous armed operations on land, and he was in fact sadly perplexed by the news that he heard from the north when he reached Monterey on the 2nd of July. Whatever the official secret of Captain Frémont's action was, Sloat was not in it. To judge the Bear Flag affair, we must then consider it in and for itself, and not in connection with its accidental good fortune as an undertaking that received a timely support from the navy. The first success that it desired and rightfully might hope to get was only a success as an independent and apparently unofficial revolution in California. This success once reached, California might pass over into our hands whenever the war came; but until the war had been formally begun, Captain Frémont had no reason to expect the support of his distant government. The navy simply knew nothing about his plans and had no sort of authority to help him; and the wide deserts separated him from all possible military support. The boldness of such an undertaking, with Captain Frémont's sixty men, and with only the doubtful aid of the settlers, must surely strike the reader forthwith; the mys-

terious carelessness of our government in utterly failing to provide for Captain Frémont any effective armed co-operation
from our squadron must add to our perplexity in case this
fourth plan actually was the real plan; and what we are hereafter to learn of the official instructions to the squadron itself,
as they were later printed in congressional documents, will only
make our problem harder. But it is at least necessary to remember that the show of official support that Commodore Sloat's
seizure of Monterey would seem to have given to Captain Frémont was in fact but an accidental outcome of other events and
was not in the least contemplated by our government in its
official instructions to the navy. Nor yet may one fancy even
that these seemingly independent undertakings — namely, Captain Frémont's and Commodore Sloat's — were so well timed
by the government that, although the official instructions of the
squadron made no mention of the expected operations on land,
the actual co-operation of Sloat with the Bear Flag movement
was silently predetermined at Washington. That hypothesis,
natural as it may so far seem, is absolutely excluded by evidence that I shall in due time present. There had been no provision for such co-operation, and if accident had delayed the
outbreak of the Mexican War a little longer, or if the news had
failed to reach Sloat when it did, the Bear Flag affair would
have developed itself into all the natural results of irregular
warfare, without any support or amelioration through the interference of the navy. The settlers, in numerous individual cases
if not as a body, would have dealt with the Californians after
the fashions and customs of irregular combatants, and the Californians would have done what they could to thwart the
rather inadequate force in the field against them. One may feel,
indeed, fairly confident that, with their poor arms and their
lack of discipline, the Californians could not easily have destroyed the resolute little Bear Flag army; but one can also
feel quite sure that the Bear Flag, in view of the small force
supporting it and of the bitter passions that it at once aroused,
could not possibly have given to the distracted land peace and
good order. The fact must be understood, therefore, that if the
cabinet authorized Captain Frémont's operation, it took no

sort of pains to prevent this province from falling into the hopeless anarchy of irregular warfare, until such time as the course
of events on the remote Atlantic coast should have led to the
beginning of legitimate war and the news thereof should have
been able to reach Sloat's squadron. Surely the reader will
agree that the problem as to how any government could thus
risk its own most obvious interests becomes not a little puz-
zling. If we were to get California, we surely needed to get it as
little as possible marred by anarchy, by destruction of property,
or by the just anger of its inhabitants. Yet Captain Frémont's
movement, strong enough to begin an irregular warfare, but
certainly not nearly strong enough to govern and pacify this
immense territory, would seem, if the fourth plan is the real
one, to have been authorized or ordered in Washington and to
have been left without any immediate provision for adequate
support! Surely something is wrong here.

IV. *The Mystery as Formerly Expounded by Captain Frémont's Friends*

BUT possibly, in insisting so exactly as I have done upon
the consequences and significance of this supposed fourth
plan for the acquisition of California, I may appear to be overlooking a somewhat different hypothesis as to this Bear Flag
affair, a hypothesis whose very existence, as we shall later see,
enables us better to understand the real conduct of Captain
Frémont, although in itself the hypothesis is utterly unfounded.
The friends of Captain Frémont, namely, did not, either then
or later, admit our fourth plan as the sole cause of his action.
They often used forms of speech that, on the one hand, seemed
to put more personal responsibility for what happened upon
the young captain's own shoulders, but, on the other hand,
made his conduct less the result of Gillespie's mission than of
the circumstances of the place and of the moment. He had to
do what he did, they have sometimes said, not so much because his secret instructions counseled just such acts as because
Castro, by warlike movements and threats, forced him to take
the field to save the American settlers from imminent pillage

and massacre. I must speak of this explanation a little because it has been so often advanced, is so audaciously inaccurate, and is, in consequence, so instructive.

In its first form, the story that the Bear Flag operations were forced upon Captain Frémont by the aggressions of Castro reached the public through Senator Benton himself, whose statement was founded upon letters received at home from the Senator's gallant son-in-law. The letters themselves were published in the *Washington Union* in the autumn of 1846, but have somehow come to be almost totally forgotten by the public. They are very valuable for us; yet, as they disappeared in the busy life of the moment and gave place to what Senator Benton had found in them, I must not reveal their contents just yet, but must repeat at this point the curious account, tainted with geographical absurdity, that the venerable Senator sent out to the world as an official statement of Captain Frémont's acts and motives.[19]

"At the middle of May," says the Senator, "Captain Frémont, in pursuance of his design to reach Oregon, had arrived at the great Tlamath [Klamath] Lake, in the edge of the Oregon Territory, when he found his further progress completely barred by the double obstacle of hostile Indians, which Castro had excited against him, and the lofty mountains, covered with deep and falling snow. These were the difficulties and dangers in front. Behind, and on the north bank of the San Francisco Bay, at the military post of Sonoma, was General Castro assembling troops, with the avowed object of attacking both Frémont's party and all the American settlers. Thus, his passage barred in front by impassable snows and mountains . . . menaced by a general at the head of tenfold forces of all arms; the American settlers in California marked out for destruction on a false accusation of meditating a revolt under his instigation; his men and horses suffering from fatigue, cold, and famine; and after the most anxious deliberation upon all the dangers of his position and upon all the responsibilities of his

---

[19] I quote in the following Senator Benton's letter as given in Cutts: *Conquest of New Mexico and California* (Philadelphia, 1847, p. 152).

conduct, Captain Frémont determined to turn upon his pursuers and fight them instantly, without regard to numbers, and seek safety for his party and the American settlers by overturning the Mexican government in California."

It is indeed entertaining enough to conceive of Castro at Sonoma "menacing" Captain Frémont on the banks of Klamath Lake and "pursuing" him at a distance of some three hundred miles in an air line, or more than four hundred by the trails, especially when one remembers that the country between was for most of the way an uninhabited wilderness, for one third of the way a mass of mountains, and almost wholly unknown to Castro, who had no burning desire, one may be sure, to have any close intercourse, not to speak of intrigues, with the Klamath Lake Indians. For the rest, Castro was himself in fact not at Sonoma, but alternately at Monterey and at Santa Clara, or in their vicinity, all through this time, and Sonoma itself was wholly innocent of any armed force. But, however that may be, nobody will now suppose that the gallant young captain himself could have felt driven to bay on the Klamath shore by the mythical army of ten times his force at Sonoma. The venerable statesman's documents and his eloquent imagination were, in their combination, for this once, a trifle unhistorical.

But in Senator Benton's *Thirty Years' View*, chapter clxiv, the story is once more told. At the approach of Gillespie, Captain Frémont, now no more driven to bay on the Klamath shores by the overwhelming odds at Sonoma, appears in a somewhat different light from the one cast upon him by Senator Benton's previous account. The situation, although still requiring Senator Benton's noblest eloquence, is less tragic. Although surrounded by hostile Indians, Captain Frémont is depicted as happy, and as comparatively peaceful in his work until the romantic coming of the brave Gillespie. He reads the heavens with his telescope, gauges the temperature of the air with his thermometer, sketches with his pencil "the grandeur of mountains," paints "the beauty of flowers," and with his pen writes down "whatever is new or strange or useful in the works of nature." In short, he pursues science, shuns war, and, if we may add to Senator Benton's eloquence a more modern phrase, he shows that his capacity for innocent enjoyment is just as great as any other man's. But Gillespie came. The letters and messages, with their contents, are described much as in the testimony before the Claims Committee. But Senator Benton adds significantly that "it was not to be supposed that Lieutenant Gillespie had been sent so far, and through so many dangers, merely to deliver a common letter of introduction on the shores of Tlamath Lake," and points out that what was communicated bore the "stamp of authority."

While the obvious design of this is once more to give to the Gillespie mission a large share in determining what followed, Senator Benton still lays stress upon the violent measures of Castro, as furnishing at least the immediate occasion for Captain Frémont's action. "He [Captain Frémont] arrived," says the Senator, "in the valley of the Sacramento in the month of May, 1846, and found the country alarmingly and critically situated. Three great operations fatal to American interests were then going on and without remedy if not arrested at once. These were: (1.) The massacre of the Americans, and the destruction of their settlements, in the valley of the Sacramento. (2.) The subjection of California to British protection. (3.) The transfer of the public domain to British subjects. And all this with a view to anticipate the events of a Mexican war and to shelter California from the arms of the United States. The American settlers sent a deputation to the camp of Mr. Frémont in the valley of the Sacramento, laid all these dangers before him, and implored him to place himself at their head and save them from destruction. General Castro was then in march upon them. The Indians were incited to attack their families and burn their wheat-fields, and were only waiting for the dry season to apply the torch. Juntas were in session to transfer the country to Great Britain; the public domain was passing away in large grants to British subjects; a British fleet was expected on the coast; the British vice-consul, Forbes, and the emissary priest, Macnamara, ruling and conducting everything, and all their plans so far advanced as to render the least delay fatal." Under these circumstances, which are all thus represented as then known to him, Captain Frémont, much as he regretted his necessity, had no alternative. "He determined to put himself at the head of the people and save the country."

Of this account one must first say, in passing, that mere dates show the impossibility of any knowledge concerning the so-called "Macnamara scheme" on the part of Captain Frémont at the moment of his action, and that, whatever these supposed "English schemes" were (whereof I shall say much later), they could have had no share in authorizing or in hastening the aggression of June 1846. So that all this portion of Senator Benton's account is quite without historical significance for our present problem, which is simply why Captain Frémont moved when he did.[20] We must therefore here dismiss these English schemes for the present, and speak of them hereafter, as supplying a supposed justification, after the fact, for Captain Frémont's energy.

But the intended massacre of the Americans and the purposed burning of their wheat-fields — what of all that as motive and justification for the hostilities? The only way to solve this problem is to find out in how far any genuine knowledge or fear of immediate hostilities from Castro was present to well-informed American settlers. Motive this hostility was for Captain Frémont in so far as he believed it to be an immediate source of danger. If he had it not in mind as a pressing peril, then there is no doubt that the messages brought by Gillespie were alone able to furnish valid motive for his operations, and then, one would surely suppose, the fourth plan will have established itself as the actual one. Yet we must not anticipate. At all events, the curious tendency just noticed, sometimes to magnify and sometimes to leave in ambiguous indefiniteness

[20] With these two accounts of Senator Benton's one should compare Captain Frémont's own explanations, the one before the Congressional Claims Committee, when he applied for the payment of the expenses of the Californian battalion (see Sen. Rep. 75, 30th Congr., 1st Sess., pp. 12 and 13), and the other before the Kearny court-martial (Sen. Doc. 33, 30th Congr., 1st Sess., Vol. V, pp. 373, 374). The two explanations are both of them cautious, but tend to convey the impression that both the secret instructions and Castro's hostility co-operated to produce the action.

the importance of Castro's hostility, suggests that the friends of the hero of our tale may well have felt somewhat oppressed by the delicacy and the secrecy of the official information that according to the fourth plan would be the real motive of his conduct; so that they may henceforth have felt it their duty to the government to shield the latter by cautious and doubtful language. Should this in the end appear to be their motive, doubtless the reader will appreciate their discretion and their delicate patriotism and will judge them generously.

V. *Californian Hostility as a Cause for War*

MEANWHILE, however, the bare matter of fact whereto this reported hostility as a motive for Captain Frémont's conduct must be reduced may be investigated under two heads. First we may ask whether Castro actually did gather any armed force to assail the American settlers. And secondly we may ask whether the great body of peaceable American settlers believed at the moment in the imminence of his attack so as to be aroused or terrified. To inquire into these matters is not to cast a shadow on the just-mentioned discretion and patriotism that may have forced General Frémont's friends ever since to put too strong an accent upon the reported hostility of Castro. By our questions as to Castro's conduct we shall only put that discretion and that patriotism in a stronger light, *in case,* indeed, the fourth plan actually proves in the end to be the government plan, as heretofore we have seemed to find very probable. Only *in case* the fourth plan were not the government plan should we feel these questions delicate.

Well, as to the first of our two questions, the answer is very simply a flat negative. Whatever Captain Frémont's informers may have told him at the time, there certainly was no truth in the stories about Castro and his anti-American warlike demonstrations. Since Captain Frémont's own departure for Oregon in March, Castro had made no preparations to drive any Americans from the department. He had issued no proclamation ordering the settlers to be expelled or threatening them with expulsion. He was not marching against them with an army;

he had no force at Sonoma, none anywhere on the north shore
of San Francisco Bay. He had no present intention of sending
a force thither, or of prosecuting in that region any hostile purpose. He feared, indeed, a coming American invasion at some
time in the future; but he knew that he could now do little or
nothing to avert it, and meanwhile he was busy in his quarrels
with Governor Pio Pico and the south. He made some warlike
preparations; but they were chiefly against Pio Pico, partly
with remote reference to possible invasions. He plotted; but
the American settlers of the Sacramento Valley were not in
danger from his plots, nor were they the ones plotted against.
His controversy with Pio Pico, had he been let alone by the
Americans, might indeed have resulted in an open combat; but
then all he would have asked of the Americans for the moment
would have been neutrality and indifference. Captain Frémont's operations were therefore in fact purely aggressive,
and would have been explicable as a defensive movement
solely on the ground that Captain Frémont had been misinformed about Castro. But, as we shall also later see, he was *not*
so misinformed by any respectable and trustworthy person.

All this is a question of fact and can easily be decided by anyone who is now well informed about the situation of that moment. Mr. John S. Hittell has spoken quite sensibly and plainly
on the matter, so far as he goes into it at all, in his *History of
San Francisco*, pp. 102, 103, where he merely says that the "un-
meaning threats of a few ignorant native Californians irritated
and perhaps alarmed the Americans north of San Francisco
Bay"; and adds, with regard to Castro's supposed proclamation, that "the governor of California had issued no such proclamation, nor was such a matter" as the forcible expulsion of
the American settlers "thought of." Mr. Hittell has long been
in a position to judge this matter intelligently, although he
gives in his book no proofs. But the documentary evidence in
full concerning the situation is in Mr. Hubert Howe Bancroft's
hands. I have no concern in this book with the details of the
native politics of the moment, and the reader, if so disposed,
must look for many such tales, as I do myself with a good deal
of interest and curiosity, to that forthcoming volume of Mr.

Bancroft's history which will deal with this period, and to Mr. Theodore Hittell's anticipated discussion of the same period in his forthcoming *History of California;* yet enough can be shown for our purpose by a few considerations. Mr. Thomas Larkin, the consul, was busy just then in giving the government at Washington every attainable fact about the state of the country. He was well acquainted with José Castro, with the whole town of Monterey, and with all the prominent Californians. He was, strange to say, engaged himself at the moment of the outbreak in intrigues to secure — but of that hereafter. Enough, he knew about the Californians, by daily intercourse, just what the captain of the surveying party at the Buttes could not know. In his voluminous correspondence with the State Department there is a great deal bearing on the situation just at this juncture. By Mr. Bancroft's courtesy, I was able, when in California, to examine this correspondence in the Bancroft Library volumes of the archives of Larkin's consulate, volumes whose nature the previous chapter has described. I have since received, by the courtesy of Secretary Bayard, official copies of some of these letters, as the originals are preserved in the State Department, and I have these copies before me as I write. The facts thus shown by Consul Larkin's personal and daily knowledge are utterly inconsistent with the supposed hostile preparations of Castro. It is quite impossible that when all the birds in the Sacramento Valley were twittering the news of the approach of Castro from bough to bough, and when his proclamation was already in the hands of the settlers, these sources of information should, although authentic, have possessed and delivered news that was sealed to a man who was on the spot at the time, in daily personal intercourse with the very Californians most concerned themselves, and who was on the alert to get information.

Other documentary evidence in Mr. Bancroft's hands shows plainly enough what Castro did mean to do. He meant to thwart and defeat Governor Pio Pico in regard to matters at issue between them. The possibilities of a future American invasion were indeed known, both to him and to Pico, as well as to all the other prominent Californians, and fear was felt. Preparations were freely discussed and begun, to be ready in time for such an invasion if it ever should come. But these preparations not only had no immediate reference to the Sacramento Valley settlers, but also were not in an advanced state. One lacked, for instance, powder. One lacked, above all, money. And one spent one's time meanwhile in petty domestic quarrels, such as brought one but little nearer to a real state of readiness. At such a time, for a busy politician, with plenty of enemies at home, as it were in his own household, with very limited military resources accessible to him, with fears for the future, with doubts and native intrigues darkening the air all about him — for such a man, who had so recently declined to attack Captain Frémont's party, now deliberately to undertake to go out into the Sacramento Valley and borrow yet more trouble at the mouths of the settlers' rifles would have been the most absurd and impossible of ideas. Only ignorance of the real situation could have attributed to Castro any such design. It is perfectly certain that he had no such design.

There was, then, no danger to the settlers from Castro. But did the settlers perchance believe, in their own minds, however mistakenly, that there was danger? And were their fears the basis of Captain Frémont's determination?

Mr. William N. Loker, one of the settlers at Sutter's Fort, and later an officer in the California battalion, testified before the Claims Committee (see p. 40 of their Report) that he actually posted in public sight himself, and at Sutter's Fort, a translation of the *"banda"* whereby the authorities ordered all American settlers out of the country on pain of a forcible expulsion.[21]

---

[21] Ide preserved a copy, as he tells us, of an unsigned American proclamation that was handed to himself on June 8, "between the hours of 10 and 11 a. m.," as he very exactly adds. (See the Ide Family *Narrative*, p. 113.) It read: "Notice is hereby given that a large body of armed Spaniards on horseback, amounting to 250 men, have been seen on their way to the Sacramento Valley, destroying the crops, burning the houses, and driving off the cattle. Captain Frémont invites every freeman in the valley to come to his camp at the Buttes immediately; and he hopes to stay the enemy, and put a stop to his" — ("Here," says Ide, also on p. 113, "the sheet was

Now, as we have seen, no such *"banda"* was ever officially pro-
mulgated at all, and what Loker posted must have been, if
anything, a forgery. The question before us is: were such for-
geries, or other false statements, whatever their source, actually
believed among the better-informed American settlers? And
did the belief of the settlers influence the captain to act? These
questions seem to me to admit of a demonstrably negative answer. I shall here lay no stress on the curiously unsatisfactory
nature of the parol evidence on this topic that was presented
to the congressional committee at Washington. It is indeed true
that those Americans who were in a position to know best about
the actual state of the Californian public were *not* the men to
whom the Claims Committee appealed for information as to
the current American belief about the situation at the moment
of the outbreak; but then, to be sure, not everybody could be
got in Washington as a witness at just the desired time. One
must remark, however, in passing, that much of the parol
evidence of settlers that was produced at Washington is historically quite worthless, expressing the vague and not disinterested views of men who either were in no position to understand the facts or were themselves decidedly indisposed to let
other people understand the facts. But such testimony we need
not even criticize. Ours arranges itself under several heads.

In the first place, then, well-informed and trustworthy settlers,
men of property and position at that time, of honorable career
and notable reputation since, have given in more recent times
testimony to the point. Especially satisfactory is the elaborate
refutation of the traditional view about Castro's hostility that I
have before me, as I write, from the pen of Mr. John Bidwell,
of Chico, California, a man whose position then as a trusted
assistant of Sutter at the fort, and whose residence in the country for some years before that date, give us good ground for
thinking him well informed; while his high public reputation

---

folded and worn in two, and no more is found.") The genuineness
of this memorandum seems certain. Of course this proclamation itself, whoever wrote it, was utterly false in its statements about the
"armed band."

in California ever since those times also assures us that we have in him an upright, cautious, and able observer. For Mr. Bancroft's library Mr. Bidwell prepared a lengthy statement, which I have used in the former chapter and which also treats of this time. But in addition to this, by the kindness of the editor of the *Overland Monthly*, Miss M. W. Shinn, I have obtained a copy of a MS. now in her possession, a part of certain records on early California history that the Rev. Mr. Willey has lent to her for her own use. This MS. answers questions of Mr. Willey's, put to General Bidwell, about the Bear Flag affair, and is full and definite. It was not at first intended for print, but for the Rev. Mr. Willey's use. I use it, by permission, here.

For a long time, says Mr. Bidwell, in fact almost ever since he reached the country, settlers in the valley were accustomed to tell and hear all sorts of wild stories about the Californian government and its plans, about coming war, or about some attempted expulsion of Americans, or about a fight for independence. These rumors would gather, from time to time, a number of people at Sutter's Fort, who would talk it all over and again disperse quietly, to be aroused once more in six months or a year. Especially the floating population of the territory, landless men of no fixed dwelling-place, trappers, deserters from ships, often precious rascals, would enjoy and spread this warlike talk. They especially hated all Californians, who well returned the hatred. "But these rumors," says Mr. Bidwell, "had this effect, Americans had learned to be always on guard. They — I mean the more considerate class — had learned to weigh signs of danger, and put, to a considerable extent, a true value on them. Those who had property, and had settled in the territory, were generally in favor of peace; while those who had little or no interest here were, as a rule, always ready and anxious for war." By 1846 these Americans of all classes were already too numerous to have any serious fear of being driven out, and the Californian leaders were known to them as men of too much shrewdness to attempt such a movement.

Mr. Bidwell, in discussing the feeling at the moment of the outbreak, then goes on to say that, after Captain Frémont's departure for Oregon, in March, "all was quiet again." "There

were no hostile demonstrations, or even threats, to my knowledge. We in the Sacramento Valley felt entirely secure. Others
dispersed throughout the country nearer the coast were wholly
exposed in case of danger, and would have fled to Sacramento
on the least notice. But there was not a whisper of trouble.
Americans would surely have given the alarm at Sacramento
long before Arce reached there with the horses, had Castro inti-
mated, by word or act, a purpose to expel them." "Is it not
strange," Mr. Bidwell adds, in another connection, "that if Castro was about to make war against American immigrants or settlers, and these so excited about it as to ask Frémont's aid, I
should have known nothing about it, and been looking for a
saw-mill site, with only one man, and he proposing to find his
way alone to Sonoma?" Mr. Bidwell was at the moment absent
from Sutter's Fort for two or three days, with Dr. Semple,
searching for a site for that sawmill which, when afterwards
built, was the occasion of the gold-discovery. "The valley,"
when he set out, just before the seizure of Arce's horses, "was
peace and quiet. No settler, the truth of history compels me to
say it, had any apprehension of danger. I was making ready to
start to Los Angeles on business."

We must indeed remember that Mr. Bidwell is not an authority for those settlers who were just then near the camp at
the Buttes, or directly under Captain Frémont's or Lieutenant
Gillespie's influence, men such as later testified before the
Claims Committee. That these may have had sincere fears in
many cases and at this time is certain. But Mr. Bidwell is good
authority for the state of feeling at Sutter's Fort. "There was,"
then, "no excitement, no danger, till Frémont began the war by
sending the party which attacked Arce, captured his horses,
and let him and his escort go with a defiant message to Castro.
If Americans really were in danger, is it possible to conceive a
more unwise thing than the beginning of war at such a time
and under such circumstances, without giving them notice?"
"Therefore," concludes Mr. Bidwell, "I say that Frémont, and
he alone, is to be credited with the first act of war. Truth compels me to say, the war was not begun in California in defense
of American settlers. It may be there was a drawn sword hang-

ing over their heads, but if so they did not know it, and Frémont must have the credit of seeing it for them. Frémont began the war: to him belongs all the credit; upon him rests all the responsibility."

One must carefully limit, as I have tried to do, the extent to which Mr. Bidwell is a satisfactory authority. He could not know, of course, as much about Castro's designs and movements as was known at the camp in the north, because he, like the American consul at Monterey, was nearer to Castro, and consequently farther from the only genuine sources of traditional knowledge about Castro than were Captain Frémont's excited informants northward at the Buttes, or on Bear River. But Mr. Bidwell, in his ignorance, may certainly be supposed to represent the state of mind of those average, respectable American settlers who had fixed interests in the country and no extraordinary sources of information about the imminent dangers that threatened. As for the evidence in the claims pamphlet about the reports at Sutter's Fort, Mr. Bidwell's testimony shows how much that is worth.

I have seen, in Mr. Bancroft's collection of statements, others, of good authority and much value, that give the same impression of the situation.

In the second place, however, as proving that not good information of danger, but private purposes of his own led Captain Frémont to act as he did, we have the important and demonstrable fact that Captain Frémont took no trouble to verify the stories of Castro's hostility before acting, but, on the contrary, behaved precisely like a man who felt authorized to act on his own initiative. For there was one person who could have told him the truth; and that was Larkin, with whom, for the rest, Gillespie was bound by his own instructions, as we shall later see, to keep up a good understanding. Yet to Larkin *no* appeal was made for any information whatever on the matter. And if Larkin seemed too far away, and if, in his credulous acceptance of false stories, Captain Frémont feared to wait long enough to get an answer from Monterey, he could equally well have got information from Yerba Buena that would have made a peaceable leader very loath to act hastily. He did, in fact, send Lieutenant Gillespie, for supplies, to San Francisco Bay, dispatching him only a week before hostilities began. And before Gillespie returned, hostilities had been begun. These facts forbid us to think Captain Frémont desirous of a warrant for his acts in any knowledge of Castro's hostility, and show us that he was certainly in no sense anxious to know the exact truth about the state of the country.

Of Gillespie's real relation to Larkin at that moment I need now only say that it was an important one, such as should have ensured mutual confidence and certainly very good faith and plain speech from Gillespie to Larkin. On the other hand, moreover, if Captain Frémont was anywhere to learn the real state of the country, or the real dangers in which he stood, it surely was from Larkin that he might expect authentic information. Now, however, a dispatch from Larkin to the State Department, dated June 1, proves that Captain Frémont first wrote to Larkin from the Sacramento Valley, giving not the least sign of any sense of his own danger, nor the least hint of the supposed danger to the settlers, but, on the contrary, saying, in a perfectly unwarlike fashion, that he meant to go East at once. After thus writing, and before he could have time to get an answer from Larkin, he began his hostilities. This is not the conduct of one who has heard reports of the hostility of a government with which he is properly at peace and who prudently wants to find out the truth and then act accordingly. It is, however, the conduct of a man who feels authorized to act quite independently and who chooses to give no sign of his purposes to even the most properly interested persons. On June 1, then, to specify, Larkin's letter to the State Department says that Larkin has just received an express from Gillespie and Captain Frémont, who have returned to the Sacramento Valley from Oregon. "Captain Frémont now starts for the States. By the courier," he goes on, "I received a letter for Hon. Thomas H. Benton, which I inclose in this." [22] The letter thus enclosed gave Mr. Benton, as we shall see, the same information about the captain's intentions to go East. If, then, Captain Frémont's intention to go East was sincere, his change of intention that led

[22] This seems to be the letter of May 24.

to the attack before he got or could get any reply from Larkin was based on a very hasty and ill-conducted examination into the mythical warlike preparations of Castro. If, however, as is possible, this intention to go East was not sincere, but was put into the letter to Mr. Benton and into the letter to Larkin for the sake of deceiving any Californian into whose hands the letters might perchance fall, still the same considerations remain as to the insignificance of that supposed hostility of Castro as motive for the captain's act. For whether the attack upon the Californians was already determined upon or not, the same thing is shown by this Larkin letter: namely, that Captain Frémont took no trouble to learn from Larkin, as he might in any case safely and prudently have done, whether an assault upon himself and the settlers was imminent, and from his side gave to Larkin no hint of his own supposed danger. On the contrary, he acted precisely like a man with a secret that either could not be trusted on paper at all, or, if it could be so trusted, still could not be even remotely hinted to the person who had the best right to know.

But our next piece of evidence is absolutely conclusive. Lieutenant Gillespie, as he testified before the Claims Committee (p. 26 of their Report), left Captain Frémont's camp on the 28th of May, after the return to the Sacramento Valley from the north, and only about one week before the seizure of Arce's horses, "to proceed to San Francisco to obtain supplies [of food] for the men." On the 30th, at Captain Sutter's, he learned, as he says, of Castro's expected attack on the settlers and on Captain Frémont. The attack, however, was not so imminent but that he could go down in a launch to San Francisco without fear, expecting to get and bring back supplies in no very secret way. He "did not reach San Francisco until the 7th." Here he got supplies from Captain Montgomery of the *Portsmouth,* and returned to Sutter's Fort on the 12th. On his return he heard of the seizure of Arce's horses. Of course, *before* he set out on this expedition, Gillespie must have known, or at least must have suspected, that the supplies that he sought were meant not only for pressing necessities, but also for an intended war. This war now is to be, according to the self-defense theory, something forced upon Captain Frémont by threatened hostilities. The knowledge of such impending hostilities Gillespie shall have brought down to Yerba Buena. But here, as it chanced, he talked quite freely with an American, who at once wrote a letter, dated June 10, from Yerba Buena; and this was later printed in a paper in the Sandwich Islands.[23] The letter begins: "There are strange things in this world, happening every day, but none to me more so than that I should find myself in California, and writing a letter to be taken to you by the first overland express, and certainly the longest ever attempted in America. A friend has kindly volunteered to put this into the hands of the gallant Captain Frémont, who is now encamped in the Sacramento, and about to proceed directly to the United States." This "friend" is evidently Gillespie himself; for the letter-writer goes on to tell how he has just heard, from the lips of the very gentleman who brought an express to Captain Frémont from the States, of the meeting on the shores of Klamath Lake; of the night of danger that followed; of the Indian attack; of the hair-breadth escape; and of the return to the Sacramento Valley. And now the Frémont party are preparing *to return to the States!* Plainly, Gillespie well kept his secret about the coming conflict from his fellow countryman. This is quite intelligible *if the plotting was going on from the American side,* but unintelligible if the pressing danger to the American settlers was now a matter of public knowledge or yet of public report. In that case the correspondent surely could not have been persuaded to send a letter overland to the United States by the hands of Captain Frémont on this mentioned information that the latter was at once to leave the land, and peacefully. As to the state of the country, meanwhile, the correspondent, in his innocence about coming events, gives us, through this wholly accidental letter, a beautifully unconscious refutation of all stories about the fears of the Americans that were well in-

---

[23] I have the letter before me in the copy made from the *Friend* into the *Sandwich Island News,* of Honolulu, December 2, 1846, a copy that I had the good fortune to find by a mere accident, and, independently, in a Harvard College Library file. I do not know for what American newspaper the letter was first written.

formed. For this letter-writer is no friend of the Californians; on the contrary, he speaks ill of them, and hopes that "a day of reckoning" may some time come for certain supposed old-time injuries. But yet his whole account of these people attributes to them a present condition, not of dangerous and hostile readiness, but of lazy impotence and inefficiency. The facts that he relates are many of them quite inconsistent with any prevalent fear of imminent war against any Americans. He says, for instance, that Castro is supposed to be quarreling with Pio Pico, "but his [Castro's] conduct *meets with such universal contempt from all classes that he cannot raise over forty men now, where a few months ago he was supreme.*" This is indeed a formidable army, "of all arms," such as Senator Benton tells us of! The letter-writer does indeed know that it is "even reported" that Castro is inciting Indians to burn up American wheat-fields; but so little does he lay stress on this mere rumor that, immediately after repeating it, he adds that all Sutter's American laborers *have left the fort before the harvest time "and gone to work for themselves, taking his cattle to pay the amounts due them.*" Thus people always behave, let the reader remember, in a time of dread of imminent "pillage and massacre"!

And so this intelligent observer, some days after the seizure of Arce's horses, but still before the news had come of this first cloud of war, had not the least notion of impending hostilities, and, after a very free talk with Gillespie, only knew that Captain Frémont was about to go East, and that there was some rumor about Castro's wish that the Indians would burn up American wheat. This writer did *not* know that Castro had threatened any armed attack on Americans; he did *not* lay the least stress on the rumor about the wheat; and what he says shows that there was *no* general "excitement" of a hostile character, such as certain of the Claims Committee witnesses pretend to know about, at Yerba Buena or anywhere else near the bay. How, if there were, could Gillespie be spinning yarns on shore so quietly to his countryman, although the bold lieutenant was, in fact, already well known at Yerba Buena to be a messenger to Frémont and a disguised American officer? For the rest, the same correspondent, in a later letter, after hostilities had begun, attributes the whole trouble to the settlers themselves and considers it their aggression. All this, then, shows both the absurdity of the current stories in the north, the carelessness of Captain Frémont about the actual state of the Californian public mind, and the determination of the captain to do his own share of plotting.

Captain Frémont's own letter of July 25, 1846 [24] to Senator Benton, the letter on which the venerable Senator's first account was founded, does indeed assert the hostility of Castro as a ground for action, but it gives no reason to doubt the validity of the foregoing reasoning. In the first place, it may have been written, as we shall see, in a sort of private family cipher. If taken literally, however, it implies that Gillespie, who set out on May 28 from the camp in the north to go to Yerba Buena for supplies, already knew of Castro's hostility and of the captain's purpose, and that officers in the United States navy, to whom Gillespie told the news, approved openly of the captain's intended course. It also implies that the account of their approval *brought back* by Gillespie was one motive of Captain Frémont's final action itself, although, to be sure, this action, as it also shows, took place *before* Gillespie's return. It implies this inconsistency and several other doubtful matters, which may be due to the haste in which the letter was written. Imperfect as it thus is for historical uses, this letter nevertheless shows plainly enough, if it shows anything, that between May 24 and June 6, and without waiting for sound advices from even Yerba Buena, Captain Frémont resolved of his own will to instigate an attack on the utterly defenseless Californians north of San Francisco Bay, giving as his warrant an entirely unfounded report (or pretext) that they were already in arms against himself. Taken in connection with the foregoing contemporaneous evidence, this fact must be viewed as forever disposing of the notion that Captain Frémont could have learned, after careful inquiry from any competent persons, that good evidence existed of immediate danger from Castro. For the letter itself shows that he took no time to make such

[24] See *National Intelligencer* for November 12, 1846.

inquiry. On the contrary, we now see clearly that the reports about Castro, such as the forged proclamation that Loker posted or the paper that Ide saw, issued from some source very near to Captain Frémont's own person, and that *if* he himself was deceived about the matter, he took no trouble to avoid such deception and acted wholly without good evidence of danger. In view of the above-mentioned evidences that somebody was decidedly interested in spreading false written reports of Castro's intentions, there can be very little doubt remaining as to the actual relation of Captain Frémont and Lieutenant Gillespie themselves to the reports that are so often said to have justified their aggression. Rather must it be hoped that the orders from Washington justified the use of these reports.

Let the reader still not for one moment misinterpret our present result. *If* the fourth plan *was* the government plan, and was so included in instructions brought by Gillespie that Captain Frémont, as a confidential officer of the government, could not escape from the duty of performing his official trust by carrying out this plan, then let the necessary means used be charged one and all to the moral responsibility of the government at Washington. The morality of such devices is, in such cases, obviously an affair for the government, not for the confidential agent, to judge. *If* the Gillespie instructions *were* so worded as to require this interpretation under the circumstances, then all the deception and all the aggression used by Captain Frémont must be pardoned or even praised, in so far as it all was an official act authorized and demanded by his government. And furthermore one must pardon, in that case, the aforesaid patriotic delicacy also that led the young officer's friends in later times to shield the government, by repeating to the American public statements that were originally of use in arousing the trappers and sturdy vagabonds of the Sacramento Valley. Even if such evidences were used before Congress to secure appropriations for the expenses of the conquest, one may still suppose the administration responsible for the somewhat singular means employed for this end. *In case* the fourth plan was the government plan, it is indeed impossible to hide from ourselves its wantonly aggressive and cruel character; but it is still easy to justify and to extol the energy of the spirited agent. So that now all still turns for us upon this question: *was* the fourth plan really the government plan, and did Captain Frémont's instructions, received from Gillespie, warrant and require him to carry it out?

VI. *The Mystery as Now Expounded by General Frémont*

STUDENTS of a scene in history must not be moved by personal interests; but I confess that from *a priori* considerations I was prepared, when I first came to the study of this subject, to form a very high opinion of the work of the gallant Captain Frémont in the acquisition of California; and later, when facts upon which we are soon to dwell had already very seriously affected my enthusiasm, I still turned, with strong hopes of discovering new facts that would vindicate him, to General Frémont himself for personal explanations. I have not promised General Frémont to agree with him in any of my results, nor have I assured him of anything but the fairest possible statement of his side also in its place in this book, along with whatever other facts, opposing or favorable, I might learn in connection with the matter. So far the facts here brought forward certainly have seemed to make Captain Frémont's responsibility at the moment of his action a very serious one, in case he was not fully supported by his instructions. He brought war into a peaceful department; his operations began an estrangement, ensured a memory of bloodshed, excited a furious bitterness of feeling between the two peoples that were henceforth to dwell in California, such as all his own subsequent personal generosity and kindness could never again make good. From the Bear Flag affair we can date the beginning of the degradation, the ruin, and the oppression of the Californian people by our own. In all subsequent time the two peoples, as peoples, have misunderstood and hated each other, with disastrous effects for both, and especially for the weaker. No doubt, as we shall later see, some great evils were, under the circumstances, inevitable. Yet much of this hatred might have been saved, had we come peaceably and openheartedly. We came, as it seemed to them, by stealth, and we used unprovoked violence. The memory of this led in part to the revolt in the south and to the bloodshed of that conflict; and so all the rest followed. Undoubted is the personal goodwill and generous appreciation that General Frémont has since shown to many native Californians, and the devotion that he later exhibited to some of their interests. With all that we have here nothing to do. His act as aggressor in the Bear Flag War began the bitterness. And in that, I say, he assumed a very serious responsibility. Now, however, we are to see how, from his own point of view, he today regards this long-past story and what he now feels at liberty to say for his personal justification.

An interview that I had with General Frémont in December 1884 forms the basis of the present statement of his side of the matter. I took copious notes at the time, submitted them later to General and Mrs. Frémont for correction, and have promised them an opportunity to see the proofs of this present version. The reader may then feel tolerably sure that, however I shall later have to criticize General Frémont's past acts or present views, the general's final and definitive account of those matters at issue, concerning which I expressed my doubts and questions to him personally, is, at this point, stated to his own satisfaction in so far as it has been possible for me so to state his views.

In answer to my general questions, at our interview, about his purposes in the expedition of 1845–6, General Frémont replied that his main object was to find the shortest route for a future railroad to the Pacific, and especially to the neighborhood of San Francisco Bay. Yet he was not without other thoughts at the time of his departure from the East. For Senator Benton, who had long devoted much attention to projects of further extension of our territory in the West and Southwest, and who, of course, had been deeply interested in the previous expedition to California, had often talked with the young captain, before the beginning of this new expedition, concerning the value that the territory would have to the United States whenever it should come, as Senator Benton was firmly determined to have it come, into our possession. War with Mexico was already probable. And so, said General Frémont, "at the time I set out, I felt that opportunity was apt to make probability a certainty, and I was determined to be prompt to act upon this feeling, and to take advantage of any opportunity to serve the country in this way."

Mrs. Frémont, at this point during the interview, kindly added some explanations concerning what she knew of the intentions of the government during Captain Frémont's absence on this expedition. After the expedition was on its way, she frequently made part in consultations between her father and Secretary Buchanan concerning California. Buchanan, as she feels sure, was very much, if not altogether, under her father's influence and agreed with Senator Benton as to all important points in the whole affair. What the character of their discussions was the subsequent instructions to Captain Frémont showed, and also the subsequent events. Yet if I desired a summary of the conversations concerning California, as she remembered them, she would express their substance in the single sentence: "Since England intends to take California, we must see that she does not." Meanwhile, of course, the certainty of a coming war with Mexico was laid at the basis of all the discussions.

General Frémont, resuming his own statement, added that he himself knew, of course, very accurately, during his absence, the great extent of the influence that Mr. Benton's long experience and position as chairman of the Military Committee of the Senate, as well as his personal powers and his political eminence, gave him with the administration. General Frémont remembers, also, how the coming of the Mexican War, in view of Mr. Benton's views and influence, was already considered by all the family as a certainty. And naturally all these facts influenced his own subsequent conduct.

After he reached California, the unfortunate difficulty with Castro took place. This, General Frémont assured me, was in no wise occasioned by his own fault, nor was it any part of his intention. For as yet no further information had reached him that could warrant him in getting into any voluntary difficulty with Castro. He remembers no incident that could have caused trouble from his side, or by the act of any of his party. Castro, as he now remembers the matter, had promised him the privilege of accomplishing one of the immediate objects of his surveying expedition, by "being allowed to travel through the country, and to become acquainted with the passes to the coast." The privilege of "resting the party and getting supplies" was merely an addition to this main request. The main request was clearly understood on both sides. The permission of Castro was indeed not put in writing, but the matter was clear enough. And the subsequent order of Castro was also clearly a breaking of the latter's promise, a complete change of policy, unprovoked and unexpected. That Captain Frémont should resist this order as much as he did was, the general assured me, merely an expression of his indisposition to submit to an affront. He was willing to give Castro an opportunity to attack, although he himself had still no authority to attack Castro. The retirement after three days was leisurely, and surveys were made all along the way until Klamath Lake was reached, the Indians showing no hostility until the fatal night of Gillespie's coming, when they attacked the camp and killed three men.

Gillespie's coming and his messages formed, of course, the main subject of my conversation with General Frémont; and the discussion upon this matter was quite full. Gillespie, according to the general's statement, brought a dispatch to him from Buchanan in oral form, having destroyed the original before he passed through Mexico, to prevent its possible capture. He also brought, as has always been said, letters from Senator Benton and Mrs. Frémont to Captain Frémont. These, indeed, were private letters, but they related in part to the same subject as Gillespie's dispatch. Senator Benton gave, in fact, to Captain Frémont, by his own letter, a more explicit expression of the wishes of the government than was given in the dispatch. But this could safely be done in the letter, because "the private letters were in a manner in family cipher, so full were they of prearranged reference to talks and agreements known only at

home." [25] That this information as to the wishes of the government was, under the circumstances, as authoritative as the
official dispatch itself is clear to General Frémont from the previously stated facts concerning Senator Benton's relations to the
administration.

Between the private letters and the dispatch General Frémont made in his statement only this distinction: that the letters were "much stronger and fuller than the dispatch, —
stronger and fuller to the one point *of taking and holding possession of California in the event of any occurrence that would
justify it,* leaving it to my discretion to decide upon such an
occurrence." The substance, however, of letters and dispatch
together was *that it was the desire of the President that Captain Frémont should not let the English get possession of California, but should use any means in his power, or any occasion
that offered, to prevent such a thing,* looking always to the imminent probability of a war with Mexico. And so what was
afterwards done *was in strict conformity to these instructions,
in view of the circumstances of the case.*

General Frémont expressed his certainty that the dispatch
brought by Gillespie was addressed to him directly. And here a
discussion took place at our interview that the reader will later
find noteworthy. I brought up Mr. J. S. Hittell's assertion as
made in his *History of San Francisco* to the effect that the Bear
Flag affair was a blunder whereby a certain important and authorized plan of Consul Larkin's to gain possession of California by peaceful means was violently thwarted. In view of this
and of what I called an apparently well-founded opinion about
Gillespie's dispatch, I asked whether it was not true that the
message from the government as brought by Gillespie was
really directed to Consul Larkin, or was at least ordered to be
repeated to him. Concerning this point General Frémont's recollection was very decided and his opinion quite clear. He was
sure that the Gillespie dispatch as he knew it was directed to

---

[25] The words quoted here are Mrs. Frémont's, added by her, for
the sake of fuller explanation, to my MS. notes of the interview.

him personally; and he was firmly of the opinion that Gillespie could not have had any important secret instruction directed to Larkin or to anybody else in California save Captain Frémont himself. Nor did it seem at all probable to him that the government would have entrusted to Larkin any part of the business. Mr. Hittel's interpretation he considered as utterly unfounded in fact. Mrs. Frémont, who later, in 1849, had frequent opportunities for conversation with Larkin concerning past events, and who felt sure that under the circumstances he would have had no objection to telling her all about the matter, never heard — so she at this point kindly assured me — any hint from him of any such secret mission. She thought that "there could hardly be a more improbable idea" than the one suggested by Mr. Hittell — namely, the idea that Larkin could have been instructed to get California by peaceful intrigue with its inhabitants. The plan could not have been carried out; Mr. Buchanan would never have dreamed of entrusting such a plan to a man of the imperfect education and small experience of Consul Larkin; the idea of such a plan was inconsistent with the wishes of the government as made known to Captain Frémont and discussed in her presence in Washington.

General Frémont also held this same view of the matter. He said, indeed, that Larkin might have been given some special instructions about conciliating the Californians, but insisted that no part of the real purpose of the government in California could have been entrusted to him or to any other agent in California save Gillespie as messenger and Captain Frémont himself as principal agent. California could not have been gained by peaceable means in the way supposed; and the actual purpose of the government as known at the time to Captain Frémont included the use of such means as were actually employed in view of the circumstances. The whole affair had indeed to be carried on, in part, out of the range of official business; and much was left to Captain Frémont's responsibility, so that he was obliged to act on his personal knowledge of what the government wanted — a knowledge not wholly communicated by official channels. However, so much is certain to him: that Larkin could not have had any important trust in the matter without the knowledge of the captain, while in fact the latter had no such knowledge.[26]

I dwelt perhaps unnecessarily, in the interview, on the question of the exact coloring of the official instructions and the exact sense of his position which General Frémont remembers himself to have had at the moment of action. No doubt, I was repeatedly assured, could exist as to the purpose of the government to take California *if there should be the least chance, "and by force if necessary."* The government wanted and intended to push the war with Mexico and instructed accordingly. As to his own feeling at the moment of action, General Frémont said, in nearly the following words: "It is not to be supposed that an officer of the government would act as I did unless he had the sense that his authority for his act was sufficient under the circumstances. I felt that the certainty of war would place me in a position to have the government behind me in all that I might do; but that if no war took place I would so assume the responsibility as to leave the government free to disavow me if it was needed. I was in a position where I might render great service to the government by taking upon myself a possible personal risk which the government knew I was taking." [27] There is at all events no chance, insisted General Frémont, that anyone acquainted with his official instructions could fairly and truthfully accuse him of *disobeying* their letter, notwithstanding the *relative freedom* with which, under the circumstances, it was his duty to act. When I referred to the summary of the situation casually given by Mr. Barrows in his *Oregon*,[28] according to which the young captain did good service by prop-

---

[26] The same view was insisted upon, later, in letters to me written for the general.

[27] The analogy of General Komarov's recent position and action in Afghanistan, as the European public have interpreted the matter, will at once occur to any reader's mind. As this interview took place in December 1884, that particular analogy of course, could not have been thought of in our conversation on this occasion.

[28] William Barrows: *Oregon: The Struggle for Possession* (Boston, 1883), in the American Commonwealth series, p. 273.

erly disregarding "red tape," General Frémont accepted the description as very fair and satisfactory.

General Frémont now continued as to subsequent events. When Gillespie overtook the party at the head of the Sacramento Valley, Captain Frémont already fully intended to return from Oregon after he should have spent some time in making surveys. When he should return he expected to remain in the territory and to "watch events." Already he hoped in this way to have part in the acquisition of California. The difficulty with Castro had diverted him for the moment from his original plans, but had not affected his ultimate purposes. From the time of the return to the Sacramento Valley until the first act of hostility, Captain Frémont waited in the valley watching events; the coming of Arce's horses seemed to him to bring the right moment for action, and so he chose it. General Frémont finds it now, of course, hard to say just in how far there was a clear understanding between him and the settlers before this first hostile act. Such men as he needed he instructed in what was needful for them to know. He took no care to prevent the misunderstandings that must arise when such a movement has to be made by an officer with confidential instructions. Merritt, who was a "good man," [29] had the instructions about taking Arce's horses and about the subsequent seizure of Sonoma and of the four notable prisoners. All that was therefore done by Captain Frémont's order. As for the Bear Flag men at Sonoma, before the party of Captain Frémont joined them, the general said that he neither knew nor cared what they did in the way of "government" at Sonoma, save indeed that their arbitrary seizures of property and similar acts seemed to him to be bad and were blamed by him when he came down to Sonoma. General Frémont, in answer to one further question, said that he saw no proclamation of Castor's ordering American settlers out of the country, or threatening them; nor does he know whether there was one. I ought here to add that although at this first interview General Frémont gave me to understand

---

[29] I fully suppose and believe that General Frémont must be here understood to use "good" as a relative term, — relative, namely, to the business of taking horses by violence.

that he had taken ample time to go over his recollections and records of that period; although he himself, in fact, chose the time of the interview and was previously advised by letter of what I aimed to know; although, moreover, he himself on this occasion referred me more than once to the Claims Committee Report, heretofore frequently quoted; and although I definitely set before him at the time as a difficulty Mr. Bidwell's assertion that the settlers had nothing to fear, still he made in the whole interview no mention of the traditional danger to the settlers or of aggression from Castro as in any wise an *important* reason for his operations, but on the contrary distinctly gave me to understand that his duty as a confidential servant of the country itself fully warranted his action. Mr. Bidwell, he assured me, was as a settler of course unaware of the purposes of the government and was therefore an incompetent critic of a confidential agent's conduct. The whole interview tended to this one result, that the instructions were the decisive element in determining the conduct of the captain, while the stories about Castro soon seemed to me so completely out of sight for General Frémont that I made, after the introduction of Mr. Bidwell's view and the asking of the question about Castro's proclamation, no further attempt to press the matter, confident that General Frémont now felt at liberty, in view of the long-past public interests involved, to leave out of account those motives that his duty to his country seems to have once forced him to make so prominent. I considered the interview as in fact decisive upon this matter, and for some time had no reason to change my view of General Frémont's present opinion. Of course I may herein have entirely misunderstood the general.

In justice to General Frémont, though with serious regrets for the cause of historical simplicity and definiteness of result, I am forced, however, to add that in a subsequent interview, in which he kindly undertook to help me about a few further difficulties, General Frémont returned once more, in answer to questions then put, to the expression of his opinion that he was at that time trustworthily informed of Castro's imminent hostility. Possibly to the natural inconsistencies of the human memory, which General Frémont himself freely declared to be,

after forty years, a troublesome obstacle to historical thoroughness and accuracy, may be attributed the whole of this last
difficulty of mine. At all events, as we have seen, there is good
reason for doubting any memory that may now assure General
Frémont of well-sifted and trustworthy information then possessed by him about any imminent danger to his command or
to the settlers from Castro. He could have had no such trustworthy information, since there was none to have. If he was
actually deceived by a conspiracy of settlers, or by some odd
accident of circumstances, very definite documentary evidence
would now be needed to substantiate the fact. And the whole
tendency of my principal interview is to show that the chief
and clearer memory of General Frémont has reference to his
instructions, and not to Castro. Whether even this clearer memory is accurate, we have now to see. I think that the danger
from Castro ought at all events forever to disappear from the
determining motives of the affair. The operation was once for
all a pure aggression, and there will never again be a chance
of making it appear otherwise. Such, then, is General Frémont's
present account.

VII. *The Mystery Deepens*

A GOVERNMENT is responsible only for instructions that it
actually gives. However near or dear the venerable Senator Benton was to the government, he was not in the government, and his private advices to Captain Frémont in a "family
cipher" cannot be viewed as committing our administration to
any policy that it did not actually authorize that distinguished
statesman to convey to his son-in-law. It would need no disavowal to save the government from the responsibility of such
acts; they would be *ipso facto* a family plot, unless the cabinet,
or at all events the President, previously knew of them and
approved them. All this is axiomatic.

In view hereof I fully appreciate the importance for General
Frémont of the discovery of sufficient proof that Senator Benton's "family cipher" letter contained nothing in opposition to
the wording of the official government dispatch brought by

Gillespie. The fourth plan was, if General Frémont is right, in the dispatch itself, although it was more fully stated in the letter. The letter from Senator Benton has never seen the light; but if we had it and the dispatch both before us, with the "cipher" interpreted, there are but four possibilities as to their relations: (1) If they disagreed, then Senator Benton's letter could have no authority, but would express only a family plot to thwart the government; and this would be true however loving and confidential the daily intercourse between the venerable statesman and the cabinet may have been. (2) But the two might perfectly agree, or the letter might be less explicit than the dispatch; and then the letter from Senator Benton would not help us at all in our judgment. (3) Since the letter, however, is said to have been *more* explicit than the dispatch, this *more* in the letter might be unauthorized exhortation, and would then again be worthless. (4) Or this *more* might be authorized, and then the best way to prove the fact would be to show the perfect agreement of letter and dispatch in contents and in spirit, *so far as the dispatch went*. In all ways, therefore, we see how vastly important it is to know what the dispatch said; and how comparatively unimportant it is, *before* we know what the dispatch said, to speculate about the private opinions of even Senator Benton concerning the conquest of California. The best way to show that his views were decisive with the cabinet is to find out the actual expression of the cabinet's views; since a government is distinguishable by the fact that even its most halting and vacillating and foolish views are for its agents always authoritative, while a person *not* in the government is distinguished by the fact that his wisest and seemingly most influential and most far-seeing and most friendly advice is worth not the waste paper needed to write it to a faithful agent of the government unless this agent knows from the government that this advice receives its own sanction.

Can we, however, find out what the dispatch said? Let us try both indirect and direct means. We have General Frémont's memory of the dispatch and of the letter, and of their agreement. But now, if the dispatch contained what was essentially the fourth plan, how could a sane government have sent it, while, both about the same time and later, sending instructions to Sloat that not only did not contemplate any support from his fleet to Captain Frémont's operations,[30] but gave him definite orders that in so many words said things utterly inconsistent with the notion of what we have called the fourth plan? This latter inconsistency appears as follows: [31]

As far as they have been published, the earlier instructions issued required Sloat, not, unless absolutely driven thereto, to attack the government of California as such, but only in case he should hear of a declaration of war to seize upon the ports, especially the port of San Francisco, but if possible without a struggle with the government. Sloat was meanwhile both first and last carefully instructed "to preserve, if possible, the most friendly relations with the inhabitants" and to "encourage them to adopt a course of neutrality." In an instruction that did not reach him before he acted, but that expresses intentions that he ‧must well have known by other means when he acted, he is assured that "a connection between California and the present government of Mexico is supposed scarcely to exist." He is instructed, "as opportunity offers," to "conciliate the people in California towards the government of the United States," and to "endeavor to render their relations with the United States as intimate and friendly as possible." He is to "hold possession of San Francisco, even while" he encourages "the people to neutrality, self-government, and friendship." Or again, in another likewise late-coming instruction, he is ordered to "endeavor to establish the supremacy of the American flag without any strife

---

[30] This point, heretofore dwelt upon, Colonel Frémont was himself at no small pains to prove before the Claims Committee, where he and Gillespie testified to Sloat's perplexity and confusion of mind concerning the unexpected and incomprehensible conduct of the young captain in the north. Colonel Frémont at that time desired to show the energy and momentous consequences of his acts.

[31] A convenient place to find Sloat's instructions together is in Ex. Doc. 19, 2nd Sess., 29th Congr. (Assembly), or again in Cutts: *History of the Conquest of New Mexico and California* (Philadelphia, 1847), in chap. vii and in the appendix.

with the people of California"; and "if California separates herself from our enemy, the central Mexican government, and establishes a government of its own under the auspices of the American flag," Sloat is to "take such measures as will best promote the attachment of the people of California to the United States." He is to bear in mind "that this country desires to find in California a friend, and not an enemy; to be connected with it by near ties; to hold possession of it, at least during the war; and to hold that possession, if possible, with the consent of the inhabitants." There is no reason for supposing these later instructions directed to Sloat to have been in any wise at variance with his earlier orders, not all of which have been published. It is plain, then, that Sloat had a very curious and delicate commission entrusted to his care. He was to get possession of the port of San Francisco whenever war should have begun; yet *even then he was not, unless absolutely forced thereto, to levy war against the inhabitants of California.* He was, on the contrary, to treat them as friends, who had unfortunately become involved in the Mexican difficulty by reason of their merely nominal connection with the central government. He was to invite them *to continue their self-government,* while he was to urge them to separate peacefully from Mexico and to come over to the side of the United States. He was to cultivate their goodwill, and as far as possible to confine himself to a naval occupation of their ports. If the reader sees herein anything of a nature to perplex and paralyze Sloat's mind whenever he should learn the contrast between his instructions and the policy that on his arrival he found under active process of development by Captain Frémont and Lieutenant Gillespie, as a consequence of the latter's secret mission, we must frankly admit that we cannot explain the variance by any hypothesis consistent with wisdom in plotting and fidelity in execution. We must indeed add that yet later instructions to Sloat — namely, those prepared July 12, 1846, after instructions had already been issued to General S. W. Kearny for an overland expedition to California — more explicitly contemplate an occupation of the whole department of Sloat's force. For by the time these instructions were issued, the Mexican War was well under way, and the government was unwilling to risk any further delays. In these instructions, then, Sloat is expected, under the rights that belong to his country as belligerent, to take entire possession of Upper California, so that, at the conclusion of peace, there may be no doubts as to such actual possession. And *now*, indeed, he is required, as he was not before, to establish a civil government of his own in the territory. But still he is assured that "in selecting persons to hold office, due respect should be had to the wishes of the people of California," as well as to the actual possessors of authority in that province." And finally, August 13, 1846, he is instructed to give the people "as much liberty of self-government as is consistent with the general occupation of the country by the United States."

But perhaps, as someone will object, when the government said that "a connection between California and Mexico is supposed scarcely to exist," they referred to their secret expectation that Captain Frémont would, ere Sloat acted, have severed the "connection." When they talked of "neutrality," they meant the kind of "neutrality" that Captain Frémont would by this time have enforced by the aid of rebels and rifles. When they talked of "self-government," they meant self-government as administered by Captain Frémont's surveying party. And when they talked of "the wishes of the people" and of "friendship," they were simply employing a little irony. The text of Commodore Sloat's dispatches, if given in full as Mr. Bancroft wrote them, would completely refute this view. The opposition of the Sloat instructions and of the fourth plan must be perfectly evident to anyone who will read the instructions, and the matter would be inexplicable, and would give rise to problems that we might forever and very blindly discuss, were there not now a very different and shorter road out of our perplexities about what the government wanted. But let this opposition have at least its obvious weight.

I have dwelt so long on all the indirect means of getting at the government's plan for the sake of reducing certain doubts and of cutting off certain questions that would otherwise come before us when I at length mention the one direct, long-hidden, now finally accessible, authoritative expression of the government's plan itself. I refer to the instructions that Gillespie brought from Secretary Buchanan, and in all noteworthy probability to the only official instructions of which Captain Frémont could have had any knowledge at the moment of acting. Whether by Gillespie's own deliberate and unheard-of treachery they were falsified to the captain, whether because of the "family cipher" letter he concluded to neglect them, whether he determined of his own will to take the risk of the moment and disobey them, whether he never even listened to find out their plain meaning, or, if he did, by what very natural misfortune of memory he forty years later came to misconceive them in his statement to me,[32] and by what wondrous good fortune he has so long occupied a position such that no government official could venture to confront him with the facts — all these questions I prejudge not and discuss not now. The historical fact about the instructions is the important thing. I have given General Frémont's view, and I must also give the facts.

VIII. *Only One Dispatch Contains the Secret Mission*

No doubt can properly exist that Gillespie brought *one* official dispatch, and one only, to any agent in California. He was sharply questioned about the matter by the Claims Committee and went over the ground several times. He was then speaking before people who were quite able to control his statements by confidential inquiries at the government offices and who in fact did get a confidential copy of the very instructions carried. He was also testifying in Colonel Frémont's own case and in his favor. If he had had two sets of instructions, one to Larkin and one to Captain Frémont, there was every reason, for the sake of the credit of the hero of the occasion, why Gillespie should have stated the fact. But he does not state such a fact in his recorded testimony before the committee. What he distinctly says is that he had a dispatch to Larkin, and repeated it to Captain Frémont, having been instructed so to do. And for

---

[32] He did not misstate them before the Claims Committee, but he was cautiously reticent about them, as we have seen, in this and in all his earlier official expressions.

Captain Frémont he had his own letter of introduction, which imported nothing but the trustworthiness of the bearer; and he had the Benton packet. That is all [33] save, to be sure, Gillespie's own personal instructions, which he communicated to Captain Frémont, and which undoubtedly were, as he says, "to watch over the interests of the United States in California." How he was to "watch" we shall learn. He was, however, as we shall see, *to co-operate with Larkin.*

Gillespie's testimony makes clear, then, that he can have had but *one* dispatch, in addition to his own personal instructions. Even if he had had two official dispatches, one to Larkin and one to Captain Frémont, not only his silence about the latter as a separate dispatch would be inexplicable, but the position of Captain Frémont at the moment of action would be precisely the same as with only one dispatch. For Gillespie's words, uttered, be it remembered, in Colonel Frémont's own cause and behalf before the committee in 1848, while the whole matter was fresh in all their minds, are as just quoted: *"I was directed to show to Colonel Frémont the duplicate of the dispatch to Larkin."* So that although General Frémont so kindly took the trouble to demonstrate for me, in our recent interview, that Larkin could not have had any secret mission from the government through Gillespie, the plain evidence is that, unless Gillespie was guilty of wanton and unheard-of treachery, the Larkin mission must have been at the time perfectly well

---

[33] Claims Committee Report, p. 30: "I was bearer of the duplicate of a dispatch to the United States consul at Monterey, as well also a packet for J. C. Frémont, Esq., and a letter of introduction to the latter gentleman from the Honorable James Buchanan. The former I destroyed before entering the port of Vera Cruz, having committed it to memory. The packet and letter of introduction I delivered to Captain Frémont, upon the 9th of May, 1846, in the mountains of Oregon." P. 31: "I delivered my letter of introduction and the packet intrusted to me to Captain Frémont, and made him acquainted with the wishes of the government, which were the same as stated above for my own guidance." P. 32: "I was also directed to show to Colonel Frémont the duplicate of the dispatch to Mr. Larkin."

explained to the young captain, who has since so completely
forgotten it and who now so sincerely deems it impossible.

That the Larkin dispatch was, however, the *only* official dispatch brought to California by Gillespie in this affair is shown,
not merely by Gillespie's own testimony, but by every scrap of
older testimony that I have been in any wise able to discover
bearing on this question. Although Gillespie testified in Colonel
Frémont's own cause to the delivery at Klamath Lake of the
Larkin dispatch, Colonel Frémont at that time gave, in his own
testimony, no hint of having received *two* official dispatches,
such as he must have received in case he had his own independent official dispatch. He merely left out Larkin's name in
his testimony. Furthermore, while the secret Larkin mission can
be traced, as mentioned, more or less covertly, in numerous
public documents, no public document can be found, I think,
that contains any trace of a record of a mission to Captain Frémont. By the courtesy of the present Secretaries, I have official
answers from the State, War, and Navy Departments which
assure me that in all of them careful search fails to reveal any
record of any instruction to a secret agent in California at that
time, save the Larkin dispatch; while this, notwithstanding its
very delicate and confidential character, remains yet on record.

As an absolutely insurmountable evidence, however, on this
point, I have at last to present Captain Frémont's own original
confession to his father-in-law, in the before-mentioned letter
of May 24, 1846. I should have presented it earlier were it not
that the captain, after all, is supposed, as we have seen, to have
corresponded in those days with the venerable Senator in a
"family cipher." What he said *might* therefore, taken alone, be
viewed as containing some secret meaning. But the coincidence
of the statement now to be quoted with the whole mass of the
historical evidence as just presented is simply overwhelming.
The literal meaning of the young captain's words is undoubtedly to be accepted, and therewith ends forever the theory of a
separate dispatch, not identical with the Larkin dispatch, and
brought by Gillespie to Captain Frémont in person. "Your letter," says the captain to the Senator, "led me to expect some
communication from him [Buchanan is the antecedent of *him*],

"but I received nothing." The italics are as printed in the copy before me.[34]

How completely our memories frequently mislead us! General Frémont not only assured me, but even demonstrated to me, as above shown, that he was, save Gillespie, the only secret agent of the government in the territory who was entrusted with this business, Larkin being an almost impossible person for the purpose. But the indubitable facts of the record are that *no* secret official commission was brought by Gillespie to anybody but Larkin, and that Captain Frémont himself confessed, in writing, in 1846, that he had no secret mission from the government, while, as Gillespie's testimony shows, Captain Frémont *must have known of Larkin's mission!*

IX. *The Mystery as Expounded by the One Dispatch*

ONE official dispatch, then, and one only, was brought to any secret agent, and this, the Larkin dispatch, would still be as inaccessible as ever, and our quandary as hopeless, were it not for the enterprise and good fortune of Mr. H. H. Bancroft. In his excellent and now often herein named treasure, the Larkin papers, are two copies, both authentic, of the Larkin dispatch as brought by Gillespie. One is the original, sent around the Horn by the Congress. It came with Commodore Stockton and arrived after its days of immediate usefulness were numbered. The other copy is the one written out by Gillespie from memory when he landed at Monterey. This copy is accurate save in one or two wholly unimportant verbal respects. The gallant lieutenant, certainly, so far told the truth. These documents have been pointed out to me at the Bancroft Library, and it was there that my attention was first attracted to their significance. Much as I have since labored to make this investigation my own, much as I have weighed for myself and arranged and rearranged all the evidence that I could find with a view to being as independent as possible, much as I have toiled to get wholly new evidence, I must still frankly admit, as

[34] See, as before, the *National Intelligencer* of November 12, 1846.

I gladly do, that without Mr. Bancroft's documents I should have been as unable to find my way out of the labyrinth as have been all past investigators of this matter. Even the new evidence that I have now found would in large part have been sealed to me. And in the end I can prove nothing that gives any other significance to these documents than the reader is already quite prepared, after the foregoing, to give them himself as soon as he comes to know what they contain. It is a curious fact in this matter that, the clew once found, absolutely all the disinterested evidence is seen to point in the same direction; while until the clew is found, the evidence looks like a mass of confusion. Yet without all the foregoing, and without some hint of the interests that have for a generation forbidden the true state of the case to come to the public knowledge, and that have at last ended in giving the hero of the tale such a curiously mistaken personal impression and memory of his own share in the matter, no reader could appreciate the solution of the mystery, or understand its historical significance as a mystery, or enjoy the true humor of this lifelong effort of a disobedient officer to seem to himself a hero.

Here, then, to sum it all up, is our country's honor involved in a violation of the laws of nations, under circumstances of peculiar atrocity: a war brought among a peaceful and, in part, cordially friendly people; anarchy and irregular hostilities threatened and begun without any provocation, and with consequences that were bad enough, as it happened, and that would have been far worse had not regular warfare just then, by a happy accident, announced its robust and soon irresistible presence. These irregular deeds are the immediate work of a gallant, energetic, and able young officer, who thenceforth gets general credit as faithful secret agent of his government and heroic defender of his countrymen, as well as savior to us of the territory of California. His reputation gained in this affair nearly makes him president in 1856. The warfare in question is also thenceforth publicly justified by unfounded reports of Californian hostility. All this is authorized, as the story goes, by a government that thus orders sixty men to distress a vast and ill-organized land, without providing any support whereby the work of their rifles can be promptly utilized to found any new and stable government in place of the one that they are commanded cruelly to harass, without warning to assault and thus unlawfully to overthrow. The official authority for all this is one dispatch and the contents of the "family cipher," in case they were officially authorized. The dispatch was brought, as the Claims Committee Report shows, to Larkin, and repeated to Captain Frémont by Gillespie at Klamath Lake. Is all the foregoing a true interpretation of the dispatch? Such is the delicate personal problem.

The solution is that Consul Larkin was, by this dispatch, instructed peacefully to intrigue for the secession of the department from Mexico, by the will of its own inhabitants, as expressed by their own constituted authorities. He was to be discreet, cautious, and alert; and he was to intrigue to this one end, and with authority also. He was made secret agent for that purpose, and permitted to draw a special salary as such (six dollars per day). He was to assure the Californian authorities of the goodwill and sympathy of his government in their controversies with Mexico; to induce them, if possible, to separate voluntarily from that country; to promise them, if they did separate, our "kind offices as a sister republic." He was to warn them against European agents and intrigues, and to assure them that we would help them against the encroachments of any such foreign power, and that we would fight side by side with them against any European invader. By all such means he was to commit us to friendship and to a policy of peace and goodwill towards the Californian people. He was to draw them to us by fair speeches. He was thus, indeed, to anticipate, as is evident, our coming troubles with Mexico (which, of course, are kept in the background here); but he was to anticipate these troubles, as we can now see, by saving the coming naval commanders any vexations when they arrived to seize the ports. Although, very naturally, no reference is made to these future events in the dispatch, a single reference in our own minds to the previously quoted instructions to Sloat will show

us how these two sets of operations fit, like the halves of the
broken ring in the old ballad-story, into the unity of one plan.
Who lost the one half of the ring we now know.
The language of this dispatch is characteristic of Buchanan.
It is very cautious, but still, in view of the nature of the case,
very plain. It begins with a reference to the information that
Larkin has long been giving to the Department about California. The government is deeply interested in all this, for the
United States take great interest in California. And the United
States government has reason to fear European aggressors
there, for Larkin has warned the State Department of the signs
of such. To counteract these, Larkin must appeal, says the
dispatch, to the people of the country; must let them know
where their interest lies, and who are their true friends. "On all
proper occasions you should not fail prudently to warn the government and people of California of the danger of such an interference to their peace and happiness; to inspire them with
a jealousy of European dominion; and to arouse in their
bosoms that love of liberty and independence so natural to the
American continent." And, farther on: "If the people should
desire to unite their destiny with ours, they would be received
as brethren, whenever this can be done without affording
Mexico just cause of complaint." Ah, soothing Buchanan! Nobody's loyalty shall be shocked! Again, the United States government "would vigorously interpose to prevent" California
"from becoming a British or French colony. In this they might
surely expect the aid of the Californians themselves." And yet
more, the government is glad to hear how friendly the Californian authorities have recently been: "You may assure them
of the cordial sympathy and friendship of the president, and
that their conduct is appreciated by him as it deserves."
To carry on the "prudent warning" with effect and authority,
Larkin is thereupon made secret agent. He is to exert his influence very prudently and is to avoid arousing suspicions on
the part of English or French agents. He is to collect diligently
information about American interests in the department. Gillespie, "a gentleman in whom the president reposes entire confidence," has seen these instructions and will "coöperate as a

confidential agent with you in carrying them into execution."
Among other things that these two are to treat in their information to the Department is mentioned a description of the "character of the principal persons" in the Californian government
"and of other distinguished and influential citizens." And a
general requirement is made to collect all possible information
about all matters that can interest the Department. Captain
Frémont's name is not once mentioned in the dispatch.

I almost fear to insult the reader's intelligence by pointing
out at too great length the utter impossibility of any kind of
reconciliation between this and the now dead and lamented
hypothesis of the "fourth plan" of our list. Shall we say that it is
unnecessary to make careful and expensive inquiries about the
personal characters of prominent Californian officials if one
sends by the same messenger an order to chase them all out of
office by means of an improvised armed force? Do you have to
know at Washington the character of a "distinguished and influential citizen" in order to put a bullet into him in California?
Shall we ask whether expecting "the aid of the Californians
themselves" against the supposed European agents in the territory means requiring as many of the Californian chiefs as are
within reach to be taken prisoners and shut up in a fort by the
first set of rovers that will volunteer to do it? Shall we wonder
whether these were the President's delicate means of expressing
his "cordial sympathy," and his "appreciation" of the friendship that Larkin has described, and that the Department fully
believed in, and that even until the very moment of the outbreak was always experienced in California by all Americans
save some vagabonds and their friends and this aggressive
armed surveying party itself? But are these questions at all
necessary? Nay, of opposition we need not speak. That is too
plain. But of the perfidy and the treachery we may speak, of
which, of course, nobody need be called actually guilty, but of
which our government would have been guilty if, by any conceivable wantonness of folly, it had at once given countenance
to the fourth plan and to the plan of the Larkin dispatch. Such
treachery would indeed have disgraced any petty Oriental
prince in a war with a neighbor worthy of his meanness; and

yet just such would have been our national treachery had we, say through Senator Benton, instructed the gallant captain in the plan in which a false tradition (and his own memory) declare him to have been instructed, and had we meanwhile ordered Larkin to use his position as consul, as old resident, and as personal friend to lull to sleep all possible suspicion in Californian breasts and to persuade the people and the officials to lay aside, as it were, their arms, lest haply they might have wherewithal to resist the gallant captain whenever his hour should come for defending his countrymen against the "oppressors"! And this perfidy, this unheard-of treachery, what under heaven would it have been worth to us? To exasperate beyond endurance a friendly people, to ensure all the possible causes that could combine to make their chief men hate us forever and the people fight us as savagely as they could — this would have been our aim. Not even the most cold-blooded of tyrants could have rejoiced in such a prospect; because, as we were situated, we wanted California to come to us as prosperous and as peaceful a land as possible. If we desired to steal our neighbor's fine horse, why should we first coax him into confinement and then scourge him with whips in his stall, to make him break his bones? Yet such destructive and atrocious folly would be precisely the thing involved in the choice of a situation with Larkin at Monterey intriguing under orders and developing perfectly obvious designs, assuring officials in private that we were the true friends, seeking to persuade them to declare their independence and to come over to us as a "sister republic"; while the gallant Captain Frémont, not driven to bay, nor pursued, nor in danger, should be quietly, yes, stealthily, getting supplies from the coast, on a representation to the United States naval officers that he is going East, and should be "watching events" until he saw a chance to attack. Given a little longer delay of the coming of Sloat and of the regular war, and what horrors might not such a fashion of beginning a war have produced, by arousing popular passions? And if such things had been suggested to the cabinet at Washington, where the true impotence of the Californian military power was of course unknown, what possible company of fools could have chosen this useless and dismal perfidy? Obviously we shall suspect *no* man of deliberately planning any such situation, least of all the men whose personal interests carelessly brought it to pass. The cabinet could not have planned it. If Senator Benton advised Captain Frémont's operations, he too must surely have done so in ignorance of the cabinet plan and cannot have planned the situation as it resulted. And that Captain Frémont and Lieutenant Gillespie themselves should venture on producing such a situation can be explained as possible only on the ground that the plan of their willfully disobedient operations so occupied their minds that they gave no sort of rational consideration to Larkin's position and work or to the situation itself. Folly it may have been in Captain Frémont, or only a result produced by the "family cipher." For the government it would have been the foulest and silliest of treacheries to ordain these two things at Washington in one cabinet. No reader can even dream that it was done.

X. *Supplementary Evidence and Summary*

So much for the significance of the dispatch. All the credit of our knowing about it today belongs, as I have said, to Mr. Hubert Howe Bancroft. His enterprise in collecting rescued the original from utter loss to the world. The exhaustive researches into the California documents of the time, undertaken under his direction, made clear to him its significance, which I, however independently I have tried to study the matter, can in the end only accept as obvious. His library is the truly original source here, and my research, although otherwise independent, is at this one most important place but a following of his already beaten trail. And only by his permission do I here summarize a document that I still feel to be his property. But yet in using the document I have been able to discover a few new facts that throw light upon its origin and relations. When I had seen and considered it at his library, I was indeed as sure of its authenticity as everybody must be who examines it. But still I felt that an opponent might possibly assert it to be, say, a production of Larkin himself in after time, in a fit of jealousy toward General Frémont. Or again, some discoverable paper in Washington archives might put it in a modified light, or might supplement it by something valuable. I determined, therefore, to apply in person at Washington, and did so with a general result, through the courtesy of the departments, that has already appeared in this chapter. The Larkin dispatch is on record at the State Department, but there is no trace of any other secret instruction concerning this business there or elsewhere in Washington department records. This largely negative result is in itself, however, highly important.

This further fact, however, I must record. While the Secretary of State kindly let me see the Larkin dispatch as a whole, there was one portion that, as I at first learned, was still regarded as confidential, that could not be shown, and that accordingly was covered. As I had with me a copy taken in San Francisco from Mr. Bancroft's original, which of course included this covered passage, I was able to submit this copy to official inspection, and so to get a courteous permission, in view of the fact that the document was actually no longer a secret, to inspect finally the whole of the precious official manuscript. Since then I have received a regularly certified copy of all but the purely business details at the end. This inspection and copy prove that the authenticity of Mr. H. H. Bancroft's document not only is in itself certain, but is a matter of permanent official record.

I venture to repeat this otherwise unimportant fact about the still remaining trace of secrecy at the State Department as a collateral evidence that the document has been considered to retain its genuine and confidential importance ever since its original production. The covered passage was one especially referring to Larkin's most significant intrigues. Of course this Larkin intrigue was itself no very noble project for a great government to engage in, and there is obvious reason for the delicacy wherewith a veil has been kept over its face from that day even until now. It is evident also that without Mr. H. H. Bancroft's previous help my curiosity at Washington could not properly have been fully satisfied, notwithstanding the marked goodwill of all persons concerned in answering my application.

He has therefore still the full credit of making the paper accessible.

I must now add from my Washington investigation one of the most curious and amusing scraps of minor documentary evidence that it was ever my good fortune to hear of. The light that it throws is indeed not very dazzling, but it is wholly accidental and unexpected; and yet what it shows is something of exactly the sort that we might have expected in case all the foregoing view is true, but not in case the common tradition of the past is true. In the ordinary "Letters to Consuls" of the State Department, in a volume that seemed not to be of an especially confidential character, I found two business letters, apparently mere bits of routine, both of them surely as free themselves from any trace of a secret nature as well could be. My eye was attracted by the familiar names. The letters, oddly enough, though copied (like all other consular letters, as I suppose) into the regular books, were this time marked "*Cancelled,*" each for itself, the word being written across the lines of the letter. That is, very plainly, after being entered, the originals were not sent but destroyed. Thus a mere accident preserved the record of a little change of mind at the State Department. And these superseded letters, what said they? The first is dated October 27, 1845, and runs:

JOHN BLACK, Esqre., *U. S. C. Mexico*

SIR, — Enclosed is a communication for Thomas O. Larkin, Esqre., Consul of the United States at Monterey, California, which you are requested to forward to him, *via* Mazatlan, by some early and safe opportunity.

I am sir, etc.,
JAMES BUCHANAN

The second letter has the same date and was evidently to be a part of the enclosure of the first. It was to have a second enclosure inside itself.

THOMAS O. LARKIN, Esqre., *U. S. Consul, Monterey*

SIR, — I enclose herewith a package for Captain Frémont, of whose movements you may be enabled to obtain some information, and request that it may be transmitted to him by the first safe opportunity which presents itself, or retained by you for delivery, according as the state of your information may suggest.

I am sir, etc.,

JAMES BUCHANAN

Absolutely innocent appear these two letters. Yet properly interpreted they tell an odd story. If anything is essential to General Frémont's view, as his memory still frames it for him, if anything is essential to the traditional conception of the whole affair, it is that the Benton packet, with its "enigmatical" letters, was a part of the administration plan, was an officially designed supplement to the dispatch, and conveyed to the captain the wishes of the same government that commissioned Gillespie to carry it. Now since the Department knew not exactly where Captain Frémont's party would be when Gillespie should reach California, it would be essential to the success of any plan that depended on the packet, on Gillespie's official dispatch, on Gillespie himself, and on Captain Frémont, all at once, that their combination should be ensured by the simple device of having the same messenger carry the dispatch, the packet, and the letter of introduction to Captain Frémont. Whatever tends to separate the packet from Gillespie's mission tends to make the traditional view that the "enigmatical" letters were of official significance more and more incredible.

Now, however, mark this: On October 17 the Department had commissioned Gillespie to go to Larkin. For on that day the Larkin dispatch is dated, both in the original and in the copy in the Washington archives, and Gillespie is mentioned in the dispatch. Ten days after this, Gillespie still not having set out, being detained, as it would seem, by the non-departure of the vessel that was to carry him to Vera Cruz, the Department has a packet in its hands for Captain Frémont, whose name, we remember, was not mentioned at all in the Larkin dispatch. This packet must be the Benton packet. The circumstances and dates make this as certain as can be expected in such a matter. Now, how does the Department regard this packet? As an important part of the undertaking wherein Gillespie is already commissioned to act? Nay, not so; for it decides to forward this precious packet, with all its "enigmas," by the uncertain means of the ordinary Mexican mails, under care of Consuls Black and Larkin. No sign is there in this that the packet is of official importance. If it is, why is not Gillespie, the trusted messenger of the secret mission, the first thought of the Secretary who, ten days ago, chose him for the work? Why risk an essential part of the secret mission by the uncertain Mexican mails when the expensive confidential agent, already entrusted with the fateful business, is on the point of departure? Larkin is to do whatever he conveniently can to deliver the packet, "as the state of his information may suggest." But Gillespie, who has it, according to tradition, as his main task to seek, to arouse, and to co-operate with Captain Frémont — he is to do nothing at all, so far, with the precious packet. It may reach California as soon as he, or it may not. It may be delivered, or it may be kept at Monterey, "as the state" of Larkin's information may suggest. Six days later, November 3, Gillespie receives his non-committal letter of introduction to Captain Frémont, and now, indeed, has the packet handed to him to deliver. Can there be a better proof than this that Gillespie's mission had originally no essential connection whatever with Captain Frémont, and that his momentous meeting with the latter resulted from an afterthought, possibly, of course, through Benton's own influence exercised at the office? "We have commissioned Larkin," the Department, at any rate, however influenced, must have said, "to intrigue for us in California. Now we have this private package for Captain Frémont. Why not let Gillespie, as a part of his duty, hunt up the captain himself, deliver the packet, and acquaint him with the intrigue? This young officer, who is doubtless on friendly terms with the Californians, can help to give the affair a show of power, by being present to support the seceding Californian authorities with his force, to render in fact 'our kind offices as a sister republic,' in case California declares its independence, or to offer aid against any dreaded British invasion. This is a fortunate completion of the plan." All this is a natural interpretation of what Buchanan and the government may have thought. Absolutely worthless, however, seems any interpretation that supposes the government to have first determined to send a secret agent to

California on vastly important business and to have then deliberately thought of sending an essential part of his secret mission not through him, but through the expected enemy's own uncertain mails. And there is no known evidence that there was any duplicate of Benton's packet. Plainly the stars in their courses now war against the traditional view of this thing. The least significant document that you accidentally find bearing on the matter indicates the same as the greatest. The published and the unpublished disinterested evidences are positively all of them on one side.

I have submitted the result of my Washington investigation to General Frémont in a long letter and in a similarly lengthy second interview. I tried to point out, both in the letter and in the interview, as well as I could, the difficulties that now assailed his view of his official mission. Without troubling him with the whole mass of evidence brought together in this chapter, I still tried to make clear to him that, unless he could put everything in an entirely novel light, it would be impossible for me to defend him against any captious critic who should put all the responsibility of his hostile action in California upon his own shoulders. I assured him of my anxiety to do him justice myself, of the fact that his previous demonstration of the impossibility of Larkin's mission would now make his case harder to defend than ever, and of my hearty wish that his courtesy to me should not finally result in merely increasing the delicacy of his position. I begged him, therefore, to let me know of any further evidence, and if possible of any documentary evidence, that should put things in any new light. In reply General Frémont was extremely patient and courteous, but he disclaimed all power to unravel the mystery, which to him also, as he asserts, is now mysterious. He knows, he insists, only what he learned of the wishes of the government through Gillespie and the "family cipher" letter. What else the government may have done or said, what other instructions it may have given to its other servants — for that he is not responsible. He did his duty, as he still imagines, and no doubt other people did theirs. But to him it is still entirely a novel thing that Larkin should have had any important part in all this business. He never heard of Larkin in so prominent a place. He feels sure, for the rest, that no peaceful intrigues could have won the Californians. All his information was of their imminent and serious hostility; and he knows that the English would have got California had he not acted when he did. The government may have had some plan including Larkin; but then this plan must have been concealed from Mr. Benton, who certainly never knew of it and never could have advised such an unwise scheme. General Frémont meanwhile knows that his instructions, while leaving much to his discretion, certainly authorized such force as he used under the actual conditions. This is as near to the whole truth as he personally is able to guide me. For other facts I must look elsewhere, and, while regarding my efforts with the most courteous interest, General Frémont regrets his inability to give me further help in the desired direction.

Such is General Frémont's present memory and understanding of the affair, as I have gathered them from him; and the reader will certainly join with me in appreciating his personal good humor and patience in following so long as he did my wearisome research. If I were not just now studying an important historical problem, whose significance is enormously greater than the interests of any one man, I should be glad to do General Frémont the courtesy, such as it would prove, of my silence. For the rest, that would have no real effect, as Mr. H. H. Bancroft has access already to the most essential document and had his mind made up about its significance long before I ever thought of the matter. And I have meanwhile the perfect consolation of knowing that the personal reputation of a distinguished public man such as is General Frémont, who has been a household name in our nation for a generation, is quite independent for good as well as for evil of what I may happen to choose to write here. At all events, I have no desire to judge any further the personal character of the well-known and picturesque pioneer hero of this present tale. What inner motives led him to this rash and in its consequences most disastrous act, which once for all did whatever one agency could do to set over against each other in deadly enmity the Americans and the Californians, it is not mine to know. The "family cipher" letter doubtless suggested some of the motives. But if the deed was a family matter, the family is always and everywhere sacred, and especially so when it is engaged in making a plot. What we desire to know is not the inner motive, but the actual historical responsibility for this first fatal scene of the conquest of California; and we have found out very clearly where that lies, the gallant general's clearest memory and sincerest impressions to the contrary notwithstanding.

One thing only I must say in leaving finally the field of direct personal criticism: namely, that save for the cause of historical certainty as such I am heartily sorry to have troubled General Frémont's courtesy for help about this matter. For although what he has told me makes the matter clearer by cutting off all hope that he has yet behind some entirely new official revelation to make, that would plainly put the responsibility for his action elsewhere than on his own shoulders or on his father-in-law's, still this remains true: he took trouble to help me, partly for the sake, I suppose, of putting himself in a fairer light; whereas what he has told me has made his position more delicate than ever, has deprived his memory of all its possible authority as a witness in the matter, and yet meanwhile has made his act, as such, easier to judge than it would otherwise be, since every possible defense seems now cut off. I cannot suppress this fact, although I frankly regret it. I have tried in every way to do General Frémont justice; and I am not the one to blame if the result is unfavorable. After all, however, I cannot forget that our country's honor is here involved much more than the personal glory of any one man.

We must turn to other and equally characteristic scenes of our early life in the land that we were now to seize upon.

Chapter III

THE CONQUEST COMPLETED, THE INTER-
REGNUM, AND THE BIRTH OF THE STATE

THE DISCERNING reader has seen in the foregoing something more than a study of individuals. These hostile undertakings and these intrigues are as characteristic as they were fateful. The American as conqueror is unwilling to appear in public as a pure aggressor; he dare not seize a California as Russia has seized so much land in Asia or as Napoleon, with full French approval, seized whatever he wanted. The American wants to persuade not only the world but himself that he is doing God service in a peaceable spirit, even when he violently takes what he has determined to get. His conscience is sensitive, and hostile aggression, practiced against any but Indians, shocks this conscience, unused as it is to such scenes. Therefore Semple and Ide, and the cautious Secretary of State, and the gallant captain, and the venerable Senator, all alike, not only as individuals, but also as men appealing for approval to their fellow countrymen at large, must present this sinful undertaking in private and in public as a sad, but strictly moral, humane, patriotic, enlightened, and glorious undertaking. Other peoples, more used to shedding civilized blood, would have swallowed the interests of the people of twenty such Californias as that of 1846 without a gasp. The agents of such nations would have played at filibustering without scruple if they had been instructed to adopt that plan as the most simple for getting the land desired; or they would have intrigued readily, fearlessly, and again without scruple if that plan had seemed to their superiors best for the purpose. But our national plans had to be formed so as to offend our squeamish natures as little as possible. Our national conscience, however, was not only squeamish, but also, in those days, not a little hypocritical. It disliked, moreover, to have the left hand know what the right hand was doing when both were doing mischief. And so, because of its very virtues, it involved itself in disastrously complex plots.

119

I. *The Conquerors and Their Consciences*

A LL the actors concerned worked, namely, in the fear of this strictly virtuous, of this almost sanctimonious public opinion — a public opinion that was at the same time, both in the North and in the South, very sensitive to flattery, very ambitious to see our territory grow bigger, and very anxious to contemplate a glorious national destiny. Moreover, all these our agents not only feared the public, but participated themselves in the common sentiments. Hence we find the Polk cabinet elaborately considering, not merely how to prosecute successfully their intended aggressive war, just as the leaders of any other rapacious nation would have considered such a matter, but also how to put their war into harmony with the enlightened American spirit. And, in the autumn of 1845, their pious plans were apparently well formed. To Mexico the Slidell mission should be sent, with its offer to purchase California. This would be a liberal offer and, if it ever became public, would set us right as a powerful and generous nation in the eyes of the world, while it would give us in the meantime a chance to get California for nothing, by the completion of our intrigue in that territory and by the act of its own people. The beautiful and business-like compromise thus planned would set at one our national conscience and our national shrewdness; it would be not only magnanimous, but inexpensive. Yet even this compromise must be carefully expressed by the honorable Secretary of State in such language as would not offend the sensitive American spirit in case, by some accident, the whole scheme should some day come plainly to light. Larkin must be instructed that we had "no ambitious aspirations to gratify," and that we only desired to arouse in the Californian breast "that love of liberty and independence so natural to the American continent." It was all very kindly, this desire, and poor Mexico ought to have been thankful for such a neighbor, so devoted to the cause of freedom, and so generous to the weak!

But this combination of the Slidell mission with the Larkin dispatch, a combination whose genuine character has not hitherto been properly understood by the historians of the Mexican War,[1] was not more characteristic of our nation than was the combination by which the pious plan was defeated. One active and not overcautious young agent who had good reason to know the importance of the crisis and who was not altogether unwilling to turn it to account for various private ends was in California just then and received certain advices in a confidential "family cipher"; and these advices somehow, whether wholly by his own fault or also by the fault of his father-in-law, led him to thwart the carefully prepared plans of the government. In acting as he did, he not only became for the moment a filibuster, pure and simple, but endangered our whole scheme by, perhaps unwittingly, doing his best to drive California directly into the arms of England. Either because England really was not anxious for California just then, or because her agents in the Pacific were not sufficiently on the alert, this result was averted, yet not in consequence of the gallant captain's undertaking, but only through Sloat's arrival with the news of those hostilities on the Rio Grande which superseded all previous plots and pretenses, and which, "by the act of Mexico," as our veracious President declared, forced us, unwilling, conscientious, and humane as we were, into an unequal contest with a physically puny foe.

Meanwhile, the gallant captain's undertaking, although a plain violation of his orders, was itself not un-American in its

[1] What light the Larkin dispatch throws on the true intent of the Slidell mission one can best judge by comparing just here von Holst's interpretation of the matter, made in necessary ignorance of the true nature of the Larkin dispatch, on p. 113 and p. 229 of his *Constitutional History*, Vol. III (American edition, covering the period from 1846 to 1850). For Slidell's instructions, see 30th Congr., 1st Sess. House Ex. Doc. 69, Vol. VIII, pp. 33 ff. On p. 41 of these instructions is a significant reference to the Larkin intrigue, which, now that that intrigue is known, shows clearly the connection of the Slidell and Larkin missions in the minds of the cabinet. Slidell is to counteract possible foreign schemes for getting California, and, to help him in this work, he is to have a copy of the Larkin dispatch forwarded him, and is to correspond freely with Larkin upon the whole subject, taking care to transmit his letters secretly.

forms and methods, at least in so far as they were reported to the public. He felt himself, after all, to be a peaceful and scientific gentleman, who shunned war and loved the study of nature. He was a type of our energy and of our mild civilization, in the presence of crafty and wily Spaniards, who, as he somehow persuaded either himself or his followers, had incited the Indians of the unknown Klamath wilderness against him, had threatened the ripening wheat-fields of his countrymen, and at last had begun marching against his own party with an armed force. This armed force marching against him was indeed not at the moment to be seen in the whole territory by any human eye; but its asserted existence nevertheless thenceforth justified him in the clearer eyes of heaven and his absent fellow countrymen. So at least he himself and the venerable Senator would seem in all sincerity to have felt; and the public, by the nomination of the young hero to the presidency in 1856, and by the large vote then polled in his favor, set their seal of approval also upon the verdict of his conscience. And both he himself and the public, as we have seen, ever afterwards considered his methods of procedure to have been as noble and unaggressive as they were fearless and decisive; while all concerned thought our national energy and kindliness finely represented by the acts of this party of armed surveyors and trappers, who disturbed the peace of a quiet land and practiced violence against inoffensive and helpless rancheros.

But when hostilities had once begun, the men who were not in the state secrets were as American and as moral as those who were initiated. To them the whole thing appeared partly as a glorious revolution, a destined joy for the eyes of history-reading posterity, a high and holy business; and partly as a missionary enterprise, destined to teach our beloved and erring Spanish American brethren the blessings of true liberty. The Bear Flag heroes interpreted the affair, in their way also, to a large and representative American public; and these heroes, like their betters, show us what it is to have a national conscience sensitive enough to call loudly for elaborate and eloquent comfort in moments of doubt, and just stupid enough to be readily deluded by mock-eloquent cant. The result of the whole thing is that although, in later years, the nation at large has indeed come to regard the Mexican War with something of the shame and contempt that *The Biglow Papers* and other expressions of enlightened contemporary opinion heaped upon the unworthy business, still, in writing California history, few have even yet chosen to treat the acts of the conquest with the deserved plainness of speech, while, in those days, the public both in the South and in the whole of the West, together with a considerable portion of the public elsewhere, was hood-winked by such methods as were used, and so actually sup-posed our acquisition of the new territory to be a God-fearing act, the result of the aggression and of the sinful impotence of our Spanish neighbors, together with our own justifiable energy and our devotion to the cause of freedom. It is to be hoped that this lesson, showing us as it does how much of con-science and even of personal sincerity can coexist with a mini-mum of effective morality in international undertakings, will some day be once more remembered; so that when our nation is another time about to serve the devil, it will do so with more frankness and will deceive itself less by half-unconscious cant. For the rest, our mission in the cause of liberty is to be accomplished through a steadfast devotion to the cultivation of our own inner life, and not by going abroad as missionaries, as conquerors, or as marauders, among weaker peoples.

II. *Sloat, the Larkin Intrigue, and the English Legend*

BUT with July 7, 1846 the conquest proper is only begun. Sloat, who had arrived from Mazatlán on July 1, naturally hesitated at Monterey when he heard of the confusion pro-duced by the gallant captain in the north. He could not un-derstand this. He had been led to expect a peaceful California, whose ports he was to seize as Mexican property, but whose inhabitants he was, if possible, to conciliate. He heard, as

Larkin says,[2] "for several days nothing but distracting reports of foreigners and Californians collecting people and preparing to fight." Sloat seems to have been unwilling to commit his government to the direct support of what naturally at the very first sight appeared, as he heard of it, to be an irregular insurrection. As he had been instructed to get into peaceful relations with the Californian government, and so to detach the country from Mexico without a collision, he doubted, apparently, whether his instructions, so far as received, authorized him to do what would now almost certainly involve an armed struggle with an angry people. The relation of Captain Frémont to the whole affair was of course to Sloat, as to Larkin, still an inexplicable mystery. Sloat was of a very vacillating temperament, and the situation involved more than he could for the moment meet with confidence and firmness. But at length he was persuaded, by more voices, it is said, than one, and certainly by numerous motives, that he must raise the flag.[3] He was understood by Captain Frémont and Lieutenant Gillespie, according to their Claims Committee testimony, to declare, when he soon after met them, that he had raised the flag "on the faith of" the doings in the north; that is, so soon as he was convinced that Captain Frémont was really concerned in the matter. He expressed, they tell us, great disappointment when the captain refused to name his authority. For, as they want us to understand him, he had felt sure that Captain Frémont must have some official sanction for the Bear Flag doings, and that it would be well to support him. But while I do not pretend to be able altogether to unravel Sloat's much-perplexed mind in those days, the reader will probably share with me no small hesitation, under the circumstances, when he is asked to suppose this now traditional account of Sloat's

---

[2] In Larkin's own letter to Buchanan of July 18, 1846, contained in copy in the Bancroft-Larkin papers, and known to me also in the official copy furnished by the State Department.

[3] Larkin (loc. cit.) expresses the matter thus: "In this state of affairs, and the knowledge of the Bear Flag having been hoisted, fearing perhaps that some other foreign officer might do it, he hoisted the United States flag in this town."

motives, as interpreted by Captain Frémont, to be a complete one. For Larkin, who was much with Sloat at the time of the raising of the flag, does not so understand the matter, as we see by his letter just cited; and there are obvious reasons for thinking Larkin, who carefully obeyed his own orders as he received them, a fairer witness on the points at issue than the gallant captain, who, having disobeyed his orders, was now deeply interested in believing that his disobedience had been both helpful and inevitable. To be sure, the raising of the Bear Flag, while it very seriously perplexed Sloat and so hindered his action, did before July 7 furnish of itself a motive to overcome his hesitation. But this motive was not the one that Captain Frémont understood Sloat to express. The motive obviously was that, by violence or not by violence, immediate action was now needed to save the distracted land from anarchy and from seizure by any foreign power that might choose to regard interference at such a moment as humane. No one, however, can understand Sloat's hesitation or his final decision who thinks of him as coming to California with the intent to make war on the inhabitants. As we have seen, he had no such intent; and hence the operations of the gallant captain in the north cannot have been operations on whose "faith" he would be ready to act, since they were utterly opposed to his purposes and to his instructions. He came, on the news of hostility with Mexico, to "encourage" its inhabitants "to adopt a course of neutrality." Such were his already cited instructions of June 24, 1845. To exceed these instructions by deliberately beginning an open struggle with the people, he did not desire, and hence he hesitated when he found such a state of affairs as seemed to necessitate a struggle in case he interfered. When at last he saw that he must seize the country to escape yet worse troubles, he tried with almost pathetic earnestness to come to an understanding with Castro and with Pio Pico, in order, as he quite sincerely said, to "avert the sacrifice of human life and the horrors of war." He invited both chiefs to a council at Monterey; he assured them both that he came as the "best friend of California"; and his language to them was in strict and undoubtedly sincere compliance with his instructions. To a hostile governor whom one purposes violently to overthrow, one does not write as Sloat did to Pico, in the tone of one rendering account, as it were, to a person who is to be conciliated: "I assure your excellency that not the least impropriety has been committed [by the Americans at Monterey], and that the business and social intercourse of the town have not been disturbed in the slightest degree." Such a spirit and such conduct could not have been inspired by "the faith of" Captain Frémont's doings. As for Sloat's relation after July 7 to Captain Frémont, the friends of the latter, not without their usual audacity, tried to show before the Claims Committee, by a singular misuse of documents, that Sloat was as anxious as he really was to get Captain Frémont's co-operation only because Sloat sought in the captain's supposed private official authority a guarantee of the propriety of his own course in raising the flag at Monterey. Now, Sloat was a morally timid man; but the published documents show clearly enough that he, whose instructions were to avoid a collision, was not living in the hope of any reassurance from the gallant captain who had brought on a collision, but was hoping so to get control of the latter as "to stop the sacrifice of human life in the north." For this reason he was indeed glad to get the co-operation of the captain at once, and he used every effort to that end.[4] Thus here, as through all the subsequent months, Captain Frémont's

---

[4] The proof here is clear, (1) in that, as just pointed out, Sloat did not want a fight with the Californians, and so could not have been seeking for a warrant for his relatively peaceful undertaking in the violence of the captain; and (2) in that in his letter to Pico, July 12, 1846 (a letter which clearly shows that he still hoped for peaceful submission from the Californians and was anxious to get it through the most friendly advances), Sloat promises to Pico to do his own best to quiet the troubles in the north. For the rest, all the other relevant documents collected in Sen. Ex. Docs. 1 and 19, 2nd Sess., 29 Congr., if taken together, plainly show the true reason of Sloat's haste to get word of Captain Frémont. This reason is as plainly not the one somewhat vaingloriously assumed by the latter in his own account of the matter. Captain Frémont was to the commodore first of all a very disturbing force, which he indeed hoped to convert very soon into a useful force.

conduct in the north remained effective as a serious hindrance in the way of the true conquest of California. It delayed the. raising of the flag a full week after Sloat's arrival by making him uncertain how to apply his instructions to the anomalous conditions; and when Sloat had begun to act, the greatest obstacle to his work lay in the results already produced by the gallant marauders at Sonoma. I know not how much Sloat, who was in communication with Larkin, ever came to know of the true nature of the official intrigue, which the latter, so far as I know, thenceforth very faithfully kept secret, but both Sloat and Larkin must have shared to some extent the knowledge of what at that moment had been lost by the folly of the Bear Flag movement; for this knowledge concerned matters that were in part, at least, no secret to many well-informed people at Monterey and elsewhere.

For Larkin, the man who, of all Americans concerned with California during that crisis, best did his duty; the one official whose credit, both private and public, is unstained by the whole affair; and who personally, if desert be considered, and not mere popularity, is every way by far the foremost among the men who won for us California — Larkin had not been idle, not before Gillespie came, and much less afterwards. He had obeyed his orders. If he was no trained official and no cultivated man, he was at least a faithful patriot, a shrewd man of business, and a cautious servant of his government; a man well acquainted with the place, the people, and the methods of work that must be employed. As an intriguer, he was distinctly successful, and no drop of blood need have been shed in the conquest of California, no flavor of the bitterness of mutual hate need have entered, at least for that moment, into the lives of the two peoples who were now jointly to occupy the land, had Larkin been left to complete his task. And although Sloat's coming would indeed have found the work still incomplete, it would, without the captain's utterly mischievous doings, have been well enough advanced to ensure with almost perfect certainty the peaceful change of flags.

For see what had been done already. In the short period of less than two months, before the beginning of the Bear Flag absurdities and after Gillespie's coming, Larkin had so far developed his intrigue as to have, first of all, the direct assurance of Castro's own aid in a plan to declare the country independent of Mexico "in 1847 or 1848." [5] "Some," says Larkin, "may have no faith in assertions of this kind from these people. The undersigned does. From twelve years' experience he believes he knows them." And his knowledge of what a Californian's promise meant was, after all, the knowledge of a shrewd Yankee trader, to whom Californians for these twelve years had been owing numerous debts, and making, of course, numerous promises. And so his opinion is worth more in these matters than even the opinion of the captain of the transient surveying parties of 1844 and 1846. But this was only the beginning. The same intrigue had been cautiously suggested to leading men all over the country. The very fact that they themselves, in later times, never publicly confessed this shows that the intrigue was, as far as it had time to develop itself, relatively effective. Had they rejected Larkin's scheme at once, they would have been free to avow their knowledge of it, both then and later. But after they once had entertained the notion, the disgrace that was inflicted upon them when they later found themselves betrayed, through what Castro himself called "the despicable policy of the agents of the United States in this Department," sealed their lips as to the plot that had at first seemed to them a generous offer from a "sister republic," but that, after the gallant captain's undertaking, could be remembered by them only as the foul treachery of a heretical nation of tyrants and robbers.

The intrigue had, however, reached a yet higher stage. In his letter of June 1, written *before* the outbreak at Sonoma (and cited, also, in the previous chapter), Larkin says: "From a dread of something, they hardly know what, and to devise some means to reinstate the deplorable condition of affairs of this country, the towns, by order of Governor Pico and the assembly, on the 30th ultimo elected eighteen members, who, with the seven members of the assembly and five military offi-

---

[5] See Larkin's letter to Buchanan, July 20, 1846: B. MS. and State Department Archives.

cers, are to convene in the town of Santa Barbara on the 15th instant.[6] Four members are chosen for Monterey. There are many opinions on what ought or in fact what can be brought forward for this meeting to act on. Some wish to call on some foreign nation for protection; others wish to declare themselves independent."

Larkin then goes on to say that he is actively intriguing with the delegates to get the junta to prepare a memorial to the central government, setting forth the grievances of the department, and so preparing the way for a later declaration of independence. His reason for advancing no further at the moment in his propositions to the delegates is the resistance that he meets from the patriotism of some people, to whom the idea of independence seems a doubtful and dangerous one. For an English intrigue he is on the watch, and of course, as we see, he has his proper fears of England; but he also has good reasons, at this moment, reasons that he gives at length, for regarding the English plans as not now imminently dangerous, in case the country remains quiet. Forbes, the English consul, is, namely, in his private capacity, a man having settled interests in the land and business connections with Americans, and, as such, he is desirous of a quick and permanent settlement of all doubts about the country's future. He is not anxious, therefore, in this private capacity, for any but an American occupation of the country. Whatever his official instructions may be, he is consequently not apt to be very zealous in the English cause. Thus, in view of the whole situation, Larkin feels sanguine of success within a year or two, and with the cordial consent of the people of the country.

All such intrigues as Larkin's are, in their very nature, matters of no mathematical surety. In view of the whole situation, however, so far as I can appreciate it, there seems no serious

---

[6] This proposed assembly appears in the Claims Committee Report as an important and altogether hostile junta, whose purpose was solely to turn the country over to England, and whose nefarious schemes shall have been thwarted by the gallant captain. In fact this junta never met, and its purposes were certainly not definite in any direction.

reason to doubt Larkin's judgment. There. is simply no evidence, as we shall soon see, that the English desire for California had ripened at that moment into any plan capable of resisting the course of events that was now steadily leading California away from Mexico and into our own possession. Had the Mexican War been postponed a few months or a year, and had the gallant captain not appeared on the ground in the north, California would have been ready to drop into our basket like a mellow apple. And without the gallant captain even the coming of the Mexican War, at the time when it came, would have been, in all probability, no source of serious trouble to our plans. The Larkin intrigue would have been prematurely closed, indeed, but not with bloodshed.

When I say this, however, I am venturing to treat with conscious contempt two of the best-known and best-believed of the popular legends of the conquest. One of these legends is that the "Macnamara scheme" was nearly ripe, and that, without the gallant captain's decisive interference, this scheme would have lost to us much, if not the whole, of California. Macnamara was, in fact, an Irish priest, who had evidently taken very ardent part in the then familiar and manifold schemes for relieving the burden of Ireland's distress by colonization. The magnitude of such schemes anybody can see by reference to the English Parliamentary Papers of that time, and Macnamara's scheme is plainly to be judged as one of the number. His plan was to put several thousand Irish families into the San Joaquin Valley; and the English government, very surely with an ardent desire to get rid of some thousands of Irish families, and probably also not without a willingness to do its part in a very safe way towards the introduction of British subjects into California, in view of future possibilities there, helped him so far as to give him transportation in one of the vessels of the English squadron while he was engaged upon his business of trying to get a great land grant. In Mexico itself he met with some opposition; it was very plainly pointed out to him by at least one person that while he pretended to be anxious to save California for Mexico and from heretical American influence, he would in fact only ensure the transfer of California to America if he introduced there numbers of Irish peasants, who, though Catholic, would surely gravitate to the United States rather than to Mexico. This was, for the rest, so plain in itself that if Macnamara had really been a chosen agent, working with a desire to secure California for England by a process of colonization, neither he nor his superiors could have failed to observe the fact so pointed out. To use Irish colonists as a barrier against American aggression would be a scheme that no English government would coolly resort to, if engaged in immediate and earnest efforts to secure California for England herself. Any British subject in California might possibly, of course, be the cause of complications that would end in the transfer of the country to England. But it is plain also that neither Macnamara nor his English patrons could have had such remote contingencies in mind as their main object. What they first and most wanted was to find a place to settle poor Irish families in order to help relieve the pressure of Irish famine. And such a place seemed to be offered to them in California, in case they could obtain favor with the central government of Mexico and with that of the department itself. With the particular fortunes of the Macnamara scheme we have little to do. It is sufficient for our purpose to note that the plan of getting the grant sought was incomplete at the moment of the conquest and would have been so even had the gallant captain never seen California, a fact that appears only the more plainly from his own testimony before the Claims Committee. For therein he says that the movement of Governor Pio Pico in the Macnamara matter in the month of July was probably determined, or hastened, by his own assault in the north. In other words, had there been an imminent danger to American interests from Macnamara, the gallant captain himself would have been the one who did all that was possible on his part to increase the danger and to hasten its consummation. There was, however, no such serious danger,[7] because the

---

[7] Señor Coronel (a native of respectable position, both at that time and since, and good authority on these matters) says in his statement, B. MS., that the scheme encountered great popular opposition from Californians in the south.

Macnamara grant would have had yet more ordeals to go through before it could have been effective. It was a scheme of altogether unprecedented and irregular character in California, and as such could not have worked quickly.

The other popular legend makes the danger from England yet more pressing, by declaring: first, that Sloat was watched (as he undoubtedly was), at Mazatlán, by Admiral Seymour, who with the *Collingwood* is known to have followed Sloat to Monterey, reaching that place a few days after the raising of the flag; second, that Seymour had orders to put California under English protection so soon as hostilities should begin between the United States and Mexico; third, that, in pursuance of these orders, he raced with Sloat to Monterey, arriving too late by reason of Sloat's skill in eluding him; and, finally, that if he had reached Monterey in time, or if Sloat had hesitated longer, Seymour would have seized California and would have established an English protectorate over the country. This story has always been somewhat thoughtlessly repeated by General Frémont's friends, although if it were true, it would of itself give us yet another and a direct condemnation of his violent efforts to harass and overthrow the existing Californian government by a course that, unless supported by the purest luck, would have only served to drive California into the arms of the coming English force instead of preparing California to resist the English. But the story is almost certainly a mere legend. And this I say after a most careful effort to understand the accessible evidence, and especially the evidence upon which the legend most relies. The whole thing is most probably a fine instance of the capacity of the public to be fooled by whatever has an air of mystery and of deep significance. Seymour *may* have had such instructions, but if he did we have *no* good evidence of the fact.

The evidence given for the legend is as follows: First, in general, England is known to have been jealous at that time of our "manifest destiny" on the Pacific and to have been unwilling to see us get California. And so far there is indeed no doubt about the matter. English travelers' books, English magazines, and English newspapers of that day express this feeling. But, in just the same sense, England was unwilling to see us get Oregon; and yet, just at that very moment, England was deliberately, if unwillingly, yielding to us more than she had originally meant to yield in Oregon. Unwillingly, I say, England did this, but did so *because Oregon was not considered to be worth a war.* Even so, however, there can be little doubt that California also was not then thought by England to be worth a war. Yet to order the seizure of California, even while the Oregon negotiations were pending and while the relations of America and England were strained, would have been, in view of our known determinations and ambitions, merely to ensure a war. If England, however, was willing to fight for California, *why did she not fight,* especially when her force then present in the Pacific was already, as is usually admitted, fairly able to cope with ours? But these general considerations are, by themselves indeed, far too vague. We can only say from them that either the English government must have ordered Seymour to get California by violence if necessary (but then he would have used violence); or else his orders cannot have gone much farther than a direction to use his discretion in *accepting* a proposition from the Californians themselves to take them under his protection. But, in the latter case, he "raced," if he did race, with Sloat, not to raise his own flag at once, but to watch events, and to accept, as he did, the inevitable results of the American action in case it should be decisive and should not be preceded by a request from the Californians for his protection. For the rest, where has anyone ever found or produced the evidence of any sort of agreement between England and Mexico, looking towards an alliance or towards a protectorate, in the event of a war between Mexico and ourselves?

In the second place, however, the legend knows that Seymour himself confessed to American naval officers, in friendly conversation, and while his own vessel lay in Monterey Bay, just after the raising of our flag, that, had he come first, his flag would have been flying over the fort in place of ours. The officers to whom Seymour said this usually speak to us through third persons. Who they were the legend generally says not, unless it avers, as it sometimes does, that Sloat was one of them. That Seymour may have said anything one pleases, in harmless jest, after dinner or at some other social meeting, and that American officers, and even Sloat himself, may have been very ready to misinterpret his jest to the credit of their own exploits, is indubitable; but that he actually, and in any earnest speech, revealed his instructions about so delicate a matter is rank nonsense. He of course did nothing of the sort. Even if he did speak in a seemingly earnest tone, we could not believe him about a matter that his duty as an officer would have forced him to conceal. His instructions, whatever they were, have never been revealed; but in Parliament, in a conversation held in the autumn of 1846, before the news of our conquest had reached England, Lord Palmerston used language about our troubles with Mexico that was utterly inconsistent with the existence of any plan such as would have seemed likely to embroil England and our own land in a controversy about California. If, then, there *was* such a plan existing, and if Lord Palmerston knew of instructions to Seymour that might lead to a quarrel with us concerning California, he felt bound to give no hint of the matter to Parliament.[8] In that case, however, the thing was strictly confidential; but then Admiral Seymour did not blurt it out to the first American officer whom he met in a social gathering. Or if he pretended to do so, then so much the more reason for doubting the fact that he pretended to confess.

The legend, in the third place, appeals to the concurrent impressions and testimony of all the American navy men on the coast at the time, from Commodore Sloat down to the common seamen. All alike seem to have given the one interpretation to Seymour's presence — an interpretation that of course highly flattered their own vanity. They all felt that they had beaten the whole English nation without striking a blow. They

---

[8] The conversation in question is found in *Hansard*, 3rd Series, Vol. LXXXVIII, p. 978. The substance is that while the Oregon difficulty was pending, England could not offer mediation between Mexico and ourselves; while now, since there is no longer fear of contest or friction between England and ourselves, such mediation is feasible.

certainly had done this in so far, namely, as they had taken California against England's openly expressed desire that we should not take it. But that England had determined to do more than to look with disfavor upon our seizure of California, Sloat and the sailors could only guess, even in case it was true. They were not in the state secrets of England. Who were they, that they should know what Admiral Seymour was about? Did he know all that *they* were about? And yet their gossip has been the infallible guide for the legend ever since.

But, in the fourth place, the legend itself more directly and triumphantly asks: what, then, was Seymour doing, if not racing with Sloat for California? The one answer plainly is: the Oregon matter was still, so far as Seymour and the rest knew, an unsettled matter. How soon the two nations might find themselves at war, neither of the commanders could at the moment tell. It was plainly Seymour's duty to watch Sloat narrowly, to know where he was and what he did, and to follow him, moreover, with an adequate force. Might not Sloat's movements, for all Seymour could know, have some relation to Oregon also? And *if* the Oregon difficulty should lead to war, then, indeed, Seymour would be bound to prevent by force Sloat's seizure of California as well as any other of Sloat's undertakings. All this he must have had in mind, and this sufficiently explains his movements.

And so, finally, the legend has to fall back on a sort of continuity of tradition and has to assert that everybody has always somehow known since July 1846 that we won California from the very jaws of the lion. Here is the true humor of the tradition, that, in the end, it is only an expression of that infallible sense which guides all our American frontiersmen and sailors, and talkers generally, to an intuitive and accurate knowledge of the details of English foreign policy. If you want a true sense of what our neighbor across the water thinks and means and is and does, you must listen to the average speculative American who has never read an English journal. He feels in his soul the wicked plans, the ambitious and oppressive purposes, of that perfidious old tyrant of the seas so fully and earnestly that, given such a fact as an English man-of-war with an

admiral on board, following our fleet when it went to seize
California, he can at once read all that England meant and
ordered.

As for me, I know naught of the instructions of Admiral Seymour in 1846, save what one very indirect piece of evidence
indicates, in a purely negative way, as to the plans that they
must have expressed. This one evidence is contained in the remarks of Lord Palmerston just cited. This is the single important objective fact amongst the wreck of legendary trash
about the English official designs upon California in 1846. And
what this evidence indicates I have already suggested. I think
it quite inconsistent with any purpose on the part of the English government to risk a struggle with us for the sake of the
wildernesses of California. It is not indeed as if Lord Palmerston had announced directly whether he had or whether his
predecessors had had designs on California. A direct mention
of California he evaded. His remarks are important, however,
since while he does not mention California at all, he does distinctly mention and promise a course of public action concerning Mexico and ourselves that would have been absurd and
impossible if he had already determined (or if his very recent
predecessors, who must have instructed Seymour, had determined, in such a way as now to bind his conduct) that California should be seized at the risk of a conflict with us and in
the face of our own open armed preparations to take the territory upon the outbreak of a war with Mexico, this war itself
being just as openly a part of our program.

This, I say, is all that I know of relevant evidence bearing
upon the instructions of Admiral Seymour. Whatever they
were, it is very improbable, therefore, that they resembled
those mentioned in the legend. And the evidence that the legend gives in support of its own claims is merely amusing in its
self-confident inconclusiveness.

Legends are plenty in this part of our story, and we have
here yet to notice, as bearing on the problems of the moment
of the conquest, a tale that Lieutenant Revere [9] first told, from

---

[9] *Tour on Duty in California*, p. 24.

a source that he does not name, concerning a mysterious junta held at Monterey in May 1846, wherein certain principal men of California, including, among others, Governor Pio Pico (who was not in Monterey or near it at all during this time) and General Vallejo, shall have discussed the situation and shall have advised together whether California ought to pass over to the United States or to some European power. The speeches of these dignitaries are given at length by Lieutenant Revere, much in the taste of the ancient historians; and the same speeches have been slavishly repeated by numberless writers ever since, until General Vallejo has been himself induced, in recent years, to remember that the story, save as to Pio Pico and some other minor matters, is substantially true, even down to the details of General Vallejo's own speech. There is little reason, however, to doubt that the story is substantially legendary, for General Vallejo, among other things, remembers the meeting as one public enough to be attended by the various foreign consuls, and, if I am not mistaken, declares it to have been held at Larkin's own house and to have been officially reported by the well-known official Hartnell. Yet no official or other contemporary MS. record of such a meeting is known to Mr. Bancroft's library, nor is such a record, as I learn on questioning at Mr. Bancroft's library, discoverable in the archives; and as for Larkin, he, who could not possibly have been ignorant of such a junta, knows absolutely nothing about it, as appears from his letters to the State Department.

III. *The Wolf and the Lamb*

TREATING Macnamara's scheme, Admiral Seymour's undertakings, and, in general, the salvation of California from the lion's mouth, with the indifference that, in the present state of the historical evidence, these matters seem to deserve, we return to the objectively verifiable facts of the conquest, which we must sketch with continued regard for our special interest in the narrative. We are studying these, like other events, as facts of importance for the social future of California and as characteristic of our nation.

Sloat raised the flag at Monterey without opposition, and
Captain Montgomery, at Yerba Buena, did the same. Castro
was in the interior, and Sloat wrote him, as has been said, begging him to come to terms without a contest. Castro attempted
no resistance, but retreated southward, disgusted with the
agents of this unintelligible power that, as it seemed to him,
had been deliberately trying to entrap him by a mixture of
soft words and treacherous violence. In his replies to Sloat [10]
he gave the latter to understand that such a moment, with the
Bear Flag people disturbing the north and hostile ships lying
in the harbor of Monterey, was not the occasion for peaceful
negotiations,[11] and we, who know now how our nation, through
its representatives, had been treating Castro, cannot blame him
for his mood. He seemed still to be not unmindful of the possibility of explanations from Sloat that might make negotiation feasible; but he had little hope of anything but force and
treachery. On his way southwards he met Pio Pico, who, full
of the domestic quarrels of the times, and ignorant of the exact
situation, had been coming against him with hostile intent.
The two resolved to lay aside their differences for the present
and to consider what to do for their common country. The proposed junta that had been appointed to meet at Santa Barbara,
June 15, to discuss the situation and to consider the possible
means of preparing for invasion or for other change, had been
altogether abandoned weeks before, the petty political quarrels
of the Californians being in part responsible for this result.[12]
And now the duty of the two chiefs was to consider what
should be the means to meet the entirely new conditions.
Could they resist the American invasion? Or should they seek

---

[10] Sen. Ex. Doc., 29 Congr., 2nd Sess., Doc. 1, p. 647; Doc. 19, p.
104.

[11] Castro wrote two letters, both dated July 9, from San Juan
Mission. One refuses to surrender to Sloat until after a consultation
with the authorities in the south. The other demands information
about the marauders in the north.

[12] Coronel, in his statement, B. MS., refers the abandonment of
the junta to political difficulties; but of course the troubles that had
now followed would have rendered the meeting in any case useless.

to get fair terms from a power that had just proved, by its apparent double-dealing, its determination to crush them altogether? Their discussion of these matters was broken by a somewhat characteristic dispute [13] concerning the proper person to have command of the forces of the north and the south, these forces being now united at Los Angeles, whither the two chiefs had retreated. The controversy was at length settled in Castro's favor; and an effort was made to organize some resistance to the American authorities, since favorable negotiations seemed out of the question. But of course this now distracted land, which had so often played at war, but which had never fought a real battle, had neither good weapons, nor trained soldiers, nor powder, nor supplies. A contest against the United States forces was, however one might pretend to organize one's resources, simply hopeless, and Castro knew it, although he tried to save after a fashion his personal honor, grossly insulted as it had been, by showing a bold front to the enemy, so far as words could serve him.

Meanwhile the Americans had taken possession of the main posts in the northern country from Monterey upwards, without immediate opposition of any sort. But after Captain Frémont had joined the forces of Commodore Sloat at Monterey, an unfavorable change had come over the spirit of the official American undertakings. Sloat, namely, had abandoned his command and returned to the United States, while Commodore Stockton, who had arrived in the *Congress,* took his place. Stockton had brought with him the sealed original of the now useless Larkin dispatch. He was under orders to deliver this and then to report to Sloat. On his arrival he found himself by Sloat's retirement quickly entrusted with a serious responsibility, which he used for his own glory and amusement, with becoming alacrity and with some genuine courage and energy.

A brief consultation with Captain Frémont seems to have had far more weight in his mind than what he chose to learn from Sloat's instructions. To conciliate the people of California

---

[13] Coronel, loc. cit.

without or before conquering them seemed to him, as to the gallant captain, nonsensical. He chose, apparently, to assume that the gallant captain's behavior in the north had been due to official instructions, although, at that early day, while the gallant captain's memory was still fresh concerning the whole matter, it must have been impossible that the latter should voluntarily give to the commodore such a mistaken account as he recently, through an error of memory, gave to me. But doubtless if he was silent on the subject, his silence was not free from a certain eloquence; and, at all events, when the new commodore's plans were once laid, the latter prepared a proclamation that, for effrontery, has never been surpassed by the pronouncements of any Mexican.[14] This proclamation was issued five days after the commodore had, on July 23, assumed command of the forces of the United States on the coast, and four days after he had accepted Captain Frémont's offer of the improvised force from the north and had organized the same into the "California battalion of mounted riflemen." The proclamation expressed the commodore's horror, on assuming command, at hearing of "scenes of rapine, blood, and murder" in the interior. Who was really responsible for such scenes, in so far as they were actual, he, of course, ignored; and hence found himself "constrained by every principle of national honor . . . to put an end, at once and by force, to the lawless depredations daily committed by General Castro's men upon the persons and property of peaceful and unoffending inhabitants." This proclamation of the wolf to the lamb was surely almost as good, in its way, as Ide's oration to the inhabitants

---

[14] Cf. Tuthill's remark, *History of California*, p. 186: "There was not wanting a certain Mexican flavor in this" (proclamation). Tuthill's account of the early part of the conquest appears to me, of course, in view of the foregoing considerations, very imperfect and erroneous as concerns some weighty matters, although in the better-known details it is fairly sound. Yet I cannot but refer the reader to Tuthill's pages just here, in view of the decidedly graceful style and the generally sober and excellent spirit in which he tells the story. See, further, Stockton's proclamation of July 28, 1846, in the *Annals of San Francisco*, p. 104.

of Sonoma, and the words so far used are fully borne out by the rest of the document. Stockton referred, rather covertly, to the duty that even he must have felt devolving upon him, as Sloat's successor, to treat, if possible, in a peaceful spirit with the authorities of the country. But, as he felt, he could not, much to his regret, live up to these instructions of his predecessor. So the proclamation at least suggested. What it said was: "I cannot therefore confine my operations to the quiet and undisturbed possession of the defenseless ports of Monterey and San Francisco, whilst the people elsewhere are suffering from lawless violence, but will immediately march against these boastful and abusive chiefs . . . who, unless driven out, will . . . keep this beautiful country in a constant state of revolution and bloodshed."

The California battalion had now already embarked for San Diego in the *Cyane,* that they might be landed south of Castro, to cut off his retreat, a plan that proved in the sequel ineffective. Stockton himself sailed in the *Congress* for San Pedro, the port of Los Angeles, and there landed a force, formed from the sailors and marines, with six small cannon. Of Stockton's vast courage and energy in landing such a crowd of sea-dogs to undertake a hunt on dry land, and in training them, after a fashion, for this new sort of chase, directed as it was against what he himself chose to pretend to consider a strong and well-fortified force of Californians, well used to the country — of all this, Stockton's admirers, among whom he was undoubtedly the chief, have taken no small pains to convince us.[15] We should be better convinced of this if Stockton's opportunities to learn from the gallant captain, and from others, the utter helplessness of this little nation of herdsmen and colonists had not been so sufficient, even in the very few days that passed ere his plans were formed. In fact, save by way of a certain bustle of preparation at Los Angeles, Castro and the

---

[15] See Stockton himself, in his mock-modest report to the Secretary of the Navy, in the already cited Doc. 19, p. 106 (or Doc. 1, also cited, p. 668); and the *Annals of San Francisco,* pp. 102 and 105. Cf. the much more sensible but still too good-humored account of Tuthill, pp. 187, 188.

rest could do simply nothing in the short time left them. Castro, indeed, made an effort to open with Stockton, as the latter approached, the negotiations that he still thought due to himself in view of Sloat's earlier efforts to conciliate him. But it was hoping against hope to expect Stockton, who wanted nothing but noise and a warrior's glory, either to understand his true obligations to Castro and to the other Californians or to consider such obligations as important. Castro surely, for his own honor's sake, ought not to have approached Stockton with any further shows of negotiation. Yet, for the sake, I suppose, of getting better terms for his countrymen, Castro did make such an approach, through messengers, to Stockton, as the latter was on the march towards Los Angeles. The messengers were insultingly received, and a message was sent back demanding unconditional surrender. Resistance was of course hopeless without arms or powder, and both Castro and Pico set out for Mexico.

On the 13th of August, Stockton, who had now been joined by the California battalion (which had landed at San Diego and come northward), entered Los Angeles with his full force and, unresisted, raised the flag. Shortly afterwards he issued several proclamations, on successive days, declaring the country a part of the territory of the United States and making arrangements for a provisional government. Now that he had made a glorious conquest, with his marines, in face of the aforesaid overwhelming odds, he felt at liberty to speak more peaceably, for the moment, to the inhabitants of the land. They should be allowed, his proclamations assured them, to elect alcaldes and municipal officers throughout the territory. They should be unmolested in their regular business, and if they submitted quietly, they should be considered as citizens of the territory, and protected accordingly. They should soon be governed by a regular governor, secretary, and legislative council, to whose provisional appointment he would promptly see. In the meantime, of course, there would remain a good deal of martial law about their position. "All persons who, without special permission, are found with arms outside their own houses will be considered as enemies, and will be shipped out of the country." The California battalion would remain in service for the present.[16]

As to what they expressed in so many words, Stockton's proclamations of August 15–22, if placed side by side with Sloat's proclamation of July 7, issued upon the raising of the flag, would seem at first glance to differ mainly by containing more details, such as would naturally be suggested by a more advanced stage of the conquest. Yet if one looks more carefully, one finds a serious difference in spirit, with one important, but since then seldom sufficiently recognized, difference in the pledges made. For Sloat, the Californians are the inhabitants of a nearly independent province, whom he wishes to conciliate, not only as individuals, but as a people, having a genuine political unity. California is to be relieved henceforth from the corrupt and disorderly rule of "the central government of Mexico," which Sloat, by this expression, takes care to represent as not identical with the proper government of California itself, but as rather a relatively foreign and disturbing force in Californian affairs. As for the Californians themselves, Sloat has "full confidence in their honor and integrity," and accordingly invites "the judges, alcaldes, and other civil officers" (a rather dubious form of language, which undoubtedly, however, if strictly interpreted, would have included Pio Pico and the departmental assembly, in case they had consented to be included) "to retain their offices, and to execute their functions as heretofore, that the public tranquillity may not be disturbed; at least, until the government of the territory can be more definitely arranged."

Now an essential part of the pledge thus made by Sloat, Stockton, after his interview with the gallant Captain Frémont, and before he could know of the way in which Pico and the assembly could be induced to view the matter, in case they should be wisely approached, simply tore up and flung to the winds. Personal glory did not lie for him in the direction of negotiations with the "other civil officers," nor did he, like Sloat, come as the "best friend of California," anxious to avoid

---

[16] Docs. as cited: Doc. 1, p. 669 ff; Doc. 19, p. 107 ff.

bloodshed. Sloat had written to ask both Castro and Pico to a council at Monterey, under a solemn assurance of a safe-conduct if they should consent to come. But all this was naught for Stockton. To be sure, he was not very malicious. He did not want to oppress the Californians, when once he should have conquered them. He only wanted his fun, as a gallant and glory-seeking American officer, out of the business of conquering them. Then indeed he could afford to be generous. But first he must have the fight. But as there was nobody in the territory capable of fighting him with any prospect of success, Stockton, after bullying and exasperating the defenseless provincial government and people with insulting proclamations and demonstrations, had at last to be content for the moment with such glory as these bloodless exercises could give him. And so in the proclamations of August 15–22 he has at length to treat the Californians with the condescending airs of a generous conqueror. He proclaims a blockade of the whole coast against all but American merchant vessels; he introduces several provisions of martial law; he undertakes to establish very soon a provisional governor and legislative assembly, and merely "permits" the people to elect their local civil officers. All these provisions are, of course, in perfect accord with the usages of civilized conquerors and do not exceed Stockton's temporary authority, so long as one considers him commander of a conquering force; but to convert the seizure of California into a military conquest at all, when as yet the inhabitants had made absolutely no violent resistance to the regular forces of the United States, was against the whole spirit of the plans and instructions of our government. Our official plan was to take possession of the ports, and to invite the inhabitants either to join us, or to retain, at any rate, their domestic freedom of action, while keeping the peace towards us. *If* the inhabitants had violently resisted this plan, *then* we should have been obliged to conquer them; but as yet they had never resisted us, save by the use of a few very naturally bold words, uttered in the first shock of their vexation. They had only resisted the marauders in the north, who had been in arms against the express commands of our government, as communicated to Captain Frémont by Lieutenant Gillespie. Therefore our pretense of needing to conquer the inhabitants was a mere show, got up either to justify the affair in the north or to satisfy a vain love of personal glory in the wanton mind of Commodore Stockton, or, more probably, to do both. And the only outcome of it all was the exasperation of the natives. All the assurances of goodwill and all the fine promises that in Stockton's proclamations of August give these documents at first sight an apparently close connection and agreement with Sloat's pledges of July 7 could not serve to hide by fine phrases the essential perfidy of our conduct towards the Californians. The people at large knew, of course, nothing of the Larkin intrigue. But they did know, or at least believed, that we had been long scheming to get the country, that our agents had made many promises, that we had then brutally attacked the people in the north, and that we had thereafter taken violent possession of the country, publishing proclamations in which assurances of peace and goodwill were so mingled with threats and abuse that nobody could make out more of their meaning than that they signified the use of force at present and of probable oppression in future. Henceforth all respectable and honorable Californians were apt to suspect if not to detest us, unless, indeed, they should prove very forgiving.

IV. *The Revolt and the Reconquest*

AND yet even now, by a proper behavior, we might have slowly won back something of the confidence and goodwill of the people, notwithstanding all that had happened. Of course, thus far, our ill-treatment of them had been at worst largely the consequence of a characteristic wantonness, ignorance, and personal ambition on the part of our agents, and not the expression of any deliberate determination to oppress the natives, when once we should have taken their land. Much as we had by this time exasperated them, there was a possibility of repentance. In some directions, moreover, repentance soon seemed to be taking effect.

And first on the list of those who, after this provisional com-

pletion of the conquest, began to show a desire to treat our
new subjects as fellow citizens and friends, one must mention
with great satisfaction the name of no less a person than the
gallant captain himself, the chief author of the foregoing mischief. We have throughout been ready to see, in all the serious
mistakes and evils of his conduct, rather the expression of bad
advice from home, or of wanton personal ambition, than the
outcome of any deliberate malice towards the Californians
themselves. Their interest before the conquest stood in the way
of his plans, and in so far he was guilty of immeasurable injustice to their rights and to their future prosperity and was for
the time as cruel as he was unjust. But he was still a kindly
and warmhearted man, whenever his ambitions, or his private
interests, or those of his family, were not concerned. And he
now had for the moment no need to be cruel to the fallen foe.
On the contrary, he seems at once to have foreseen an opportunity for future business and social relations with the people,
such as led him now to desire their friendship, just as he so
recently had determined upon their overthrow. He was quick
to adapt himself to their ways and soon began to win the personal friendship of many of them. Although he could no longer
stay the bitter consequences for the whole land of his folly in
the north, consequences that remain until this day, and will
yet long remain, he could already excuse himself in the eyes of
some even of the natives by neglecting to assume his full share
of personal responsibility for the outbreak; and he could meanwhile use his undoubted personal charm to win the hearts of
hospitable Californians.[17] What was evil about the matter our

---

[17] Coronel, in his B. MS. statement, contrasts the conduct of the
gallant captain in the south at this moment very favorably with that
of other American officers, after the conquest was once for the time
over: "*Frémont se entregó a las diversiones del país, se familiarizó
prontamente con los habitantes, adoptando sus trajes y modo de
vivir hasta cierto grado. El se vestía como los rancheros, y andaba
á caballo con ellos; se hicieron tan íntimas las relaciones entre él y
los del país, que ya muchos de estos le tuteaban.*" This personal af-
fability of conduct and this charm of manner could not at once,
Coronel says, conquer the objections of many of the principal fami-

government had especially to answer for, in the minds of the people, and so the captain himself began to evade personal censure; nor has he ever since left off. But at all events this new course of conduct was not only prudent, but so far as the Californians were concerned generous and just; and the gallant captain deserves all due credit for it.

With this new-found wisdom of Captain Frémont's well agrees also the more habitual conduct of such a man as the Rev. Walter Colton at Monterey, whose book *Three Years in California* [18] gives us such an excellent notion of some aspects of the days of the interregnum. He found the people good-humored and disposed to submit to their fate. He studied them thoughtfully; applied from the first a sensible and tolerant mind to understanding and to helping them, in his office as alcade; and was in all respects an example of the more enlightened American influence at its very best, in a time of transition. The people of Monterey liked him and felt generally contented with the new rule as represented by him.

Some of the new officials, also, were Americans who had long been in the country, who had not participated in the sins of the conquest, and who were the men for the place. But there were exceptions to the excellent rule thus exemplified. And the exceptions were numerous enough to keep the hatreds of the moment well alive in most parts of the country. In the eyes of men like Gillespie, in the eyes of numerous navy officers and men, in the eyes of most of the California battalion, the Cali-

---

lies; but the impression produced on the mass of the people was excellent, so far as it went.

[18] New York, 1852. The author, a chaplain in the navy, was appointed provisional alcalde of Monterey by Commodore Stockton on July 28, 1846, was formally elected by the people to the same office at the election under Stockton's proclamation, September 15, and remained in the country until after the gold-discovery. He tells us his story in diary form, and includes in it too much of his decidedly innocent inner life for the purposes of such a work; but of the condition of the country he has also much to tell that is very helpful. September 4, 1846, he held the first jury trial in California. He was throughout an efficient and popular officer.

fornians were, after what had happened, a boastful and treacherous people, given to murder and pillage, an inferior race, a people to be suspected, to be kept down with a strong arm, and to be reminded constantly of their position as the vanquished. Gillespie, however, was left in charge at Los Angeles. Other navy men were scattered along the coast. The California battalion was under arms, was expectant of its pay, and meanwhile was not perfectly contented. The result of Gillespie's intolerance was an outbreak at the south; and in this movement the whole country south of the bay more or less sympathized and took part. In the outbreak the native people gave their well-nursed exasperation vent. Helpless as they on the whole were before the well-armed Americans, they still showed of what stuff they were made by resisting on at least two occasions — namely, near San Pedro and at San Pascual — with stubbornness and not without success. They were by January 1847 a second time conquered, this time not without considerable bloodshed, and the bitterness of the conquest was thus once for all rendered chronic, and for a large part of the population fatal. For the new outbreak had, in American eyes, all the character of a treacherous revolt, while the bloodshed rendered the hatred of the native population thenceforth undying. Everywhere the result was bad, and to this second act of the conquest the subsequent general demoralization of a mass of the native population, especially in the south, may be directly traced. The whole disturbance was a fruitful mother of bandits and vagabonds, who vexed the California of later days for a score of years.

Gillespie at Los Angeles was, I have said, the immediate cause of the revolt. This distinguished and faithless bearer of dispatches was not a suitable man to conciliate the natives. He adopted Commodore Stockton's tone and made them all feel the bitterness of martial law, vexing them with unnecessary regulations; he neither knew nor cared to know the customs of the people.[19] At last, apropos of the arbitrary arrest of a

---

[19] The general feeling is no doubt fairly voiced by Coronel, who as resident, was directly aware of what went on in Los Angeles at the time. Coronel, a man of thoroughly trustworthy character, is the

citizen, a disturbance broke out; and this led to more arrests. One man whose arrest was at this time ordered, J. M. Flores, an officer under the previous government, fled from the town and began to form a party of the discontented fugitives outside. Flores was, unfortunately for his future reputation in history, a paroled military officer, and so were a number of those who joined him. The revolt, as an expression of outraged public opinion, would indeed have been justifiable enough had it not been hopeless; but the paroled men who took part in it were numerous enough to give the whole affair a character of which the contemporary American writers were not slow to take advantage in what they said of it. Yet the insurgents were not all officers, much less paroled ones. The revolt was a popular act. The incidents of the reconquests, which thus opens, are complex and exciting, and form a fruitful subject of controversy. Our purposes and our limits forbid us to dwell upon them, and above all upon the controversy that they led to — the famous controversy between General Kearny and Captain (or now more properly Lieutenant-Colonel) Frémont. These details, which would be necessary in a complete history of California, are neither so characteristic of the forces at work, nor so fateful for the future of California, as those that we have been already treating.[20]

Californian to whom Mrs. Jackson was indebted for some of the accounts of the scenes of the reconquest that she repeated in her well-known articles in the *Century Magazine*. His statement concerning Gillespie's doings at this moment runs (B. MS.): *"Gillespie . . . empezó á dictar medidas muy opresivas; per ejemplo: publicó una orden para que no anduviesen dos personas juntas en las calles; para que no se reuniesen los ciudadanos baja ningún pretexto en sus casas; para que se cerrasen las tiendas de comestibles á la puesta del sol."* "Gillespie," concludes Coronel, *"tenia á esta gente tan obstinada que se hizo una especie de tiranuelo odioso."*

[20] Authorities in print and easily accessible concerning the revolt are, of compendious narratives, Tuthill's in his *History*, Bryant's (from personal observation) in his *What I Saw in California*, Cutts's in his *Conquest of California and New Mexico*, and the story as told in the *Annals of San Francisco*. The proceedings of the Frémont-Kearny court-martial contain much original matter. Hall's *His-*

In brief, however, Gillespie's position at Los Angeles became untenable against the overwhelming numbers of the revolting party. After a lively siege, some of whose incidents Coronel recounts, in his statement to Mr. Bancroft, with much zest, Gillespie capitulated, retiring to Monterey. The revolting party labored hard to get powder and other supplies, and Flores issued vigorous proclamations. At Santa Barbara Lieutenant Talbot escaped with his men from the besieging force. The lower country was soon largely overrun by them.

Stockton promptly heard of these troubles. He was at Yerba Buena at the time, and at a banquet that had been tendered him by the Americans of the place he made a speech concerning the news, in his most brutal and boastful tone, showing not the least sense of the position and feelings of the people, announcing his intention to make quick work of the revolt, and expressing in a violent way his opinion of those engaged in it. He then set sail for San Pedro in the *Congress,* having previously sent the *Savannah* with Captain Mervine to the same place. The California battalion embarked for Santa Barbara, but had to return to get horses, which they had hoped to get at Santa Barbara. Mervine, meanwhile, had landed at San Pedro and had set out for Los Angeles, hoping to win the glory of defeating the revolters himself. His marines were met by a party of mounted Californians, who dragged with them a single gun on wheels. They had but a few charges of powder, but these they used so effectively, dragging their gun, after each discharge, out of Mervine's rifle range, that before their little supply was exhausted, several of Mervine's men had been killed and he had become discouraged and had retreated to his ship. Stockton, arriving at San Pedro, and suffering from a lack of supplies, took his force by water to San Diego, where he

tory of San José treats of the revolt in that region. Lieutenant Cooke's *Conquest of New Mexico and California* is an incomplete and one-sided but not valueless account, by one of the officers concerned in the closing scenes. Colton in his *Three Years* also gives some details, and so does Lieutenant Revere, in his *Tour on Duty.* Authorities concerning particular scenes and controversies are very numerous, and many of them still inedited.

landed in November, drove off the enemy, and established a camp.

Meanwhile the Californians, who had been hoping for help from Mexico, found themselves threatened, although, for the moment, not very seriously, from a new quarter. General Kearny, namely, was approaching from New Mexico, but with only a small detachment of dragoons. The general had already completed his little conquest of New Mexico and had now come on to California, of which he had been ordered to take possession and in which he was commissioned to found a civil government. He too had been ordered, like Sloat, to "act in such a manner as best to conciliate the inhabitants, and render them friendly to the United States," but his orders were, of course, unlike Sloat's, subsequent to the date of the declaration of war.[21] He was, however, still expected to form his civil government, as far as possible, in conformity with the existing conditions, and with all proper use of the actual native government and officers found in the territory.

On the way from New Mexico, Kearny had been met by an express conveying dispatches from Stockton and from Captain Frémont to the government at Washington,[22] and announcing the conquest of the country. In consequence of the information that he thus received as to the condition of California, Kearny had left New Mexico a part of his force, and, expecting Cooke with the "Mormon battalion" to follow soon, he had gone on with about one hundred dragoons. On his arrival in the territory, he found himself in the presence of a not very formidable but active foe, who had for weeks been straining every nerve to procure the means for fighting. Kearny's own supplies were low. He managed to send a messenger to Stockton at San Diego, and the result was that a detachment, under

---

[21] See the often herein cited Doc. 19, p. 6. The instructions to Colonel Stevenson, issued later than Kearny's, when Stevenson was sent to California around the Horn, with his well-known regiment of volunteers, were to make the inhabitants "feel that we come as deliverers" (loc. cit., p. 12).

[22] See his testimony before the court-martial, Sen. Ex. Doc. 33, 1st Sess., 30th Congr., p. 41.

Lieutenant Gillespie, consisting of about thirty-five mounted men, came to his aid. Gillespie joined Kearny near San Pascual. On the morning of December 6 the united forces, undertaking to attack the Californians at San Pascual, suffered serious loss and gained nothing. This fight, which was to all intents and purposes a defeat, although Kearny himself did not confess the fact in his official reports, left his force in a very dangerous position, from which it was rescued by another detachment of Stockton's men.

The forces of Kearny and Stockton were now united, and, without coming to a sufficiently definite agreement as to which of the two leaders, under the circumstances, ought to be considered as at the head of affairs in California, both the officers in due time set out for Los Angeles together. On the 8th of January 1847 they found the enemy, just beyond the San Gabriel River. They crossed the river in the face of the enemy's quite ineffective fire. The home-made powder of the Californians was in fact nearly useless, and the few charges of good powder that had proved so useful in meeting Mervine near San Pedro had exhausted the little stock that the Californians possessed of that kind. The commodore, who had somewhat rashly, and in ignorance of the facts about the resources of the Californians, ordered the troops to make the charge across the river, took great credit afterwards for this new triumph over a practically defenseless foe, whose harmless bullets dropped helplessly all about the men. The next day, the 9th, saw the last armed encounter of Californians and Americans. On the Mesa, north of the river, the mounted Californians undertook once more to resist their foe. But after a few spirited but quite useless attempted charges and some slight loss, they broke altogether and fled. Abandoning Los Angeles, the chiefs, with what force remained to them, retreated northward to meet Captain, or, as he was now oftener called since his battalion had been organized, Major Frémont, in order to surrender to him rather than to Stockton and Kearny, who had given notice of their intention to spare no men whose parole had been broken.

Of Major Frémont's conduct since he had returned northward from Santa Barbara I need not speak in detail. He had shown becoming energy in getting horses and supplies for his battalion and in raising further volunteers. The country, including the more peaceable natives, had had to suffer, meanwhile, from the loss of the horses and the supplies, but at the moment some such seizures were simply necessary, and there was no cash on hand to pay for them; so that the faith of the government had to be pledged instead. The misfortune that all this increased the old feeling of disgust for American rule was now, of course, inevitable, and the leader of the battalion could no longer prevent that. The further fact that many newcomers by the large and able immigration of 1846, fresh from across the plains, were enlisted in the battalion, and thus from the first moment met the Californians in a hostile spirit, was also a fact full of evil for the future, since many of the men of 1846 were destined to play no small part in the history of California and were often to be men of great authority as pioneers. And of course they thenceforth remembered the Californians as treacherous rebels and believed all the absurdities that they heard concerning the Bear Flag legend. But all this was now but one more link in the fatal chain of injustice. Beyond this, however, the northern operations during the suppression of the revolt were generally humane. The disturbances near Santa Clara and near Monterey were suppressed by detachments of our forces. The main body of the California battalion, proceeding southward, under its leader, crossed the Santa Inez Mountains on Christmas Day, in cold and storm, and then proceeded in the same direction far enough for Major Frémont to receive at Cahuenga, on January 11, in his capacity as military commandant of California, under Stockton's appointment, the capitulation of the Californian chiefs, whom, to the great disgust of Stockton, the gallant leader of the battalion was bold enough to pardon altogether, saying nothing of the broken paroles. His act was as generous as it was politic, and it had for him the advantage also of redounding to his personal glory, since in performing it he somewhat exceeded the authority that even Stockton might be supposed to have given him (so long as the latter was actually carrying on the war), and yet did so in the obvious interests of humanity and good order. Both Stockton and Kearny were forced — at least in so far as concerned the amnesty — to accept the act once executed; the amnesty was thus, once for all, complete, and the next scene was no longer one of war with Californians, but of a quarrel between Stockton and Kearny about the authority to govern the conquered territory. In this quarrel, as we know, the young military commandant of California under Stockton became involved, being appointed Governor by Stockton.

Of personal popularity the leader of the California battalion had won back, through his crowning act of clemency to the parole-breaking leaders of the revolt, more than he personally had lost by those acts in the north that the natives now generally attributed to the secret commands of his government. With not unnatural pride he later pointed out before the court-martial at Washington how he, the "conqueror of California," could thenceforth have ridden unguarded and alone through the whole length of the province without any trace of personal danger. Apparently he had atoned for his monumental mischief-making; but the atonement was only apparent. Although the native people, who knew nothing of the mystery, might fail to recognize the chain of causes that connected all their troubles with his private responsibility, the irrevocable wrong was now done. Clemency to individuals could win him great personal popularity, but it could never in fact unite the two peoples in the land whom he had now sundered in fierce hatred, nor atone for the ruin already wrought and thenceforth to follow. The very evils that his clemency moderated were all his own doing.

Of the details of the Stockton-Kearny-Frémont quarrel I have here nothing to say. In all but technical right the young Governor whom Stockton appointed appears almost throughout in a far better light than Kearny. And technical affairs of military law are of no concern here. It is enough to remind the reader that Governor Frémont was at length obliged to yield, and that in June 1847 he set out for the East, across the plains, in company with Kearny, and thereafter was, as we have already seen, court-martialed for his disobedience of Kearny's orders. He was convicted on largely technical grounds, and pardoned by the President. He declined to accept the President's clemency and resigned his commission. This court-martial only added to his popular glory and discovered to the public nothing of his real offense of an earlier date. The cabinet was bound, of course, to keep the Larkin intrigue secret. They had accepted, meanwhile, in an official document (the Report of the Secretary of War), the first theory propounded by Senator Benton in his letter to the President, founded on his earliest private advices from Captain Frémont. This aforementioned theory, as we know, gave Castro's mythical onslaught as the justification of the Bear Flag affair. The cabinet had no means, therefore, of calling the young officer to public account for his true disobedience; nor had they, probably, in view of Senator Benton's position and influence, even the wish to do so. For their purpose it was now enough that the country was ours. And so the whole matter was thenceforth, although not forever, enveloped in official prevarication and in mystery.

But the quarrel of the chiefs had been yet one more serious evil to California. Some of the important provisions of the Cahuenga capitulation, relating, indeed, not to the amnesty but to the legal status of the inhabitants, had been disregarded in later proclamations by Kearny, and were disregarded by his successor, Colonel Mason. The California battalion was refused pay by Kearny, and all the claims for its expenses remained then and for years afterwards unsatisfied, to the great displeasure of both American and native inhabitants.[23] Nor was the situation immediately improved by the rapid and rather confusing increase of the American population during this period. Stevenson's regiment, together with some other United States forces, arrived by water. Cooke's "Mormon battalion" came in from New Mexico during the quarrel of the chiefs. The immigration of 1846 was all in by the time the Donner party had been rescued, in the early months of 1847; and in

---

[23] Larkin, in a letter to the State Department, June 30, 1847, in his somewhat rude speech, but still with effect, sets forth the distracted condition of the land just after the end of the quarrel of the chiefs.

July 1846 there had appeared unexpectedly at San Francisco a shipload of Mormons, who had come from New York, by way of the Sandwich Islands, hoping to find refuge in this foreign land, which they now found to be, after all, an American land. The leader of these Mormons was the spirited, energetic, and coarse-fibered Samuel Brannan. The diversity of the purposes that had brought all these different companies of people hither; the need of finding for all alike, both soldiers and civilians (now that the war in California was done), employment and support; the uncertainty of the future in a country that, of course, could not technically be called ours before the campaigns in Mexico were done — all this, together with the incapacity of the newcomers themselves to understand perfectly their own delicate political situation, made this whole period of the interregnum a time of doubts, of problems, of complaints, and of weariness, as well, of course, as a time of most important and historically influential social life.

V. *The Conquerors as Rulers and as Subjects; Quarrels, Discontent, and Aspirations*

FOR it is at just such moments that the American nature shows its best qualities. Amid all the mistakes and the foolish words that abound in such a time, one is surprised to note the general and instinctive moderation of the Americans concerned, considered as a community. They seem always on the point of trying to solve their social problems by violent and revolutionary methods; and yet they refrain, not from fear, but by virtue of self-control. The American newcomers in California, under the new condition of things, naturally took the lead in everything. The natives, weary of the recent struggles, and generally hopeless and sullen, were glad to be let alone, and for the time they had little to say. It was the American who now complained bitterly of all the political, commercial, and social evils of this transition state; who loudly called for a stable government; who sometimes threatened to disregard United States authority altogether and go back to Bear Flag conditions; and who, in general, gave his soul free vent in his newly founded newspapers.[24] Yet it was the American who, in the midst of his private discontent, and in fact by virtue of this discontent, prepared the way for the birth of the sovereign state in 1849.

For the constitution of 1849 was not, as people usually conceive it, the product solely of the suddenly formed good resolutions of the new-coming gold-seekers. Had these men of the interregnum not preceded the gold-seekers, California would have had no state constitution in 1849. The constitutional convention was formed, as we shall see, partly of men that had lived in the territory through the interregnum, and only partly of newcomers that had political ambitions. In settling the problems of the convention, the men of the interregnum, despite their general ignorance of the politician's arts, were highly influential, and about many matters their influence was decisive. To see, therefore, why California was ready for a constitution in 1849, we must consider the controversies of the interregnum itself. Otherwise the convention of 1849 seems like a social miracle, as in fact it has often been treated by historians.

Technically, at the beginning of 1847 the department of California was still a bit of Mexican territory, under the military rule of an occupying force of our own hostile army. The law of nations, as the United States officers themselves pointed out, gave the conqueror under such circumstances authority to ordain such temporary laws and executive regulations as he might choose. But seldom is a conquered country in such a condition as was California in 1847. For the most active and

---

[24] These have been already mentioned: the *Californian* (first published in Monterey and later in San Francisco), and the *California Star*, published in San Francisco. The first of these papers was for a good while conducted, as we know, by Semple, and was founded in 1846. The other, the *Star*, was founded by Brannan, at the beginning of 1847, and, although variously edited, remained under his influence through 1847. Both papers were interrupted in their publication by the gold-discovery, which, in the summer of 1848, sent everybody to the mines. The *Star* I have used in the Bancroft Library file; the *Californian* in the San Francisco Pioneer Library file.

prominent of the population were now of the nation of the conquerors. That Western settlers, and the Mormons who had sought for a refuge in the California wilderness, should be disposed to be treated as Mexicans that had been conquered by an American army is not natural. But if these settlers were of the conquering, and not of the conquered, party, and if the country was to be American, they naturally wished to enjoy the benefits of the conquest, and to be governed, after American fashion, by themselves. Their wishes were for the time inadmissible and even dangerous; but their desire was, in itself considered, a laudable one. Technically, therefore, these settlers were a conquered people, like all the voluntary residents in any conquered province that is under military occupation. Actually, however, they thought themselves free as air, had in many cases themselves assisted in the conquest as members of Major Frémont's temporary battalion, and felt a healthy contempt for all military men and for that little brief authority wherewith military men are too commonly puffed up. Moreover, the government, as represented by General Kearny, had declined to pay at present the claims of the men of the California battalion. This led these men, who were now civilians, to feel no exceeding love for the military government. And, worst of all, they lived from day to day under what they thought to be a very inconvenient system: namely, the so-called Mexican law. This system was indeed in an amusingly dilapidated condition at that time in the department of California. If you take away all of a watch save the coiled mainspring and the main axle with its bearings, the watch goes for a second well enough, but you would not think it a valuable instrument. Now all that was left in California of the Mexican system of law was the local alcalde in each center of population. His action might be prompt, for the mainspring of his will was indeed there; but how usefully he might act, or how thoughtfully, depended on the conditions into which this fragment of legal machinery might momentarily be brought. If something, say the judge's personal good sense, held on to the axle, the watch might run down more deliberately; and if the hold was just right, the watch might even in some fashion be said to keep time. But the uncertainty was disheartening; the vigor of the law was often very unpleasant; and there was no immediate prospect of improvement. Very naturally the popular mind often turned to thoughts of self-government under a formulated constitution.

The alcalde was the sole judicial officer whose functions were perfectly familiar in the daily life of the natives of California. The simplicity of provincial litigation, the imperfect organization of society, the jelly-like unsteadiness of the native government of the department, had long united as causes to make the ordinary native regard a direct appeal to the alcalde in all cases of need as the principal, if not the only way in which a private and non-political citizen could, of his own choice, have to do with the authorities. When the conquest came, the office of the alcalde, therefore, alone survived the downfall of the very uncertain governmental institutions of the country. But when the alcalde survived, the Mexican laws could not be said to survive with him. Nobody in California had been at much trouble to learn or to apply to daily life any code of laws whatsoever. The known functions of the alcaldes had long been recognized by mere tradition. Beyond those known functions the alcaldes had possessed very great practical freedom of individual judgment. Their offices were not well supplied with lawbooks. The conquerors, in fact, found at first practically no books at all. The alcaldes appointed or elected after the conquest followed the devices of their own hearts. Not only were they commonly judges both of the law and of the evidence, but their position was often practically that of legislators. No wonder that their arbitrary powers aroused in the American mind many longings for self-government. These new alcaldes were often themselves Americans, and both at San Francisco and at Sonoma, as well as in one or two other places, they ruled communities that were now almost wholly American. One could appeal from their decisions to the Military Governor,[25] but practically, in respect of most minor matters,

---

[25] During most of 1847 and 1848 this was Colonel Mason, successor to General Kearny, an able and careful officer, whose personal character is well depicted for us in the *Memoirs* of General W. T. Sherman, then, as lieutenant, his adjutant and secretary. See

one had to submit to them. Was it, then, much to have helped conquer this vast land for one's beloved free country if one found oneself forthwith under an authority more arbitrary and unintelligible than even the native authority itself would have been?

The longings thus aroused were somewhat encouraged by the promises that Sloat, acting on the original official theory of our relations to California, had made to the inhabitants in his proclamation of July 7, 1846. The inhabitants of California were to enjoy, as we have seen, "the privilege of choosing their own magistrates and other officers for the administration of justice among themselves," and Sloat, for reasons that had now become unintelligible to his successors, had invited the "judges, alcaldes, and other civil officers to retain their offices, and to execute their functions as heretofore." Although the revolt and its suppression had made Sloat's doings now seem very ancient history, the spirit of his proclamation was still remembered by the Americans. He had not intended to come as conqueror, even to the natives themselves. Yet now the very people for whose benefit and by whose help the actual conquest had been made could not get for themselves nearly as much as he had freely offered to the natives. If the letter of his proclamation could not be executed, why might not the spirit of it be regarded? And yet, as the Americans felt, the later military governors had taken back nearly the whole of these promises of Sloat's, both in letter and in spirit. In several instances they interfered with the popular will concerning the choice of alcaldes; [26] and they claimed yet more powers than they used.

But this authority of the military government and of the alcaldes was not only arbitrary, but also, as I have suggested, somewhat vague, even in the definitions that were given to the

the *Memoirs*, Vol. I, chap. i, p. 29 *et passim*. Mason's own official records, as published in the California Documents of 1850, are historically very important.

[26] See General W. T. Sherman's *Memoirs*, Vol. I, p. 30. Also see the California Documents of 1850 (1st Sess., 31st Congr., Doc. 17), pp. 318, 321, 325, for letters of Colonel Mason bearing on this matter.

public from official sources. If Sloat's proclamation only aroused delusive hopes, Stockton, on his part, before he abandoned his position of authority, had given to these Americans a perplexing explanation of their position when he had told them that the country, as a province under military occupation in time of war, must indeed be governed by a military man, but that in the relations of the inhabitants with one another they must be governed by the "former laws and usages" of the department. Now, that position of Stockton's was obviously a perfectly sound one in theory, but unfortunately, as we have just seen, no American settlers knew or could just then find out what the former usages and laws had been. The conquerors were ignorant of Mexican law, even if that had ever been practically known or applied in the territory. Litigants, if they were natives or old inhabitants of the country, had a fashion of swearing to usages that they always interpreted in a sense wholly inconsistent with the claims of the opposing party; and the result produced in the American settler's mind, when he heard these strange "laws and usages" talked over, was a certain longing to get back once more to the law of nature, by which, as we know, the Western settler often used to mean the Constitution of the United States. Doubtless he was yet more fixed in his idea that the Constitution of the United States is the law of nature when he perceived that in some respects it was certainly very much opposed to the nature of the native Californian, whose former usages, whatever they might have been, seemed to the American settler to be the usages of a priest-ridden, downtrodden, ignorant, and altogether unnatural set of creatures, whom providence had created to be replaced by the Americans.

The discontent thus excited in the settler's breast finds expression in the discussions of the situation that are contained in the *California Star* for 1847 and 1848. I have found the old file very fascinating reading, not because it contains very deep wisdom, but because it illustrates so well the popular feeling.

The *Star* opens the conflict, in no very dignified way, with its very first number, January 9, 1847. Under its first editor, Mr. E. P. Jones, the *Star* even permitted one of its correspondents, Mr. C. E. Picket, later notorious in California, to go so far as to bring the liberty of the press into danger, by causing someone apparently Captain Hull, who was in charge at Yerba Buena, to threaten that the military government would interfere to prevent further publication unless greater prudence were shown in speaking of the condition of things. The time was in fact a rather critical one. In the south at that moment Stockton and Major Frémont were busy with the revolt, and no recent news had been received from them. General Kearny's arrival in the department was still a mere rumor at Yerba Buena. Alcalde Lieutenant Bartlett was in the hands of a party of Californians, who had captured him during his absence from the town. Mr. Hyde was acting alcalde. At such a moment as this the editor declares that everybody is already tired of being subject to the whims of an alcalde, and insists that somebody shall at once find somewhere "the written laws of the territory," which shall be enforced "without regard to the statements of A, B, or C, in relation to certain customs which probably never existed." Surely "the written laws of the country," he thinks, "can easily be obtained and published." This is the sanguine speech of an impatient man. Two years and more later General Riley found and published what he supposed to be these written laws, and then the people were nearly ready to supersede them. On January 23, 1847 the editor, again taking up his parable, expresses strong objection to the tendency of alcaldes to make laws and rules having the force of law. The alcaldes, he maintains, never had such power in the olden time and ought not to have it now. "We heard a few days since that the alcalde of Sonoma had adopted the whole volume of Missouri statutes as the law for the government of the people in his jurisdiction. If this is allowed, we will have as many legislatures in California as we have alcaldes or justices of the peace, and the country will be thrown into more confusion in a short time than ever existed in any part of the world inhabited by civilized men." But, the editor goes on, if an alcalde cannot make a code, then surely he cannot make a single law, nor yet even a rule having the force of law. His business it is to find the law of the territory and to enforce it. Surely this editorial remonstrance against the omnipotence of the alcaldes seems very reasonable. Yet it was almost vain.

But, fair as much of this criticism was, there was another side to the situation. The subsequent stages of the controversy illustrate this other side, since they naturally lead us to a very important and fateful problem, which here for the first time looms up before the new-coming Americans. One thing that already made these newcomers especially restive was the uncertainty of landownership. It is tragic to think of the handful of settlers in 1847 hoping to get pretty soon some definitive settlement of the terrible land question, which was to cost so much in blood and treasure for a generation to come; but at all events one can see how naturally an American settler's mind would turn to popular self-government as the immediate way out of the perplexities concerning land that the conquest had brought with it. It is also plain that the existence of a military government, uncomfortable as such a government then was, was the only guarantee of the native Californian population against simple spoliation on the part of the American settlers. Without treaty of guarantees, without time to impress on the American mind of the newcomers of 1845 and 1846 the nature of their native customs and of their claims, the Californian landowners would have had a poor chance in a squatter legislative assembly in California just then. That the danger was no illusion further facts shall forthwith show.

On February 27, 1847 there is an editorial article in the *Star* on the civil government: it rejoices that the government has passed into such good hands as those of Shubrick and Kearny; and it hopes that something will be done for the new settlers, in allowing them to settle at once on vacant lands, with the understanding that these shall be secured to them when the territory is ceded. One notices easily how dangerous it would have been to landed property in California to let an American settler decide what then constituted vacant land.

On March 13, 1847 a correspondent of the *Star*, signing himself "Paisano," writes to the editor a very ably stated and still a very dangerous letter on land grants, to the effect that the settlers coming in expected their tracts of land and are sorry to find such great and indefinite grants already coverning the face of the country. The indefiniteness that he describes is of the sort so well known to us since. "Those," he says, "who have recently emigrated to this country came here with the well-founded [?] expectation that under the Mexican laws they would be enabled to secure a tract of land immediately upon their arrival; but they have been disappointed; and shall I state the cause of that disappointment? Are the powers that be prepared to hear it? . . . It is simply this: The United States have acquired possession." This is a sad evil, resulting from so great a good. The remedy is, according to Paisano, "that the legislature be organized without delay, and that immediately upon their organization they proceed to the enactment of a law upon the subject. Let this law provide that every man shall be entitled to a certain quantity of government land; and let it further provide that, in order to acquire a legal right to the possession of the same, it shall be necessary for the claimant to have his lands recorded and surveyed. A law of this kind, I apprehend, would remove at once the chief cause of discontent among the people. But it will very likely be urged by those who take a more limited view of our legislative powers that they when organized, will have no authority to interfere in any manner with the disposition of the public lands; yet it will be observed that nothing more is here suggested than to give to each individual a possessory right to a certain tract of land, upon certain conditions. But this suggestion is not made because it is supposed that the legislature will lack the power to go farther, for, in my opinion, this legislature, when organized, may enact all laws which the public exigence may require."

The author of this letter I am able to identify as L. W. Hastings, a lawyer, later a member of the constitutional convention, an active man, and an emigrant leader, and prominent in emigrant affairs. Hastings is to be praised for what he earlier and later accomplished of good. But this particular scheme of his means on the face of it spoliation. This man, who "hopes," as he says about this time in an advertisement of his law office, to acquire some day soon a knowledge of the Mexican land law and its applications to Californian land, now, even while he admits that the face of the country seems covered with land grants in the very parts where men want to settle, still coolly proposes to settle the matter, not by the courts, but by the action of a legislature that would be under the control of the settlers themselves. The very grievance that he states is so stated as to show too clearly the remedy that he has in mind: Let the settlers, he says, "apply wherever they may, and to whomsoever they may, and the result is invariably the same: they are repulsed with an indignant 'This is all mine.' This all-embracing occupant, after the very expressive and exclusive declamation here alluded to, goes on to describe his unbounded premises. 'That mountain,' says he, 'on the east is the southeast corner of my farm, and that timbered country which you see in the distance is my northwest corner; the other corners of my farm are rather indefinitely marked at present, but I shall endeavor to have the ROPE applied to them also, as soon as the ALCALDE is at leisure.' " Well, if this indefinite state of affairs is the grievance — and it is plainly a grievance — what shall be thought of a man whose plan for settling the difficulty is not first of all a patient judicial examination of the traditions, usages, laws, and grants under which these claims are made, but the calling of a land-hungry legislative assembly of the intruders themselves to apply the precedents of the unoccupied Oregon wilderness to the settlement of the ancient problems of California land law? As for the facts, Mr. Hastings makes the common settlers' blunder, found also in Ide's proclamation in the spring of 1846, according to which the Mexican government had somehow guaranteed to every American settler a tract of land immediately upon his arrival. This was a very bad blunder, since in fact every foreign settler upon Mexican territory who brought with him no passport was at that time, from the moment he crossed the boundary, a violator of Mexican law and legally subject to expulsion from the territory. There had been, indeed, for years no enforcement of this law in California; but this act of grace, or of neglect, had been absurdly interpreted by the American intruders, through some curious inner transformation, as an official guarantee of land grants to all of them. Finally, as to practical judgment, Hastings's scheme is of the wildest possible character, in view of the endless litigation that such arbitrary acts of a self-constituted territorial legislature in California must ultimately have brought about. We have suffered many things of land in California; but how much more should we not have been forced to endure if Mr. Hastings's territorial legislature had begun to tear down and to build up in 1847?

Thus, then, one may see something of the other side of this question of government. To the settlers' rights must be opposed the need of patience. I have dwelt at length on this matter of Mr. Hastings's discussion of the land question because it shows the state of opinion concerning governmental needs and prospects in California at that time and helps us to trace the steps that led to the constitutional convention of 1849. The general dissatisfaction that existed among the American settlers, the reasons for this dissatisfaction, the plans that were proposed as a solution, the considerations pro and con concerning these questions of settlers' rights, are all important if one wants to understand the fine political talent that was soon to shine out so well in the actual political organization of the state.[27]

These discontents were as embarrassing to the really well-meaning military government as they were valuable in organizing the popular sentiment and in preparing the way for a state government. Mason himself was doubtless as just under such conditions as he could be. His influence was strictly conservative. He tried, for instance, to protect landowners from squatters and accepted any reasonable *prima facie* evidence of

---

[27] The *Californian* is not behind its rival in any of these complaints about the situation, although its opening numbers had given a promise of a strictly pacific editorial policy. For instance, on June 5, 1847 it complains bitterly of "military despotism"; on June 12 it expresses freely the general discontent with the United States government in view of the non-payment of the California battalion claims; on July 17 complaints are renewed of the inefficiency of the military government; and on October 27 the editor proclaims that alcalde government is far worse than direct martial law. Desires for a territorial legislature are renewed and ably defended January 5, 1848 and again in the summer of that year.

legal ownership as sufficient for his temporary purposes.[28] He could not grant what the people desired in the way of self-government, for of course he now had no authority to do more than to govern the land as a military conqueror. For since the conquest had actually involved force, the government, on hearing of the facts through the official reports, had now instructed accordingly,[29] and there was no thought of carrying out anything corresponding to the original cabinet plan about California. The land must wait until a treaty of peace before Congress could do anything for it. Meanwhile it was to be regarded as Mexican territory in our military possession. Mason's duty was thus clear.

But his position, nevertheless, was delicate. The changing instructions that were received from Washington concerning a war tariff in California did not tend to make people more content with the government, but deeply displeased both the merchants and the consumers. The force at Mason's command was furthermore limited, and the state of the country was politically disheartening: conquerors and conquered mixed confusedly together, discontent either loudly expressed or sullenly half concealed, and numberless social and legal problems demanding immediate solution — problems about solemnizing marriages, about giving divorces, about the treatment of the Indians, about the titles to town lots, about everything.[30] Mason was a good executive, but he would have been a great statesman also if he had been adequate to all this work.

Vexatious as all these things were, they were yet very val-

---

[28] See the Cal. Doc. as cited above, pp. 322, 324, and elsewhere.

[29] See Cal. Doc. cited, pp. 244–6.

[30] In Cal. Doc. as cited, p. 338, is a letter from Mason to the Adjutant General at Washington, dated September 18, 1847, narrating the discharge of the Mormon battalion and the present difficulties of Mason's position, with "but two companies of regular troops, both of which are rapidly being diminished in strength by deaths and desertions." "All other troops," he says, "must claim and will receive their discharge the moment peace with Mexico is declared." As for the problems before Mason, their variety may be judged by reading letters (loc. cit.), pp. 335, 344, 349, 355.

uable events for the future commonwealth. For the people learned something of the real problems that the new social order would have to meet, and, in thus learning, these American newcomers, so to speak, aged rapidly in their ideas and plans. By 1849, as we shall see, they had bcome strict conservatives themselves, as against the hordes of the newcomers of the great year. And their conservatism it was that made a sound constitution possible. Had there been no troubles in 1847 and 1848, there would have been much less order possible in the early years of the state government, and in 1849 there would have been no constitution made at all.

VI. *The Beginnings of the American San Francisco*

MATERIAL prosperity slowly but surely grew in the active little community in the very midst of all this political confusion. The center of the growth was already at the village of San Francisco. To the little cluster of houses that within about ten years had grown up at Yerba Buena Cove was given, early in 1847, by the consent of all concerned and by the decree of the alcalde, the name that was its proper due, the historic name of San Francisco, which the bay, the mission, the presidio, and the district had all long since borne. The immediate occasion of the change of name from Yerba Buena to San Francisco was the projection and beginning of a new town called Francesca on the northern shore of the bay, a town that its projectors, Semple and Larkin, intended to make a commercial center for this future great country of California. The Yerba Buena people were clever enough to see the possible importance of identifying in name their own town with the great bay, and the dangerous advantage of the name Francesca in comparison with their own present local name. They had the first and best right to the name San Francisco and were not slow to adopt it. They were, in fact, within the boundaries of the then legally existent pueblo of San Francisco.[31] The

---

[31] See, on the matter of the name, the *Annals of San Francisco*, pp. 178, 188; J. S. Hittell's *History of San Francisco*, pp. 110, 111. The legal existence of the pueblo at this time was, as is well known,

name of the projected Francesca was hereupon changed to Benicia.

In March 1847 General Kearny had authorized by proclamation the sale of the beach and water-lots on the east front of San Francisco, and the alcalde, then Edwin Bryant (the author of *Three Years in California*), gave notice of the sale on March 16. Kearny had, of course, no real legal authority in the matter, and the proclamation was issued, in response to the request of the people of San Francisco, chiefly in order to give the sale a show of authority.[32] The sale itself seemed to the people a necessity for the growth of their town, and the titles thus conveyed, while in later years giving rise to no small question and difficulty, were finally recognized, through both legislative and judicial action. Further sales of town lots and the new O'Farrell survey of the town streets marked yet more steps in the progress of the settlement during the summer and autumn of 1847. By the census of August 1847 there were 459 persons in the village, which still excluded from its limits the mission settlement. Of these, 51 were under five years of age, and 32 more between five and ten. Of the whole number, 138 were girls or women.[33]

The drawings of the village and of its surroundings, which are preserved to us from that early day, have no small interest to anyone who knows the present great city and suggest many comparisons, as well as many reflections on what might have been. One finds woodcuts from some of these drawings in the *Annals*. The little cluster of houses stood for the most part a short distance back from the low, curving beach of Yerba Buena Cove, a cove very early filled up by the busiest portions of the city of the gold period. Telegraph Hill loomed up close

---

not proved to the satisfaction of our courts until long afterwards; but the application of the name to the bay, presidio, mission, district, was an old story.

[32] See the *Annals*, as cited, p. 181; Hittell's *History of San Francisco*, p. 113; Cal. Documents of 1850 (as cited), pp. 291, 302, 333.

[33] *Annals*, p. 176. On the further sales of lots and O'Farrell's survey, see *Annals*, pp. 182 ff., and Hittell's *History of San Francisco*, pp. 114 ff.

above the village on the north side. Southward the distance was greater across the lowlands to Rincon Hill and to the point that in that direction bounded the cove. Going westward from the beach, one almost immediately began to ascend those steep hills over which, in the present day, the characteristic cable street-railroads of San Fransisco carry numberless passengers towards the now fine dwelling-house regions of the "western addition" beyond the hills. These steep hills, then covered with the low shrubbery of the peninsula, are now at one point' crowned by those tediously vast "palaces" of certain million-aires, which a true San Franciscan points out from the bay to the newcomer on the ferry-boats as among the most noteworthy landmarks of the place.

The peninsular region in which this village of 1847 lay was a sad and desolate one save for the glorious outlook northward and eastward, to be gained from the hills above the village, and save also for the ruggedly graceful outlines of these hills themselves. In the hills lay, in fact, a great opportunity for the possible future building of a truly stately city. They together formed several fine amphitheaters between their curving sides, they presented noble contours to the traveler approaching by the bay, and they left enough level ground at their bases to make, with the addition of land to be formed by the inevitable filling in of the cove (and, in time, of Mission Bay also), ample room for the necessities of the commercial life of the city. But otherwise the place, through all the dry season of the year, was one of the most windy, barren, and dismal spots that could well have been found in a temperate climate. Over the stately and graceful Twin Peaks, beyond the mission, the gray ocean fog, then as now, slowly crept eastward, in the chilly summer after-noons, towards the shivering town, while the sharp sand was driven by the brisk wind both along the shores and amid the gloomy low sand hills to the southwest, towards the mission, and while one could see from any hill the white-capped waves gleaming all over the great bay to the north and east. The al-most treeless peninsula at such times was a place to which anchorites might well have resorted to meditate in windy soli-tude upon the woes and sins of an accursed world, amid this

monotonous wilderness of low shrubbery, of drifting sand, and
of steep hill-slopes. Even now, with all the cheerful noise and
strife of an exceptionally active city to distract one's mind from
gloomy topics, a summer afternoon out of doors in San Francisco is a bitter penance to everyone but the most devoted of
San Franciscans. And meanwhile nearly all the fine opportunities that the hill-contours offered, to compensate by dignity of
aspect for the dreariness of the summers, have been wasted and
are now gone forever, unless indeed the city should some day
undergo a revolutionary change not only of architecture, but
also of plan. It is characteristic of the progressive American
that in most parts of the East and throughout the great West,
at least in all those regions where there are neither bluffs or
hills to be dealt with, he destroys a landscape in just so far as
he builds a city. Well-planned cities, however, would ennoble
the landscapes. At San Francisco there was but one great natural beauty in the situation of the city that the builders could
ruin. They could not ruin the wonderful outlook eastward and
northward from the hills, for that was beyond their reach; and
they could not ruin either many trees or streams at the point
where they built their city, for there were few to ruin. But they
could in large measure ruin their hill-contours and the beautifully curving amphitheaters that these bounded. This, of
course, they did, and so for all time they have defaced what
might have been the foundation for a most stately and imposing city. As one now comes to San Francisco by water, one begins to see at once what was done with the rugged dignity of
the somber hills that surrounded the old village of 1847. These
hills have been outraged and insulted with manifold cruelties:
never finished grading undertakings have uselessly torn them
in some places; in others one has given them over to dirty and
degraded little houses; and where the houses are either truly
excellent or only pretentiously grand, the perfectly straight
streets disfigure, as with long, cruel stripes, the sturdy forms of
the noble hills. For these streets pass over the hills in merci-
lessly undeviating parallel lines, and by the sides of the streets,
on the breathlessly steep ascents, the wooden houses seem to
be perpetually toppling, while they still find some mysterious

way of holding their desperate places on the slopes and of keeping still in their stiff military array. The village of 1847, from the moment it began to grow, planned an impious assault upon the hills by means of these straight streets, and the life of the town was for years a savage struggle with the landscape. Nor has the struggle ever ceased. Even now, if one walks out a little beyond the mission, one finds very much such a region as that in which the Yerba Buena village was first set down: desolate, windswept hills, with fine contours, with a magnificent outlook towards the bay, and with often beautifully outlined amphitheater valleys between adjacent hills. Into this region the southwestern part of the city is now growing, with just the same cruel prejudices about straight streets, with just the same determination to hack and hew, to bruise and to torture these hill-contours, until the city shall become in this region also what in its older parts it now inevitably seems at first sight from the bay: a planless wreck of a city instead of what those who study its map suppose it to be — namely, a very well-laid-out and well-arranged city. For the geometrical simplicity of the plan on paper means brutal confusion of aspect when applied to these hills. In the "western addition" one finds today very many beautiful features; but all the rest of the city is, as to general plan, a lost opportunity.

Such fashions of building cities are characteristic of our people everywhere. Commercial necessity, it will be said, built San Francisco and left no time for seeking beauty. But, as the ancient writer said to those who complained of the tedious preparation required in studying an art, "we ourselves make our own time short." If the San Franciscan had never wasted time or money on wholly useless mutilation of his hills, or on wholly worthless enterprises in street-grading, his spare time for improving the general aspect of his city would have been longer. And the great art of at least letting alone such portions of the land about or in a town as one does not actually need until such time as one shall be able to beautify them is an art unknown to us Americans, who can, slowly indeed, and with many mistakes and troubles, build at length one work of art, and one only — namely, a well-constituted state — and who ruthlessly deface nearly every other object that comes in our way. For the ugliness of most of our cities we bear a national responsibility. San Francisco is far better than many.

The village from which all this was to grow lived, in 1847, a life not only of considerable commercial activity and of many political anxieties, but also of much private joviality and good-fellowship. The people had their social gatherings, their balls, their dinners, and their suppers and already tasted the social freedom characteristic of California life. The 4th of July, and also the 7th, were celebrated in 1847, the second of the two anniversaries commemorating, of course, the raising of the flag. Nor were the inhabitants altogether careless about a school for their children. The subject was agitated in 1847, and a public school was actually opened in April 1848. The general commercial and agricultural development of the country was meanwhile the object of much interest at San Francisco. The energetic Sam Brannan already knew no limit to his hopes or to his plans. A number of the *Star,* prepared under his direction in March 1848 for circulation in the East, contained an article by Dr. Fourgeaud on the resources of California — an article that reads like a prophecy of what would be said many years later, after the gold excitement had passed by and when the agricultural development of the state had fairly begun.[34] The article dwells on the certainty of a great agricultural future for the territory, and naturally makes agriculture the mainstay of future prosperity, remarking meanwhile that the mineral wealth of the territory is believed to be also great. By the middle of March, 1848, the little village had a population of above eight hundred, and contained about two hundred houses.[35] And now came the great news.

---

[34] See Hittell's *History of San Francisco,* p. 97. This number of the *Star* is not infrequently to be met with now in Eastern libraries, and is in fact the only number of this paper that is at all common in collections of California material.

[35] *Annals,* p. 200.

VII. *Gold, Newcomers, and Illusions*

THAT gold had been discovered some time before the importance of the discovery was generally understood, even in California; that until April 1848 little excitement was occasioned in towns on the coast; that then the excitement about the gold rapidly grew and soon almost depopulated the villages; and that thereafter the summer of 1848 was full of a new and infinitely wondrous life, amid adventures, good fortune, and hardships — all this every reader of California annals knows without long explanation. And every such reader knows, too, the tale, so simple in its main incident, so confused, contradictory, and tangled in its details, about the first discovery of the gold. How Sutter's mill, near the later town of Coloma, was just being prepared in the wilderness for the work of sawing the wood to be brought from the mountain forests near by; how, in January 1848, Marshall, as superintendent of the work, tried to enlarge his tail-race by little successive artificial freshets of water sent down through the race; how the water washed out into sight a few gold particles along the banks of the race; and how Marshall found them and tested them — all this story is the property of every pioneer. How, furthermore, Marshall took the news to the incredulous Sutter and forced him to believe it; how the workmen at the mill came to know, in their turn, of the gold; how various efforts were made to keep the matter secret from all but a few, and how the efforts failed — these, indeed, are details about which the traditions somewhat differ, but these are things of only antiquarian interest. Marshall himself, who got such a factitious fame by the event that made him rather than another the purely accidental discoverer of that which he had taken no pains to find and which somebody must inevitably have found very soon — Marshall, poor fellow, won, besides fame, little but sorrow from the accident, and his recent death has left the numerous writers of obituary biographies with absolutely nothing to say about him save that he did succeed in picking up the gold grains and that he did prove himself thenceforth to be an utterly incapable man. For the visionary Sutter, too, the discovery was to be a calamity, although, again, largely by his own fault. But at the moment the discovery, once appreciated, seemed to all concerned as wonderful and good a thing for their personal prospects as it actually was for the fortunes of California, of the United States, and of the world. These sanguine early discoverers could not yet know that great gold mines, while they vastly benefit the world, are for the communities that possess them tremendously severe moral tests, and for by far the most of the individual miners inevitable ruin.

We are, in fact, now and henceforth to deal with a California that was to be morally and socially tried as no other American community ever has been tried, and that was to show as we Americans have not elsewhere so completely and in so narrow compass shown both the true nobility and the true weakness of our national character. All our brutal passions were here to have full sweep, and all our moral strength, all our courage, our patience, our docility, and our social skill were to contend with these our passions. Whoever wants merely a eulogistic story of the glories of the pioneer life of California must not look for it in history, and whoever is too tender-souled to see any moral beauty or significance in events that involve much foolishness, drunkenness, brutality, and lust must find his innocent interests satisfied elsewhere. But whoever knows that the struggle for the best things of man is a struggle against the basest passions of man, and that every significant historical process is full of such struggles, is ready to understand the true interest of scenes amid which civilization sometimes seemed to have lapsed into semi-barbarism. It is, of course, impossible to read this history without occasionally feeling a natural horror of the crimes that for a while were so frequent; but one's horror is itself a weakness, and must give way, for the most part, to a simple realistic delight in the jovial fortitude wherewith this new community bore the worst consequences of its own sins and, after a remarkably short time, learned to forsake the most serious of them. Early California history is not for babes nor for sentimentalists; but its manly wickedness is full of the strength that, on occasion, freely converts itself into an admirable moral heroism.

For the moment the gold excitement simply deprived the settlements outside of the gold mines of all significance. In the course of May and June nearly everybody went to the mines — from San Francisco, from Monterey, from San José, from all the settlements.[36] The military officers alone resisted the temptation to abandon present engagements for the new work of mining, and the officers themselves could to some degree satisfy their natural curiosity in a proper way by visiting the mines for official purposes. So it was when Colonel Mason, duly escorted, examined the mining region in June and July of 1848 and gathered facts for the famous letter of August 17, which, when it became known in the East, formed, with Larkin's letters to Buchanan on the same topic, the official and authentic basis for the great California gold excitement in the East during the following winter and spring.[37] The skilled miners in the territory were very few, but men happened to begin with the discovery of certain very rich placers. Men like Marshall and Sutter, or like the well-known settler Sinclair, or like John M. Murphy of San José, employed or attempted, with greater or less success, to employ Indians to do the work of gold-mining for them, and all together the individual strokes of good fortune in the summer of 1848 were very numerous. In the mines, meanwhile, were many deserting soldiers and sailors, and the executive arm of the provisional government grew daily weaker. The miners were, indeed, already declared on good authority to be trespassers, since they were mining on what the expected treaty would make United States public land; [38] and

---

[36] See the *Annals*, pp. 202 ff.; Hall's *History of San José*, pp. 190 ff.; Tuthill's *History of California*, chap. xviii; Colton's *Three Years*, chaps. xviii and xix; and General Sherman's *Memoirs*, Vol. I, pp. 40 ff., for accounts of the immediate effects of the first gold excitement. Other authorities could easily be given. The newspapers, indeed, soon fail us, for the excitement stopped both of them.

[37] See Mason's letter in the Cal. Doc. of 1850, pp. 528 ff., and the same in the beginning of Foster's *Gold Mines of California* (New York, 1849) and Larkin's letters in Foster, op. cit., pp. 17 ff.

[38] The treaty of peace between the United States and Mexico was not officially known in California before the issue of Mason's

when the treaty became known it only made the legal aspect of the matter clearer. But then, for the present, the executive was powerless to prevent this trespassing; and as to the future, the miners were destined to remain, by their own choice and by the tacit permission of our government, unmolested trespassers on the public lands until the passage of the act of 1866, authorizing the survey and sale of the mineral lands of California.

The tempting subject of the social condition and of the adventurous fortunes of the mines during that first golden summer I must here postpone. It would lead us into questions that our next chapter can best consider in their due connection with the general history of the crises of the early mining life. We are still concerned with the territory at large, and must ask ourselves first what social changes the gold-discovery brought upon the country from without, and then how the reaction led the already well-prepared men of the interregnum to insist upon leading the newcomers to submit to a state constitution. For the state, as I have already declared, was the child of the men of the interregnum; while the newcomers furnished only, on the one hand, a few professional lawyers and politicians to help in the deliberations of the convention and, on the other hand, the tacit assent of a crowd of generally careless miners, most of whom took far too little present interest in anything but a quick fortune and an early voyage home. These newcomers could have done little in the first year if the men of the interregnum had not been fully ready for the work of state-building; but, at the same time, the coming of these vast crowds forced the hand of the executive and so helped to give the men of the interregnum the popular government for which they had so long been striving.

The newcomers, by sheer force of numbers, must, however, in any case thenceforth give to the state its character. It is important for us to understand what manner of men they were and in what spirit they came. They were, in the first place, as all who describe them are never weary of telling us, a very

proclamation of August 7, 1848, announcing the fact. See the Cal. Doc., p. 590.

miscellaneous company, containing people from all parts of the world. Yet we shall never understand them if we suppose that the cosmopolitan character of the mass as a whole resulted in a truly cosmopolitan social life. The effective majority in all the chief communities was formed of Americans, and here, as everywhere else in our land, the admixture of foreigners did not prevent the community from having, on the whole, a distinctly American mode of life. The foreigners as such had, of course, no political powers, made no laws, affected the choice of no officers, and had no great tendency to alter the more serious social habits, the prejudices, or the language of Americans. The mass of the Americans in California never grew to understand the foreigners as a class, any more than we have elsewhere understood foreigners. A pioneer tradition one indeed finds, expressed in various ways, to the effect that the Americans in the mines "talked a language half-English, half-Mexican"; but this tradition must be understood to mean simply that the majority of these pioneers mispronounced a large number of Spanish proper names and several of the commoner Spanish words and phrases and were very proud of the accomplishments that they thus showed. No one who has grown up in California can be under any illusion as to the small extent to which the American character, as there exemplified, has been really altered by foreign intercourse, large as the foreign population has always remained.

The foreign influence has never been for the American community at large, in California, more than skin-deep. One has assumed a very few and unimportant native Californian ways, one has freely used or abused the few words and phrases aforesaid, one has grown well accustomed to the sight of foreigners and to business relations with them, and one's natural innocence about foreign matters has in California given place, even more frequently than elsewhere in our country, to a superficial familiarity with the appearance and the manners of numerous foreign communities. But all this in no wise renders the American life in California less distinctly native in tone. The theater, the opera, and the out-of-door amusements of the early American population were, as far as I can see, the social institutions most affected by foreign influences; and the foreign people have indeed had great effect upon these matters ever since. But that resulted, and still results, from our own naturally earnest, bare, and unæsthetic national life. An amusement is usually something external to us, something that as a nation we cannot invent and that we therefore have to accept, with little independent criticism, from foreign sources. So in early California the foreigners soon furnished not only the good music and some of the theatrical performances,[39] but also numerous bull-fights and many gambling-halls. We accepted all these delights indiscriminately and submissively and supported them very generously. In time we outgrew the bull-fights and abolished the public gambling-halls; but we have always in California remained indebted to the foreign population for much amusement of the other and higher sorts, of which, indeed, they have given us a great many really excellent experiences. An amusement, good or bad, remains, however, to the last an external addition to the average American's life, and you cannot call a community of Americans foreign in disposition merely because its amusements have a foreign look. The causes that began to work in early California, and that have now rendered the modern American California as distinct and original a community as it is, must be sought elsewhere than in the influences furnished from foreign sources.

More important, then, both for the life of the early community and for the growth of the state ever since has been the fact that the Americans present represented all parts of the Union. The native American Californian grows up today with some Northern or Southern sympathies, since his parents have taught him to have them, but usually without strong Northern or Southern animosities. If he pretends to have such, a short change of dwelling-place to a suitable community is enough to remove them. The old feelings that have ruled a warring generation east of the Rocky Mountains he cannot enter into. Much of the old bitterness amuses him, too, as he hears of it also at

[39] Although, indeed, the American theater also was better developed in San Francisco in the early years than was any other form of American amusements.

home. For many early settlers, Northern and Southern men of the old days before the war, have not forgotten in California their ancient quarrels, and they yet express their sectional feelings in many emphatic ways, although scarcely with the ardor still known in some older parts of the country. But with the young Californian these old differences, save when viewed as matters of history, are little more than mere phrases. He has seen these Northern and Southern men together all his life, and to him they are what they are, simply Californians, with various trainings and tastes and prejudices, and with numberless political and private quarrels, but very much alike notwithstanding. He may join in repeating the bitter phrases himself, but you see at once, by the mechanical glibness wherewith he uses them, how little they mean to him.

Very early, however, this relatively peaceful mingling of Americans from North and South had already deeply affected the tone of California life.There was never a thought of border warfare in the early days of California. There were no such troubles as those later in Kansas. One object of very many at first was to forget the unhappy sectional quarrels that had prevailed at home. California fell into the ranks of free states without any sort of struggle carried on upon her own soil. There were numerous plots, no doubt, for a future division of her territory and for the introduction of slavery into the southern half; but these plots related to the future. For the moment California was nonpartisan. This purely nonpartisan stage in politics was indeed brief. By 1851 the Democratic Party was well organized, and thenceforth, until the war, it ruled the state. In the days of its rule Southern politicians predominated in the state's affairs, and sectional intolerance was often enough and bitterly enough expressed. But there was still this to be noted in California: the hotter the Southern politicians grew, the greater, on the whole, seemed to wax their political influence over the Northern men. The Northern men were, however, all the time in a majority, but they submitted to the dictation of Southern politicians. They did this partly because, as Californians, they had everything to gain by avoiding bitter sectional conflicts, and partly for the simple reason that the Southern politicians were, as a class, by far the ablest politicians in the field. There was, for instance, nobody in California before the war who could cope on equal terms, as a skillful party leader, with Senator Gwin save one, David Broderick, and he was by family and training a characteristic Irish-American, not a typical Anglo-American at all. So, just because they were abler managers, the Southerners remained nearly always at the head until the war came. Then, indeed, the Northern business men of the state were far too patriotic, not to say far too clever, to be led into secession by any politicians, however, skillful, and for the entire war period they kept down all Southern influences with becomingly stern majorities; yet only to give a large place once more to these same influences from almost the outset of the reconstruction period. Since then California has been a "doubtful state" in politics.

In short, then, the North, despite all quarrels, grew from the outset nearer to the South in California than it has done elsewhere. Americans came to understand one another as Americans; and in doing so, the Northern men proved more plastic than the Southern. The type of the Northern man who has assumed Southern fashions, and not always the best Southern fashions at that, has often been observed in California life. The Northern man frequently felt commonplace, simple-minded, undignified, beside his brother from the border or from the plantation. There was an air of sometimes half-barbarous but always, in some mysterious fashion, dignified freedom about this picturesque wanderer from the Southern border, who was doubtless often able to seem of much more social significance abroad than he could have dared assume at home. The Northern man admired this wanderer's fluency in eloquent harangue, his vigor in invective, his ostentatious courage, his absolute confidence about all matters of morals, of politics, and of propriety, and his inscrutable union in his public discourse of sweet reasonableness with ferocious intolerance. The Northern man was fluent, too, but with a less sustained eloquence, with more of a certain formal mildness and good humor in his public behavior. He had great confidence in all good public speakers; he had a strong disposition to compromise public differences; he indeed could not be fooled about a matter of business by any Southerner, but both the sweet reasonableness and the ferocious intolerance overcame him in debate. He often followed the Southerner, and was frequently, in time, partly assimilated by the Southern civilization.

It is because of this intimate union of Northern and Southern men that I think early California so good a place for showing the American character as distinguished from any local character. Yet how this American character was at first shown we can understand only in case we remember the wandering and fortune-hunting spirit in which all these men alike came.

Families there indeed were among the early immigrants. One who, like myself, is a son of pioneers of 1849 is not disposed to forget the fact that there were such families. Yet the women are universally known to have been at best very few. The men, therefore, had generally left their responsibilities elsewhere. I shall have so many occasions to remind the reader of this familiar fact henceforth that I need only touch upon it here. Yet the resulting irresponsible and adventurous mood of the community can best be understood by a few references to contemporary sources.

For nearly all these men expected, of course, to go back soon to their homes, vastly wealthy. The gold fever of 1848–9 in the East, after the news reached the Atlantic, has often been described. All energetic and progressive men were apt to be affected by it. The life promised was wholly new, adventurous, golden — a fine contrast to the commonplace work of the older American communities, a perfect satisfaction to our wandering race instincts. But of course this natural excitement was not left to itself. There were people interested in increasing it by deliberate lies. The false dreams of hopeful youth were thus supplemented by forged documents, which seemed to prove the truth of golden wonders that were in fact mere inventions. I have before me, as I write, such a lying document, printed in New York, and dated 1848; a pamphlet, namely, purporting to be written by one H. I. Simpson, of Stevenson's regiment,[40] and called *Three Weeks in the Gold Mines.* I have traced to a source in an authentic letter, published first in the *Californian* at San Francisco, July 15, 1848, and reprinted in Foster's *Gold Regions of California*,[41] a part of the material used by the writer of the pamphlet, who has misunderstood his sources in such wise as to make amusing geographical and other blunders.[42] Yet his literary skill is admirable, and his lying is so circumstantial and his stolen authentic information is often, meanwhile, so elaborate and accurate that one reads him with a feeling of profound respect.

Our interest in such pamphlets is the kind of mood to which they appealed, and which they inflamed. "Simpson" describes a life of leisurely gold-gleaning. His creator knows how not to seem too extravagant, even while lying. In the course of the "three weeks" one goes in quite impossible stages from Sutter's Fort to the foot of the "Shastl" peak (evidently Mount Shasta) and returns. One walks so far, not because the gold is scarce (on the contrary, one finds it lining stream-bottoms all about), but solely because one wants to get a notion of the size of the gold region. Ten days of these "three weeks" are, however, spent by two men, with almost no implements, in picking up $50,000 of gold. During the rest of the time the yield is much more moderate, just because one is wandering, or is talking

40 According to Mr. H. H. Bancroft's Pioneer Lists, there is no such name on the rolls of Stevenson's regiment. The pamphlet was printed by Joyce & Co., of 40 Ann Street, New York, and the copy known to me is in Harvard College Library.

41 Page 27 of the book, as heretofore cited.

42 The writer of the authentic letter above cited, who had gone to the mines in May or early in June, correctly described the country passed over as then "covered with the richest verdure, intertwined with flowers of every hue." The lying pamphlet copies this expression with slight verbal variations, but incautiously makes "Simpson" apply it, in the forged letter, to the road from San Francisco to San Jose *in the latter part of August!* "Simpson" also makes (p. 6 of the pamphlet) this road to San Jose pass through the "delta" formed by the Sacramento and San Joaquin rivers, and he finds San Jose itself lying in this "delta"!

over theories about the great central gold vein, whence all this gold no doubt "streamed" or was "thrown out," in the old "volcanic" days.[43] Of course one has to work for one's gold. One does not exactly pick the lumps "off the ground," as the song *Susanna* stated the case. "Simpson's" creator is too clever to say that. The great point is that one's labor is certain to be easily and vastly and steadily rewarded, and that one's first simple guesses about where the gold is to be found prove perfectly correct. One's wandering merely verifies all predictions. One's companions are also the best of fellows. The life is perfectly happy. Why should not all one's friends come, too, and make their fortunes among these inexhaustible treasure-houses? All this tale is presented not vaguely, nor with merely stupid exaggerations. The extravagance is veiled with a skillfully false show of manly reserve and moderation. One admits that there are some varieties of fortune. One adds meanwhile to the actually absurd and mendacious tale multitudinous little facts — descriptions of landscape, of people, of geographical matters, with names and dates also freely given; and the names and the local facts are often real, and are then easily verifiable through the current authentic descriptions of California, from which they are in fact derived. So that, in fine, the pamphlet is very persuasive and plausible and is a type of the sort of thing that in those days led thousands of trusting and incapable young men to a miserable death in the wilderness or in the degraded and demoralized drinking and gambling camps of the wilder days.

Men, whether capable or incapable, who read such things were not in the mood for sober state-building and would have

---

[43] An interesting chapter could be made up of the theories, framed on the basis of the popular geology then current, that were discussed by miners in those days, in their efforts to understand the sources and disposition of the gold, theories in which "volcanoes" had a very large part. The Rev. Dr. Benton amused himself with a number of them in his very entertaining *California Pilgrim* (Sacramento, 1853), pp. 231 ff. Others one finds in various communications to the early newspapers. Men spent much time and money in disproving them before becoming satisfied.

to learn much ere they could attain that mood in the land whither they went. From that land many of them would indeed return, more or less defeated, poor and broken-spirited; many would die early deaths; the survivors would for the most part stay in the new land as hard toilers and poor men; a few only would reap great fortunes, and of these few only a part would ever again see the old home. The average net income per man throughout the whole mining community, even in the best days, was, in view of the high expenses of living, seldom more than equal to treble the wages of an unskilled day laborer at home, and was usually much less than that. The miners themselves were the least likely of all men in California to become wealthy. The high wages naturally meant, for the miners, seldom the inducement to save for their families at home, but almost always the temptation to extravagance. Meanwhile the unsteady life affected the whole community in lamentable ways. For such realities, then, the golden dreams were preparing the dreamers.

VIII. *The Ways to the New Land*

THE NEWCOMERS reached California either by water or by the emigrant trail across the continent. In the former case they generally came either by Panama (often, later, by Nicaragua), and so by the new steamers that just before the gold-discovery had begun to do mail service in the Pacific, or else around Cape Horn, and in that case by whatever good or wretched sailing-vessel could be chartered for the purpose. Steamers and sailing-vessels came for some time as overcrowded with passengers as the passengers' brains were overcrowded with illusions.[44] Especially amusing is the state of things at the moment when the first gold-hunters from the Atlantic coast had reached Panama and were there waiting for

---

[44] For the Cape Horn voyage and the illusions, well described, see Dr. Stillman's fine record, from contemporary letters, in his *Seeking the Golden Fleece* (San Francisco, 1877). Some few of the newcomers crossed central Mexico, more used the Isthmus of Tehuantepec; but these were routes of minor importance.

the first steamer, the *California,* which was to carry them to the golden land. The *California* had left for the Pacific Ocean before the gold was heard of, to go around the Horn and to begin the new mail service. She reached the South American ports just at the moment of the beginning of the gold excitement as felt there, and she made San Francisco February 28, 1849, after first stopping at Panama and then at Monterey. At Panama she had to take up all who could be crowded aboard. Yet ere she reached Panama, the people there had already had time to live through much excitement and perplexity. The steamer *Oregon,* a little later, found yet larger crowds of these unhappy ones. The climate was fatal to some and unhealthy to many more, and everyone was enraged to find such imperfect means of transportation ready on the Pacific side. Of the new life in California everybody present had also the wildest notions, and fretted at each hour of delay.[45] But meanwhile the American spirit hunted for suitable expression. After the *California* had passed, a newspaper, the *Panama Star,* was begun on the spot by the impatient watchers for further steamers. This paper was well filled with bitter complaints about the expenses of this weary life on the way, about the poor accommodations attainable at Panama, and about the deceit practiced by the steamship companies that had brought the people here.[46] In the same *Star,* meanwhile, Protestant church exercises are also announced, and accounts are given of a recent celebration of Washington's birthday with a becoming dinner, with speeches and with toasts. What the wanderers ate at this dinner does not appear; but as they say in the *Star* that nearly all the preserved meats brought from New York have been spoiled, and as they seem in general a very hungry crew, one is disposed to imagine that on Washington's birthday they dined off bananas and drank such brandy as Panama afforded.

[45] The Rev. Mr. Willey, in his excellent statement, B. MS., has vividly described the situation at Panama at this moment, and I am much indebted to his account.

[46] The *Panama Star* of February 24, 1849 is the number that I have used and that is now preserved in the Pioneer Library at San Francisco.

Their American citizenship, at all events, these sorrowing wanderers could not forget. When the *California* came, those who were already on the spot were shocked to find that she brought with her not less than seventy-five Peruvians as steerage passengers. For the Peruvians also had caught the gold-fever. Now even a Peruvian, as is unhappily obvious, so far presumes upon the fact that God made him as to take up room, a truth that one thousand American citizens, waiting for a chance to get on board a steamer that was made to hold at most, perhaps, one fourth as many men, deeply and with obvious justice resented. The reasons for their resentment were further enforced by the truly righteous reflection that these base South Americans were actually trying to go and steal gold in California — gold that plainly belonged solely to Americans. What could be done? General Persifer F. Smith, as it chanced, was waiting at Panama also, and was to go with his little escort on the *California,* to take command of our forces on the Pacific coast. He was heaven's messenger at this time to his perplexed countrymen. He could vindicate the eternal justice. To make him a better messenger of heaven just then, he had, as his letters to the government show, quite lost his head for the nonce and was at the mercy of the prayers of his furious fellow citizens. Accordingly he entered into their feelings entirely. He reflected that all the gold-miners in California were, and would for some time remain, trespassers on public lands, and that it was his solemn duty, as military commander of the Department of the Pacific, to keep them all off. He also reflected that he could not keep them all off, as they were many and his force would be small. He further reflected that if he could not keep them all off he might keep some of them off, for the benefit of the others, thus at once protecting the public lands, pleasing the favored trespassers, and keeping out the foreigners. For, as he concluded, these Peruvians, and men like them, would be somehow more genuine trespassers on the public lands than his countrymen would be. For of course trespassing is a thing of degrees and is tolerable if the trespasser is a good fellow. The foreigners, therefore, he determined to exclude, and so announced in a proclamation, whose sole immediate intent was to clear the steerage of the *California* of those insolent and space-consuming Peruvians.[47] But the latter refused to leave the ship, and Smith's worthless thunder afterwards died away before he had fairly settled to his work in California. All miners were alike trespassers, and all alike needed peace, and protection from the government, which could not possibly have excluded them if it had desired. This the general soon recognized, and he did his best thenceforth to secure good order.

The proclamation, however, called forth an eloquent letter in the *Panama Star,* from an American gold-seeker — a letter far too good to be lost. This correspondent, chafing in his enforced idleness at Panama, calls upon his future American fellow trespassers to prepare to help enforce Smith's proclamation against foreigners whenever California shall be reached. It is plain to him that the matter is one of simple right. Not, of course, that he means ill by the foreign miners.

"If foreigners come, let them till the soil and make roads, or do any other work that may suit them, and they may become prosperous; but the gold-mines were preserved by nature for Americans only, who possess noble hearts, and are willing to share with their fellow-men more than any other race of men on earth, but still they do not wish to give all. I ask of them who have left their homes, their comforts, their wives and children, and other dear relatives, if they would be willing to share all the hopes with the millions that might be shipped from the four quarters of the globe. I will answer for them and say no.

---

[47] The proclamation is to be found in the *Panama Star* as cited. The Rev. Mr. Willey gives the mentioned motive as the real one in his statement. P. F. Smith's letters to the War Department, Cal. Doc. of 1850 (as cited), pp. 704 ff., themselves further show sufficiently both the clouded state of his own judgment at the moment and the true motives for his proclamation, whose text is given here also, on p. 716. On p. 712 Smith announces his intention, March 15, now that he has actually reached California, to enforce his proclamation, but on p. 720 he acknowledges that he can do nothing. General Riley's view, a short time later, in his capacity as Governor of California, appears from p. 789, in a letter of August 30, 1849, where he shows a very sensible willingness to abandon all such foolish distinction between trespassers.

We will share our interest in the gold-mines with none but American citizens."

All this unconsciously brutal mixture of greed with mock justice would seem to us excellent fooling if we did not remember that such ideas took form later in California in the Foreign Miners' Tax Law of 1850 and in the numberless indecencies, vexatious regulations, and atrocities that marked our treatment of the foreigners in early mining days. The next chapter will teach us to give the words of such men as this correspondent a very serious meaning.

This voyage by Panama had, during all the early years, until the isthmus railroad came, its peculiar dangers and excitements. The tedious passage up the Chagres River and across the low mountains, the lazily clever natives, with their endless thieving and cheating devices, the frequently long waiting at Panama, the terrible cholera, the equally terrible Panama fever, the weariness, the heat, the degenerate life of many of the watching travelers, and then the sickly passage on the crowded steamers northward, the fogs on the California coast, the untrustworthy charts that made everybody uncertain how near shipwreck one might at any moment be, and the final joy when the Golden Gate appeared, and when one sailed through the long, narrow strait into the magnificent harbor and anchored in front of the strange new city of tents — all these things we may read in numberless narratives of the early golden days and may still hear from the lips of many pioneers.[48] The Panama voyage, however, remains in its character largely a tale of adventure, although not indeed without some very educating experiences. More important still for the social education of thousands of newcomers was, however, the seemingly monotonous life of the long voyage in crowded vessels around Cape Horn. For quarrels with incompetent or dishonest sea-captains, and quarrels among the passengers themselves, were common enough in this vast fleet of hastily chosen and often improperly manned and governed vessels. One thus learned

[48] Bayard Taylor's *Eldorado* tells of the voyage in the earliest days. Other pioneer accounts are too numerous to be catalogued here.

tedious lessons of unavoidable tolerance and of self-government; but one also grew somewhat indifferent to the forms and machinery of government as practiced on land and became disposed to think a direct appeal to the community the best form of popular administration. Furthermore, one saw much, in the various ports, of foreign peoples and customs. One reached California after long months of sailing, trained in independence, and with a comparatively wide experience of men. Some of the newcomers around the Horn have since been among California's most significant citizens.

On the plains journeyed, meanwhile, in the summer of 1849, and in a number of subsequent summers, vast crowds of weary emigrants, who faced disease, hunger, and Indians for the sake of the golden land. Their life also has been frequently described; most fully and successfully, perhaps, in the contemporary record of Delano (Old Block), himself one of them, and a man of mark later in the pioneer community.[49] As my own parents were of this great company, I have taken a natural interest in following their fortunes, and have before me a manuscript, prepared by my mother for my use, wherein, as an introduction to her own reminiscences of early days in San Francisco and elsewhere in California, she has narrated, from her diary of that time, the story of the long land journey. Her diary and recollections are not as full as Delano's, but contain many incidents very characteristic of the whole life. The route taken and the general sequence of events in the early part of the journey do not vary much in her account from the ordinary things narrated by all the emigrants of that year. There was the long ascent of the Rocky Mountains, with the cholera following the trains for a time, until the mountain air grew too pure and cool for it. A man died of cholera in my father's wagon. There were also the usual troubles in the trains on the way, among such emigrants as had started out in partnership, using a wagon in common, or providing, one a wagon, and another the oxen or mules. Such partnerships were unstable, and to dissolve them

---

[49] A. Delano: *Life on the Plains and at the Diggings*, Auburn and Buffalo, 1854. The journey across the plains is given from the author's diary.

in the wilderness would usually mean danger or serious loss to one of the partners. In settling these and other disputes, much opportunity was given to the men of emigrant trains for showing their power to preserve the peace and to govern themselves. There was also the delight at length, for my mother as for everybody, of reaching the first waters that flowed towards the Pacific Ocean. And then there was the arrival at Salt Lake, the meeting with the still well-disposed Mormons, and the busy preparation for the final stage of the great undertaking.

From Salt Lake westward my parents, with their one child, my eldest sister, then but two years old, traveled apart from any train, and with but three men as companions. Their only guide-book was now a MS. list of daily journeys and camping-places, prepared by a Mormon who had gone to California and back in 1848. This guide-book was helpful as far as the Sink of the Humboldt, but confused and worthless beyond. The result was that, after escaping, in a fashion that seemed to them almost miraculous, an openly threatened attack of hostile Indians on the Humboldt River — an attack that, in their weakness, they could not for a moment have resisted — they came to the Sink, only to miss the last good camping-place there and, by reason of their vaguely written guide-book, to find themselves lost on the Carson Desert. They erelong became convinced that they had missed their way and that they must wander back on their own trail towards the Sink. It was a terrible moment, of course, when they thus knew that their faces must be turned to the east. One was confused, almost stupefied for a while by the situation. The same fatal horror of desolation and death that had assailed the Donner party in the Truckee Pass seemed for a while about to destroy these emigrants also. They knew themselves to be among the last of the great procession. Many things had occurred to delay and to vex them. It was now already October, and there was not a moment to waste. To turn back at such a crisis seemed simply desperate. But the little water carried with them was now nearly exhausted, and their cattle were in hourly danger of falling down to die. Dazed and half senseless, the company clustered for a while about their wagon; but then a gleam of natural cheerfulness returned. "This will never do," they said, and set about the work of return. On the way they met by chance another lonesome little party of emigrants, who, with very scant supplies, were hurrying westward, in fear of the mountain snows. These could not help my father, save by giving him a few new directions for finding water and grass at the Sink and for taking the right way across the desert. As the slow wagon neared the long-sought camping-place, my mother could not wait for the tired oxen, but remembers hurrying on alone in advance over the plain, carrying her child, who had now begun to beg for water. In her weariness, her brain was filled with nothing but one familiar Bible story, which she seemed to be dreaming to the very life in clear and cruel detail. But the end of all this came, and the party rested at the little pasture-ground near the Sink.

These details I mention here, not for their personal interest, but because they are so characteristic of the life of thousands in the great summer of 1849. My mother's story goes on, however, to yet another characteristic experience of that autumn. Once supplied at the Sink, my parents, still as nearly alone as before, set out once again across the forty-mile desert, and, after more hardships and anxiety, reached the welcome banks of the Carson. But the mountains were now ahead, the snows imminent, and the sand of the Carson Valley, under the wagon-wheels, was deep and heavy. On October 12, however, they were opportunely met by two mounted men detailed from Captain Chandler's detachment of the military relief party that General Smith had sent out to meet and bring in the last of the emigration. The newcomers, riding at full speed, seemed to my mother, in her despair, like angels sent from heaven down by the steep, dark mountains that loomed up to the westward. They were, at all events, men of good mountaineering experience and of excellent spirit, and they brought two extra mules, which were at once put at my mother's own service. By the peremptory orders of these relief men, the wagon was forthwith abandoned. What could be packed on the still serviceable animals was taken, and the rest of the journey was made by the whole party mounted. They arrived safely in the mines a little before the heavy snows began.

General Smith's energy and humanity in sending out the relief, of whose work these two men were but a single detached instance, is worthy of all praise. Still more important than the relief on this Carson route was the detachment sent northward to meet the ill-starred emigrants who had chosen the Peter Lassen trail, in the hope to escape the desert west of the Humboldt Sink by passing north of it. Their numbers were, at this last moment of the season, far greater, and their suffering more immediate and desperate. As the reports [50] show, Chandler and the others on the Truckee and Carson routes relieved, indeed, many cases where the actual suffering was much greater than even the worst that my own parents underwent; yet this whole relief party dealt largely with straggling parties at the rear of a great column, while the Lassen route contained just then great numbers of people, who suffered fearfully and as a mass. Delano himself ably describes the situation on this northern route.[51]

Socially considered, the effect of the long journey across the plains was, of course, rather to discipline than to educate; yet the independent life of the small trains, with their frequent need of asserting their skill in self-government, tended to develop both the best and the worst elements of the frontier political character: namely, its facility in self-government, and its overhastiness in using the more summary devices for preserving order. As for the effect on the individual character, the journey over the plains was, at least as a discipline, very good for those who were of strong and cheerful enough disposition to recover from the inevitable despondency that must at first enter into the life of even the most saintly novice in camping. Where families were together, this happy recovery happened, of course, more quickly. One learned, meanwhile, how to face deadly dangers day by day with patience and coolness, and to strongly religious minds the psychological effect of this solitary

---

[50] Official reports of the relief expedition one finds in Ex. Doc. 52, 31st Congr., 1st Sess., p. 96 ff.

[51] Op. cit., p. 234. Delano himself got in early. Both in this year and later, many emigrants also took a southern route from Salt Lake to Los Angeles, and yet others came via Santa Fe.

struggle with the deserts was almost magical. One seemed
alone with God in the waste, and felt but the thinnest veil
separating a divine presence from the souls that often seemed
to have no conceivable human resource left. This experience
often expresses itself in language at once very homely and very
mystical. God's presence, it declares, was no longer a matter of
faith, but of direct sight. Who else was there but God in the
desert to be seen? One was going on a pilgrimage whose every
suggestion was of the familiar sacred stories. One sought a romantic and far-off golden land of promise, and one was in the
wilderness of this world, often guided only by signs from
heaven — by the stars and by the sunset. The clear blue was
almost perpetually overhead; the pure mountain winds were
about one; and again, even in the hot and parched deserts, a
mysterious power provided the few precious springs and
streams of water. Amid the jagged, broken, and barren hills,
amid the desolation of the lonely plains, amid the half-unknown
but always horrible dangers of the way, one met experiences of
precisely the sort that elsewhere we always find producing the
most enthusiastic forms of religious mysticism. And so the truly
pious among these struggling wanderers gained from the whole
life one element more of religious steadfastness for the struggle
that was yet to come, in early California, between every conservative tendency and the forces of disorder.

IX. *The Struggle for a Constitution*

THE CONSTITUTIONAL questions that the interregnum had begun so fiercely to agitate assumed a new form in the presence of all these incoming strangers. San Francisco was already
in the summer of 1849 a great town, now very largely built of
tents, and daily growing. The end of 1849 was to see more than
one hundred thousand people in the territory. Everything
must be improvised, government included. Meanwhile anarchy
seemed to be threatening. By May 1849 General Riley had
succeeded Colonel Mason as Governor, while General Smith
commanded the Department of the Pacific; but desertions to
the mines had rendered the military power almost wholly in-

effective. Very good men were disheartened at the prospect. And if the immigrants of 1846 had fiercely objected to that fragmentary pseudo-Mexican legal system of irresponsible alcaldes, what would the newcomers of the spring, summer, and fall of 1849 hold of the same system in an even more degenerate form? Who should govern these crowds? Themselves? But then the whole theory that the United States government still held would have to be abandoned. Or should the United States Military Governor remain as before at the head of affairs? But his authority was now called in question on new grounds, and with very great plausibility, since the treaty of peace. And if he had authority, where were the soldiers to be found in sufficient force to maintain it? The social condition, then, seemed to call urgently for immediate action.

For now, just as this new social condition was establishing itself, the feeling began to grow very strong that the political situation of the country was, since the treaty of peace, a wholly new one. And here begins one of the strangest periods in California political history. What was the actual legal status of the territory of California after the treaty of peace? Congress, as we know, never passed any law for the formation of a California territorial government, and so the anomalous condition, whatever it was, continued to exist down to the time of the admission of the state of California into the Union. Now, two great and conflicting theories of the status of California were commonly held at that time. These two came into open opposition in the beginning of 1849. The one was the settlers' theory, which with full confidence regarded California as in a condition analogous to that of the territory of Oregon. This theory was the same in purport as the previous settlers' theory that had been maintained in the *Star* of 1847, but it was now urged on much more plausible grounds. The treaty of peace, it was said, had deprived the Military Governor of his legal powers. He was merely a usurper. California was a part of United States territory. In the absence of congressional action the people had a right to meet and to legislate at their pleasure. This right they derived from the nature of man and from the Constitution of the United States. The former has guaranteed to man the right to govern himself according to the principles of justice. The latter, the Constitution of the United States, as was asserted, guaranteed to the inhabitants of America a republican, and not a military, government, at least in time of peace. Had Congress furnished to the people a territorial government, the people would be bound to accept the same. But in the absence of such action the popular will, putting itself under the sole restraint of the Constitution, must reign supreme. This theory, as we see, was not without its vagueness. Exactly how the Constitution of the United States could be interpreted as including this form of the doctrine of popular sovereignty is not clear to me, nor was it made clear in the discussions of that period. The Constitution had never contemplated exactly the case of this conquered California. The very appeal to the law of nature showed a certain lack of clearness in the settler's mind about the state of the law in the statute-books. Yet the settler's instinct was a sound one, however imperfect his theory. The time was in fact nearly ripe for an expression of the popular will. The settlers of 1845 and 1846 had changed their restlessness for conservatism in the presence of the newcomers. The treaty of peace had taken the land question out of the power of local legislatures; and an additional residence of two years in the country had made the immigrants of 1846, the land-hungry men of 1847, comparatively sedate old inhabitants. They felt themselves in a sense the true Californians. They regarded the forty-niners with a certain conservative dread. They had in very many cases come to own land themselves, by purchase from the claimants under Mexican grants. They were now in most cases, when compared with the forty-niners, no longer revolutionary agitators, but sober American advocates of the older order of things, and opponents of the spoliation that they had before threatened. Therefore the squatter legislature of the Hastings plan was already a less imminent danger, although Americans had by no means sincerely determined as yet to recognize the just claims of all native Californians. Meanwhile, if the danger of violent and wholly one-sided legislation was already less, the danger of violent and wholly confused popular movements in default of legislation grew daily greater. And no way seemed open, even in the autumn of 1848, much more in the spring and summer of 1849, save to call upon the American political instinct to express itself in the form of an organized government.

But the chief opposing view of California's legal status has to be mentioned. That is the view maintained by Mason and then by General Riley, the last territorial Governor of California. Riley's view was of course in accord with his instructions. It is well known, and shall be stated in Riley's own words:

"The laws of California, not inconsistent with the laws, constitution, and treaties of the United States, are still in force, and must continue in force till changed by competent authority. Whatever may be thought of the right of the people to temporarily replace the officers of the existing government by others appointed by a provisional territorial legislature, there can be no question that the existing laws of the country must continue in force till replaced by others made and enacted by competent power. That power, by the treaty of peace, as well as from the nature of the case, is vested in Congress. The situation of California in this respect is very different from that of Oregon. The latter was without laws, while the former has a system of laws, which, though somewhat defective, and requiring many changes and amendments, must continue in force till repealed by competent legislative power. The situation of California is almost identical with that of Louisiana, and the decisions of the Supreme Court in recognizing the validity of the laws which existed in that country previous to its annexation to the United States, were not inconsistent with the constitution and laws of the United States, or repealed by legitimate legislative enactments, furnish us a clear and safe guide in our present situation. It is important that citizens should understand this fact, so as not to endanger their property and involve themselves in useless and expensive litigation, by giving countenance to persons claiming authority which is not given them by law, and by putting faith in laws which can never be recognized by legitimate courts."

That is, as one sees, according to Riley's view, Stockton's

proclamation concerning the "former laws and usages" remained as valid a statement of the situation of California after the treaty of peace as it had been before the treaty of peace. In consequence the chief military officer present is still governor of the territory, only now he is civil, and not military, governor.[52]

That Riley's view, although probably legally the correct view, was not indubitable, even from the point of view of the government itself, appears from two curious facts. The first is that the government, while it thus instructed Riley as to his legal position, held and expressed another and an opposing view of the nature of his powers. The second is that Riley himself, when the constitutional convention had once finished its work, simply abandoned his position, by giving up to the authorities that the people elected this power and responsibility which he had affirmed to be legally his own. For nothing is clearer than that an officer legally responsible for the government of a territory cannot consistently abandon his post unless an equally legal authority is ready to succeed him.

As to the first point, the alternative theory that the administration held appears in two documents. One is the President's message to Congress in December 1848, which declares that "upon the exchange of ratifications of the treaty of peace with Mexico on the 30th of May last, the temporary governments which had been established over New Mexico and California

---

[52] Riley's view is well summed up in Burnett's *Reminiscences of an Old Pioneer* (New York, 1880), p. 329. Burnett's account of this whole controversy is one of the best extant, outside of the official record as preserved in the Cal. Docs. of 1850, and apart from the contemporary numbers of the *Alta California*. Burnett himself represented the settler's view. Riley's own statement of the case, as quoted above, is to be found in the Cal. Docs. of 1850 (as cited), p. 777. A clear statement of the settler's view is further to be found in the speech of C. T. Botts, in the *Debates of the Constitutional Convention of California,* p. 11. As to the technical merits of the case, ably disputed as it was, I have no authority of my own to decide, but I am advised by good authority that Riley's position, in so far as he consistently held to it, was no doubt legally sounder than the opposing views.

by our military and naval commanders, by virtue of the rights of war, ceased to derive any obligatory force from that source of authority; and having been ceded to the United States, all government and control over them under the authority of Mexico had ceased to exist. Impressed with the *necessity* of establishing territorial governments over them, I recommended the subject to the favorable consideration of Congress in my message communicating the ratification of peace, on the 6th of July last, and invoked their action at that session. Congress adjourned without making any provision for their government. The inhabitants, by the transfer of their country, had become entitled to the benefits of our laws and constitution, *and yet were left without any regularly organized government.* Since that time, the very limited power possessed by the executive has been exercised to preserve and protect them from the inevitable consequences of a state of anarchy. *The only government which remained* was that established by the military authority during the war. *Regarding this to be a de facto government, and that by the presumed consent of the inhabitants it might be continued temporarily,* they *were advised* to conform and submit to it for the short intervening period before Congress would again assemble and could legislate on the subject. The views entertained by the executive on this point are contained in a communication of the secretary of state, dated the 7th of October last, which was forwarded for publication to California and New Mexico, a copy of which is herewith transmitted." The letter of Buchanan, Secretary of State, to which reference is made in these last words, expresses this view as follows:

"In the mean time, the condition of the people of California is anomalous, and will require on their part the exercise of great prudence and discretion. By the conclusion of the treaty of peace, the military government which was established over them under the laws of war, as recognized by the practice of civilized nations, has ceased to derive its authority from this source of power. But is there, for this reason, no government in California? Are life, liberty, and property under the protection of no existing authorities? This would be a singular phenomenon in the face of the world, and especially among American citizens, distinguished as they are above all other people for their law-abiding character. Fortunately they are not reduced to this sad condition. The termination of the war left an existing government — a government *de facto* — in full operation; and this will continue, with the *presumed consent* of the people, until Congress shall provide for them a territorial government. *The great law of necessity justifies this conclusion. The consent of the people is irresistibly inferred from the fact that no civilized community could possibly desire to abrogate an existing government, when the alternative presented would be to place themselves in a state of anarchy,* beyond the protection of all laws, and reduce them to the unhappy necessity of submitting to the dominion of the strongest."

As to the second point, if Riley's theory, held in accordance with his instructions, was the correct one, then the people of California not only were unable to form a popular government without his consent, but had no right, even with his consent, to begin their own state government before Congress should have admitted the state. Governor Riley, as chief executive, could indeed call a convention, but, from his own point of view, he could not authorize the actual formation of a sovereign state, nor properly recognize it in advance of a congressional recognition. Yet just this he did, surrendering his powers to the new state government months before the admission of the state. There was, then, simply no consistently held theory concerning the legal status of California at this critical moment.

Yet the problem involved was in the spring and summer of 1849 no mere question of theory, but an intensely practical one, which threatened quickly to become very serious indeed. Here were the people, with the Oregon tradition in their minds, anxious for self-government and loudly asserting a right of which they could give no very definite theoretical or legal account. Here was Riley, with one form of the administration doctrine in his mouth, hopefully transcribing, translating, and publishing the supposed "laws in force." Here was the President ordering through the Secretary of War that Riley should take this plan of explaining the law to the people of California, and himself meanwhile making through the Secretary of State a wholly different and inconsistent explanation of General Riley's powers, an explanation whereby the government of California is denied to be a discoverable actuality, is treated as a mere presumption, and is based upon the notion that California, being between the devil and the deep sea, must get out by the one road that providence has kindly opened: namely, the military government. Thus the settler talks of the law of nature, General Riley of Mexican law, Secretary Buchanan of the "presumed consent," whatever that may be; and meanwhile California society is looking the devils of anarchy in the face and is bravely trying to help itself. It was in those days that James King of William, as he later wrote in the *Bulletin*, heard people at Sutter's Fort talking over the situation, and speculative wanderers discussing in leisure moments before the campfires whether murder could fairly be called a crime any more in California, since there was now no law.

We have had in the foregoing to speak of the American settler's bigotry in the presence of un-American institutions, and of his injustice to the conquered population. When on the contrary one turns to his political skill as it showed itself in this crisis, one has, as we are all aware, nothing but praise. In fact, the instinctive political skill shown throughout this early history is the one thing in early California affairs of which we can certainly feel quite justly proud. Nearly all else in the early history of California after the country was in American hands is more or less under a cloud, save, indeed, so much as fortune chose to make romantic and charming. We shall see hereafter how little the political skill itself was able to cope with the moral dangers of the early days, and how only after years of toil men learned to supplement their instinctive cleverness in state-making with the necessary devotion to the more commonplace duties of citizenship. But viewed simply as cleverness, this quality, as it now shows itself, is wholly admirable.

The summer of 1849 was full of abortive lesser attempts at planning the ways and means of self-government; most of these attempts seem not to have got beyond the limits of private conversation. Some people freely talked about the Bear

Flag and a Pacific republic. Others insisted that perfect loyalty to the government at Washington was consistent with the firmest determination to resist all unconstitutional military government here. Riley repeated, in every possible official way, that his government was not military, but civil and legal, a necessary continuation in the present of the old Mexican form of administration. Congress, meanwhile, was of no service, and adjourned in 1849, as it had adjourned the year before, without having done more for this new land than to extend customs regulations over California and to establish a few post-offices and mail-routes. Why Congress thus hesitated is a matter of well-known national history. The interests of California had to be postponed while Congress wrangled over the position of slavery in the new territories. Had the Southern party more promptly undertaken to compromise matters, it might have been able to gain more for itself. The long delay ended in the total and inevitable loss of California to the slave-power.

As we shall hereafter see, all this political confusion was at the moment consistent with the prevalence of temporary good order. The summer of 1849 was a cheerful and a socially peaceful one throughout the mining and commercial region. The southern part of the territory, where the native Californians lived, was indeed already showing signs of the general demoralization that we were in time to inflict upon it. Its trade, such as there had been, languished, its people were unwelcome in the mines and unhappy at home. They had also a natural and well-founded dread as to the future of their property and were suspicious of us, as well as sometimes actively hostile. But elsewhere the life was busy and hopeful, although carelessness, dissipation, and absurdly great expectations were preparing the way for a possible future anarchy. The state organization was needed none the less in view of this present temporary social prosperity of the country. For there were dark days ahead.

As for more organized efforts at self-government: such were the abortive legislative assembly of San Francisco and similar attempts in Sonoma and in Sacramento.[53] Such were also the

---

[53] See the *Alta* for March 1, 1849 for reports from Sacramento

meetings associated with these efforts, wherein delegates were elected to meet in a constitutional convention at San Jose, without any authority from Governor Riley. But all such attempts not only were failures in themselves, but were superseded by Riley's own proclamation, issued June 3, 1849,[54] announcing, in accordance with his instructions, that as Congress had adjourned without providing "a new government for this country to replace that which existed on the annexation of California to the United States," it had become "our imperative duty to take some active means to provide for the existing wants of the country"; and calling upon the people to elect a convention to form a state constitution. In the meanwhile Riley ordered elections under the "former usages" of judges of superior jurisdiction, and of other necessary officers, to hold office until the state government should be completed and ready for its work. And he caused to be published what he regarded as the Mexican laws of the territory still in force.[55]

With hesitation and after much murmuring the people accepted Riley's call, waived their theoretical objection that he, as usurper, had no right to make the call, and elected their delegates to the convention. And thus the vexed question as to the

and Sonoma of meetings to organize district governments. For the San Francisco meetings and undertakings, see the *Annals*, pp. 208, 218, 220, and pp. 221 ff. For the general situation and an account of these movements, see also Burnett (loc. cit.). Tuthill, in chap. xx of his *History*, gives a somewhat detailed account of the matter as discussed in Congress. See also Cal. Docs., pp. 773 f.

[54] Cal. Docs., pp. 776 ff.

[55] As to the details of this action, Riley was guided by the advice of his secretary of state, the able and laborious Captain (in later years General) H. W. Halleck. Halleck's labors in preparing the way for the convention, and in the convention itself, have been well recognized and set forth by the Rev. Mr. Willey, in his interesting article in the *Overland Monthly* for July 1872, entitled "Recollections of General Halleck."

For the laws published by Riley, and for the official summary of the whole affair, as presented to Congress by the senators and representatives of California when they first went to Washington, see the volume of the *Debates of the Convention*, Appendix.

legal rights of the people of California was solved by a very illogical and yet very sensible compromise, which was made according to no theoretical principle whatsoever. The popular-sovereignty sentiment of the Oregon tradition became untrue to itself, and its upholders illogically submitted to General Riley's authority so far as to go into the convention that he called and authorized and to vote under such conditions as he ordained. General Riley, for his part, very illogically sacrificed the claim that he was the legal ruler of California and that he was subject only to the administration and to congressional legislation, by calling a convention of the people and by resigning his powers so soon as the people had elected their own officers, and long before the admission of the state by Congress. As for Buchanan's beautiful little theory about the "presumed consent" of the people of California as the source of Riley's authority, that theory was soon utterly forgotten. And so here in California was repeated that ancient proceeding of compromise in place of adherence to abstract principle which has been all along so characteristic of the Alglo-Saxon in his political life. When one sees how the ponderous machinery of the Constitution was soon afterwards in order and lightly running, notwithstanding all this wearisome preliminary wrangling among the master-workmen about plans and doctrines, one is strongly reminded of a certain grandly simple expression of the spirit of English and in fact of all Anglo-Saxon constitutional history, an expression contained in the most profound and familiar of nursery tales: namely, in the one in which there is first a seemingly hopeless difference of opinion among the characters about certain great questions of principle, so that a time of tragic uncertainty follows, until of a sudden, a compromise being happily suggested, the mouse begins to gnaw the rope, the rope to hang the butcher, and so all else to go well. This tale is a figure of the workings of Anglo-Saxon government.

X. *The Constitutional Convention and Its Outcome*

So the convention assembled at Monterey, finding no quorum September 1, 1849, but beginning its organization September 3. This first business was rather slowly accomplished, three days being consumed in purely preliminary work, and yet more time being lost subsequently in subsidiary matters, before very much was accomplished. The convention had of course great difficulties concerning printing and engrossment. Other physical difficulties are hardly worth dwelling on here. The members of the convention nearly all brought with them their blankets to Monterey; like the foxes and the birds they had to look for holes and nests, and like the foxes and birds they finally found where to bestow themselves. They speak highly of the hospitality of the little town. Larkin invited one member to lunch and one to dinner every day, and it is to be presumed that at least that member got in each case a good meal. The rest exhibited no small patience, on the whole, although occasionally the records of the votes show many absentees.

Bayard Taylor in his *Eldorado* describes the whole body with great interest and delight. Their own table of ages, etc., is the basis upon which I have constructed the following statistical analysis of the social and political character of the convention, which I give in a form quite different from theirs (cf. *Debates*, p. 478).

To understand the work of the convention, one must remember the conflicting forces present, as indicated by this table and by the debates. A strong center (if one may transfer to the body a foreign phrase) was made up of the Americans of the interregnum. They had various personal peculiarities and occasionally aired their private views at excessive length; nor were they men of any great likeness of training. But they had in common a lively interest in a permanent and strong government in California; they all had a concern in California that was prior in origin to the gold-discovery and that seemed apt to outlast any immediate good fortunes or reverses that might come to them in consequence of this discovery. They were fearful of the new-coming population, in case it were not soon restrained by fixed laws. And they were indisposed to permit the sectional interests of older states to interfere with the present destiny of California. What one may call an extreme right was meanwhile composed of the old Californians, among whom must be in-

NATIVITY			RESIDENCE		OCCUPATION				AGE			
			Resident in California for more than one year	Resident in California for one year or less	Merchants	Farmers	Lawyers	All other professions	Under 30 years	30 or more, but under 40	40 or more, but under 50	50 or over
22	New York.....		11	8	3	2	2	4	3	2	8	–	1
	Pennsylvania & New Jersey..		2	2	–	–	–	1	1	–	2	–	–
	New England...		6	5	1	2	2	2	–	2	2	1	1
	Ohio..........		3	1	2	1	–	1	1	–	3	–	–
14	Missouri.......		1	1	–	–	–	1	–	1	–	–	–
	Kentucky......		3	1	2	–	1	1	1	1	–	2	–
	Virginia........		3	3	–	–	1	1	1	–	1	1	1
	Maryland......		5	2	3	2	–	2	1	1	–	1	–
	Florida........		1	–	1	–	–	–	1	1	–	–	–
	Tennessee......		1	–	1	–	1	–	–	–	–	1	–
California..........			7	7	–	–	2	–	5	–	2	4	1
Foreign lands.......			5	5	–	1	2	1	1	1	2	2	–
Totals.........			48	35	13	8	11	14	15	9	23	12	4

cluded some of the older foreign residents. These men came to the convention as strict conservatives, loving the old order of things, wholly opposed to the formation of any state government, preferring a territorial organization, and anxious for a political separation of their own section from the northern half of the territory. When they discovered their original plans to be impracticable, they were for the time at sea, until they found a new and unexpected, although somewhat covert and certainly very insincere ally.

This was in the extreme left, as, keeping up the form already used, we may call the small but very ably led section of extreme Southerners. These men, of whom B. F. Moore of Florida was the one most unpleasantly noticeable, and among whom Jones of Louisiana (by birth a Kentuckian) was also noteworthy, were led by the most interesting politician in the convention, the since famous, and recently deceased, W. M. Gwin. Their undoubted object was, not so much to give over any part of California at once to slavery, since this hurrying life of the gold-seekers wholly forbade any present consideration of such a plan, but to prepare the way for a future overthrow of the now paramount Northern influence in the territory and so to make possible an ultimate division of the state, in case the southern part should prove to be adapted to slave life.

The very existence of this plan has been frequently denied, but one who reads the debates can have little doubt of it. The interest of the discussions lies largely in the marvelous skill with which Gwin, although unable to carry his point, still in minor matters directed the course of the proceedings and gradually gathered about himself such a following that, although he was baffled in his immediate objects, he at all events made himself a power in the convention and assured for himself a prominent position in the future political life of the state. No other man in the convention approaches him in impressiveness and in skill, as shown in these debates. A monograph on the convention long enough to give the time for unraveling the intricate skein of the debates would read in large part like a chapter from the political biography of one who intellectually was the most admirable of all the unprincipled political intriguers in the history of California.

Of Gwin himself much has been written, although not with reference to his work in the convention. Mr. O'Meara's generally admirable monograph on *Broderick and Gwin* (San Francisco, 1881) has discussed the later political life of the great schemer during the period of his struggle with his picturesque, heroic, and almost equally unprincipled foe, that remarkable representative of the Irish-American political character David Broderick. The Civil War proved to be Gwin's political grave. His public life in the South and in Mexico was thenceforth a failure, and his recent death has closed a long period of inactivity. Gwin had before 1849 already been in the House of Representatives at Washington. In California he appeared in 1849, just in time to take part in the trial of the "Hounds" in San Francisco.[56] This event brought him into public notice. He had come to the territory with the avowed determination to be a senator from the new state. He was glad, therefore, to find himself a man of mark forthwith and took advantage of the fact to get himself at once elected to the convention. To Monterey he went, armed with copies of a printed constitution: namely, that of the state of Iowa, in which he intended to make some amendments, but which he plainly regarded as an instrument that would give him especial authority in the convention. For this body, as he knew, would be without printing-press.[57] He also intended, as the survivors of the convention say, to get himself elected president of the convention. But the men of the interregnum chose Semple instead, whose eloquence was thereby a trifle checked.[58] Gwin was undaunted. In the "Committee on the plan of a constitution," he took a prominent part and in the early debates was already noteworthy, always seeming conciliatory, thoughtful, learned, and reasonable. He above all avoided directly broaching sectional topics, or matters that could arouse jealousy between classes of the people. When McCarver, who represented the Oregon tradition, with its hatred of a free Negro population, proposed in committee of the whole to supplement the clause forbidding Negro slavery in California (a clause that had already been *unanimously* adopted in committee *without debate*) by another

---

[56] Of the "Hounds" we shall hear a little hereafter, in another connection.

[57] See his own account, *Debates*, p. 24. Also Mr. E. O. Crosby's statement, B. MS., a most valuable sketch of the convention by a surviving member.

[58] *Debates*, p. 18. As Semple took the chair, he made a "few remarks," saying among other things: "The eyes of all Europe are now directed toward California." With this proud consciousness he sat down and no doubt looked every inch a president. He made in fact a very good one.

clause excluding from the state free Negroes, Gwin let the men
of the interregnum talk this matter over at their leisure, but
himself said nothing. The clause of McCarver passed in committee, but only to be overthrown later in the house, and by a
vote that, so far as it was not composed of the men of the interregnum, would seem to have been organized almost altogether outside of the proceedings of the convention, and that
remained to the end comparatively silent on this matter. Gwin
was in this silent majority.

But the true purposes of the master began to appear when
the great topic of the boundary of the future state came up. Here
was a chance for him both to join together the two extreme
wings of the convention, by conciliating the Californians, who,
so far, had suspected him, and to prevent the Northern party
from acquiring too great a control on the coast. Wholly fatal to
the plans of Gwin's party it would have been either to attempt
to introduce slavery into the constitution directly, or to have
proposed an immediate division of the southern territory from
the northern half. The newcomers, even in case they were
themselves violent Southerners, had, in general, no desire to
see slavery introduced for the present into the unsettled gold-
mining community. And the men of the interregnum were altogether opposed to any thought of a division of the inhabited
territory, in whose conquest they had taken part. Any effort,
under these circumstances, to affect the course of events by
direct means would have been fatal to Gwin's political aspirations, as well as to the cause that he no doubt had at heart. One
thing, however, remained. The Northern party might be prevented from carrying out the very natural plan of limiting the
boundaries of the state to the inhabited portions of the territory and to the Sierra region. The vast unknown country beyond, extending to the Rocky Mountains — this the men of the
interregnum were inclined to cut off once for all, although in
theory it belonged to California. If they succeeded in this purpose, however, then a compact state would be formed, having
a certain geographical unity, and perhaps resisting further
efforts to divide it. It would have the whole frontage on the
ocean, it would be a free state, and it would be a strong state,

rendering the unknown territory eastward almost certainly
worthless to the Southern party in the future. Might not all this
be prevented? Might not one insist for the moment upon keeping the territorial boundaries of California intact? Might not
one thus insist on going to Congress with a state covering this
whole vast region (wherein are now Nevada and Utah and a
large part of Arizona)? Might not one consequently secure
under any circumstances an important advantage to the Southern party? For, first, if, as was possible, Congress should refuse
to admit the whole of this great state and should determine to
divide it into a northern and a southern half, the desired result
would forthwith be secured. But one need not rely upon that.[59]
Far more important for the interests of the Southern party would
be the certainty that this great state, if it was once admitted,
would, in time, fall to pieces; and the equally manifest certainty
that, in this falling to pieces, a division of the state that would
cut part of it off from the ocean would be sure to be deemed
unjust. For, in view of these considerations, such a division
of the overgrown state would take place as would give the
Southern party their fair chance to introduce slavery into the
southern half of California, in case such introduction should
ever be found profitable.[60]

---

[59] And Gwin did not rely upon it, as he actually accepted Halleck's proviso, which proposed to permit the state legislature to accept from Congress a limitation of boundary on the east, but declined to empower the legislature to accept a division into northern
and southern halves. Yet Gwin must have known that to carry to
Congress a very large state might very easily lead to an ultimate division of the same, before admission, into a northern and a southern
half. For if Congress refused to admit the state until such division
were made, the people would be apt, in the end, to submit; and the
bigger the territory included, the more probable would be such a
refusal.

[60] For remarks of Gwin, showing that he had this plan in mind,
see *Debates*, p. 169. "If we include boundary enough for several
States, it is competent for the people and the State of California to
divide it hereafter." And, p. 196: "I have not the remotest idea that
the Congress of the United States would give us this great extent of
boundary if it was expected that it should remain one State. And

The native Californian members, however, were evidently approachable upon this matter. As people interested in the old order of things, they were glad to vote for the whole of old California as a state so long as their own much desired separation of their section from the rest could not be carried out. So they willingly joined in rejecting any new limitation of the old boundary to the eastward. Moreover, they could easily be brought to understand their own advantage. This present lavish offer of the one great state to the Union meant, as they well knew, a good chance of more future freedom to themselves, through the division of the state, and the formation of a little state or territory for their own benefit. Gwin and Jones very cleverly appeased them further by together introducing a taxation article that was supposed to promise to work in their interest. The Californians were thus captured, and readily voted for Gwin's proposition. How much Gwin really loved them, the Land Act of 1851 and Gwin's infamous supplementary land bill of 1852 will sufficiently show us.

Oddly enough, however, the Gwin plan received some cooperation in the convention from the least expected quarter: namely, from Riley's secretary, Halleck, and from the other ad-

---

when gentlemen say that they never will give up one inch of the Pacific coast, they say what they cannot carry out. So far as I am concerned, I should like to see six States fronting on the Pacific in California. I want the additional power in the Congress of the United States of twelve senators instead of four; for it is notorious, sir, that the State of Delaware, smaller than our smallest district, has as much power in the Senate as the great State of New York. It is not the passage of a bill through the House of Representatives that makes a law; that bill has to go through the Senate, and in that body the State of Delaware has as much power as the State of New York. And the past history of our country, sir, develops the fact that we will have State upon State here, — probably as many as on the Atlantic side, — and as we accumulate States we accumulate strength; our institutions become more powerful to do good and not to do evil. I have no doubt that the time will come when we will have twenty States this side of the Rocky Mountains. I want the power, sir, and the population. When the population comes, they will require that this State shall be divided."

ministration agents in California, whose influence in the convention was decided, although their votes were few. Their purpose, indeed, was not Gwin's; and it was a very odd one. Thomas Butler King, a direct representative of the administration, who had come to California on a tour of observation, to make a report on the condition and resources of California, a report that was later printed, and who, meanwhile, expressed in private the President's views on topics connected with the convention, had said to some of the members — to Semple among the rest: "For God's sake, leave us no territory to legislate upon in Congress!" That is, as he meant to be understood, "relieve us from the need of further discussion about slavery in the territories by presenting to us a complete California, ready for admission, extending to the Rocky Mountains, and excluding from its boundaries slavery." The ostrich-like innocence of this plan of the Whig administration of Taylor — which had sent out poor Butler King to wander about in a land that he never understood and to express views that never helped anybody — is plain enough. But votes were votes, and Gwin rejoiced in an alliance with Halleck — an alliance that, once for all, seemed to prove to the Northern public in California, whose votes, also, Gwin, as senatorial candidate, might one day need, that Gwin himself had never intrigued on behalf of slavery. For here was a Whig administration, in its imbecility, instructing its agents to do just what Gwin himself had planned.

The plan, then, seemed sure to succeed, and twice it secured a majority of votes, after long debate — once in committee, once in the house. But it failed at last, through the praiseworthy firmness of the men of the interregnum, who, driven to the wall, finally made clear that they were ready to break up the convention rather than to submit to what they regarded as a permanently mischievous act. C. T. Botts, himself a Virginian, but always, in this convention, disposed to go with the typical men of the interregnum (men such as Hastings, Semple, Brown, McCarver,[61] McDougal, Price, Snyder, and the rest), was a

[61] McCarver, an Oregon man, belongs in the list, although he had been in California but a year. For the scene in convention at the crisis of the struggle, see *Debates*, p. 440.

leader in this firm opposition. The result was that a spirit of compromise was once more developed, and Gwin's plan had to be given up in favor of the present boundary of California. But the effort, although it failed, was an important one. It first showed Gwin's skill. He had brought over to his side the Californian representatives, who had at the outset suspected him and whom he himself so little loved that he was quite capable, as events showed, of undertaking to despoil them, in legal fashion, of their lands.

The boundary question sufficiently showed the character of the forces at work in the convention. Nevertheless the body was, notwithstanding its inner hostilities, a comparatively able and patriotic group of men, and in questions not directly involving sectional problems it devoted itself with earnestness to its great task. Cruder political notions appeared but little in its deliberations, and when they appeared, instinct quietly ignored what spoken argument would often have found it hard to refute in any such way as to convert the advocates of the political errors involved. The results were thus generally wise. In general character the constitution adopted followed that of the state of New York. A noteworthy feature was the prohibition of any and all charters to authorize banks of issue, a provision ardently insisted upon by nearly all the members. As is well known, and as has before been said, the clause prohibiting slavery passed the convention by a unanimous vote.

The convention over, the constitution was submitted by its makers to the people, who languidly adopted it by a very small but nearly unanimous vote, November 13, 1849, and elected the first state officers. Riley at once gave up his office to the new Governor, Burnett, although the state was not admitted by a wrangling Congress until September 9, 1850. Thus began the life of a constitutional government that was to continue for thirty years without radical change of its organic law. The change, when it came, was for the worse.

Chapter IV

THE STRUGGLE FOR ORDER: SELF-GOVERN-
MENT, GOOD HUMOR, AND VIOLENCE
IN THE MINES

THE STATE, then, was triumphantly created out of the very midst of the troubles of the interregnum and in the excitements of the first golden days. But the busy scenes of early California life give us, as we follow their events, little time for quiet enjoyment of the results of even the best social undertakings. The proclamation of the sovereign state itself is only as the sound of a trumpet, signaling the beginning of the real social battle. Anarchy is a thing of degrees, and its lesser degrees often coexist even with the constitutions that are well conceived and popular. The California pioneers had now to deal with forces, both within themselves and in the world beyond, that produced an exciting and not bloodless struggle for order, some of whose events, as they took place in the mines, in the interior cities, in the course of the state politics, and in San Francisco, I must try to describe, selecting what will best illustrate the problems of the time from the great mass of occurrences and returning, where it is necessary, to the relation of some events that were antecedent to those last described. Of the romantic and heroic I shall have something to tell as we go on; but much of our story will concern matters that only the sternest and least romantic realism can properly represent.

I. *The Philosophy of California History during the Golden Days*

Two very familiar errors exist concerning the California of the years between 1848 and 1856, both misconceptions of the era of the struggle for order. One of these errors will have it that, on the whole, there was no struggle; while the other affirms that, on the whole, there was no order. In fact there were both, and their union is incomprehensible, save as a historical progress from lower to higher social conditions. Both the

214

mentioned errors find support, not in authoritative pioneer evidence, but in some of the more irresponsible reminiscences of forgetful pioneers, reminiscences that express little save a desire to boast, either of the marvelous probity, or of the phenomenal wickedness, of their fellows in the early days. Many pioneers [1] seem to assume that, save their own anecdotes, no sound records of the early days are extant. Yet the fact is that, valuable as the honest man's memory must be, to retain and convey the coloring of the minds and moods of individuals and parties, this individual memory cannot be trusted, in general, either for the details of any complex transaction or for an account of the whole state of any large and mixed community. And one finds this especially true when one reads some of these personal reminiscences of the more forgetful California pioneers. In one mood, or with one sort of experience, the pioneer can remember little but the ardor, the high aims, the generosity, the honor, and the good order of the Californian community. A few gamblers, a few foreign convicts, a few "greasers" there were, who threw shadows into the glorious picture. But they could not obscure it. On the other hand, however, another equally boastful memory revels in scenes of sanguinary freedom, of lawless popular frenzy, of fraud, of drunkenness, of gaming, and of murder. According to this memory nothing shall have remained pure: most ministers who happened to be present gambled, society was ruled by courtesans, nobody looked twice at a freshly murdered man, everybody gaily joined in lynching any supposed thief, and all alike rejoiced in raptures of vicious liberty. These are the two extreme views. You can find numbers of similarly incomplete intermediate views. The kaleidoscopic effect of a series of them can be judged by reading the conflicting statements that, with a rather unnecessary liberality, Mr. Shinn has added to his own much more sober, rational, and well-founded views, in some of the less authoritative citations in chapters xi and xii of his *Mining Camps.*

---

[1] E. g., the writer who calls himself William Grey, in his *Pioneer Times* (San Francisco, 1881).

But these impressions are, as individual impressions, once for all doomed to be unhistorical. The experience of one man could never reveal the social process, of which his life formed but one least element. This process, however, was after all a very simple though widely extended moral process, the struggle of society to impress the true dignity and majesty of its claims on wayward and blind individuals, and the struggle of the individual man, meanwhile, to escape, like a fool, from his moral obligations to society. This struggle is an old one, and old societies do not avoid it; for every man without exception is born to the illusion that the moral world is his oyster. But in older societies each man is conquered for himself and is forced in his own time to give up his fool's longings for liberty and to do a man's work as he may, while in a new society, especially in one made up largely of men who have left homes and families, who have fled from before the word of the Lord and have sought safety from their old vexatious duties in a golden paradise, this struggle being begun afresh by all comes to the surface of things. California was full of Jonahs, whose modest and possibly unprophetic duties had lain in their various quiet paths at home. They had found out how to escape all these duties, at least for the moment, by fleeing over seas and deserts. Strange to say, the ships laden with these fugitives sank not, but bore them safely to the new land. And in the deserts the wanderers by land found an almost miraculous safety. The snares of the god were, however, none the less well laid for that, and these hasty feet were soon to trip. Whoever sought a fool's liberty here (as which of us has not at some time sought it somewhere?) was soon to find all of a man's due bondage prepared for him, and doubtless much more. For nowhere and at no time are social duties in the end more painful or exacting than in the tumultuous days of new countries; just as it is harder to work for months on a vigilance committee than once in a lifetime to sit on a legal jury in a quiet town.

What we have here to do is to understand what forces worked for and against order in this community of irresponsible strangers, and how in time, for their lonely freedom, was substituted the long and wearisome toil that has caused nearly all the men of that pioneer community to die before their due season, or to live even today, when they do live at all, the life of poverty and disappointment. Let us name at the outset these forces of order and of disorder.

The great cause of the growth of order in California is usually said to be the undoubtedly marvelous political talent of our race and nation. And yet, important as that cause was, we must not exaggerate it. The very ease with which the state on paper could be made lulled to sleep the political conscience of the ordinary man, and from the outset gave too much self-confidence to the community. The truly significant social order, which requires not only natural political instinct, but also voluntary and loyal devotion to society, was often rather retarded than hastened in its coming by the political facility of the people. What helped still more than instinct was the courage, the moral elasticity, the teachableness, of the people. Their greatest calamities they learned to laugh at, their greatest blunders they soon recovered from; and even while they boasted of their prowess and denied their sins, they would quietly go on to correct their past grievous errors, good-humored and self-confident as ever. A people such as this age are in the long run favored of heaven, although outwardly they show little proper humility or contrition. For in time they learn the hardest lessons, by dint of obstinate cheerfulness in enduring their bitter experiences and of wisdom in tacitly avoiding their past blunders.

Against order, however, worked especially two tendencies in early California: one this aforementioned general sense of irresponsibility, and the other a diseased local exaggeration of our common national feeling towards foreigners, an exaggeration for which the circumstances of the moment were partly responsible. The first tendency pioneers admit, though not in all its true magnitude; the second they seldom recognize at all, charging to the foreigners themselves whatever trouble was due to our brutal ill-treatment of them.

As for the first tendency, it is the great key to the problem of the worst troubles of early California. The newcomers, viewed as a mass, were homeless. They sought wealth and not a social order. They were, for the most part, as Americans, decently

trained in the duties of a citizen; and as to courage and energy
they were picked men, capable, when their time should come
for showing true manhood, of sacrificing their vain hopes and
enduring everything. But their early quest was at all events an
unmoral one; and when they neglected their duties as freemen,
as citizens, and as brethren among brethren, their quest became
not merely unmoral, but positively sinful. And never did the
journeying pillar, of cloud by day and of fire by night, teach
to the legendary wanderers in the desert more unmistakably by
signs and wonders the eternal law than did the fortunes of
these early Californians display to them, through the very acci-
dents of daily life, the majesty of the same law of order and of
loyalty to society. In the air, as it were, the invisible divine
net of social duties hung and, descending, enmeshed irresistibly all these gay and careless fortune-hunters even while they
boasted of their freedom. Every piece of neglected social work
they had to do over again, with many times the toil. Every
slighted duty avenged itself relentlessly on the community that
had despised it.

However, in the early days there was also that other agency
at work for disorder, whose influence is to blame for much, although not for all, nor even for most, of the degradation that
the new state passed through. This was a brutal tendency, and
yet it was very natural, and, like all natural brutality, it was
often, in any individual man, a childishly innocent tendency.
It was a hearty American contempt for things and institutions
and people that were stubbornly foreign and that would not
conform themselves to American customs and wishes. Representatives of their nation these gold-seeking Californian Americans were; yet it remains true, and is, under the circumstances,
a very natural result, that the American had nowhere else, save
perhaps as conqueror in Mexico itself, shown so blindly and
brutally as he often showed in early California his innate intolerance for whatever is stubbornly foreign. No American of
sense can be proud when he reflects upon these doings of his
countrymen, both towards the real foreigners and towards
those who were usually confounded with such — namely, the
native Californians. Least of all can a native American Califor-

nian, like myself, rejoice to remember how the community from which he sprang treated both their fellow intruders in the land and his own fellows, the born citizens of this dear soil, themselves. All this tale is one of disgrace to our people. But it is none the less true, and none the less profitable to know. For this hatred of foreigners, this blind nativism, are we not all alike born to it? And what but reflection and our chance measure of cultivation checks it in any of us?

If we leave out the unprovoked violence frequently offered to foreigners, we may then say that the well-known crises and tragedies of violent popular justice during the struggle for order were frequently neither directly and in themselves crimes of the community, as conservative people have often considered them, nor yet merely expressions of righteous indignation on the part of an innocent and outraged society; but they were simply the outward symptoms in each case of the *past* popular crimes of disloyalty to the social order; they were social penalties, borne by the community itself, even more than by the rogues, for the treason of carelessness.

II. *The Evolution of Disorder*

I N the mines, to be sure, naked fortune was a more prominent agent than in the cities or on the coast. Plainly the first business of a new placer-mining community was not to save itself socially, since only fortune could detain for even a week its roving members, but to get gold in the most peaceful and rapid way possible. Yet this general absolution from arduous social duties could not be considered as continuing indefinitely. The time must come when, if the nature of the place permitted steady work, men must prepare to dwell together in numbers, and for a long period. Then began the genuine social problems. Everybody who came without family, as a fortune-hunter whose social interests were elsewhere, felt a selfish interest here in shirking serious obligations; and among such men everybody hoped, for his own person, soon to escape from the place. And yet if this social laziness remained general, the effect was simply inevitable. There was then no longer any divine indulgence for the indolent. The social sins avenged themselves, the little community rotted till its rottenness could no longer be endured; and the struggle for order began in earnest and ended either with the triumph of order and the securing of permanent peace or else only when fortune sent all the inhabitants elsewhere, much sadder men, but sometimes, alas, greater fools than ever, to try the same hopeless social experiment elsewhere.

The social institutions of early days in California have recently been studied in Mr. Shinn's ably conceived book on *Mining Camps*. Mr. Shinn has examined only certain aspects of the social life; he has in fact considered the camps mainly in their first and most satisfactory aspect, as immediate expressions of the orderly instincts of American miners. That this view of the mining life is correct, so far as it goes, I doubt not, and I am glad to find it so well and carefully stated as Mr. Shinn has stated it. Anyone can verify it at his pleasure by a reference to the early newspapers. But, after all, one who thus studies the matter knows the mining camp, so to speak, only in its first intention, as it was in its early months, in the flush of childish hopes, or under simpler conditions. The impression that Mr. Shinn leaves us gives us, therefore, too gentle a view of the discipline to which the gods persistently subject all men. What good sense, clear wit, and a well-meaning and peaceable spirit could accomplish in establishing a simple but very unstable order, any community of American miners did indeed quickly accomplish, at the very beginning of the life of the mining camp. When they met on any spot to mine, they were accustomed, as Mr. Shinn shows us in the evidence that he has so enthusiastically collected, to organize very quickly their own rude and yet temporarily effective government. An *alcalde* or a *council*, or, in the simplest case, merely the called meeting of miners, decided disputes; and the whole power of the camp was ready to support such decisions. Two or three of the simplest crimes, such as murder and theft, were recognized in the brief code of laws that the miners' meeting often drew up, and these crimes, once proved against any man, met with the swiftest punishment — petty theft with flogging and banishment, graver crimes with death; although every accused man was given, in all the more orderly camps, the right of a trial, and usually of a jury trial, in the presence of the assembled miners. In brief, the new mining camp was a little republic, practically independent for a time of the regular state officers, often very unwilling to submit to outside interference even with its criminal justice, and well able to keep its own simple order temporarily intact. Its general peacefulness well exhibited the native Anglo-Saxon spirit of compromise, as well as our most familiar American national trait: namely, that already mentioned formal public good humor which you can observe amongst us in any crowded theater lobby or street-car, and which, while indicating nothing as to the private individual characters of the men who publicly and formally show it, is still of great use in checking or averting public disturbances, and is also of some material harm, in disposing us, as a nation, to submit to numerous manifest public annoyances, impositions, and frauds. Most useful this quality is in a community made up of mutual strangers; and one finds it best developed in our Far Western communities.

These two qualities, then, the willingness to compromise matters in dispute, and the desire to be in public on pleasant terms with everybody, worked in new camps wonders for good order. We read, on good authority, of gold left in plain sight, unguarded and unmolested, for days together; of grave disputes, involving vast wealth, decided by calm arbitration; of weeks and months during which many camps lived almost free from secret theft and quite free from open violence. We find pioneers gloomily lamenting those days when social order was so cheap, so secure, and so profitable. And all these things give us a high idea of the native race instinct that could thus express itself *impromptu* even for a brief period.

But I must still insist: all this view of the mining life is one-sided, because this good order, widely spread as it often undoubtedly was, was still in its nature unstable, since it had not been won as a prize of social devotion, but only attained by a sudden feat of instinctive cleverness. The social order is, however, something that instinct must make in its essential ele-

ments, by a sort of first intention, but that only voluntary devotion can secure against corruption. Secured, however, against
the worst corruption the mining-camp life was not, so long as
it rested in this first stage.

For this is what we see when we turn to the other, still more
familiar picture. Violence leaves a deeper impression than
peace; and that may explain very readily why some boasting
pioneers and many professional story-tellers have combined to
describe to us the mining camp as a place where blood was
cheaper than gold, where nearly all gambled, where most men
had shot somebody, where the most disorderly lynching was
the only justice, and where, in short, disorder was supreme.
Such scenes were of course never as a fact universal, and nowhere did they endure long. That we must once for all bear in
mind. Yet when we turn away from the exaggerations and absurdities of the mere story-tellers and the boasters, and when
we look at the contemporary records, we find, never indeed so
bad a general state of things throughout the mines as the one
just described, but at all events at certain times a great deal of
serious and violent disorder in many camps. To what was all
this due? The first answer is suggested by a chronological consideration. The camps of 1848 began with orderly and friendly
life, but in some cases degenerated before the season was done.
The camps of 1849 are described, by those who best knew
them, as on the whole remarkably orderly. By the middle of
1850 we meet with a few great disturbances, like those in Sonora. By the beginning of 1851 complaints are general and
quickly lead up to violence; one looks back to 1849 as to the
golden age of good order, and one even laments the coming of
the state government, which has brought the semblance but
not the substance of law. In the older camps, 1851 thus marks
the culmination of the first phase of the struggle for order,
while newer camps are of course still in their first love. This
paroxysm of social rebirth passes, and a more stable order
seems for a time to succeed, in many parts of the mines; yet,
according to the age and the population of individual camps,
similar struggles are repeated, all through the early years. This
simple chronological consideration, which I hardly need con-

firm by detailed references just here, since it is well known and will sufficiently appear in the following, shows that disorder was *not* the initial stage of the mining camps, but was a corrupt stage through which they were apt to pass. The nature and the causes of the disorder must appear from what we can learn of the details in the newspapers and other records of the time.

III. *Pan and Cradle as Social Agents: Mining Society in the Summer of 1848*

To understand these records, however, one must remember the general facts about the origin, the growth, and the aspects, physical and social, of any mining camp. A camp, at first an irregular collection of tents about some spot where gold had been discovered, assumed form, in time, by the laying out of streets; and if its life continued, for its tent were substituted, first "cloth houses," and then wooden buildings, among which, a little later, fireproof structures would begin to appear. While some camps grew upon "flats," the situations of the early camps were generally in the deep ravines, close under the vast frowning cliffs that rise on each side of the narrow canyons of the larger Sierra rivers.[2] Those in the lowest foothills were, however, sometimes surrounded only by gentler slopes, or by bluffs of moderate height. The bars of the larger rivers, the gravel in the tributary ravines, and a few gravel deposits that were far enough from water to be called "dry diggings" were at first the chief accessible sources of the gold.

Moral growth is everywhere impossible without favorable physical conditions. It has seldom been noticed by later writers that the social condition of the camps was, in the successive years and despite all good intentions, largely and almost irresistibly determined by the various successively predominant

---

[2] The seventh letter of "Shirley," in Ewer's *Pioneer,* Vol. II, p. 91, gives vivid impressions of the scenery and situation of Indian Bar, on the Feather. The letter was written in October. "At present," she says, "the sun does not condescend to shine upon Indian Bar at all." So it was all through the winter. No one who has had a glimpse of the Sierras will fail to remember such places along the canyons.

methods of mining. To understand this fact we need only to
follow some of the early accounts of these methods, associated
as many of them are with descriptions of the local habits and
customs of the moment. To the most of the newcomers all mining was novel, and they describe the mysteries of the art with
enthusiastic detail. Let us begin in 1848 with Walter Colton.[3]
"I went among the gold-diggers," he says, "found half a dozen
at the bottom of the ravine, tearing up the bogs, and up to their
knees in mud. Beneath these bogs lay a bed of clay, sprinkled
in spots with gold. These deposits, and the earth mixed with
them, were shovelled into bowls, taken to a pool near by, and
washed out. The bowl, in working, is held in both hands,
whirled violently back and forth through half a circle, and
pitched this way and that sufficiently to throw off the earth and
water, while the gold settles to the bottom. The process is extremely laborious, and taxes the entire muscles of the frame.
In its effect it is more like swinging a scythe than any work I
ever attempted." This "pan" work was at first very general, although miners did not usually work in just such places as this.
It has retained its place in the prospector's life, and in mining
in new placers, ever since, although the handling of the pan
may be made less laborious than it was to Colton's muscles. A
little more practice, and the use of a current of water, such as
usually could be found at hand or reached by carrying the
earth down from "dry diggings," helped to make the pan-washing itself no very hard toil for strong arms. The digging, however, no practice could improve, or render anything but the
most wearisome of tasks. In washing with the pan, in a running stream, one began each washing by holding the pan, half
full of dirt, a little under the current of water. Shaking or even
sometimes stirring the contents and throwing out with the
hand the larger stones, one gradually raised the pan out of
the current as the earth dissolved away and was carried off in the
stream. At last the motion and the flow of water carried off
the whole mass save a little black sand mingled with the gold
particles. After drying this, one could get rid of the sand by

---

[3] *Three Years in California*, p. 274.

blowing or, as was customary in later times, by clearing away iron particles with a magnet.[4]

At best, however, pan-mining was, in proportion to the amount of gravel washed, a slow and tedious process. Even the richest diggings were thus apt to prove disappointing, and, socially regarded, the pan, if it had remained long the predominating instrument of mining work, would have precluded any rapid or secure progress in the organized life of the camps. In 1848, while the larger and more accessible camps rapidly began the use of "machines," newer camps were still constantly being formed by men who wished to seek their fortunes through the independent use of their pans. And the easily learned art of pan-mining was a very demoralizing one so long as a great proportion of the miners could still hope to get rich by it. Colton, whose experiences lay where "machines" were less used, and pans the rule, describes to us men mining in numbers near together, sometimes within sound of numberless querulous "prairie-wolves," [5] who had not yet been thinned out or driven to be as shy as the surviving ones now are in California hills; but the men he makes as wandering, and often as discontented, as the wolves; independent of their fellow laborers; quite capable, of course, of ready and unexactingly simple camp organizations; [6] but not led to undertake any very serious social duties. Where each man toiled with his pan, he hardly needed to speak to his next neighbor, who was mainly an object of curiosity, or of envy, in case he either showed symptoms of having made some discovery or proved his greater luck by the gold he could display. The means of getting supplies from the coast in these less accessible camps were subject to all sorts of uncertainties; and so long as the pan was very largely used'

---

[4] For an account of the very simple process of "panning," see Hittell's *Resources of California*, 6th ed., p. 314. For the use of the pan in 1848, see further Foster's *Gold Regions of California*, p. 20 (Larkin's letter). Also see Brooks: *Four Months among the Gold-Finders* (London and New York, 1849), pp. 36, 37, 41.

[5] Colton, op. cit., p. 279. The "prairie-wolf" is of course identical with the "coyote."

[6] See also Mr. Shinn's *Mining Camps*, chaps. ix and x.

among implements of mining, affairs must remain so. For pan-mining left it doubtful where one's market would be, almost from day to day, a thing that no dealer could safely long tolerate.[7] Hence the enormous prices, the untrustworthy markets, and the occasional approaches to starvation in the newer mines.

The pan as sole instrument for gold-washing was, then, sociologically and morally, as well as economically considered, a great evil for the mining life; and one can be glad that its time of more extended use was so short. Already in 1848 many men, and some whole camps, were desiring and using "machines," as they are at first rather vaguely called in the accounts — e. g., as Larkin calls them; [8] and Larkin himself had one of them made for a native miner, at the latter's order, in Monterey: "a log dug out, with a riddle and sieve made of willow boughs on it," costing, he tells us, one hundred and twenty dollars, "payable in gold dust at fourteen dollars an ounce." Mason, according to his report of August 17,[9] had found on July 5 the greater part

----

[7] The local predominance of the pan over the cradle is shown by Colton when (p. 281) after describing the cradle, he adds: "Most of the diggers use a bowl or pan; its lightness never embarrasses their roving habits; and it can be put in motion wherever they may find a stream or spring. It can be purchased now in the mines for five or six dollars; a few months since it cost an ounce." This evidence of course holds only for the camps seen by Colton. The fall in price may have been due to the increasing use of the cradles; but it must be remembered that Indian willow baskets, or any other possible and easily portable substitutes for bowls, were then eagerly accepted. The restlessness of these pan-miners exceeded the well-known uneasiness of the later mining communities, just because there was lacking for them every motive to permanency in any camp save actual and continuous great success, while the rudeness of the pan as an instrument made great success almost always transient. See instances of sudden migrations and restlessness and remarks upon the fact in Colton, pp. 293, 302, 314. "As for mutual aid and sympathy," he says, "Samson's foxes had as much of it, turned tail to, with firebrands tied between." This is of course a little Coltonian.

[8] See his letter above cited, p. 19 of Foster's *Gold Regions of California.*

[9] I quote here again from Foster, p. 10.

of the miners at the Mormon or lower diggings already using the cradle: "a rude machine," "on rockers, six or eight feet long, open at the foot, and, at its head, a coarse grate or sieve; the bottom is rounded, with small cleats nailed across. Four men are required to work this machine: one digs the ground in the bank close by the stream; another carries it to the cradle, and empties it on the grate; a third gives a violent rocking motion to the machine; while a fourth dashes on water from the stream itself." — "The sieve keeps the coarse stones from entering the cradle, the current of water washes off the earthy matter, and the gravel is gradually carried out at the foot of the machine, leaving the gold mixed with a heavy fine black sand above the first cleats. The sand and gold mixed together are then drawn off through auger holes into a pan below, are dried in the sun, and afterwards separated by blowing off the sand." Essential to the success of the cradle was of course its inclined position. In the form described, it has remained in occasional use without change of principle ever since, although it is less rudely made; but in large, permanent, and steadily productive diggings it is not useful. Its position soon became a very subordinate one, and later it became a rare sight.

For the time, however, the cradle was a step in advance, physically and morally. Gravels that the pan-miner contemptuously abandoned were well worth working on this plan. Camps that would have been deserted remained, and were prosperous. The great thing, however, from the sociological point of view, was that men now had voluntarily, and in an organized way, to work together. The miner's partnership, which grew up in this second stage of mining life, soon became one of the closest of California relationships, and, as such, has been widely and not unjustly celebrated in song and story. This accidentally primitive society had passed from a state of "nature," in the old sense of the word (this state of "nature" being indeed here a state of unstable peace, not of general war) and had become a collection of mutually more or less independent, but inwardly united bands. Rapidly as the successive stages of this growth passed by, they still left their mark on the social order, as we shall soon see.

The summary of the situation in the small community of the early golden days is, then, that the first established and more crowded camps quickly passed into the second stage of mining life, substituting for the pan the cradle, while numerous dissatisfied gold-seekers were constantly hunting for new diggings and founding new camps, using meanwhile for the most part the pan. The resulting total of social condition is hard to describe, for lack of good evidence. Mr. Shinn's account above cited, although well told, and founded in large measure on a fair sort of pioneer evidence, is still one-sided and is too optimistic. I have more confidence in a direct use, as far as it goes, of the very frank and unassuming contemporary story of Dr. Brooks, also already cited. J. Tyrwhitt Brooks, an English physician, just then from Oregon, visited the gold region in the midst of the first excitement, in an improvised company from the coast region, consisting at first of six white men and one Indian and later considerably larger. The party, in the various stages of its life, contained both Englishmen and Americans and included one Californian gentlemen of some position. These partners were nearly all mutually quite new acquaintances; one was supposed to be a deserting sailor; none knew anything at the start about mining. For some time they had good luck; in the end they lost nearly all their gains; their fortunes were on the whole characteristic. The account of Dr. Brooks, as published, contains numerous misprinted dates, since the volume, which comprises the doctor's diary of the expedition, with some remarks, was sent home as a bundle of MS. for the private use of his friends and was thereupon printed without the author's supervision. Allowing for the plain misprints, the chronology of the account nevertheless agrees well enough with that of events otherwise known from the Mason and Larkin letters; and Brooks seems to be a perfectly trustworthy observer.

At the Mormon diggings Brooks "stirred" his first "pailful" of earth. He found (loc. cit., p. 36) many of the diggers there washing with "pots," others, as would seem, even washing directly from their spades, using these as very rough pans. Many, however, used cradles, and Brooks and his companions, quickly wearying of pan-work, made their own cradles out of rough boards in a day or two and worked together. The habit of employing companies of Indians to do the mining for some one white adventurer was common enough; but the mass of the miners worked either singly or in the small cradle-parties. The miners of the Mormon diggings were all conscious, even at this time, of a controlling customary law, quickly formed, as it seemed to them, but at all events derived from no one discoverable present source. Thus (p. 46) it was generally understood that a lump of gold more than half an ounce in weight, if picked up from the freshly dug earth by a member of a party mining in partnership, "before the earth was thrown into the cradle," belonged to the finder personally and not to the party. As for society, that at the Mormon diggings was quickly under the sway of a few native Californian families, of respectable and sociable character, who appeared under the protection of their heads, well-to-do native citizens, who had chosen to seek gold in good company. The wives of these men were waited on by Indian servants; they gave their usual Californian attention to bright dress and good-fellowship and held very delightful dancing-parties in the evenings "on the green, before some of the tents" (p. 47). The friendly and well-disposed camp joined largely in these parties and found it very naturally "quite a treat after a hard day's work, to go at nightfall to one of these fandangoes." Brooks gives us no impression that he ever found these entertainments at that place and time in any wise of suspicious character, although he thinks that the gentlemen sometimes drank a little more than was proper, so that the merriment was occasionally "animated and imposing" (p. 48). Of the ladies, the wives and daughters of the Californians, he had nothing but good to say.

With regret Brooks and his fellows bade farewell to these fair entertainers of society at the Mormon diggings, and on the first of July left the now overcrowded place for the North Fork, having first sold their two cradles at auction for three hundred and seventy-five dollars in gold dust at fourteen dollars to the ounce. At the site of Coloma they found Marshall mining with a company of Indians, and they spent a day or two near this place themselves, working in dry diggings and carrying the earth down to the stream to wash. Thence they went on to Weber's Creek, passing on the way Sinclair, at work with his Indians. Reaching a new camp here, whose members were scattered over the stream-bed and up the neighboring ravines, they made for themselves new cradles by hollowing out logs and began to employ Indians to help them (p. 57). Here they were when Colonel Mason visited the mines. But these diggings also were quickly overcrowded by wandering miners, of whom "about half work together in companies — the other half shift each for himself" (p. 59). The lonely men were evidently pan-miners. The Indians also crowded the place in hundreds, worked for bright clothing and whiskey, and staggered about drunk. The miners of Brooks's party grew discontented. There was doubtless plenty of gold on Bear River; a trapper told about the region and consented to guide the party thither for "sixty-five dollars and his food." The Brooks party had much trouble in getting provisions enough for their journey, as everything was "inordinately dear," so that they had to content themselves with bacon, dried beef, and coffee (p. 61). They at this time received and accepted offers from three or four strangers to join their company, which was thus strengthened against Indians. Hard toil, under good guidance, but through a very rough country, brought them over the hills to Bear River Valley, where, after finding rich gravels, they began once more to make cradles and to build a large, roughly fortified shanty for protection against the Indians. They made a stricter division of labor than before, and toiled fruitfully for some time. The life was at best a hard one, and Brooks found himself very lonesome and homesick. At night, around the campfire, the trapper-guide told great tales of the deserts beyond the Sierras and of the horrible dangers of the unknown expanse of the Great Salt Lake, on to whose "dark turbid waters," as he declared, "no living being has yet been found daring enough to venture far," owing to a mysterious whirlpool there said to exist. The country about them was rugged and still little visited, and was as romantic and bewildering to them as were the trapper's nightly yarns. Their diggings, however, proved very rich.

At this point trouble began. First some "horse-thief" Indians appeared and succeeded in galloping off with several of their horses. In a brush with these Indians one of the Brooks party was killed. Next, as the time grew near when the season would force them to forsake the lonely golden valley, sickness appeared in the camp, provisions ran low, and the mass of gold dust now accumulated in their cabin began to seem to them, after the Indian fight, a perilous wealth. For Indians too by this time desired gold to exchange for fire-water. While the trapper, with one man, accordingly set out for Sutter's Fort to get provisions, three of the party, including the Californian gentleman, were deputed to carry the gold dust to San Francisco, while the others were to toil out the season and divide gains with those sent away. Success, however, had already engendered jealousy and suspicion. The party were very near an open quarrel (p. 78) over the choice of the men to be entrusted with the gold, and one of the three actually sent, a friend of Brooks, who had accompanied him from Oregon, was intended by Brooks and some others to watch his fellow messengers.

On the way with the gold the three messengers were suddenly attacked by mounted robbers, who lassoed and badly injured this third man and escaped with his horse and saddlebags, the latter containing the bulk of the gold itself. The unjust suspicions of which Brooks frankly makes confession, by causing this man to be the carrier of most of the treasure, had resulted in the loss of nearly the whole outcome of the long toil. The robbers were native Californians and Indians; and one of them, who was killed in the fight, was, Brooks declares, on the report given by miners who recognized him, "one of the disbanded soldiers of the late Californian army, by name Tomás María Carrillo; a man of the very worst character, who had connected himself with a small band of depredators, whose occupation was to lay [sic] in wait at convenient spots along the roads in the neighborhood of the seacoast, and from thence to pounce upon and plunder any unfortunate merchant or *ranchero* that might be passing unprotected that way. The gang had now evidently abandoned the coast to try their fortunes in the neighborhood of the mines; and, judging from the accounts that one of the miners gave of the number of robberies that had recently taken place thereabouts, their mission had been eminently successful" (p. 82).[10]

This characteristic event, the outcome of the scattered condition of society at the moment and of the demoralizing old days of the conquest, led Brooks to learn of several equally characteristic occurrences of other sorts in neighboring mines. The companions of the wounded man were possibly aided in repulsing the robbers by the approach of a band of mounted miners, who opportunely appeared just after the assailants had fled. The newcomers, however, declined to take any trouble to help the wounded man, but, as the messengers related to Brooks, "coolly turned their horses' heads round, and left us alone with our dying friend, not deigning further to notice our appeals." Every man looked out for himself in those days, as one sees; and when the two messengers, after at last getting, by their begging a little, help, managed to bring their friend — not dying, indeed, but badly hurt — to a near camp, they could only return alone and disheartened to the old spot on the Bear River and tell their strange tale to the rest. The whole party thereupon spent a night about the campfire in sullen silence, broken only by occasional bitter or suspicious speeches, until the dawn found them weary, haggard, and disgusted. What gold was left they quarreled over during the morning, and having at last weighed it out in parcels, they separated finally into two parties, of which one, with Brooks, set off to the camp where the wounded man had been left. On the way they met the trapper who, with his one companion, had previously gone to Sutter's Fort for supplies. These two also had had their adventures, which they now proceeded to tell. The trapper and his comrade found flour as much as eighty-five dollars a barrel at Sutter's Fort. On the way back their pack-horses were stolen one night, with their packs of provisions. When they appealed to the miners of a neighboring camp for help in finding the thieves, they were only treated with rudeness and suspicion, and one of the miners drove them off with his rifle (p. 86). He later proved to be what his friends called a peaceably-disposed

---

[10] Of this Tomás M. Carrillo, Mr. H. H. Bancroft's list of pioneers knows only this one fact, as told by Brooks.

man, whose brusqueness of manner was the result of the large quantity of gold dust that fortune had given him and of the fact that he consequently demanded proper introduction of people who came to call on him. To be sure, his desire to be alone had already led him to feel it his duty to shoot and kill two men, so that some of his neighbors called him a "terror"; but, as appears from p. 89, others justified him, on the ground that he had shot only people who needed shooting. Such an assertion, under such circumstances, admitted of no proper verification; but, at all events, his manners lacked delicacy, and the two Brooks-party men felt aggrieved at the imperfect public spirit in this whole camp, near which their pack-horses had so mysteriously disappeared. The two had yet other sad things to tell Brooks of the state of society at this little camp; for some men there had their arms in slings, and others said that such injuries were common in those diggings after people had chanced to differ in opinion.

Brooks and his party from Bear River exchanged their own little tale of disaster with the one thus confided to them by the trapper and his comrade and then went on to hunt for the wounded friend. Him they found slowly recovering from his injuries and lying in a shanty. But the camp where he was staying was sickly. "Fever was prevalent, and I found," says Brooks, "that more than two thirds of the people at this settlement were unable to move out of their tents. The other third were too selfish to render them any assistance" (p. 87). It was even hard to find a burial-place when one was dead; for these miners "denied the poor corpses of their former friends a few feet of earth for a grave, and left the bodies exposed for the wolf to prey upon." The season, in fact, was nearly done, and men were now frantic for the gold.

All this was surely an unpleasant state of affairs; though 1848 is the season that Mr. Henry Degroot, as quoted by Mr. Shinn,[11] seems to look back upon as containing "all that was staid and primitive in or about the mines of California." But we have

[11] *Mining Camps*, p. 122. It is proper to add that Mr. Degroot, as appears by his article in the *Overland Monthly* for April 1874, arrived in 1849 and knew of 1848 only by hearsay.

already seen, in Dr. Brooks's account of the happy fandangos
"on the green" at the Mormon diggings, how capable he was of
picturing the pleasant side of this seemingly so irresponsible
and accidental life and how different the view of a man in
another camp at the same time might have been. One also sees,
however, the impossibility of doubting that, in these pan-
mining days, with only about half of a camp using the rocker,
and with no miners connected in any form of close personal
organization, save such as the rocker-parties implied, irresponsibility meant almost universal selfishness beyond the limits of
one's own party, and selfishness, in the long run, meant disorder and occasional violence, with a very bad social outlook
ahead, despite the readiness wherewith rough camp organizations could always be made for the momentary repression of
more intolerable crime or for the settlement of greater disputes.

At all events, in these last days of the season of 1848 Brooks
found everybody talking of disorder and insecurity. His friend
was, indeed, safe enough and was well cared for by a "kind
Californian nurse and her husband," whose "kind treatment of
my poor friend offered a striking contrast to the callous selfishness around." But when Brooks himself set out towards Sutter's
Fort, he heard reports of trouble all about him. Nobody left
his gold in his tent; everybody carried it on his own person;
and the number of missing men "whose own friends had not
thought it worth while to go in search of them" was considerable. One or two dead bodies were found floating in the river,
"which circumstance was looked upon as indicative of foul
play," as a gold-digger who was drowned by accident ought,
people said, to have enough gold about him to keep his body
under water. The characteristic fact that nobody was known
by Brooks to have taken any trouble to look closely at these
dead bodies, to verify or disprove, by examining for direct signs
of foul play, this *a priori* reasoning, is only indirectly indicated
by our author. "Open attempts at robbery," he adds, "were rare;
it was in the stealthy night-time that thieves prowled about,
and, entering the little tents, occupied by not more than perhaps a couple of miners, neither of whom, in all probability,
felt inclined to keep a weary watch," stole what could be found.

Going farther on his way, Brooks came to the ill-humored camp near which the trapper had lost the provisions. Here he saw a group of miners drinking brandy "at a dollar a dram." As the greater part of them were "suffering from fever," the doctor himself seriously disapproved of their course, on professional as well as on economic grounds. Nevertheless, he found time to learn a few facts in favor of the much maligned inhabitants. They were selfish and dissipated, but they meant well in their way.

Weary of such things, he reached Sacramento and then went on to Monterey, where he joined in a fruitless pursuit into the Tulare region of a robber-band, who were reported to be identical with the assailants of the gold-bearing messengers. The result of the pursuit was only more weariness and a sight of prairie, thicket, and hill. In sullen silence the pursuers at last rode back to Monterey, sick at heart. As for those who still remained together of the original party, there was nothing to do but to part. The resolution to do so "was not come to without something like a pang — a pang which I sincerely felt, and which I believe was more or less experienced by us all. We had lived for four months in constant companionship, and a friendship, more vivid than can well be imagined in civilized lands to have been the growth of so short a period, had sprung up betwixt us. There had been a few petty bickerings between us, and some unjust suspicions on my part; but these were all forgotten." The remaining gold was divided, and "the same night we had a supper, at which a melancholy joviality was in the ascendant, and the next day shook hands and parted." "On waking the next morning," says Brooks, "I found that I was alone."

In this account there is one thing to be noted: namely, that Brooks is uncommonly objective in his fashions of speech. He has no discoverable aim save to tell a plain story, and often tells things to his own disadvantage. Hence one may have a reasonable confidence in his accuracy. His own summary is especially noteworthy, as given in his introductory letter to a relative, written after the diary. Of the country itself he speaks well: "I assure you it is hardly possible for any accounts of the gold-mines to be exaggerated. The El Dorado has really been discovered" (p. 13). But of the social condition he has only a gloomy account to give: "I have worked hard and undergone some hardships; and, thanks to the now almost lawless state of the country, I have been deprived of the mass of my savings, and must, when the dry season comes round again, set to work almost new. . . . My own case is that of many others. As the number of diggers and miners augmented, robberies and violence became frequent. At first, when we arrived at the Mormon diggings, for example, everything was tranquil. Every man worked for himself, without disturbing his neighbor. Now the scene is widely changed indeed." Allowing for a little momentary depression, we may still regard the account given by Brooks, and confirmed by the details of his story, as a fair one, on the whole, so far as his own experience could guide him, and his experience is plainly no insignificant one.

How shall we reconcile this tale of transient peacefulness, followed by weary selfishness, bickering, and violence, with the much brighter picture of 1848, given on the basis of his own pioneer evidence, by Mr. Shinn? The method of reconciliation seems to me clear enough. The quickly organized and, at the first, peaceful camp of 1848 was an easily cultivated and soon withering flower, which could not well live to the end of the California dry season. There was no unity of interest to preserve its simple forms from degeneracy. The camp consisted of a perfectly transient group of utterly restless and disconnected men, who had not the slightest notion of staying where they were more than a few weeks. When a countryside was full of such groups, disorder, before many months should pass, was simply inevitable. Skill in improvising organizations could not avert the result. Moreover, the life in small partnerships involved, despite the idyllic character of the relations of "pards," almost every possible temptation that could act to make a good-humored man quarrelsome. Rough camp-life, among novices, is almost always as full of bickering as of good-fellowship. Good humor in public meetings, or in the camp at large, with private petty quarrels going on meanwhile — this was the common condition. The affray in the Donner party has already, in an earlier chapter, suggested this really very trite reflection to us, and we need not dwell on it here. The practiced camper recovers his even temper, but the novice is long subject to bearishness. The matter is largely physical. The civilized man becomes soon peevish, with the irregular meals and the monotony of camp-life, and may show, even to his best friend, a hitherto unsuspected brutality of mood and behavior.

What public spirit there was in 1848 showed itself best, as Mr. Shinn has pointed out, in the regulation of the miner's temporary land tenure and in the settlement of disputes about mining rights. But the life, on the whole, was seriously demoralizing to all concerned in it, and must remain so until more elaborate methods of mining should be introduced.

IV. *Mining Society in 1849 and 1850, and the Beginning of Sluice-Mining*

THE SMALL-PARTNERSHIP and cradle system of mining was also, as we know, the common system of 1849 and of the early part of 1850. In a noted, but now, at least in the herein cited first edition, quite rare pamphlet,[12] one finds the experience of 1848 and of the early summer of 1849 summed up in a way that is very instructive for our present purpose. On page 34 the newcomer receives advice as to his needs. First of all he is told to carry little baggage, as "it will always impede his free movement, if he should want to go from place to place. He should have absolutely nothing more than what he can carry on a beast, if he be able to have one; or, if not, what he can shoulder himself. The less one brings to the mines, the better prospect of success he may have." A change of clothing, a pair of blankets, a pickaxe, a spadé (a winding-sheet is not mentioned), a crowbar, a pan, a sheath knife, a trowel; such is the outfit for the single miner. "A washing-machine," however, "is used when there are two or more working in partnership." This

---

[12] *California as It Is, and as It May Be, or a Guide to the Gold Region,* by F. P. Wierzbicki, M.D., first ed., San Francisco, printed by Washington Bartlett, 1849, p. 60. The preface is dated September 30, 1849. The book is the first English volume printed in California.

machine is then described in its simpler form very much as above, and one recently imported improvement, the "Burke Rocker," a sort of transition to the later "Long Tom," is praised. All other devices so far known to Wierzbicki are condemned, especially, of course, those numberless and useless washers that newcomers brought and so promptly left in the rubbish-heaps of San Francisco. The result as to the value and limits of mining partnerships is very simply and practically stated (page 36): "However, according to circumstances, these partnerships are formed, it can only be said that there is no occasion for more than four persons in a company, and frequently three or two do better than four. For protection and occasional service that one may require from another, it is always better to be in partnership with a suitable person or persons." On page 45 and page 46 Wierzbicki mentions meanwhile in a casual way and as an understood fact the general good order and peace of the mines. But he shows us also on what changing stuff this good order depended. The "silent consent of all" generally is enough to ensure a miner of his rights to his "claim"; lynch law has been sometimes needed and used for murderers and robbers; but improvised judges and juries have seen the thing carefully done. The miners easily settle their own disputes about the use of land; their justice is prompt and efficacious. The population, however, "is constantly fluctuating"; and so any permanent jurisdictions seem to the writer incapable of establishment at present. One sees the outcome of all this. The miners rove about in what seems on the whole peace; there is no seriously exacting government in Israel; every man does what is right in his own eyes, subject to a simple and easily improvised popular justice. Large partnerships and extended social alliances are, however, entangling and useless. *Responsibilities must be avoided by one who wants success.*

The immediate result of this system, as applied in 1849, was, however, on the whole, remarkably free from serious public mishap. Many causes combined to postpone this year the evil results. The great numbers and high character of the newcomers are in part responsible for this. The great numbers led to vast extensions of the field of work and rendered the risks of intercommunication among the various camps less noticeable than in the previous year. By virtue of sheer mass, the community meanwhile forced upon itself a degree of hastily improvised organization that was intended by no one individual, but that was necessary for the purpose of feeding and otherwise supplying so many people. The numerous new commercial towns that sprang up in the valley regions offered fresh chances to disappointed miners and checked both their discontent and their desire to wander off alone. Thus the whole life was, for the time, far healthier than the life that Brooks saw.[13]

Bayard Taylor, who traveled through the country as *Tribune* correspondent in 1849,[14] and who saw much of the mines, is an observer sufficiently optimistic to suit the most enthusiastic. He came at just the moment of his life [15] to appreciate the young community. He was himself young, ardent, and in love; he had come to California to see great things, and he certainly saw them. There is no question of his general accuracy in telling what he really saw, and he has the power that so few of our unimaginative nation have to describe scenes, people, and things, instead of itemized and arbitrary abstractions of a numerical or technical character. Still, we must understand his mood; he saw whatever illustrated life, hope, vigor, courage, prosperity. It was not his business to see sorrow or misery. He saw, for instance, but one drunken man in all the mines.[16] Others at the same time had a less cheerful experi-

---

[13] A suggestion as to the chronology of the early settlements belongs here. The American, the Cosumnes, and the Mokelumne rivers were the sites of the early mining settlements of 1848, and here the greatest activity of 1849 also went on. By 1850 the large camps had extended northward as far as the North Fork of the Feather and into Mariposa County on the south. The next year saw much activity as far north as Shasta. Prospectors were of course always in advance of the larger camps.

[14] Bayard Taylor left San Francisco, to return to the East, just after the fire of December 24, 1849. See *Eldorado* (Household edition), p. 316.

[15] See his biography by Mrs. Taylor and Mr. H. E. Scudder (Boston, 1885), Vol. I, chap. vii.

[16] *Eldorado*, p. 312. People drink far too much, thinks Taylor,

ence in this respect. Mr. Theodore T. Johnson, for instance,[17] who was of a more melancholy turn of mind, "frequently saw miners lying in the dust helpless with intoxication," and we need no such evidence to convince us of what we well know *a priori.* Taylor's optimism, however, is not without its high value for us; for he shows us what the better spirit of 1849 really was, despite all its so fatal carelessness. "In all the large digging districts," we learn (p. 101), "there were established regulations, which were faithfully observed. . . . There was as much security to life and property as in any part of the Union, and as small a proportion of crime." This he knew partly from hearsay; although as to hearsay evidence he was indeed a little uncritical, since, just after narrating on such evidence the attempted expulsion by Americans of the "ten thousand" Sonoran miners at work in the southern mines — an attempted expulsion that he supposed to have been fairly successful, though it was not — he goes on at once to assure us (p. 103) that "abundance of gold does not always beget a grasping and avaricious spirit," and even adds that "the principles of hospitality were as faithfully observed in the rude tents of the diggers, as they could be by the thrifty farmers of the North and West," and, finally, that "the cosmopolitan cast of society in California, resulting from the commingling of so many races and the primitive mode of life, gave a character of good-fellowship to all its members." All this he tells us, not by way of irony about the recent hospitality and good-fellowship shown to the ten thousand Sonorans, but because he could "safely say," as he expresses it, "that I never met with such unvarying kindness from comparative strangers."

But, allowing for all the youthful optimism, Taylor's testimony is good evidence for the peace and hospitality that he directly experienced or heard of from trustworthy people, and his experience was large and varied. He found at the begin-

---

but somehow they do not get drunk in California. This was a not uncommon boast of early Californians; but nobody makes it in California now.

[17] See his *Sights in the Gold Region, and Scenes by the Way* (New York, 1849), p. 182.

ning of winter (p. 263) the camps in the "dry diggings" well organized, each one with "an alcalde chosen, and regulations established as near as possible in accordance with the existing laws of the country." The alcaldes had very great powers, but were well obeyed. "Nothing in California seemed more miraculous to me than this spontaneous evolution of social order from the worst elements of anarchy. It was a lesson worth even more than the gold." In his general summary (in chapter xxx) of the social condition of California, Taylor finds gambling and extravagance very prevalent, and, together with the excessive drinking of those people who never got drunk, he considers these the great evils of the land. But the simpler virtues seemed to him cheap and easy in California. Generosity, hospitality, democratic freedom from all social prejudices, energy, ardor, mirthfulness, industry: all he found alike prevalent. As he saw the easy work of the constitutional convention and took part in the preparations for the subsequent election, public spirit also seemed to him a common virtue of Californians. The signs of the too general lack of it came near to the surface of his experience sometimes; but those he never saw. On p. 252 he tells us of the scene on the Lower Bar of the Mokelumne at the first state election, in November 1849. "The election day dawned wet and cheerless." Until noon the miners lay dozing idly in their tents, unable to work and very careless about the dignity of the occasion. At last the voting began in the largest of the tents, "the inspectors being seated behind the counter, in close proximity to the glasses and bottles, the calls for which were quite as frequent as the votes." This was indeed harmless enough for the moment, and the ignorance of most of the miners about the men voted for was natural. But more characteristic was the spirit in which men voted. One of the candidates lost twenty-three votes for having been seen recently electioneering in the mines in a high-crowned silk hat. Some people voted only for known candidates. But many chose otherwise, a representative man of them saying, in justification: "When I left home, I was determined to go it blind. I went it blind in coming to California, and I'm not going to stop now. I voted for the constitution, and I've never seen the constitution. I voted for all the candidates, and I don't know a damned one of them. I'm going it blind all through, I am." This fellow was only too decidedly a type of a large class. And such was the birthday of the new state in the mountains.

In short, 1849 was a year of successful impromptu camp organizations and of general external peace; but it was as full of the elements of future confusion as it was of the strength and courage that would in time conquer this confusion. The roving habits of that year long remained injurious elements in the more exacting civilization of later years. And even the memory of the easy social successes of those days often proved demoralizing to the later communities, by begetting an impatience of all legal delays and mistakes. If we want, however, really to understand the forces of early California life, we must study the year 1851, a year that, despite the traditions of the pioneers, is of far more historical interest than 1849. The latter is the year of the making of the constitution, and that is its great historical merit; but for the mass of the population it is also the year of vague airy hopes, of noble but untried social and moral promise, of blindness, of absurd blunders, and in general of fatal self-confidence and selfishness. Its one poetical aspect, the fervor of innocent, youthful, romantic hope and aspiration among its better men, is something as brief as the "posy of a ring." 1849 is, in short, the boyish year of California. 1851, on the contrary, is the manly year, the year of clearer self-consciousness, of lost illusions, of bitter struggles, of tried heroism, of great crimes and blunders indeed, and of great calamities, but also of the salvation of the new state. It saw the truly sad and significant days of our early life, and we should honor it accordingly.

A series of changes in the methods of work, a series that began already in 1849, that continued through 1850, and that reached a first culmination early in 1851, was destined to render far more stable and responsible this roving mining life of 1849. The work done by the rocker might be made more effective by enlarged appliances, and especially by increasing the amount of water used in washing. Thus, after several improved rockers had been tried with varying success, the long tom (widely used in 1850) and, a little later, that finely simple invention, the board sluice, separately and together first modified and then revolutionized, the whole business of placer-mining.[18] Elaborate descriptions belong not here. In its typical form, however, a sluice is a very long shallow box, which may extend to many hundreds of feet, so inclined as to give a stream of water flowing through it a very good headway in the box, especially perhaps in the upper end. Along the bottom of the sluice, as it originally was made, were fastened low cleats of wood or "riffles," "at long intervals" (so runs the description in the *Transcript,* loc. cit.). Later the riffles were better arranged with special regard for durability and for convenience in removing them to "clean up." The gold particles will be caught and will settle just above the riffles. To the sluice a constant and swift stream of water must be supplied through an artificial channel, from a reservoir, or from some point where it is convenient to tap a natural stream. This free supply of running water is the essential element of sluice-mining. The sluice thus provided by one's side, one shovels the paying-gravels into it from one's claim, and so the earth is carried down to the "tailings," an assistant removing the larger stones meanwhile. One continues this process steadily for days, or even weeks, and then upon "cleaning up" one expects to find the gold particles,

---

[18] The first number of the *Sacramento Transcript* that appeared as a steamer edition, on April 26, 1850 (see 2nd vol. of the Harvard College Library *Transcript* file), contains on a single page an interesting series of letters from the various mining districts, which furnish a survey of the state of work at the moment. The tom is mentioned as in use at Auburn, but is not otherwise mentioned. During the summer it became more common. The second steamer *Transcript,* May 29, 1850, discusses mining "machinery" at length, mentioning only the various improvements of the rocker, with devices for the use of quicksilver. As late as the *Daily Transcript* of October 19, 1850 I find the rocker the chief instrument mentioned in reports from the mines, although the tom is known. Not until May 2, 1851, however, do I find in this paper an account of "sluice-washing" as a new and profitable process. It then rapidly grew in favor, and the tom became an auxiliary or wholly subordinate instrument. The northern mines took up new devices more rapidly than the southern.

mingled with a little black sand, collected above the riffles.[19] As for the "tom," in its earlier forms, it was simply a kind of very short sluice, provided with a strainer for catching large stones, and supplied with water by hand.

The introduction of the sluice, with its various auxiliaries, not only secured the productiveness of California placer mines for many years, but acted indirectly on society, as a check to the confusion and disorder that began to grow among the miners in 1850 and 1851. Although the early camps were more orderly than those of 1851, they were so, as we shall see, only because the demoralizing influences of a roving and hazardous, irresponsible life had not yet begun to work their full effects. The disorders of 1851 and later years could be checked, and were checked, because they occurred in communities that now had vested interests. As so often happens in social matters, the effects here began to show themselves when the causes were already in decline; and some of the camps of 1851 reaped the whirlwind that the wanderers of 1849 had sown. But sluice-mining meant serious responsibilities of many sorts, and so, in the end, good order. For, in the first place, men now had to work less independently and more in large companies. And water became a thing that could no longer be taken as it came, but that must be brought in a steady stream to the right place, often by much labor; and thus it acquired a market value, so much per "miner's inch." To supply it in the dry Sierra valleys became a distinct branch of industry. It might be needed to wash gravels found high up on hillsides; and in order to get it there, men must build great wooden aqueducts, or "flumes," from far up the mountain streams, so as to let the water run, of its own impulse, to the needed place. The flumes often crossed wide valleys; they were themselves the outcome of months of labor, and employed in time many millions of capital. In various improved shapes they have remained essential to the mining industry ever since.

---

[19] It is impossible to give any extended list of authorities on this topic, and needless to. Cf. Hittell's *Resources,* p. 307 (6th ed.); Capron: *History of California* (Boston, 1854), p. 208; Auger: *Voyage en Californie,* p. 107, for views of various periods.

Nor was this the only direction in which gravel-mining increased its organization and proved its power to make a possible basis for the social life of a civilized community. River-bed mining, undertaken on a small scale early and on a large scale, but with general disaster, in 1850, was in 1851 and later a great and fruitful industry.[20] It constituted one of the boldest and most dramatic of the miner's great fights with fortune. He had to organize his little army of laborers, to risk everything, to toil nearly through the summer for the hope of a few weeks at most of hard-earned harvest at the end; and often, at the very moment when victory seemed nearest, an early rain swept everything away and left absolutely no return. In this type of mining, whose operations have been very frequently described, the object was to turn the course of some one of the greater mountain streams, by means of a dam and a canal or flume. The bed would thus be left bare, perhaps for miles, while the flume carried along the whole body of the stream, whose impulse was meanwhile used to turn water-wheels in the flume, and so to pump from the stream-bed the surplus water that still interfered with active operations.[21]

To get all this ready was a slow and difficult operation. The mountain torrent, winding, cliff-bound, and swift, was no easy prey to catch and tame. One had first to wait long for its fall before beginning work. When, after months of toil, the thing was done, nobody knew what was to be found in the river-

[20] The vast river-bed operations of 1850, both in the northern and in the southern mines, are reviewed in the newspapers of that autumn. See in particular, for the early undertakings of 1849, Wierzbicki, op. cit., p. 41 and p. 46; and, for the operations of 1850, the *Sacramento Transcript* of September 30 and October 8, 1850. The causes of failure in 1850 were inexperience in doing the mechanical work, a frequent bad choice of situations, and the early, though light rains of that autumn. In 1851 the dry weather continued till nearly the end of the year and success was very general.

[21] Borthwick's *Three Years in California* contains in a plate, opposite p. 208, an original sketch of an early river-bed mining scene. Numerous others may be found in California books. Dredging the rivers was early dreamed of, but of course never succeeded in producing gold.

gravels until mining had gone on for some time. Meanwhile nothing is more whimsical than the beginning of the California rainy season. The first great black clouds and the first steady, warm southwester may come already in September, although then the showers are apt to pass by in a night. November is yet more likely to hear the moaning of the first long autumn storm. But there are years that pass away altogether before the serious work of winter begins, and so leave to the following January and February the honors of the first "clouds and flowers," and keep even through December still the weariness of the "dust and sky." This uncertainty, which in later years has so embittered the lives of farmers, was in the early days significant, although with a difference, for the river-bed miners. The great rains would at last fall, and, unless good warning had been given and taken, not only the dams would burst (as for that matter they must then in any case soon burst), but the flumes, with all their works, would go plunging in fragments down the newly born brown torrents. And so these last weeks of gold-harvesting and of danger to all the capital invested were weeks of feverish toil and anxiety. Yet on such food some of the wealthiest camps for a time subsisted. And the work taxed all the energies of hundreds of men.

Without giving further space to descriptions of mining by sinking shafts (or "coyote-holes," as the miners of 1850 and 1851 called them), and without dwelling upon the beginnings of quartz mining and of hydraulic mining, we must return to our main topic. It was necessary for us thus to examine a little the physical side of the mining industry in order to appreciate the growth of the social life. The passage from lonely pan-washing to the vast operations of the flume companies, of the river-bed miners, and later of the hydraulic miners and of the quartz-mining companies did not remove from mining its dangerous character, either considered as an investment for capital or viewed as a basis for a sound social order. But, at all events, men found in the advance of the industry to its more complex forms, in the formation of the necessary great partnerships, and in the organization of labor the thing that all men need: namely, something to give a sense of mutual duties and of common risks. The irresponsible freedom of the gay youth who had crowded the ships from the Eastern states must in all this toil be sadly limited. They had condemned themselves to one of the hardest and often bitterest of lives. But, at all events, they were now bound to build a society. Even while they organized their private schemes their camp became a town, and themselves townsmen.

V. *The Spirit of the Miners' Justice of 1851 and 1852: the Miners on Their Own Law*

WE have seen how the mining camp, from the first moments of its existence, was easily organized so as to seem a rudely but for some time effectively governed little state. The business of government, as we have also seen, was limited to keeping the public peace from grosser disturbances, to punishing theft and murder, and to settling disputes about the use of land for mining-purposes. The miners meanwhile commonly had a feeling that purely "private disputes" — that is, those that did not violently and directly assail the public peace in a general way — were not properly the concern of the community.[22] This was, to be sure, a fatally mistaken notion and could not be consistently carried out. But the effort to carry it out, by ignoring so far as possible processes for debt, and by paying little attention to gamblers' quarrels and to like displays of violence, must soon demoralize any growing community.

However, we have to consider the young mining town as it was and to ask what was the consciousness that, after the first months of entirely primitive good order, isolation, and effective self-government had passed away, the miners themselves had retained, while they still continued to apply to criminals this rude and primitive camp code. Did they suppose themselves to be still really and justly free from any immediate external authority? Were they conscious of their camp as of a properly independent community, having a right to its own laws? Did they retain this consciousness after submission to the state courts was possible? Or did they, on the contrary, feel their

[22] Cf. Mr. Shinn's *Mining Camps*, p. 126.

improvised code to be simply lynch law, the assertion of an unauthorized independence, and so an actual rebellion against the established and properly sovereign laws of the land, a rebellion only excused by the necessity of the moment? This question, comparatively insignificant in 1848 and 1849, becomes of much greater interest as soon as the new state was born.

To this question Mr. Shinn has answered, in his *Mining Camps,* on the basis of his various authorities, that the miners' organization was normally not only efficient for its purposes but also wholly in earnest in its work (p. 175), and that the miners' justice, notwithstanding its occasional lapses, was "in every important particular" sharply contrasted with lynch law (p. 230). Mr. Shinn draws at some length the contrast between miners' law and lynch law. Lynch law, as we now know it, through certain too familiar newspaper items from a number of rural districts in our South and West, is sudden in its action, creates no true precedents, keeps no records, shuns the light, conceals the names of its ministers, is generally carried out in the night by a perfectly transient mob, expresses only popular passion, and is in fine essentially disorderly. Miners' law was open in its methods, liked regularity of procedure, gave the accused a fair chance to defend himself, was carried out in broad daylight and by men publicly chosen; and when state and county organization were sufficiently developed to take its place, it gladly resigned its scepter to the regular officers of the law.

This is the strongest possible statement on the side of those who maintain the satisfactory character of the miners' code for the simple social purposes that it undertook to attain. I am very anxious to do this view proper justice. That for a while, in new and orderly camps, the law of the miners' meetings was in spirit as effective in its way as a regular code, and that those who supported it hoped in time to bring it into due subordination to the state law, I readily admit. But, unfortunately, camps were many, their primitive mood of perfect good order was brief, and the typical mining town of 1851 and later years had passed into a transition stage, where it was nominally in connection with organized state authorities and was actually desirous of managing its own affairs in its own old way. To this state of affairs Mr. Shinn's account applies with great difficulty. After 1849 all camps were nominally under the state government. New camps were still often for a little time practically quite isolated, but ere long state organization would, at least in name, overtake them. According to Mr. Shinn, the miners' meeting, or the council, or the alcalde, or whatever governed the new camp would be a conscious preparation for this coming of the regular law. As soon as the organized legal machinery became in any sense more than a name, the orderly instinct of the miners would counsel immediate submission, and they would voluntarily abandon or subordinate their organization in its old forms to these new ones. Until the state organization came, the miners, however, would be conscious of their rightful independence. But, much as this theory of Mr. Shinn's impressed me on a first reading, the direct evidence shows that after 1849 the miners, even in newly organized districts, were apt to regard their camp law, especially the criminal part of it, as a necessary but lawless device for forcing a general peace. Their contemporary accounts of it differ from their accounts of their land laws. These latter they regard as furnishing the only just and truly legal method of dealing with mining rights. They resist strenuously any legislative interference with their local self-government in these matters. They insist absolutely upon the autonomy of the miners' district as regards the land; and for years, against all legislative schemes at home and all congressional propositions at Washington, they actually maintained this autonomy. But their independence in matters of criminal law was brief and, so far as I know, was seldom, almost never, defended at the time on any such theoretical grounds as Mr. Shinn's; but was defended solely as being the last resort of isolated communities and was confessedly, in a strict sense, lynch law.

For this reason, after concrete cases of violent popular justice in the mines, we find the community, in speaking of the affair, generally more or less on the defensive. To 1849 this statement applies in but very small measure, since the camps of 1849 were, on the whole, free from any very notable general disturbances of which any contemporary record is known to me; and were in any case out of relation to higher authority. But in 1850, and still more in 1851, when the popular justice of the mines is dealing with really serious complications, one finds this feeling of the need of special justification of each such act as a lawless but inevitable deed very prevalent. Of the sharp line of demarcation between lynch law and miners' law the miners themselves are thus seen to be, at the time, largely unconscious.

It would be easy to show all this clearly enough by means of citations from those contemporary books of travel [23] whose authors are not seriously hostile to the miners' justice. But on travelers' accounts, or on other books, we need not depend. The newspaper of the time is the best source of information about the spirit of the people. The California newspapers of 1850, 1851, and 1852 generally defend miners' justice; but they show us two things: first that the miners' justice was not usually sharply distinguished from mob law, even in the minds of those concerned in it; and secondly that in the concrete instances of the use of miners' justice we can discover all possible gradations, from the most formal, calm, and judicial behavior of a healthy young camp, driven by momentary necessity to defend itself against outrage, down to the most abominable exhibitions of brutal popular passion, or even of private vengeance.

Specimen contemporary newspaper comments on the popular tribunals are not hard to find; and in tone they very fairly agree. The acts of these popular tribunals, when not outrageously unjust, are generally defended; but almost always [24] without any consciousness that they stand for a definite stage

---

[23] See in particular Capron: *History of California* (Boston, 1854), p. 228; Delano: *Life on the Plains*, etc., chap. xxv; Borthwick: *Three Years in California*, p. 223 ff.

[24] I use this qualification because of a single case where the *Sacramento Transcript*, as we shall later see, speaks of miners' justice without regret and as utterly opposed to lynch law. But this exception has a reason. No doubt other cases exist, though seldom.

of normal legal development, or are the "friends and forerunners" of the regular law; and solely on the ground that the extreme need justifies the outburst and that miners' justice is a lamentable necessity. Thus, in the *Sacramento Transcript* of February 12, 1851, after a description of a very common sort of miners' trial at Bridgeport, a town on Deer Creek, where a defaulting partner had been overtaken and brought back by his fellows, tried by an improvised court, convicted, and sentenced to a severe whipping, I find these comments: "This is the only sure means of administering justice, and although we may regret, and deem lynch law objectionable, yet the present unsafe sort of prisons we have, and the lenity shown offenders, are such as to induce us to regard such an exercise of power" (concludes the editor) with comparative lenity. Just before this issue the editor had been repeatedly complaining of the general insecurity of prisons. A considerable study of the files of this paper leads me to think this expression of opinion a fair representative of the editorial views.[25] Nor do I find any defender of popular justice in the news columns or correspondence of this paper saying anything more definite in defense of miners' lynching than this. On the contrary, I find such defenders almost always recognizing a conflict between regular law and miners' law. In practice, as appears from this evidence, the miners demanded of the regular courts more than that they should be known to exist. The miners demanded that these courts should be judged efficient by the very men who, as citizens, created them under the constitution, before the citizens could be called upon to surrender any authority to them. And if miners chose to declare a court inefficient, they felt at any time free to supersede it by their own impromptu tribunals. And then they defended these tribunals, not as normal means of punishing crime, but as abnormal necessities.

Thus, in a letter dated Coloma, May 7, and published in the *Transcript* of May 12, 1851, persons who sign themselves "The Miners" give an "authentic statement" of a recent outburst of popular indignation near that place. An honest citizen, as it seems, had lost from his wagon some packages of flour and

[25] Cf. the editorial of January 14, 1851.

butter, and the goods were traced, apparently by scattered flour, "from near the wagon to the cabin of Jones and partners" and identified by the owner. When these facts were made known, the "company present" chose a "jury of twelve men, together with one presiding officer, who coolly and deliberately proceeded to investigate the facts of the case," giving "Jones and his partners" a fair chance. The prisoners were found guilty by the jury, and the "company present, numbering about 33," concurred by unanimous vote in the verdict. Then they considered what to do. The district was the oldest in the mines, since it was in that district that Marshall had first found gold; and the courts were well established. Many of the crowd were disposed accordingly to hand over the prisoners to the officers at Coloma. But ere they had set out for the town, other voices were heard. "To deliver the prisoners to the civil authorities would be tantamount to an acquittal of them, and would do no good, further than to help fill the pockets of officers and lawyers." So it was said, and they "resolved to settle the matter without delay." The prisoners were hereupon treated very leniently, being ordered to refund the value of the property stolen, and to leave the district before the next morning, or else to be whipped and then banished in case they sought to stay. Lenient the offer was, though not strictly in accordance with the Bill of Rights. The prisoners, being given the choice, elected to leave unwhipped, or at least said so. But, possibly remembering the Bill of Rights, they concluded upon reflection to go about their business as usual and "neglected to leave." Whereupon twenty or twenty-five persons, hearing of this contempt of court, hunted up Jones the next day "and were proceeding to a suitable place to inflict the punishment, when the sheriff and his subs interfered in behalf of the law," promised to keep the prisoner safe, and "induced" the mob to give him up. "He was accordingly committed to jail, and tried next day before Justice Brooks. And notwithstanding the plain, pointed, irresistible, and unquestionable evidence of the guilt of the prisoner, he was informed by the court that the charges against him were not sufficient for conviction; and no doubt Mr. Jones now thinks that he is at perfect liberty to steal any and everything he can,

provided he can be tried by the so termed courts of justice."
Such is the "authentic statement" of the miners. But their comments are interesting, because they illustrate just the sense of
a conflict between miners' justice and the regular law which
was so common in those days. "Would it be less," continue the
signers of the letter, "than the deserts of such officers as these,
if they had to receive the dues of Jones as their own, in every
case where they let the guilty go unpunished? We have the
following to say in reference to our position in this neighborhood, as it regards lynch law: we are to a man opposed to any
such law, and we believe there is no part of California in which
the citizens would be more submissive to the civil authorities
than ourselves, could the laws as designed by our legislature be
executed faithfully. But when we call on the civil authorities
for redress, we are repulsed. Indeed, sirs, we would not be surprised if the present administrators of the law in this part of
the country should make the whole community a mob. . . . So
long as this evil exists to the extent that it now does, we will
find our citizens looking to themselves for protection."

But we need not depend on any one newspaper. In the *San
Francisco Herald* for April 4, 1852 [26] is a letter from a "special
correspondent," plainly a resident, at Mokelumne Hill, a prominent camp in the southern mines. A vigilance committee had
been formed there for about two months. Since its formation
there had occurred but one murder. "The strong current of
crime" that had theretofore swept "everything before it," and
that the regular courts had never checked, had been checked by
the committee, and order had begun to reign on the hill. Some
weeks had passed without disturbance, "and it was supposed
that the committee were no longer on the lookout." But alas!
this tale of prosperous peace was a short one.

"A number of robberies have, within the last ten days, been
committed." "Scarcely a night has passed for some time but
something has been stolen, or some man robbed." At last, after
one Perkins had been robbed of forty-five ounces, a Sonoran,
by name Carlos, was found on a tent floor, apparently drunk.
The tent, as was seen, had just been cut open, Carlos had no

[26] Harvard College Library file.

business there and seemed too drunk to explain his errand. He staggered off, but was soon discovered to be sober enough indeed, was arrested by the committee, was found to have gold specimens in his possession that Perkins could identify as a part of the lately stolen gold, and was at last induced to confess himself one of the recent thieves. So "the committee deliberated what should be done with him. It was thought that if he was handed over to the city authorities, he might perhaps be committed to Jackson jail; where, if he remained twenty-four hours, it would be because he liked the accommodations, and had no fear of being convicted." To flog and release him was thought equally useless, since the committee knew his previous reputation and despaired of reforming him. "If hung, there would be one thief less," and one warning more. So the committee resolved to hang him. Carlos made no objection, but asked only for a good supper, a priest, and a glass of brandy. The committee cheerfully complied with his requests, and after having received such religious and other consolation as his poor soul desired, Carlos slept well all night, walked coolly to his gallows the next morning, and cheerfully helped about his own execution. So much for the case.[27] The comments are thoroughly characteristic.

"It is much to be deplored," says the correspondent, "that necessity should exist for such extreme measures. This execution will doubtless be condemned by many in California, and by more in the old States. The sickly sentimentalist will hold up his hands in horror; the officers of the law will be found loud in their indignation at what they will call a ruthless, illegal deed; the ermined judge who sits secure in his seat at a salary of thousands per year will be indignant that the people should presume to take any measures to protect their own life and property and punish offenders without their [*sic*] aid and sanction; but those who live in well-ordered communities, where they have officers who know their duty and dare do it, can have no idea of the situation in which we are placed. Whose fault is it?

---

[27] The main facts are confirmed by the account in the *San Francisco Alta* for April 5, 1852, steamer edition.

"The truth is, it has been absolutely and imperatively necessary for us to protect ourselves, and, law or no law, it will be done. We have a Committee of Vigilance who are determined that, until a different state of things exists, they will not disband, but will punish in the most exemplary manner all and every high-handed offense against life and property."

Any reader is struck by the force of this plea, and he fully agrees that, like "Jones and partners" at Coloma, Carlos may have been as verily a dog as the report marks him. But with Jones and Carlos in these cases we have little concern. Our interest is chiefly with the honest men themselves and with their unhappy state. The reader must have observed the curiously external point of view that the writers of the two letters just cited adopt as they discuss their own society. "People cannot understand our woes," they pathetically insist. "We have lawyers, judges, sheriffs, prisons, but, alas! no justice, unless we fight for it ourselves, treating our own law-officers as aliens, and becoming a mob. Oh, the depravity of those courts and of those lawyers!" But, as we are tempted to retort: whose gold, now hoarded by the pound in insecure tents, the prey of every vagabond, might have contributed to build a strong jail at Coloma or at Jackson? Or, perhaps, was it not of a truth felt unnecessary to build a strong jail — unnecessary just because one chose in one's heart, meanwhile, to think ropes a little cheaper than bricks, and, for the purpose, just as strong? Nay, is all the "sickly sentimentalism," or all the cant, on one side in this matter? Who whines perpetually and tediously, all through these early days, about "necessity," and "the first law of nature," and the defects of the social order, and all his gloomy social afflictions; even while, in fact, his whole purpose is to store his gold dust, to enjoy his private fun, and then to shake off the viler dust of the country from his feet as soon as possible? Who but the poor outraged miner himself, whom necessity, if not manhood, will ultimately compel to apply himself to his duty and to stop his whining?

Nothing is capable of clearer demonstration from contemporary documents than the color of the sentiments of a community, in case one can find the very words of a representative people. The details of transactions it is harder to state accurately. In passing from the motives of the miners' popular justice to its methods and more characteristic incidents, we shall be much at the mercy of our witnesses. Yet of this the reader may be assured. What I have here further to narrate about miners' justice will rest, as far as possible, like the foregoing, on contemporary evidence. For what a pioneer can say, after many years, about the incidents of a given affair is worth little or nothing in comparison with any fairly objective contemporary evidence, unless, indeed, the pioneer in question was himself directly concerned in the very incidents that he relates. And for our purposes just here, no vague generalizations about the early justice will serve such as are so familiar in the later books and essays, by romancers and pioneers, on those early days. We must go afresh to the sources.

VI. *Miners' Justice in Action — Characteristic Scenes and Incidents*

ALL gradations, I have said, can be found in the popular justice of the mines, from the most orderly and wisely conducted expression of outraged popular sentiment that is in any way possible outside of the forms of law, down to the most brutal and disgraceful outbursts of mob fury. I wish that the latter class of incidents had been rarer than one actually finds them. But the day for either vindicating or condemning by a labored argument the pioneer life as a whole has long since passed. The true vindication of those days — their only possible vindication — is the great and progressive state that grew up upon that soil and that thenceforth was destined to do for our land a very real service. But, after all, neither to vindicate nor to condemn the whole community is our desire; we want, for the sake of our own instruction in political duties, to study the various individual events and tendencies that determine social life and to let our praise or our blame fall upon them.

The more regular and orderly popular justice of the mines took place especially in the newer and more isolated camps, although circumstances might bring it to pass almost anywhere in the mines. We find it expressing itself often in very quaint forms, using, generally, considerable severity, but keeping up a show of good temper throughout. Where it was thus free from passion, its verdicts seem, at all events, to have been generally in accordance with the facts, whatever we may say of the wisdom of its sentences.

A study of the lynching affairs thus directly from the sources seems to me to throw a wholly new light upon the character of which they were the too frequent expression. Many of the popular legends about lynching that have influenced the more modern and romantic tales of the early days distort very curiously the true motives of the miners. A mining camp is presented to us in such stories as a community that always especially delighted in its lynching parties and that went about them with all the jovial ferocity of young tigers at play. But when the lynching affair was once begun, then, as the story-tellers will have it, the popular court was easily moved by purely sentimental considerations. A timely offer of drinks, a good joke, or, far better still, an ingenious display of ruggedly pathetic eloquence might suffice to turn the court aside from its dangerous undertakings. The whole affair was a kind of great and grim joke, and sentimentalism could always take the place of the joking mood and, if it did so, might save the prisoner. In the dramatic presentation of such scenes many writers have amused themselves. Thus the lynching affair, even if tragic in outcome, is, throughout, enlivened, according to these accounts, by absurdly conventional humor; and often, when the outcome is to be less terrible, the tragedy is averted by conventional eloquence. To take a very recent instance of such story-telling, I read not long since, in the *Overland Monthly,* a pretended sketch of an early lynching scene in which the prisoner's life is at length saved by the ingenuity of his volunteer defender, an old man whose reputation for veracity stands very high in the camp where this scene is supposed to take place. This veracious defender, namely, who has never before seen the prisoner, concludes to save the latter's life by making an exception in his favor and lying about him. The prisoner's face is pock-marked, and the defender accordingly

makes up, on the spur of the moment, a long story about how
this poor wretch once nursed a very unfriendly man, well
known to the defender himself, through an attack of smallpox
and so caught the infection. The defender's tale is made as
harrowing as possible. Its effect is electric. The prisoner stands
accused of a very serious crime, and the evidence against him
is strong; but all is forthwith forgotten. Judge Lynch offers him
tobacco, gives him a drink, and sets him at liberty, on the
ground that so saintly a man as one who volunteers to be a
smallpox nurse under very harrowing circumstances is at liberty to do a little occasional mischief in those diggings without
question.

Now, such sentimentalism as this is utterly foreign to the
typical miners' lynching affair, whether orderly or not. The
typical lynching occurred, indeed, in a community of Americans where everybody was by habit disposed to joke in public
and seem as cheerful as he could and to listen to all sorts of
eloquence; but the affair itself was no expression of this formal
joviality, nor yet of this submissiveness to oratorical leadership.
It proceeded from a mood of utter revulsion against the accustomed good humor of the camp. It was regarded as a matter
of stern, merciless, business necessity. It was unconscious of any
jocular character. Disorderly lynching affairs in some few cases
do, indeed, appear to have been mere drunken frolics. But
nearly all, even of the disorderly affairs, and that, too, where
their cruelty was most manifest, had in them no element of the
merely jocular. They expressed an often barbarous fury; but
they pretended to be deeds of necessity, and a sentimental
speech in a prisoner's favor would have done nothing save, possibly, to endanger the prisoner's life yet more, or even to endanger that of his advocate. No one understands the genuine
lynching who does not see in it a stern laying aside of all these
characteristic American traits of good humor and of oratorical
sentimentalism themselves for the sake of satisfying a momentary popular passion aroused against the forces of disorder. Just
because the miner was accustomed to be so tolerant and easy-
going, these moments of the outburst of popular fury found
him, whether orderly or not, in all typical cases merciless, deaf

to all pathetic appeals, unconscious of anything save the immediate public necessity. What element of comedy remained in some of these affairs was generally an unconscious element.

And so, while not all the lynching scenes are equally tragic, a large class of them is doubtless well typified by the following very gloomy tragedy, which suggests, if one wants to reflect upon it, a world of horror behind the scenes. This is, namely, a trial for murder, occurring in 1851 at Shasta, then the center of a newer mining region. I use the report communicated from Shasta to the *Sacramento Transcript* of April 3, 1851 and give the details at some length just because the affair is so characteristic.

At Oak Bottom, about ten miles from Shasta, there lived, in March of that year, two partners,[28] Easterbrook and Price, who had come from the lower mining region together, a few months before, leaving on their way a third partner, disabled by poison oak, at Grass Valley. The two had left families at home in the East and were come to California to win fortunes for them, Easterbrook, in particular, expecting, like so many others, to raise the mortgage from his farm. Nobody seems to have questioned their respectability, or their mutual friendship. One evening in March the two went together to the "residence of Mr. Isaac Roop," as it is called in the report. This was next door, in fact, to their own tent, and was a "residence" where one drank "ardent spirits," as the report in its exact way calls the drink there found, where one also played cards, and where one had to pay a bill at the end of the evening. As the hours went by, Easterbrook, whom nobody seems to have accused afterwards of being a habitual drunkard, grew a little excited and quarrelsome, and after some minor difficulty with a third person, he found himself refused more liquor by the cautious Mr. Isaac Roop. Thereupon Easterbrook called for his bill and began to quarrel over the amount of it. Price, meanwhile, had gone to their tent near by and had lain down on his blanket, whether drunken himself or no does not appear. At all events, hearing

---

[28] I give real names only to guarantee the accuracy of my report. After so many years there is little danger that the persons will be recognized.

Easterbrook's voice, he called out, as Easterbrook at last proceeded to pay his score: "Don't be paying out other people's money." Easterbrook started at the insult, rushed back to the tent in fury, cursing, and told his partner to prepare for death. Price had been only joking and was not moved by the threat. "*Lay down,*" he was heard to say quietly, "*lay down and go to sleep.*" An eyewitness saw, by whatever dim light there was, that Easterbrook dragged out a gun from under some baggage. In an instant one heard a report, and Easterbrook himself was fleeing from the tent into the night. When the bystanders, who at once pursued, had caught him in a little time, he said, apparently with the air of one waking: "Have I shot Price?" And when they said that he had, he replied: "Do as you please with me; it was an accident, and I was drunk." Price lay gasping; he never spoke again and died in about an hour.

The next day Easterbrook was brought, guarded, down to Shasta, over the ten miles of new miners' road. There, just after midday dinner, a meeting of the citizens was called. Perfect decorum prevailed; a ghastly air of ordinary and businesslike propriety pervades the stiffly written report. There were doubtless lawyers present. The assembled people first chose a chairman and secretary and then a committee of three to select a trial jury of twelve men "to try the cause before the people." They also passed a resolution summoning the witnesses and guaranteeing to the accused a fair and impartial trial;.and they then appointed an officer "to carry into effect the verdict of the jury, and summons to his aid as many persons as might be necessary to release or execute the prisoner." The chairman swore in the jury and called the witnesses; and now at length the story of the homicide was heard. The prisoner was thereafter asked what he had to say in defense. He replied briefly, but not without some natural and terrible pathos. He had been in the mines only since the 29th of the last July. Never before this one time had he in all his life "had words" with any man. Never had he "done anything to cause a blush." Standing now as one on the verge of the grave, he could declare in God's name that he felt in his mind "guiltless of any premeditated intention to

kill Mr. Price." ("Mr." has its sadly formal ring as applied to
the dead partner at this moment.) Mr. Price was a "good man."
The prisoner had never had any feeling against him. And Price
had left "a wife, and a daughter who is now married." But, as
for the prisoner himself: "I have a wife and three children. The
eldest is nine years of age. My circumstances are such, that,
should I leave the world, my wife and children will be penni-
less. I have a farm which is incumbered, and without my return will be sacrificed. It is not for myself, but my wife and
children that I plead. Taking my life would not bring to life
Mr. Price. It would only make one more widow, and three more
orphans, and on their account only do I plead for mercy, as
any of you would, were you in the same unfortunate condition."
This defense seems to have been noted down by the secretary of the meeting, for the newspaper report is very formally
worded and is called official. There were no other arguments
heard on either side, the jury feeling no need of further advice. Shasta was not a place for tears, nor for pity; and the jury,
after a brief consultation, brought in a written verdict, signed
by each one, declaring Easterbrook guilty of murder in the first
degree and sentencing him to "be punished immediately by
hanging by the neck until he is dead." The meeting had con-
vened at two o'clock. It was now after four. The prisoner was
given about an hour to set his affairs in order and was hanged
between five and six. — The *Transcript* editor regards this as a
truly wonderful case, finds in it a fine spirit of law and order,
and calls it "an exhibition of the power of the American mind
over that which we have heretofore known as mob law." The
reason for this exceptional and benevolent mood on the editor's
part is a recent occurrence in Sacramento itself, the "Roe"
lynching, which had for the moment made popular justice seem
to him of vast importance. Usually, as we have seen, he was
less enthusiastic.

I know not whether the story of "The Outcasts of Poker
Flat" was founded, as report has declared, upon some oral
tradition that reached the author years later, of a real incident
of early times. If so, then the real incident itself may have been

the expulsion from this same town of Shasta, in August 1851, of all the so-called "suspicious" characters of the town, "seven men and two women." [29] A "hay yard" had been burned down, and report made the act the work of an incendiary. All suspicious characters were at once ordered out of town; "they complied," and passed down towards a brook called "Whiskey Creek." Now as these nine went by the way, they met, oddly enough, coming down from Oak Bottom, our friend Mr. Isaac Roop himself, at whose "residence" the two partners had passed the fatal evening some five months before. I know not what general disgust with respectable gentlemen who had "residences" to leave when out for their airings, or what feeling of recklessness it was, that moved these nine; but one of them hereupon shot at Mr. Roop. Were this only a book of fiction, they would have killed him, by way of ending the story well. But this is history, and one is bound to say that, according to the report here cited, they missed Mr. Roop altogether, who went his way, probably with more than his accustomed quickness, into Shasta and told what they had done. Whereupon the miners of that town sent out an armed party, who very firmly and leniently escorted the nine southward to the border of the county, with the intent of sending them thence into banishment; and of their fate, and of Mr. Roop's, in subsequent days, I know nothing. This, then, must suffice as concerning the justice of the people of Shasta in 1851. — Here, at least, there was no trace of the sentimental or the jocular.

Our next case is less gloomy than Easterbrook's, and takes place later, and in a less severely primitive locality. It is a case of larceny this time. In the *San Francisco Herald* of March 22, 1852 I find a report, apparently officially furnished by mail to this and other papers, of a miners' meeting at Johnson's Bar, where one "Dr. Bardt," whose title is very considerately preserved throughout the report, was arraigned for theft.[30]

---

[29] *Alta California* of August 20, 1851.

[30] The comedy of this scene, be it noticed, lies not in the conscious behavior of the miners, who were as business-like and merciless as the judges of Easterbrook, but in our point of view as spectators.

"The meeting having been called to order, Mr. Campbell was appointed chairman, and Cyrus Hurd, Jr., secretary.

"On motion, it was resolved, that Dr. A. Bardt be whipped for the said thefts.

"On motion, it was resolved that Dr. Bardt should receive thirty-nine lashes on the bare back and leave the mines in three days.

"It was moved and seconded that Dr. Bardt should be cropped. The motion, on being put, was negatived unanimously.

"On motion, it was resolved that Dr. Bardt be whipped by the constable, Mr. Thompson, with a rope.

"On motion, it was resolved that the constable should proceed immediately to the discharge of his duty.

"On motion it was resolved that the secretary be requested to furnish a copy of the proceedings to be published in the California papers.

"The punishment having been inflicted, it was, on motion, resolved that the meeting do adjourn sine die."

Since the thefts are spoken of as the "said thefts," one is disposed to compare this case to the above cited Coloma case of "Jones and partners," and to suppose that "Dr. Bardt" had tried to set a previous verdict at naught.

Severe, unsentimental, and in the sharpest contrast to their daily joviality was the mood of the lynching miners as we have so far examined it. The cause of this contrast we have also begun to see. The miners' justice, however, even where the evidence was clear and the trial orderly, was often not merely severe, but atrociously cruel. In the *Transcript* for January 30, 1851 one finds the record of a trial at Mississippi Bar, where a thief, "in consideration of his youth," was not hanged, but was given one hundred and fifty lashes, and a brand "R" on the left arm, after having his head shaved on one side. One is surprised to find how people who at home, in those philanthropic days, would very likely have been under the sway of sentimentalists and would have shuddered at severe penalties of all sorts now behaved when they were away from home. For the change their own sense of irresponsibility is largely to blame, the same sense of irresponsibility that led them to tolerate the causes that led to these social disasters.

The two punishments, flogging and death, as penalties for theft have invited much comment from critics of early California mining life. It is too obvious to need much special discussion here that to flog and banish a thief from a given camp was to do worse than nothing for the good order of the mines at large. The thief went out into the mountains a very poor, desperate, and revengeful man. He had, meanwhile, all the vague chances ahead that were offered to him by a possible entrance as a stranger into some new camp. Hope in any cheerful sense these chances would hardly give him; but in his despair they would promise him that in the new place he might possibly avenge, on people who did not know him, the blows that he had suffered from those who had found him out. Or, again, the sight of the lonely mountain roads might offer to his despair the proper suggestion for a new life of crime. In any case, the camp that banished him had only, as Capron's informants put it,[31] "let loose a fiend." And the friendly interchange of their respective fiends among the various camps was obviously the whole outcome of this prevailing system of flogging and banishment.

Those miners who chose to hang the notorious thieves of their camps were therefore, so far as the direct effectiveness of their work was concerned, wiser, since they got rid of at least one rogue. A dead thief steals no more; and as I have above shown, this book has no sort of sentimentalism to expend over dead thieves, although, for other reasons, this plan of lynching thieves was a bad one. Where the miners' courts were orderly, careful, sensible in examining evidence, and certain of the habitual and intolerable roguery of the thief before them, it was far better, under the circumstances, to hang than to flog and banish him, and less cruel also. Nevertheless, the real objection to the habitual hanging of the thieves by the people, as practiced in those days, is none the less cogent. I have already suggested where this true objection lay. The thief himself, as an individual, was indeed often enough a worthless hound and

[31] Capron's *History*, op. cit.

deserved all that he got. As against the interests of society at large, his interests were naught. But it was precisely the interest of society that was in the long run most injured by the habit of hanging the thieves in these rude, irregular miners' courts. For the popular conscience was debased by the physical brutality of the business, and so soon as the lynching habit was once established, this conscience was put to sleep by a false self-confidence, engendered of the ease wherewith justice seemed in such cases to be vindicated. And society, which, with all its fancied honesty, was, in its own way, an obvious accomplice of the thief himself, was prevented for a while from appreciating the enormity of its offenses. For it was society that encouraged these rogues and that, with every month, made them worse rogues than ever. By its careless spirit, by its patronage of gambling-saloons, by its jolly toleration of all private quarrels that did not go so far as once for all to enrage the public, by its willful determination to spend no time on self-discipline, and no money on so costly a thing as a stable public order, and, above all, by its persistently wicked neglect to choose good public officers, the mining society made itself the friend and upholder of the very roguery that it flogged and hanged. Its habitual good humor ensured the necessity of occasional fury and brutality. And so long as it flogged and hanged in this rude popular way, it could not be convinced of its errors, but ever and anon, after one of these popular outbursts of vengeance, it raised its blood-stained hands in holy horror at crime, lamenting the fate that would doubtless force it still in future to continue its old business of encouraging this bloodshed. All this criticism of mine may be merely moral commonplace; but I am sure that I should never fill these pages with such platitudes were it not for the outrageous effrontery with which the average mining community of those days used to defend itself, in the fashion cited above. The single act was indeed often in itself defensible. It was the habit of risking such emergencies that was intolerable.

So far did this trust in hanging as a cure for theft go that in the second legislature, that of 1851, an act was passed making hanging for grand larceny a penalty to be thenceforth regularly

imposed at the pleasure of the convicting jury.[32] So easy is it
for men to sanction their blunders by the help of a little printers' ink, used for the publication of a statute.

The familiar reply of the pioneers to all these criticisms is
that if the miners' justice reformed nobody, it at least effec-
tually intimidated every rascal. And much nonsense has been
repeated by writers on those early days concerning the terrible
magnitude and swiftness, the certainty, the simplicity, and the
consequent deterring effect of lynch law. But one who repeats
this nonsense forgets first of all that axiom of criminal justice
according to which the magnitude and the frightfulness of a
penalty are of but the smallest deterring power in comparison
with the certainty of the penalty; and such a one also forgets
that mob law can never be certain. While a vigilance committee in the mines was in full course of vengeance, crime
would indeed be terrified. But at the very instant the committee
relaxed its vigilance, the carelessly open tents, the gold, the
scattered wanderers prospecting in the hills or finding their way
along the roads, all suggested to the thief his old chances. And
what had he, after all, to fear? No vigilant police, no conscien-

---

[32] I am somewhat perplexed to find Mr. Shinn, *Mining Camps,*
p. 228, note, referring this law to the first year of the life of the state,
and to the legislature of 1850. The matter is one of plain record, and
is of some importance, because it shows that the law did not first encourage the lynchers, but that only after the extravagances of popular justice had for some time flourished, it was found possible to load
the statute-book with an entirely useless and demoralizing penalty —
useless because its uncertainty made it of no deterring power,
and demoralizing because all useless and obsolete penalties are
mere opportunities for whimiscal popular vengeance, not expressions of the dignity of the social order. The best possible comment
on this law is a case where a thief was tried under it at Monterey,
as reported in the *San Francisco Herald* for June 26, 1852. The jury
brought in a verdict finding the prisoner guilty as charged, sentencing him to death, *but recommending him to the mercy of the court.*
The court was puzzled; but as the prisoner was a native Californian,
the jury got the benefit of the doubt, and the prisoner was formally
sentenced to death.

tious public spirit, no strong jails. Only a momentary and terrible outburst of popular justice was, at the worst, to be dreaded. If he escaped that, by flight or by even temporary concealment of his crime, there would be no detectives to hunt him down, no permanently accessible evidence to be produced against him. No witness would be public-spirited enough to wait an hour longer than might be convenient for a chance to testify. In a few weeks the witnesses who could hurt him might be scattered far away and the whole thing forgotten. Under such circumstances could the bare chance of even one hundred and fifty lashes with a branding, or even the possibility of being hanged, deter a rogue from his work? The analogy of the case of England at the close of the last century, with the ineffectiveness of the capriciously executed death penalty as there ordained for lesser offenses, at once suggests itself. Criminals, like savages, scatter to their hiding-places after any sudden defeat; but they are not thereby civilized, and constant vigilance is needed as much after their defeat as before. And when the vigilance committees scattered the rogues of a given camp, the result was very like the one that takes place when a lonesome wanderer in Californian wildernesses scatters the coyotes that have gathered at night around his campfire. The coyote loves to hold parliament, in such a case, just beyond the circles of the firelight, for the benefit of the poor wretch who, rolled up in his blankets, is trying to rest from his labors beside his fire. With unearthly noises the vile beasts drive away from him sleep, for a prostrate and almost motionless man, all alone, the coyote regards as a deeply admirable object. And the man occasionally starts up, perchance, and dashes out into the dark with ineffective ravings, while the whole pack vanish yelping in the night. But, alas, when he returns to his fire and lies down, the gleaming eyes are soon again near, and he has nothing to do but to curse away the hours until dawn, helpless against his tormentors as Gulliver bound in Lilliput. As anyone can see by a chronological study of the newspapers of 1851 and 1852, just such was the experience of many camps with their rogues. Of unhanged rogues a community rids itself only

by ceasing to nourish them; while if you nourish rogues, you
cannot hope to hang them all, nor yet to hang the most of
them.[33]

A chronological study of the newspaper files, I say, proves
this inefficacy of mere lynching, in so far as such a study can
of itself make any social tendency clear. In the spring of 1851,
in fact, and also far into the summer of that year, one finds
much lynching going on. That autumn there seems indeed to
be once more general peace and good order in the mines; but
for this not merely past popular violence must be held responsible, but many other influences as well. The dry season continued until late, and vast river-bed operations, great tunnels,
flumes, dams, ditches, were occupying men's attention. Labor
was organized as never before in the mines. The vested interests of the various communities were great and increasing;
the yield was large, but the responsibility serious. At such a
moment the community was on its good behavior. Moreover
(and this is a deeply significant fact), the violence of the spring

---

[33] The reader should compare here again Mr. Shinn's discussion
of our whole topic and the instances that he cites. He has often
failed to give his sources, and he seems to me one-sided in the choice
of facts; but his is the only effort published before the present one
to discuss systematically the whole subject of popular justice in California, and his view is much more favorable than mine. For further
instances of moderately orderly popular procedure in the mines I
must content myself here with referring to the *San Francisco Alta* of
1851 (Harvard College Library file), in the numbers for May 21
(where a horse-thief at Nevada was allowed by the "crowd" to
choose, himself, who should give him the thirty-nine lashes); July 11
(where a Sonora correspondent describes the caution with which a
vigilance committee proceeded in trying a Mexican horse-thief, who
was given a whole day in which to prepare his case and produce his
witnesses, and who was then convicted and flogged, a collection being afterwards taken up for his benefit); and October 22 (where the
passengers on a Marysville steamboat tried and convicted in regular
miners' form one of their number who had committed a theft on
board, and sentenced him to pay a large fine in gold dust to a sick and
destitute man who chanced also to be on board). All these incidents
are characteristic.

and summer had reacted on the honest men even more than on thieves. The need of vindicating lynching, a need that these people almost always felt, showed that they were capable of being shocked by their own deeds of popular vengeance. For, after all, these honest men had very often been well brought up at home and were still new to bloodshed. In their lives the lynching affairs were, despite their recent frequency, still terrible and wholly exceptional events. And so they may be fairly presumed to have taken, for a while at least, the ordinary precautions of decent citizens. They did not so easily tolerate minor disorders, nor by their good humor encourage ruffians to live in their camps. Probably they gambled less frequently themselves, drank less, acted more soberly. To these causes quite as much as to the temporary fright of the rascals must we attribute the comparative good order of that autumn. Yet the rascals were neither dead nor gone from the state nor reformed, though many of them had left the mines. Just after two horse-thieves had been sentenced to death under the new law at Stockton, the *Stockton Journal* of about October 25, 1851 [34] "again complains," as the *Alta* says, "of the increase of crime and rowdyism at that place." The complaint asserts that disorder prevails to a lamentable extent in Stockton, that "every day is marked with some scene of violence; and the night becomes frightful, from the hideous iniquities perpetrated under the shadow of its obscurity." "All quiet," continues the *Stockton Journal*, "is banished from the place, for no citizen feels safe, unless he is armed for any emergency. Might is the only protection a man can claim in these perilous times." Now, these words are a trifle passionate and rhetorical; but they have no doubt a very real foundation. Some of the banished rogues had gone to Stockton, although that city had not been unaffected by the general popular struggle for order in the summer of 1851. These wretches had found the moment favorable in that city, and the sentence of death just legally passed on the two horse-thieves had not awed them into submission. Yet this was in the comparatively peaceful closing season of the great year of popular justice, which was indeed a valuable

[34] Quoted in the *San Francisco Alta* for October 27.

year, yet not, in general, because of its violence, but because of its organization of labor.

To see the utter transiency of the effects of brute violence, as a suppressor of crime we must, however, look onwards to the newspapers of 1852. Surely, if mere warning by frequent lynchings were enough, the warning of 1851, with the constant readiness of the people to follow it up, on occasion, by new lynchings, ought to have produced a reign of peace in the mines, lasting longer than through the autumn and winter following. But consider the facts. We have already seen how, in the spring of 1852, things went on at Mokelumne Hill. I have before me in a file a number of the steamer *Alta* of June 15, 1852. This number has an astonishing catalogue of crimes, reported from the mining regions both north and south, together with lynchings; and the editor declares that, were he to give all the particulars to be gathered from his mining exchanges of one day, he could fill a number of his own daily edition. And then he adds a significant quotation from an interior paper of the southern mines. "The 'Calaveras Chronicle,'" he says, "complains of the alarming increase of crime in that section within the past few weeks. The grand jury have found ten indictments. 'Summary examples' (*i. e.*, lynching examples), says the 'Chronicle,' for capital and minor offenses have been frequently made; but the *canaille* would scarcely lose sight of the scaffold, the tremor which a malefactor in the agony of death cast through their frame would scarcely have ceased, until they caused the public ear again to be greeted with intelligence of more outrages, more robberies, more assassinations." As for the state of the mining public in that part of the country at the moment, it appears, from several items in that number of the steamer *Alta*, that a "Mexican" at Jackson, having been accused, without any evidence of which an intelligible account can be given, of being the murderer of two Frenchmen who had been slain in their tents near there, was brought before a drunken justice of the peace and was by him committed to prison; and that the "crowd" thereupon, without giving him a fair chance to be heard further in his own defense, took him from jail and hanged him, after a desperate struggle, in the presence of his pleading mother and sisters. Now, this affair, which is very confusedly reported, and which, of course, may have been distorted in the telling, sufficiently indicates, at all events, that the lynching habit was as demoralizing as it was useless.[35]

VII. *A Typical History of a Mining Camp in 1851–2*

MORE orderly expressions of popular justice, of the sort heretofore frequently recorded, were impossible, as we now see, without results that must be far worse than mere mistakes. A mining town was not standing still. It was a growing or else a decaying organism. In alternating between universal optimistic good humor on the one hand and grim vengeance upon wrongdoers on the other, it was, however, either stunting its true growth or dooming itself to decay and corruption. Fortune has preserved to us from the pen of a very intelligent woman, who writes under an assumed name, a marvelously skillful and undoubtedly truthful history of a mining community during a brief period, first of cheerful prosperity, and then of decay and disorder. The wife of a physician, and herself a well-educated New England woman, "Dame Shirley," as she chooses to call herself, was the right kind of witness to describe for us the social life of a mining camp from actual experience. This she did in the form of letters written on the spot to her own sister [36] and collected for publication some two or

[35] I have not wished to burden these pages with a complete list of the very numerous cases of lynching that I have collected from the contemporary newspaper files. The foregoing cases, as far as they go, are to my mind typical, and I believe my choice to be a fair one. At all events such directly verifiable data have far more worth than the confused memory of the pioneers before referred to.

[36] These *Shirley Letters*, found all through the numbers of Ewer's *Pioneer* (published at San Francisco in 1854–5), have already been once cited. Of their authenticity we are assured by the editor. The internal evidence is to the same effect. "Dame Shirley's" interest is not at all our particular one here; and she is quite unconscious of the far-reaching moral and social significance of much that she describes. Many of the incidents introduced are such as imagination could of itself never suggest, in such an order and connection. There

three years later. Once for all, allowing for the artistic defects
inevitable in a disconnected series of private letters, these
"Shirley" letters form the best account of an early mining camp
that is known to me. For our real insight into the mining
life as it was, they are, of course, infinitely more helpful to us
than the perverse romanticism of a thousand such tales as
Mr. Bret Harte's, tales that, as the world knows, were not the
result of any personal experience of really primitive conditions.

"Shirley" entered the mines with her husband in 1851 and
passed the following winter and the summer of 1852 at Rich
Bar and Indian Bar successively, both of them busy camps,
near together, on the North Fork of the Feather River. The
climate agreed with her very well, and on the whole she seems
to have endured the hardships of the life most cheerfully.

Rich Bar [37] was, in September 1851, when she first saw it, a
town of one street, "thickly planted with about forty tene-
ments"; tents, rag and wooden houses, plank hovels, log cabins.
One hotel there was in it, the Empire. Rich Bar had had in its
early days a great reputation for its wealth, in so much that
during its first summer it had suddenly made wealthy, then
converted into drunken gamblers and so utterly ruined, several
hundred miners, all by giving them occasional returns of some
hundreds of dollars to the panful. It had now entered into a
second stage of more modestly prosperous and more steadily
laborious life; it was a very orderly place, and was inhabited
partly by American, partly by foreign miners. Some of the latter were South Americans. "Shirley" on her arrival found herself one of five women on the bar, and was of course very pleas-

---

is no mark of any conscious seeking for dramatic effect. The moods
that the writer expresses indicate no remote purpose, but are the
simple embodiment of the thoughts of a sensitive mind, interested
deeply in the wealth of new experiences. The letters are charmingly
unsentimental; the style is sometimes a little stiff and provincial, but
is on the whole very readable. The real name of the author, according to *Poole's Index,* is Mrs. L. A. C. Clapp[e].

[37] *Pioneer,* Vol. I, p. 221.

antly and respectfully treated by those miners whom she had occasion to know.[38]

In the Empire, the only two-story building in town, built originally as a gamblers' palace, but, by reason of the temporary industry and sobriety of the bar, now converted into a very quiet hotel, "Shirley" found temporary lodgings. The hotel office was "fitted up with that eternal crimson calico, which flushes the whole social life of the 'Golden State' with its everlasting red." [39] In this room there was a bar, and a shop of miners' clothing and groceries. The "parlor" was behind this room, on the first floor: a room straw-carpeted, and furnished with a big mirror, a red-seated "sofa, fourteen feet long," a "round table with a green cloth, red calico curtains, a cooking-stove, a rocking-chair, and a woman and a baby, the latter wearing a scarlet frock to match the sofa and curtains." Upstairs were several bedrooms, with immense, heavy bedsteads, warped and uneven floors, purple calico linings on the walls, and red calico curtains. The whole house was very roughly and awkwardly pieced together by a careless carpenter, and cost its builders eight thousand dollars. It was the great pride and ornament of the camp.

The landlord was a Western farmer, his wife yellow-complexioned and care-worn. The baby, six months old, kicked and

---

[38] The popular stories of absurd displays of sentimentality by early miners who chanced to be reminded of home through the sight of a woman or of a child never find much corroboration from the statements of women who were actually in the mines at the time. Most women were of course uncommonly well treated by the whole community, and any man's services would have been instantly and gladly at their disposal in case of any need. They were met with even effusive politeness; but miners were not such fools as the storytellers like to make them. "Shirley," soon after her arrival, was greeted in her husband's office by one of his friends who insisted on making her sip champagne on the spot at this friend's own expense, in honor of his first sight of a woman for two years. But Shirley did not hear that anyone ever danced about a woman's cast-off bonnet or petticoat.

[39] *Pioneer,* Vol. I, p. 174.

cried in a champagne-basket cradle. The woman cooked for all the boarders herself. Of the four women who besides "Shirley" were in town, another kept with her husband the "Miners' Home" and "tended bar." Within about a week after "Shirley" came, a third of the four, whom she had not met, died, and "Shirley" attended the funeral,[40] which took place from a log cabin. This dwelling was windowless, but with one large opening in the wall to admit light. The funeral scene was characteristic of the social condition of the moment. Everything about the place was "exceedingly clean and neat" for the occasion. "On a board, supported by two butter-tubs, was extended the body of the dead woman, covered with a sheet; by its side stood the coffin of unstained pine, lined with white cambric. . . . The husband held in his arms a sickly babe ten months old, which was moaning piteously for its mother. The other child, a handsome, bold-looking little girl, six years of age, was running gayly around the room, perfectly unconscious of her bereavement." Every few moments she would "run up to her dead mother, and peep laughingly under the handkerchief." "It was evident that her baby-toilet had been made by men; she had on a new calico dress, which, having no tucks in it, trailed to the floor," giving her a "dwarf-womanly appearance." After a long and wandering impromptu prayer by somebody, a prayer that "Shirley" found disagreeable (since she herself was a churchwoman and missed the burial service), the procession, containing twenty men and three women, set out for the hillside graveyard, "a dark cloth cover, borrowed from a neighboring monte table," being "flung over the coffin" as a pall. It was the best pall Rich Bar could have furnished for anybody. The coffin-lid was nailed down, as there were no screws, the sharp hammer blows on the hollow coffin shocking the solemn little assembly with their uncanny noise. "Shirley" tried, a few days later, to amuse the little motherless girl, who was then about to leave the camp with her father for Marysville, and offered her a few playthings. The little one chose with ecstatic delight some tiny scent-bottles, which she called "baby-decanters."

Among the miners perfect good humor prevailed on the bar.

[40] Ibid., Vol. I, p. 347.

On the anniversary of Chilian independence Yankee miners walked fraternally in procession with the Chilians, every member of the procession "intensely drunk," [41] and yet there seems to have been no quarreling. The people on the bar used profane language to an unpleasant extent on the commonest occasions; but they were well-meaning about it and called it only a "slip of the tongue." "Shirley," as woman of cultivation and curiosity, took a friendly interest in their less disagreeable manners and customs, and especially in their rich and to her at that moment very novel slang. She recorded with amusement how they ended a discussion upon business questions with: "Talk enough when horses fight," or "Talk enough between gentlemen"; how they assured themselves of one's sincerity by questioning: "Honest Injun?" (which she spells, with Yankee primness, *Indian*); and how they would ask one of another: "Have you a spare pick-axe about your clothes?" or say that they "had got the deadwood on" somebody.[42] Take them for all in all, they seemed to her far oftener amusing than coarse or disagreeable. And many of them she plainly found delightful men, men of education no doubt, and of good social position at home.

Before October had fairly begun, she had moved with her husband to the neighboring Indian Bar, where he had many personal friends. The scenery here was wilder, but the society was much the same in its busy and peaceful joviality. Here were some twenty tents and cabins on the bar itself; other houses were on the hill, the whole place evidently growing very fast; and other inhabited bars were near. The whole region was full of activity; dams, wing-dams, flumes, artificial ditches, were to be seen all about. "Shirley" now began to live in her own log cabin, which she found already hung with a gaudy chintz. The one hotel of Indian Bar was near her cabin — too near, in fact; for there much drinking and music, with dancing (by men with men), went on. "Shirley" found and improvised very amusing furniture for her dwelling, trunks, claret-cases, three-legged stools, monte-table covers, and can-

---

41 Ibid., Vol. I, p. 274.
42 Ibid., Vol. II, p. 24.

dle-boxes furnishing the materials for her ingenuity. In her
little library she had a Bible, a prayer-book, Shakespeare, and
Lowell's *Fable for Critics*, with two or three other books. The
Negro cook of the hotel, who for some time did her own cook-
ing as well, played finely on the violin when he chose, and was
very courteous to "Shirley." She speaks of him often with in-
finite amusement. Prominent in the society of the bar was a
trapper, of the old Frémont party, who told blood-curdling
tales of Indian fights; another character was a learned Quaker,
who lectured at length to "Shirley" on literature, but never
liked to listen to her on any subject, and told her as much very
frankly. The camp had just become possessed also of a justice
of the peace, a benevolent-looking fat man, with a big head,
slightly bald, and a smooth fat face. He was genial and sweet-
tempered, was commonly supposed to be incompetent, and
had got himself elected by keeping both the coming election
and his candidacy a secret, save from his friends. Most of the
miners, when they came to hear of him and of the election,
thought such an officer a nuisance in those diggings, as the
camp could surely keep order without his help. But so long as
he had nothing to do, he was permitted to do it, and to be as
great a man for his pains as he liked. Late in October one case
of supposed theft occurred, the trial taking place at Rich Bar,
before a miners' meeting. The "Squire" was allowed to look on
from the platform, while the improvised popular magistrate,
sitting by his side, administered justice. The thief, as "Shirley"
heard, was lightly flogged and was then banished.[43]

Not until December, however, was the general peace broken
further. But then it was indeed broken by a decidedly barbarous case of hanging for theft. The "Squire" was powerless
to affect the course of events; the "people" of Indian Bar, many
of them drunken and full of disorderly desire for a frolic, tried
the accused, whose guilt was certain enough, although his previous character had been fair; and when he had been found
guilty, the "crowd" hanged him in a very brutal fashion. He
was himself drunken to the last moment. The more reckless

---

[43] Ibid., Vol. II, pp. 151, 214.

people of the bar were the ones concerned in this affair, and all "Shirley's" own friends disapproved of it.[44]

General demoralization, however, set in with winter. There was little to do on the bar; the most of the men were young; the confinement of the winter, on a place "about as large as a poor widow's potatoe-patch," was terrible to them. Christmas evening saw the beginning of a great revel at the hotel near "Shirley's" log cabin.[45] Days had been spent in preparing for it; the bar of the hotel had been retrimmed with red calico; brandy and champagne in vast quantities had been brought into camp; and, what was most wonderful of all, the floor of the hotel had been washed. An oyster and champagne supper, with toasts and songs, began the revel. "Shirley" heard dancing in the hotel as she fell asleep that night in her cabin; and next morning, when she woke, they were still dancing.[46] The whole party now kept themselves drunken for three days, growing constantly wilder. They formed a mock vigilance committee to catch and bring in the few remaining sober men of the camp, to try them, and to condemn them to drink some stated quantity. Some of the wildest revelers were the most respected men on the river. At last they all reached the climax: as "Shirley" heard the thing described, they lay about in heaps on the floor of the hotel, howling, barking, and roaring. All together "Shirley" thought the letter describing this affair the unpleasantest of her series so far. Strange to say, no fights are recorded at this time. But thenceforth confusion seems to be somewhat noticeable in the social affairs of that vicinity. In March a man at a camp near by was stabbed in the back during a drunken frolic, and without any sort of cause. Yet people took at the time no notice of the affair.[47] In April a Mexican at Indian Bar asked

---

[44] Ibid., Vol. II, p. 351.

[45] Ibid., Vol. III, p. 80.

[46] These "balls," attended by men only, because there were only men to attend them, were not uncommon in the mines. Borthwick, in his *Three Years*, has preserved, opposite p. 320, a sketch of one of them, made on the spot, and worth pages of stupid description. See also his excellent sketches, from life, of gambling-scenes.

[47] *Pioneer*, Vol. III, p. 220.

an American for some money due the former. The American promptly stabbed his creditor; but again nothing was done.[48] The Mexicans were in fact now too numerous for comfort at Indian Bar, since Rich Bar had just expelled all foreigners, who therefore now came to this place. The public houses, which now were noisy with gambling, drinking, and fighting, had increased from one to seven or eight, and on Sundays they were "truly horrible." But summer began without any further great outbreaks of mob violence. On the Fourth of July, however, the "gradually increasing state of bad feeling" recently shown by our countrymen towards the foreigners culminated, for the moment, in a general assault, the result "of whiskey and patriotism," on the Spaniards near one of the saloons, of whom two or three were badly hurt.[49] "Shirley" confesses that, as she learns, the people of Spanish race on the bar, many of whom are "highly educated gentlemen," are disposed to base an ill opinion of our whole nation on the actions of the rougher men at Indian Bar. "They think [very oddly] that it is the grand characteristic of Columbia's children to be prejudiced, opinionated, selfish, avaricious, and unjust. It is vain to tell them that such are not specimens of American gentlemen." Our democratic airs as shown in the mines, "Shirley" thinks, deceive them. They fancy that we must be what we choose to see — namely, all alike. But the men who really so acted as so unfavorably to impress the foreign gentlemen were, she declares, the gamblers and rowdies of the camp. "The rest of the people are afraid of these daring, unprincipled persons, and when they commit the most glaring injustice against the Spaniards, it is generally passed unnoticed." "We have had," says "Shirley," wearily, "innumerable drunken fights during the summer, with the usual amount of broken heads, collar bones, stabs, etc." These fights usually took place on Sunday; and not otherwise could "Shirley" always have been sure of remembering the day of rest. Things were sadly changed from those bright days of her early stay at the bar.

The vengeance of the gods, which was thus gathering over

---

[48] Ibid., Vol. III, p. 355.
[49] Ibid., Vol. IV, p. 24.

Indian Bar, descended with sudden stroke on Sunday, July 11. "Shirley" had been walking with a party of friends in the beautiful summer woods; but when she returned, the town was in a fury. A "majestic-looking Spaniard" had quarreled with an Irishman about a Mexican girl ("Shirley" for the first time, I think, thus showing a knowledge of the presence at Indian Bar of those women who seem, in the bright and orderly days of her first arrival, to have been actually unknown in the camp). The Mexican, having at last stabbed and killed the other, fled to the hills; and the Americans were rushing about, shouting: "Down with the Spaniards!" "Don't let one of the murderous devils remain!" and other similarly enlightened words. "Shirley" was conducted by her husband for safety up on the hill and to a house where there lived a family containing two women. Here from above, gazing directly down on the bar, she watched "a sea of heads, bristling with rifles, guns, and clubs." In this vast confusion a gun was accidentally discharged, during a scuffle, and two men were wounded. This recalled the people to their senses, and they forthwith elected a vigilance committee. They were then pacified for the day.

But the next day the committee tried five or six Spaniards, "supposed to have been ringleaders in the drunken mob of Sunday," and sentenced two to be flogged and all to be banished, their property "being confiscated for the use of the wounded persons." "Shirley" was obliged to hear, from her cabin, the flogging of the two men, and found it, naturally, very highly disagreeable. One of the two convicted men, a "gentlemanly young Spaniard," begged in vain to be killed rather than whipped, and finally swore the most awful vengeance on all Americans henceforth. These sentences of the committee were, after all, very lenient; for the mob had demanded the death of the prisoners. Thus began the rule of the Committee of Vigilance.

Within the next week there was a murder by a Negro, and he was hanged for it at Rich Bar. Fights went on more wildly than before. Yet another Negro is named, who cut his own throat and created much excitement thereby, since at first one of his fellows was accused of having done the deed. As for the state of society, "it has never been so bad," "Shirley" writes, two or three weeks later, "as since the appointment of a committee of vigilance." It was now almost impossible to sleep. The rowdies paraded the streets all night, howling, worrying their enemies, and making great bonfires — all the men of this crowd of roughs being constantly drunken. "The poor, exhausted miners . . . grumble and complain, but they — although far outnumbering the rioters — are too timid to resist. All say, 'It is shameful: something ought to be done,' etc., and in the mean time the rioters triumph. You will wonder that the committee of vigilantes does not interfere. It is said that some of that very committee are the ringleaders." A duel took place during this time at a neighboring bar. "The duelists were surrounded by a large crowd, I have been told, foremost among which stood the committee of vigilance!" [50]

The mining operations that summer were not a distinguished success at Indian Bar, and in autumn there was what miners call a "general stampede from those diggings." The physician and his wife took leave of the miners not unwillingly. "Shirley's" health, to be sure, had wonderfully improved. In closing her mining life she notices that "the few men that have remained on the Bar have amused themselves by prosecuting one another right and left." "The 'Squire,'" she adds, "comes out strong on these occasions." His recent course in these litigations "has been so fair, candid, and sensible, that he has won golden opinions from all, and were it not for his insufferable laziness and good-nature, he would have made a good justice of the peace." [51] This criticism applies so well, also, to all the honest miners of Indian Bar and vicinity (men who formed an undoubted majority of the community) that we need no better summary than these words give us of the life of that year on the bar. These native Americans of good character would have little real trouble in preserving the peace of the camp, had they not chosen, one and all, to show such detestable "laziness and good-nature."

"Shirley's" well-sketched pictures have passed before us, and

---

[50] For the immediately foregoing, see *Pioneer*, Vol. IV, p. 103 ff.
[51] Ibid., Vol. IV, p. 347.

the series is complete: easily secured peace, then carelessly criminal tolerance, then brutally intolerant degeneracy, and then the final wretched dissolution. There can be no doubt that the story is typical of the life of many camps. With "Shirley" we rejoice at last to leave to its triumph the majesty of the benevolent law, personified in the fat-faced squire, as it works to the edification of that handful of impecunious and litigious fellow citizens who were forced to stay on the bar.

VIII. *The Warfare against the Foreigners*

I HAVE now disposed, I hope forever, of the familiar pioneer theory that makes the "foreign criminals" the one great cause of the trouble of the miners. The rapid degeneration of the weaker young men of all sorts in those times has been commonly enough noticed in the accounts of the mines. The foreigners, too, had their share in the effects of this tendency, and the Spanish Americans most of all, because they were most abused and least capable of resisting the moral effects of abuse. Many of them were also bad enough to begin with, and that there were great numbers of foreign rogues in California is, of course, certain. But for the rapid degeneration both of individuals and of communities the honest men were chiefly to blame, because they knew the danger and neglected for a time, in the mines, every serious social duty. The honest men were, at the worst, a fair majority, and were usually an overwhelming majority of the mining communities. Had they not been so, California would never have emerged from the struggle as soon as it did. Since they were so, it is useless for the survivors now to remind us of the undoubtedly honorable intentions of these good miners of early days and to lay all the blame elsewhere. Not everyone that saith Lord! Lord! is a good citizen.

But if the foreign criminals were not the great source of mischief, the honest men certainly did all that they could to make these foreigners such a source. The fearful blindness of the early behavior of the Americans in California towards foreigners is something almost unintelligible. The avaricious thirst for gold among the Americans themselves can alone explain the corruption of heart that induced this blindness. Some of the effects we have already seen. We must look yet a little closer at this aspect of the struggle.

The problem of the future relations of foreigners and Americans in California was, at the moment of the birth of the state, undoubtedly perplexing. A mixed population of gold-seekers was obviously a thing to be feared. Left to themselves, American miners, as it seemed, might be trusted to keep a fair order. With all sorts of people thronging the territory, danger might be apprehended. This problem, then, as to the future, was sure to trouble even the clearest heads. But, after all, clear heads ought quickly to have understood that this perplexing problem was not for any man, but, in its main elements, only for fortune to solve; and that the work of sensible men must be limited to minimizing the threatening evils by caution, by industrious good citizenship, and by a conciliatory behavior. The foreigners could not, on the whole, be kept from coming. One could only choose whether one would encourage the better or the worst class of foreigners to come to the land, and whether one would seek to make those who came friendly and peaceable, or rebellious and desperate. But the California public and the first legislature chose to pass an act to discourage decent foreigners from visiting California, and to convert into rogues all honest foreigners who might have come. This was, indeed, not the title of the act. It was the Foreign Miners' Tax Law of 1850.

Its avowed purpose was as far as possible to exclude foreigners from these mines, the God-given property of the American people. Its main provision was a tax of thirty dollars a month (levied by means of the sale of monthly licenses) upon each foreigner engaged in mining. At the time when it was passed, there were already several thousand Sonoran miners in California; and, as we have also seen, there had already been difficulty with them in the southern mines, a difficulty that, as we learn from Bayard Taylor,[52] passed off peaceably enough at the moment, because the Sonorans would not fight. Taylor's

---

[52] See also Riley's letter (Cal. Docs. of 1850, p. 788) as corroboration.

mistake lay in supposing the Sonorans to have been seriously discouraged. In the next year they were more numerous than ever. So the public and the legislature were forewarned. The common talk about our national divine right to all the gold in California was detestable mock-pious cant, and we knew it. The right and duty that undoubtedly belonged to us were to build up a prosperous and peaceful community anywhere on our own soil. But you cannot build up a prosperous and peaceful community so long as you pass laws to oppress and torment a large resident class of the community. The one first duty of a state is to keep its own peace, and not to disturb the peace. The legislators must have known that to pass the law was to lead almost inevitably to violent efforts at an evasion of its monstrous provisions, and was meanwhile to subject the foreigners to violent assaults from any American ruffians who might choose to pretend, in the wild mountain regions, that they were themselves the state officers. Violence must lead to violence, and the state would have done all it could to sanction the disturbances.

Seldom is a political mistake so quickly judged by events. The next legislature, little wiser about many things than its predecessor, was still, in this matter, forced quickly enough to withdraw its predecessor's absurdity from the statute-books. The *Alta California* breathes with a sigh the general relief on hearing that this is done.[53] But ere it could be done, untold

[53] See the weekly *Alta,* in the Harvard College Library file, for March 15 and March 22, 1851. As appears from remarks and news herein contained, the repeal of the tax was, like all political action, the product of manifold motives. San Francisco felt bitterly, as the chief port of the state, the loss of commerce that the act directly and indirectly entailed. Business men, in Stockton and the southren mines, complained of the loss of customers. Everyone by March 1851 was weary of the insecurity produced by the bickerings with the foreigners. And at a public meeting held (as the *Alta* reports) in Stockton, March 6, 1851, and addressed by several speakers, among others by one "Terry," whom I supposed to be the well-known judge of later years, the discussion is made to touch on the vital national question of north and south. The tax law is called a scheme to depress the enterprise of the southern mines, and so of

mischief, which added fearfully to the sorrows of the struggle
for order, had been caused by the unlucky act.

No adventurer, no gambler, no thief, no cutthroat, who had
desired to come to California from Mexico, or elsewhere
abroad, could be prevented by a threat of taxing him thirty
dollars a month for mining. Many a cautious, sober, intelligent
foreigner might be warned away by the exorbitant tax, as well
as by the hostility that it indicated. For, when levied not upon
the uncommonly lucky miner, with his two ounces or his pound
a day, but upon the ordinary poor devil, with his ups and
downs, whose "wages" per month were in only a very few
months more than enough to support him at the prices that prevailed, and in the winter months were often nothing at all, the
thirty-dollar tax was a monstrous imposition. And when levied
on men who had come already in 1848, and who had often felt,
before the passage of the act, that the Americans hated them
merely for being the more skillful miners, this tax was a blow
that their hot spirits were sure to resent.

Trouble came at once, and quickly culminated in the difficulties at Sonora, in 1850. From his sources Mr. Shinn has
given, in chapter xviii of the *Mining Camps*, an account of this
disturbance.[54] He regards it as a "case where indignation
against foreigners had much justification." I am prepared to believe that whenever it is proved, but what I have been able to
gather from the contemporary newspaper files makes me prefer
to express the matter by calling the affair a not wholly unprovoked, but still disgraceful riot on the part of Americans. They
were undoubtedly harassed by foreigners of the poorer sort,
and a number of murders were committed by such, but when
the Americans turned upon foreigners as a class, and especially
upon Sonorans and South Americans, and tried to exclude them
from the mines in a body, by means of mob violence, supported

---

the southern portion of the state, whose sectional sympathies were
well known.

[54] His chief source, I suppose, is the *Miners' Directory of Tuol-
umne County* (Sonora, 1856), which he cites in his *Land Laws of
Mining Camps* and elsewhere. This pamphlet I have not been able
to use.

by resolutions passed at miners' meetings, the undertaking was a brutal outrage, and the good sense of decent Americans quickly rebounded, for the moment, from the mood that could be guilty of such behavior. The result was, however, meanwhile, that many foreigners were rendered desperate and were turned into dangerous rascals, and that many more were driven violently away from the mines; but that, nevertheless, the body of the foreign miners remained in the mines at their work, ill-humored, suspicious, and ready for the worst; so that the last state of "those diggings" was far worse than the first. There is here no space for a discussion of the sources bearing on this topic; and these Sonoran difficulties form one of the many still almost unstudied topics that abound in California history and that invite monographic treatment. I can give only the result of what I so far can make out. When, early in the summer of 1850, the collectors came for the foreign miners' tax, they found the foreigners surly and suspicious and did what was possible to make them more so. A number of murders were committed by "Mexicans," and then the American miners began to meet and to pass resolutions, not against murderers, nor in favor of a firm organization of the regular machinery of law, but against foreigners. One famous set of resolutions, quoted in all the authorities on this affair, pronounced in favor of a committee of three Americans in each camp to decide what foreigners were "respectable" and to exclude all others by a sort of executive order, meanwhile depriving those who remained of all arms, save in cases where special permits should be issued. One is reminded once more, by this procedure, of poor Ide and the "blessings of liberty." Other resolutions passed in those days, and often later in various camps, excluded foreigners altogether, sometimes giving the obvious intentions of providence as the reason for this brutality. There followed numerous assaults upon Mexicans and several riotous assemblages of Americans.

It is impossible to judge how far the newspaper reports of foreign outrages in that region and time, outrages such as robberies and murders committed upon Americans, are truthful. Any mysterious outrage was attributed to "Mexicans"; any

American wretch who chanced to find it useful could in moments of excitement divert suspicion from himself by mentioning the Mexicans in general or any particular Mexicans as the authors of his crimes. And in "those diggings" there were, undoubtedly, numerous Mexicans who well deserved hanging. But the story as told by the foreign population is not known to us. We can see only indirectly, through the furious and confused reports of the Americans themselves, how much of organized and coarse brutality these Mexicans suffered from the miners' meetings. The outrages committed by foreigners were after all, however numerous, the crimes of individuals. Ours were the crimes of a community, consisting largely of honest but cruelly bigoted men, who encouraged the ruffians of their own nation to ill-treat the wanderers of another, to the frequent destruction of peace and good order. We were favored of heaven with the instinct of organization; and so here we organized brutality and, so to speak, asked God's blessing upon it. The foreigners were often enough degraded wretches; such drank, gambled, stole, and sometimes murdered. They were also, often enough, honest fellows, or even men of high character and social position; and such we tried in our way to ruin. In all cases they were, as foreigners, unable to form their own government or to preserve their own order. And so we kept them in fear and, as far as possible, in misery.

So ill we indeed did not treat them as some nations would have done; we did not massacre them wholesale, as Turks might have massacred them: that treatment we reserved for the defenseless Digger Indians, whose villages certain among our miners used on occasion to regard as targets for rifle-practice, or to destroy wholesale with fire, outrage, and murder, as if they had been so many wasps' nests in our gardens at home. Nay, the foreign miners, being civilized men, generally received "fair trials," as I said, whenever they were accused. It was, however, considered safe by an average lynching jury in those days to convict a "greaser" on very moderate evidence if none better could be had. One could see his guilt so plainly written, we know, in his ugly swarthy face, before the trial began. Therefore the life of a Spanish American in the mines in the early days, if frequently profitable, was apt to be a little disagreeable. It served him right, of course. He had no business, as an alien, to come to the land that God had given us. And if he was a native Californian, a born "greaser," then so much the worse for him. He was so much the more our born foe; we hated his whole degenerate, thieving, landowning, lazy, and discontented race. Some of them were now even bandits; most of them by this time were, with our help, more or less drunkards; and it was not our fault if they were not all rascals! So they deserved no better.

The Sonora troubles of 1850 would be less significant if they had expressed only a temporary mistake and had given place to a proper comprehension of our duty to foreigners. But although the exorbitant foreign miner's tax was repealed in 1851, and although, when a tax was reimposed later, it was of comparatively moderate amount, still the miners themselves were not converted from their error until long afterwards, and, in numerous individual cases, they were never converted at all. The violent self-assertions that from time to time were made of the American spirit over against the foreign element accomplished absolutely no good aim and only increased the bitterness on both sides, while corrupting more and more our own sense of justice. Instead, therefore, of justifying themselves as necessary acts of "self-preservation," the miners' outbreaks against foreigners only rendered their own lives and property less secure. Two years after the Sonora troubles, one finds in the summer of 1852 the same weary business going on in the southern mines, less imposing, no doubt, in its expressions of wrath, but none the less disgraceful and demoralizing.[55] The later the year, the more certain it is that all molestation of foreigners who had been in the peaceful possession of claims meant simply confiscation of valuable property that had been

---

[55] See in the steamer *Alta* (Harvard College Library file) for July 13, 1852, the account of the expulsion of foreign miners, French and Spanish American especially, from expensive and valuable claims in Mariposa. See, also, resolutions of miners at Sonora, passed October 12, in the steamer *Alta* of November 1, ordering foreigners out of the mines.

acquired by hard toil. For such claims, in these later times, were often river-bed claims, or "coyote-holes," or similarly laborious enterprises. So, in the disturbance in July 1852 in Mariposa, referred to in the foregoing note, the foreign miners, as appears from the report, had undertaken all the work of turning the course of a river, and their property was confiscated as soon as it was perceived to be valuable.[56] And the turpitude of such conduct is especially manifest from the fact that the foreigners (as Auger, just cited, admits in the case of his own countrymen) were in any case, and even under the fairest treatment, at a serious disadvantage in all operations of an extensive sort, by reason of their comparative deficiency in the character and training required in order to improvise, amid the confusion of a new country, greater organizations of labor and capital. The Frenchmen, says Auger (p. 106), in case of great mining undertakings, "*ont toujours cédé au découragement qui remplaçait chez eux une ardeur immodérée ou aux divisions intestines qui les séparaient brusquement au moment de recueillir les fruits de leur enterprise.*" He excepts only the one greater case cited, where the Americans did the work of dissolution for the Frenchmen.[57] Thus, however, the very instinct and training of which we in this land have such good reason to be proud aggravates, in the present case, our disgrace. Because we knew so well how to organize, we were not the weak nor the injured party, but had these foreigners at

[56] E. Auger, in his *Voyage en Californie* (Paris, 1857), p. 112, gives an account from hearsay, whose correctness I am unable to control, of one of the earlier difficulties between French and American miners in the southern mines, and remarks in that connection, very accurately, that among the miners "*La justice favorise généralement les Américains aux dépens des étrangers.*" On page 106 the author recounts from hearsay another quarrel at this time over a river-bed claim, "*sur le Stanislaus-river,*" where his countrymen were violently dispossessed. This may be the Mariposa case misplaced.

[57] Borthwick, op. cit., p. 369, cited also by Mr. Shinn, in the *Mining Camps,* p. 155, contrasts finely the organizing power of the American miners with the gregarious habits of the seldom organized French miners and makes the fact illustrate national peculiarities.

our mercy; and for the same reason our outrages upon them were organized outrages, expressions of our peculiar national combination of a love of order with a frequently detestable meanness towards strangers.

The northern mines, however, are often supposed to have been not only more orderly, but also more tolerant. This is probably, on the whole, the case. As there were fewer foreigners present in the northern mines, the temptations to abuse them were less frequent. In some cases, however, proof can be found even in the southern mines themselves of very great earnestness in the enforcement of the rights of foreigners. An amusing account is given (in a book that contains a series of well-written and apparently substantially truthful sketches of California life, by a Canadian) of a demonstration in a camp on the Stanislaus, as late as 1856, by the whole force of the camp to protect certain Chinamen in their rights as miners.[58] This camp, Shaw tells us, was inhabited mainly by miners from the northern states of the Union, and where the influence of such was paramount it may have been, in general, a somewhat more tolerant influence. Yet, once for all, our American intolerance towards the unassimilable foreigner is not a sectional peculiarity, however often it may appear somewhat more prominently in one section of our land than in another. And the northern mines show us numerous cases of it. "Shirley's" experiences, we remember, were in the northern mines. It was in the same mines, and in the same summer of 1852, that miners' meetings at Bidwell's Bar, at Foster's Bar, at Rough

[58] Pringle Shaw: *Ramblings in California* (Toronto: James Bain; date of publication not given, but apparently not far from 1858), p. 72 ff. An American miner sold his claim to Chinamen, who were dispossessed by three "gaunt long-haired fellows" from Arkansas. Shaw was himself the recorder of claims in the district, appointed to his office by the miners' meeting. The Chinamen complained to him; he remonstrated with the "jumpers" and was insulted and threatened by them. He then called out the force of the camp, about one hundred men, who marched in military order to the disputed claim, under arms, and gave solemn warning to the Arkansas trio to leave it in five minutes. The order was obeyed.

and Ready, and elsewhere passed resolutions excluding foreigners.[59] This shows how the same vain and demoralizing undertakings were still believed in at the north that had been so disastrous at the south. And one sees in another form how little reliance can be placed upon the impression that the baseness of the foreigners in California was to blame for the chief troubles of the struggle for order in the mines. But, as a crowning illustration of the position of the northern miners in this matter, the fact remains that in Downieville, far up in the northern mines, was committed in the summer of 1851 the most outrageous act of lynch law in all the pioneer annals, the entirely unnecessary hanging of a woman, whose death, under the circumstances, was plainly due, not merely to her known guilt, but quite as much to the fact that she was not an American. And the deed was not only done but defended by American miners.

IX. *The Downieville Lynching of July 5, 1851*

VERY obvious considerations lead civilized men, in times of social disturbance even more than in times of peace and good order, to be lenient to the public offenses of women. A man who gravely transgresses against order is necessarily viewed first of all as transgressor, and only in the second place do his fellows remember that considerations of mercy, of charity, or of his own personal merit may enter to qualify the sternness of justice towards him. But a woman, however she transgresses against law and order, is necessarily regarded first of all as a woman, and only in the second place does one remember that even in her case justice must have its place. Therefore all the considerations that may render lynch law a temporary necessity among men in an unsettled community have,

---

[59] Steamer *Alta* for May 31 and June 15, 1852. In the meeting at Bidwell's Bar the miners expressed great indignation at "all merchants and shipping agents engaged in transporting a countless number of villains from all parts of the world to California." So the *Alta* (steamer edition of June 15) expresses their view, partly in their own words.

obviously, absolutely no application to the few women who may chance to be there. If they become intolerable, a quiet expulsion of them must serve, until such a time as the community, having made up its mind to behave sensibly, has provided prisons to confine them.

However, the people of Downieville, in July 1851, were once led to think differently. The incident has been frequently mentioned in books and essays about the early times and has often been regarded with horror and often, also, explained and even defended as a necessity of the moment. Garbled accounts of it are found, sometimes, in the later pioneer reminiscences.[60] Of the newspapers of the time that I have been able to use, but one, so far as I know, has an extended account of the affair coming directly from an eyewitness. This paper is the *Daily Pacific Star*, of San Francisco, whose version, I believe, has never yet been employed for historical purposes. I had the good fortune to come upon this version while consulting a partial file of the paper in the Mercantile Library in San Francisco, and upon it I have here largely depended. Other newspaper reports, such as the *Alta* account, or that in the *Sacramento Transcript*, I have seen; but they are brief and unsatisfactory. On the whole it is plain that the newspapers, even in those plain-spoken days of early California, were disposed to hush the matter up as soon as possible. One of the editors of the *Star* happened to be in Downieville at the time; hence this particular report in the *Star* for July 19, 1851.

On the night of July 4, one Cannan, apparently an American,[61] was walking home with some friends, in a state of mind and body appropriate to the occasion, when they passed near the house where, as they well knew, there lived, together with her Spanish paramour, a young woman of Spanish American

---

[60] See, for example, the otherwise generally inaccurate essay of Mr. H. Robinson, on "Pioneer Times in California," in the *Overland Monthly* for 1872, Vol. VIII, p. 457. See, also, Borthwick's unconsciously unfair version, from hearsay, op. cit., p. 222.

[61] If Mr. Robinson, in the essay cited, can be viewed as trustworthy, he was a man of good position among the miners, and member of an influential order.

race. She was, it would seem, a person whose associates were mostly gamblers; just how irregular her life was does not appear, save from this one item about her paramour. To judge by what is stated, she may therefore have been of at least pretended fidelity to him. All accounts make her a woman of considerable beauty, of some intelligence and vivacity, and of a still quite youthful appearance; and she seems to have been a person not at all despised in the camp. At this moment her house was dark, and the occupants were sleeping. But Cannan, in passing by, stumbled and fell, as his companions say, against the door of her house; and the light, rude door giving way, he fell half inside. One of his companions pulled him back, saying: "Come out; hush up; there's a woman in that house," or some such words. As Cannan rose, he had, in a drunken whim, picked up something from the floor, just inside the house door — a scarf or some like article; and his companions with difficulty got it away from him to throw it back. Then they all found their probably devious way homewards.

Next morning Cannan, with one of the same companions, passed by the house and announced to his companion his purpose to apologize to the woman for having made the disturbance of the night before. Cannan could speak Spanish, which his companion did not understand, so that we have, in this respect, no competent witness surviving the following scene. At all events, as Cannan's companion testifies, the companion of the woman met them at the door as they approached, and seemed angry with Cannan and was understood to threaten him. A moment later the woman herself appeared and spoke yet more angrily. Cannan continued the conversation in what seemed to his companion a conciliatory tone; the woman, however, grew constantly more excited at his words, whatever they were, and erelong drew a knife, rushed quickly upon him, and stabbed him to death at a stroke. Whether Cannan really gave any momentary provocation by violent and insulting language addressed to the woman, this American witness is of course unable to testify. Both the woman herself and her paramour afterwards asserted that he did, and that it was his abuse, used

in the course of the quarrel, that drove her to the act, in an outburst of fury.

The deed was quickly known throughout the town, and the
citizens at once organized a popular court, in the ordinary
lynchers' form, with an elected judge and a jury. The woman
and her paramour were brought before the court, the crowd
feeling and showing meanwhile very great excitement. Some
shouted: *"Hang them;"* others: *"Give them a trial."* Our eyewitness heard a number also shout: *"Give them a fair trial and
then hang them,"* a compromise that seems perfectly to have
expressed the Great American Mind as represented by these
particular townspeople. A gentleman present, named Thayer,
protested indeed openly, during the excitement, against this
popular violence, but he was ordered by the crowd "to consult
his own safety and desist." The trial began in the presence of
the impatient crowd. The disturbance of the previous night
was recounted, Cannan's friends insisting that there was no
intention on their part to trouble the woman, and that what
happened was due to a drunken accident and a frail door. The
murder was described by Cannan's companion, and the two
accused, being called upon, both gave, as the woman's sole
justification, her rage at Cannan's midnight disturbance and at
his abuse. The man had evidently had no part in the murder,
which was the work of the instant.

Then followed, it would seem, a recess in the trial and thereafter a little more testimony for the defense. A physician, Dr.
Aiken, was called by the woman, and gave it as his opinion
that she was with child in the third month. The doctor made,
as the editor tells us, a very unfavorable impression on the people. The only reason given for this unfavorable impression is
"that he seemed desirous, so it was thought, to save the prisoner." Never before this in California, and never since, so far
as I know, has Judge Lynch been called upon to deal with the
delicate question now presented to this court. The Great American Mind suggested, under the circumstances, a consultation
of physicians, and another physician was called, who, with Dr.
Aiken, retired into a house, taking the prisoner. The Great
American Mind itself, meanwhile, grew intensely excited out-

side the frail structure in which the consultation was taking place; and this mind induced the crowd who represented it to threaten fiercely, and in no whispers, the offending Dr. Aiken, and to fill the air with shouts of *"Hang her."* The result whereof was that at this very orderly and decent consultation of scientific experts, while Dr. Aiken seems not to have been convinced of his error, the consulting physician kept his own and his fellow's skin safe by announcing what we may hope to have been a sincere, and even by chance a well-founded, opinion, which differed altogether from Dr. Aiken's. Hereupon the jury soon quieted the tumult of the Great American Mind by declaring their verdict of guilty against the woman and by themselves passing sentence of death upon her, while they acquitted the man. As it is an old trick of hypocritical flatterers of public opinion in this land to attribute all outrages and riots to our foreign fellow-residents, I do only justice if I remark that the names of the jurymen at this trial are given, and are as native to our language as are the names of Bunyan's jurymen at the trial of Faithful. In this instance, then, they are such names as Burr, Reed, Woodruff, and the like.

One who fancies that the fair prisoner was overwhelmed with abject terror all this while does not know her race. That same afternoon she was to suffer, and when the time came, she walked out very quietly and amiably, with hair neatly braided, stepped up to the improvised gallows, and made a short speech, in which she bade them all a cheerful farewell and said that she had no defense for her crime save that she had been made very angry by Cannan and would surely do the same thing again if she were to be spared and were again to be as much insulted by anybody. Then she adjusted her own noose and cheerfully passed away.

This account, in so far as it is due to the *Star* editor, is not the account of an enemy of the Downieville people or of an angry spectator. The *Star* says, editorially, that it cannot very heartily approve of this hasty lynching of a woman, but that it expects the moral effect of the act to be on the whole good. Downieville had been much troubled with bad characters, and a necessity existed for some action. "We witnessed the trial, and feel convinced that the actors desired to do right." They had in fact themselves solicited this publication. One is reminded, as one reads, of the saying attributed to "Boss" Tweed in his last moments. *"He had tried,"* he declared, *"to do right, but he had had bad luck."* The people of Downieville obviously had bad luck.

X. *The Attainment of Order*

YET, after all, the effect of these outbursts of popular fury was indirectly good, although not in the way that many pioneers like to dwell upon. The good effect lay in the very horror begotten by the popular demoralization that all this violence tended to produce. While a part of the community was debased by all these doings and was given over to a false and brutal confidence in mob law, a confidence that many individual men have never since lost, the better part of every such mining community learned from all this disorder the sad lesson that their stay in California was to be long, their social responsibility great, and their duty to devote time and money to rational work as citizens unavoidable. They saw the fearful effects of their own irresponsible freedom. They began to form town governments of a more stable sort, to condemn rather than to excuse mob violence, to regard the free and adventurous prospecting life, if pursued on a grand scale, as a dangerous and generally profitless waste of the community's energies, to prefer thereto steady work in great mining enterprises, and in every way to insist upon order. The coming of women, the growth of families, the formation of church organizations, the building of schoolhouses, the establishment of local interests of all sorts, saved the wiser communities from the horrors of lynch law. The romantic degradation of the early mining life, with its transient glory, its fatal fascination, its inevitable brutality, and its resulting loathsome corruption, gave place to the commonplace industries of the later mining days. The quartz mines and the deep placers were in time developed, vast amounts of capital came to be invested in the whole mining industry, and in a few years (by 1858, for instance) many mining towns were almost as conservative as much older manufacturing towns have been in other states. For all this result lynch law in the mines, after 1850, was responsible *only* in so far as it excited in the minds of sensible men a horror of its own disorderly atrocities. Save in the newest camps, and in those most remote from regular courts, one can say almost universally that in so far as the lynch law had been orderly, it had been at best the symptom and outcome of a treasonable popular carelessness, while in so far as it had been disorderly, it had been brutal and demoralizing and in itself an unmixed evil. Almost everywhere, moreover, as we have seen, it was not an externally produced necessity, forced from without upon the community by the violence of invading criminals; but it was the symptom of an inner social disease. For this disease the honest men themselves were the ones most responsible, since they were best able to understand their duty. The lesson of the whole matter is as simple and plain as it is persistently denied by a romantic pioneer vanity; and our true pride, as we look back to those days of sturdy and sinful life, must be, not that the pioneers could so successfully show by their popular justice their undoubted instinctive skill in self-government — although indeed, despite all their sins, they showed such a skill also — but that the moral elasticity of our people is so great, their social vitality so marvelous, that a community of Americans could sin as fearfully as, in the early years, the mining community did sin, and could yet live to purify itself within so short a time, not by a revolution, but by a simple progress from social foolishness to social steadfastness. Even thus a great river for an hour defiled by some corrupting disturbance purifies itself merely through its own flow over its sandy bed, beneath the wide and sunny heavens.

Chapter V
SOCIAL EVOLUTION IN SAN FRANCISCO

THE CONSERVATIVE social elements are apt to escape our notice as we study any time of great activity. They are too commonplace to fall under the easy observation of eyes that have become accustomed to bright lights and to strong contrasts of color. Yet we must study them also, and especially as they showed themselves, side by side with some of the worst elements of disorder, in the early life of San Francisco.

For in San Francisco, after all, the great battle was to be fought and the victory won for the cause of lasting progress in California. Elsewhere the struggle was either in smaller and more nearly separate towns or else in the wide but dependent rural districts. But upon the city by the Golden Gate all the permanent success of the good cause depended. Here the young state was, so to speak, nourished. Here the ships and a great part of the immigrants came. Here was from the first the center of the state's mental life and to a great extent of its political life. Here good order must be preserved if any permanent order was to be possible elsewhere. And so of course the progress of San Francisco was to be largely identical with the progress of the whole of the new state.

In the mines, as I have said, the great and comparatively permanent business interests of the years after 1851 and the consequent rapid establishment of all the institutions of town life rapidly wrought to transform the more successful camps into thrifty, orderly, and respectable American communities. I have said little of the details of such transformations, because one can best study the same process, only on a larger scale, in the case of San Francisco, where from the first there were large business interests; where, soonest of all places in the growing parts of the country, there were to be found numerous families; and where the most justly influential men were not wanderers only, but often merchants of high character, of conservative aims, and of extraordinary ability. San Francisco best illustrates the mechanics of the growth of good order. Naturally, how-

297

ever, we are here, as before, driven to consider many dramatic
incidents that belong to the painful side of the struggle for
order.

I. *The New City and the Great Fires*

EXTERNALLY the San Francisco of 1848 underwent almost
magical changes within the next three years. They have
been so often described by enthusiastic travelers and sketch-
writers that one need spend no very long time on them here.
At first the newcomers, in San Francisco as in the mines, would
temporarily bestow themselves in tents. But there are reasons
why a tent in San Francisco, even in the dry summer-time, in
the cold sea-breezes, is not an agreeable dwelling. Hence the
rapid growth of very lightly and rudely built houses, half
wood, half cloth. All of these brought enormous rents.

Wierzbicki, in the pamphlet once before cited, page 49,
writes: "Four months ago" (this is written in August or September 1849) "the town hardly counted fifty houses, and now
it must have upwards of five hundred, and these are daily increasing. . . . From eight to ten thousand inhabitants may be
afloat in the streets of San Francisco, and hundreds arrive
daily; many live in shanties, many in tents, and many the best
way they can." Bayard Taylor's account of his first view at
nearly this same time [1] runs: "The view extended around the
curve of the bay, and hundreds of tents and houses appeared,
scattered all over the heights, and along the shore for more
than a mile. A furious wind was blowing down through a gap
in the hills, filling the streets with clouds of dust. On every
side stood buildings of all kinds, begun or half finished, and
the greater part of them mere canvas sheds, open in front, and
covered with all kinds of signs, in all languages. Great quantities of goods were piled up in the open air, for want of a place
to store them. The streets were full of people, hurrying to and
fro, and of as diverse and *bizarre* a character as the houses."
He then mentions the various nationalities that he could pick
out in the throng. They were not a few, Asiatic and European.

[1] *Eldorado*, p. 55.

An example of the better sort of house in the new town was the Parker House, an ordinary frame building, which, before winter, was in part rented to gamblers, who are said to have paid at the rate of sixty thousand dollars a year for their part of it. Even higher is the sum that they are declared by Bayard Taylor and others to have paid. As for the character of all but the best of the hotels, the early sketches are never weary of describing to us their enormous prices and their fearful accommodations — the dirt, the fleas, and the other numberless miseries of a crowded and hasty life.[2] And even the best of the hotels were poor indeed, although what they furnished in the way of food was better than their other accommodations.[3] Between the hotel, as the home of the well-to-do wanderer, and the bed on the sand, under the stars, men found all sorts of intermediate fashions of living, according as luck guided them. Labor, during the whole summer of 1849, commanded, of course, the highest prices in San Francisco and was hard to get at those; so that none of the newcomers needed to starve, while even the wealthiest man had to do some hard handiwork for himself.

Before the beginning of the rainy season piers were creeping out into the bay,[4] while the chaparral growth on the hillsides above the town was rapidly driven backward by the houses, while warehouses were building along the shore, and while the daily growing forests of masts in the bay gave proof of the general abandonment of their ships by the impatient crews. These deserted sailing-vessels rotted, many of them, for years in the harbor, the price of labor for a good while hardly permitting any undertaking to man them for a return voyage, while the clippers erelong rendered the older vessels finally worthless. Only the steamship company could during this summer of 1849 undertake to maintain its regular trips to and from Panama, carrying the mails and the crowds of new-coming isthmus passengers.

---

[2] *Annals,* p. 247.
[3] Bayard Taylor, loc. cit., p. 60.
[4] See Bayard Taylor's second view, loc. cit., p. 109; J. S. Hittell's *History of San Francisco,* p. 146.

This confused and hurriedly built town, crowded between the steep hills and the bay, with all its tents and its rude warehouses and its flimsy gambling-palaces set down at random, the "water coming up to Montgomery Street," as the old pioneers are never tired of telling one,[5] and the vast fleet of seaworn vessels lying beyond, and idly rotting in the bay — this strange picture will never be forgotten. But within the town itself the scene, upon the approach of winter, was yet further confused by the great rains of 1849–50; by the miserable, unimproved streets, full of fathomless mixed sand and clay mud; and by the increasing crowds of idlers, whom the rainy weather brought back to the town from the interior. To a newcomer the San Franciscans at this moment, living in their rag palaces, or renting them at figures that would have sounded possible in the *Arabian Nights*, and doing all this even while the mining industry itself was suspended by the rains, and while the source of all the wealth was thus temporarily cut off, seemed more like madmen than ever. A correspondent of the *New York Evening Post*, under date of November 15, 1849, gives with a half-serious fury and contempt an amusing account of the landlords of San Francisco at this moment: [6]

"The people of San Francisco are mad, stark mad. . . . A dozen times or more, during the last few weeks, I have been taken by the arm by some of the *millionnaires* — so they call themselves, I call them madmen — of San Francisco, looking wondrously dirty and out at elbows for men of such magnificent pretensions. They have dragged me about, through the mud and filth almost up to my middle, from one pine box to another, called mansion, hotel, bank, or store, as it may please the imagination, and have told me, with a sincerity that would have done credit to the Bedlamite, that these splendid . . . structures were theirs, and they, the fortunate proprietors,

---

[5] Montgomery Street, at that time running along the edge of Yerba Buena cove, towards its northern end, was erelong separated from the bay by the filling in of the whole cove, and is now a number of blocks from the water.

[6] I find the letter quoted in the *National Intelligencer* of January 3, 1850.

were worth from two to three hundred thousand dollars a year each. . . . There must be nearly two thousand houses besides the tents, which are still spread in numbers. . . . And what do you suppose to be the rental, the yearly value, of this card-house city? Not less, it is said, than twelve millions of dollars, and this with a population of about twelve thousand. New York, with its five hundred thousand inhabitants, does not give a rental of much more than this, if as much."

In fact, these rag-palace owners no doubt were moderately insane, not so much in their estimate of the wealth of the new land as in their tacit assumption that rags would not burn. And accordingly in December 1849 there came the first great San Francisco fire, which burned a million dollars' worth of the rags and of the wealth that had been stored in the houses made of them. Nobody ventured to mourn very long over this disaster; and very soon the burned district stood rebuilt, in the full glory of wooden bandboxes that were to be rented once more at the rates that would have befitted kings' houses. The 4th of May 1850 saw, however, the second great fire, which was much more disastrous than the first to the business interests of the place, since it affected less the gamblers and more the warehouses of the merchants than the first fire had done, and since withal it destroyed three millions instead of one million of property. A third fire, of which much the same may be said, took place on June 14. Rags were thenceforth prohibited [7] within the fire limits of the town; which resolved to be staid and sober thereafter, and to use as building material nothing more combustible than kindling-wood. The hills of San Mateo County, to the southward, were, accordingly, yet more rapidly stripped of their fine redwood trees, and the city nailed together the light boards more busily than ever and grew with vast rapidity. September 17, 1850 was indeed marked by another serious fire, but not one of enormous size. And, indeed, not until May 4, 1851, the anniversary of the second fire, did the citizens find fresh and sufficient reason to repent of their conduct.

Meanwhile, during 1850, both the domestic business of the

---

[7] J. S. Hittell, op. cit., p. 157.

state and the commerce by sea came to get a more rational
character. The Eastern merchants grew somewhat accustomed
to their California trade and began before the end of 1850 to
build their famous swift clipper-ships to supply it; and, of
course, their plans now included sufficient wages to attract and
to hold trustworthy crews for voyages to the waters of the
golden land. Thus the San Francisco market soon came to get
a better and more steady supply of what was needed. The
land, which had, so far, to import from distant places nearly
everything, including breadstuffs, potatoes, and butter, had
suffered already terribly from the wild fluctuations of prices
that had characterized its San Francisco markets, and that, of
course, had resulted from the lack of any definite source or
method of supply. The ships had brought as cargoes everything and anything, in the wildest confusion and amid the ut-
most general ignorance of shippers both about what California
needed and about the storage of goods for such long voyages.
Cargoes of coal, for instance, were sent from Baltimore in bulk,
and without proper means for ventilating the holds during the
long voyage around the Horn. Many such cargoes consequently
took fire and were lost.[8] Preserved articles of food were sent
that on arrival proved to be tainted and worthless. Whole
houses — some of wood, others of corrugated iron — were
shipped in pieces, and were in some cases serviceable, but
were also often worthless. Elaborate gold-washing machines
came, which might be adequate to every possible sort of investigation of mud save such an investigation as would show
whether there was any gold in it, but which never showed that.
Of the things actually and seriously needed in California there
might at one moment come twenty times too much, and shortly
thereafter there might be nothing at all of the kind needed
discoverable in the market.[9] To all this confusion the clipper-

[8] See Mrs. Bates's account, in her *Four Years on the Pacific Coast*
(Boston, 1858), of her voyage to California. She was three times in
succession in coal-carrying vessels, all of which were burned. She
escaped each time quite safely and reached her goal at last, a little
nervous, of course, about coal as an article of commerce.

[9] According to the *Post* correspondent, above cited, bread had in

ships, making swift and regular, though of course still far too long, voyages, could not put an entire stop; but they improved the state of things very much, as merchants could correspond with Eastern shippers by steamer and then be sure of getting their invoices in some fairly determinate time by means of the clippers. The clippers erelong rejoiced in large size, in fine outlines, in poetical names, in wonderful records for speed, and all through the years before the war they were the glory of our American commerce. Long since, as we know, they have vanished from the seas.[10]

The year 1851 brought its further great material changes to San Francisco. Foremost in importance was the fire of May 4, which destroyed, at the very least estimate, some seven millions of dollars' worth of property [11] and was thence called "the great fire." The account given of the causes that conspired to make it so great is, as one finds the tale in the *Alta* (loc. cit.), worthy of note. The chief engineer, with numbers of firemen, was away that fatal night between May 3 and 4 at Sacramento. There was, just then, a kind of interregnum between two city councils — the old one having adjourned and the new not having been sworn in: therefore nobody felt empowered to

---

November 1849 risen from twenty-five to fifty cents a loaf, the price being for a small loaf, not much larger than a breakfast roll. All business at that moment, as he declares, is pure gambling; so that whether one is in the gambling-places or out of them, one finds the whole town a vast gambling-hell. One often pays, in fact, ten per cent a month for money.

[10] The commercial life of San Francisco, from this early period down to the completion of the Pacific railroad, was characterized by the institution known as "steamer-day"; i. e., the day preceding the departure of each Panama steamer. On this day collections were made, correspondence with the East prepared, and an enormous mass of business done in connection with the importing trade. The special "steamer editions" of the papers were prepared on these days.

[11] See J. S. Hittell, op. cit., p. 168, whose estimate is founded on that of the *Alta* of the date of the fire, known to me in the steamer edition of May 15. The *Alta* editor was, however, himself disposed to think this estimate too low.

order the tearing down of buildings to check the flames. Some of the engines lacked hose; all of them lacked water. The wind was high. Among the spectators "there was generally a great want of concentrated effort." In short, as one sees, the whole affair was a perfect 'expression of the civilization of the moment. Sixteen entire squares of houses were consumed, with parts of several others, and several lives were lost. The municipality of this mushroom place, as one may remark, was at that moment in debt, for the expenses of the city government, over one million of dollars; and this calamity of the great fire was surely a fitting work for such a municipal organization to accomplish overnight.[12]

The great fire was met with the same general and heroic good humor that had always been shown before. There were, of course, men who were utterly crushed and crazed by it. But the community as a whole was soon as cheery as ever, and at least a trifle wiser than before; not so much in its immediately following conduct as in its plans for the future. The *Alta* of that date begs the city authorities not to pass at once any ordinance restricting or forbidding the building of frame houses within fire limits, since such a measure at that moment would drive away too many who are now hesitating whether to risk another trial of their fortune in the city. Everybody, says the editor, is now convinced of the need of fireproof buildings. Let the merchants, however, build temporary sheds on their lots at once and begin business afresh. Then they will soon be able to build better structures. And, in fact, the commercial part of the city was erelong much better built, and the portion of the city that had suffered from the greatest of the fires remained thenceforth comparatively free from such calamities.

But higher up the hillside and among the dwellings of the town the last of the great fires was still to do its work. On Sunday, June 22, 1851, the *Alta* newspaper opened the day with a fine editorial on the delights and the duty of a truly religious Sabbath rest. It added, indeed, to this editorial the an-

---

[12] See the *Annals*, p. 328, for the city debt, and p. 329 for the fire. The *Annals* make the loss from ten to twelve millions of dollars.

nouncement in its local columns that this same Sabbath evening there would be presented at the Jenny Lind Theater (a
famous place of amusement, which had been built on the site
of the old Parker House) "three laughable farces": namely,
The Widow's Victim and two others, together with "dancing
by Señorita Abalos." At half past ten o'clock that morning an
alarm of fire was sounded at the corner of Pacific and Powell
streets, just as the church bells were tolling. People on their
way to church, as well as the idlers of Sunday morning, were
soon in crowds about the fire. But there was little to be done
to check it. The city had still no proper or adequate water supply; a few "reservoirs" there indeed were, lower down, in the
now nearly rebuilt business portion of the city, where the May
fire had raged, but here, among the dwelling-houses, there was
no water, and the little one- and two-story buildings burned,
says the *Alta,* like shavings. The genial summer sea-breeze of
San Francisco, which usually amuses itself with merely filling
one's eyes with sand, had now something better than sand to
drive before it, and quickly warmed to its savage work. In a
little time it had become a gale. The fire-engines came, but,
since they had little or no water, they could only stand by as
silent exponents of the city's official disapproval of fires. People tried to check the flames by tearing down the little houses
that stood in the track; but, as we know, one can more easily
burn an old box than tear it to pieces, and the nails were the
only sound part of these houses. Hence the fire soon drove off
the defenders. By the time the office of the *Alta* itself was
reached, on Washington Street, the presence at that point of
a good private fire-engine and of plenty of water in a tank,
and even the blowing up with powder of the adjoining building, did not save the *Alta* building, with the types and the
presses, from total destruction. About the Plaza the flames
raged fiercely. Three or four men lost their lives in the course
of the day. A very sick man was saved from his burning lodgings by his friends and carried on his bed into the middle of
the Plaza for safety; and there, amid the burning heat, the
cinders, and the bitter smoke, he died, his body lying in plain
sight, among the crowds and the heaps of goods, during the

day. These heaps of goods themselves several times caught fire
as they lay. The "old adobe" on the Plaza, of which we shall
hear in another connection, was destroyed. It was the last remaining relic of the old village of Yerba Buena. The city hos-
pital was also burned, the ninety patients then in it being safely
removed for the moment to a vacant lot.

Señorita Abalos did not dance on the stage of the Jenny Lind
Theater that Sunday night, nor did people laugh at *The
Widow's Victim* and the other laughable farces. For the Jenny
Lind Theater was once more a heap of hot ashes, and on the
hills above the town hundreds or even thousands of homeless
wretches shivered, amid the chaparral bushes, over whatever
remnants of their little store of household goods or of treasure
they had been able to save.

The fire of June 22 was emphatically a poor man's fire. The
great fire of May 4 had burned the business part of the city
and had destroyed vast wealth. But this last fire burned chiefly
the houses of people who had little else but their houses to
lose. The total loss was indeed not above three millions of dollars, some ten squares of these board hovels being totally destroyed, with parts of several other squares. But the immediate
suffering was possibly very nearly as great as that caused by the
fire of May 4. "Thousands of people," says the *Alta* next day,
"are homeless. We are sick with what we have seen and felt,
and need not say any more." The *Alta* itself was printed that
next morning on borrowed presses and from borrowed types
set up in the office of one of its fellow newspapers. Its page had
shriveled from seven columns to five, and the columns were
some five inches shorter than on the previous day.

Thenceforth, as we learn from the *Annals*,[13] "many of the
buildings" showed "a wonderful improvement in strength and
grandeur." An improvement in "grandeur," above that shown
in a board hovel, meant, in the business part of the city, the
building of substantial and generally very modest and useful
brick buildings, supplied with double iron shutters and with
large tanks of water. These same buildings still in a great number of cases remain in use. On its old site the Jenny Lind Thea-

---
[13] Page 345.

ter was rebuilt and during the next year was sold to the city for an exorbitant price and converted into the city hall, which still remains on the Plaza, although the new city hall, far out on Market Street, has in recent years superseded it as the municipal headquarters.

Outside of the business part of the city wooden houses have, however, always remained the favorites of the San Franciscan. One prefers them in view of the character of the climate, and, one trusts, with a now well-founded confidence in the energy and ability of the large and efficient fire department of the city as one's security against all fires. In the early years, also, and long before the modern paid fire department was organized or thought of, the lessons of these great fires were well taken to heart, from the middle of 1851 on, and the fire organizations of San Francisco were always strong and devoted.[14]

These, then, were the great transformations that the city underwent by reason of the early fires. In another and more healthful way, also, the city meanwhile transformed the appearance of its most important parts by rapidly carrying on the work of extending its water-front towards deep water, through the filling in of the old Yerba Buena Cove. This was done by carrying sand over temporary tracks, in cars drawn by small engines. The busy water-front of 1851, with its numerous long wharves extending far out into the cove, with its hurrying crowds in which all nationalities were still represented, and with its steam-cars occasionally rushing recklessly by, transporting their loads of sand, presented a scene far different from that of the confused heaps of merchandise and the cloth houses of 1849; but it was still a characteristic early Californian scene. From the "Happy Valley," which lay to the south, the railway track, in July 1851, ran along Market and Battery streets, transporting the sand to the rapidly filling water-lots.[15] Towards the end of that month, an accident having occurred whereby a man was run over by the cars, losing his leg, an ordinance was proposed in the board of aldermen "to restrict the speed of the cars to six miles an hour." This restriction, however, would not

---

[14] See the enthusiastic chapter in the *Annals*, p. 614 ff.
[15] *Alta* of July 19, 1851.

have been enough of itself to check the evil; for when, July 30, a man was killed by the same cars, on Market Street, the coroner's jury found that the accident might have been prevented "if the car in front of the man conducting it had not been loaded higher than his head, thus preventing him from seeing the track." [16] One's load, carried in front of one, was usually higher than one's head in California in those days, and one seldom saw the track ahead, whatever might be one's business. Hence the disasters, individual and social, of the early days. But amid all the confusion the progress towards physical stability, towards sound buildings, good and safe docks for ships, well-organized fire departments, and comparatively clean and decent streets, was sure. One great physical evil remains to be mentioned as explaining many social evils. In the early years the streets, like those of London in the last century, were, save very near the Plaza, wholly unlighted at night.[17]

II. *The Moral Insanities of the Golden Days*

WE pass from physical to social conditions. Society in these years was affected first of all by certain obvious and general mental disturbances of individual lives — disturbances that had a decidedly pathological character. Most of the citizen were young men, and homeless. Their daily and most sober business was at best dangerously near gambling, and their nerves were constantly tormented by unnatural and yet for the time inevitable excitements of a perilously violent sort. They differed, moreover, from the miners in that their life was as a rule comparatively sedentary and in that they worked far more with their brains than with their hands. Hence these nervous excitements told upon them all the more seriously. Their problems, too, were far more complex and brain-wearying than those of the miners. The miner was apt to degenerate for lack of healthful mental exercise of any sort. As he was often a clever and educated man, he found his hard manual labor intolerable;

---

[16] *Alta* of July 31, 1851.
[17] *Alta* of July 19, 1851.

and at night he drank or gambled for the sake of forgetting the inanity of his toil. But the San Franciscan of property and position was differently beset. He had all the mental labor that a man could need, and much more besides, and he had little or no true relaxation. Able and cultivated business men, who at home would have passed their evenings with their families or in some other pleasant social intercourse, or perchance in lecture rooms or in theaters, here toiled every night until ten or eleven o'clock over their accounts, and began afresh on each new morning, as soon as the light shone over the far-off blue summit of Mount Diablo, the old fierce struggle with the confusions of their business undertakings. The self-absorption of this life was often something monstrous, and the consequences are no matter of mere theory. The insane asylum, which the state had very early to equip at Stockton, gave ample proof of the effects of this terrible nervous strain. The great number of patients at this asylum made a frequent subject of remark among the early writers about California.[18] Indirectly, however, one sees the same dangers illustrated even in the case of perfectly healthy and normal men, who stood the mental if not the moral strain as well as possible, and liked it. The life between 1849 and 1852 or 1853 has often seemed to such men, as they have looked back on it, like a wild dream. Even in so early a book as the *Annals*, published in 1855 and in part written in 1854, one finds the life of 1849 and 1850 regarded in this same dreamlike and unsubstantial fashion. One collected, indeed, for this book, any number of trustworthy data from the newspapers; but one often commented upon them in the most confused and forgetful fashion possible. These things seemed to the author of the *Annals* to have taken place ages ago. In the old home the young girl graduate of 1849 might, in 1854, have been quietly preparing for her early wedding and for the very beginning of her life. But in California, as the *Annals* show us, these young men of 1854 already talked of the days of 1849 as

---

[18] See, for example, the remarks of the well-known pioneer "street-preacher," "Father" Taylor, in his *California Life Illustrated,* p. 133. He gives official statistics. The asylum was founded in 1852.

they might of a romantic and almost forgotten ancient history.[19] And a delirious history it indeed became for the authors of the *Annals,* as soon as the writers left their newspaper records and began to repeat their memories or the hearsay evidence of others. One can remember, as these men tell us, all sorts of confused emotions, but, as we judge from their wild and whirling words, one can remember nothing rational. Everybody, for instance, used to gamble; so one seems to remember. And gambling in the big saloons, under the strangely brilliant lamplight, amid the wild music, the odd people, the sounding gold, used to be such a rapturous and fearful thing! One cannot express this old rapture at all! Judges and clergymen used to elbow their way, so one remembers, to the tables and used to play with the rest. The men in San Francisco who did not thus gamble were too few to be noticed. If you condemn this gambling, so the historian continues, that is because you do not know the glorious rapture aforesaid, the rapture of gambling in a place where gambling is the only perfectly respectable amusement. But one's memory does indeed reach beyond this respectable amusement and is equal to the description of decidedly worse things, in which of course everybody was also engaged! There were some women in the city in 1849, but they were not exactly respectable persons, yet they were the sole leaders of society. They too gave it even in later years a certain grace and gaiety that makes one speak of them, with a curious sort of reverence, very frequently in the course of the *Annals.*[20] Just as one cannot easily remember who the men were that did

---

[19] *Annals,* p. 217, p. 665 *et passim.*

[20] See p. 259, p. 368 (where these persons are spoken of in a curiously close connection with the "upper classes"), p. 503 (where San Franciscans are declared to be of the "conscientious" opinion that, "after all, their wild and pleasant life is not so very, very wrong," and where the general degeneracy of the women in the city is reaffirmed), p. 504, p. 507 ("the trains of lovely women"), *et passim.* The especial merit of a book previously cited, Grey's *Pioneer Times in California,* is that it points out these absurdities in the *Annals,* although, in doing so, the book itself makes various inaccurate statements.

not gamble in those days, so one fails to recall in looking back on the early years the women who were respectable. Doubtless such existed; but then they had that curious quality of respectable women — namely, they were somehow not conspicuous, especially in the public crowds. Hence, as the authors of the *Annals* seem, for some probably sufficient reason, to have been personally unable, in early days, to secure the honor of their acquaintance, the existence of these good women fails to become a matter of historical record in the reminiscences with which so much of the confused volume is filled.

Now, however, side by side with these wild memories of a society where every man and woman, without any notable exception, went to the devil on his or her own chosen primrose path, one has to record, as sober fact, taken from one's newspapers, such things as a very goodly array of pioneer churches, supported by active and not poverty-stricken societies. And "now" (in 1854) "the city is full of [church] societies." [21] In fact, "such an array of churches and societies are surely evidences enough of the sincerity, zeal, and success of the early spirit of moral reform." [22] These societies have also done a large amount of charitable work; they have from the first established benevolent institutions, their exercises are well attended, and their undertakings well supported with money, so that, as one concludes (p. 701): "We have said enough, we hope, to prove that not all, nor nigh all the citizens of San Francisco, are lost to everything but reckless dissipation. No city of equal size — few of ten times its age — can present such a list of men and institutions, who have accomplished so much *real* good with so little of cant and hypocrisy.

These significant contradictions sufficiently characterize the spirit in which the annalists wrote their big book. San Francisco was to them a mere rubbish-heap of broken facts, and they had no conception of the sense of it. But their mood as writers depends, as I have just asserted, partly upon the pathological conditions connected with this life. Long-continued and unnatural excitement had disturbed their judgments. They were still very

---

[21] Page 697.
[22] Pages 699, 700.

active and laborious men, and the immense collection of facts
that they made for their book, from the early newspapers, will
always remain a monument of industry. But so far as their own
past experiences were concerned, the excitements of the early
years had made them simply incapable of telling any straight
or coherent story about these years. And, as one may remark,
the same infirmity has beset a good many San Francisco pioneers ever since. The cool-headed man who did not make a fool
of himself with absurd dissipations, nor destroy his health with
continuous overstrain in making haste to be rich, can indeed
give you helpful information about the early life, and such information I have frequently used in the pages of this book. But
the boastful and reckless old pioneer who imagines himself to
have seen all the heights and depths of the early life, who
knows more about it, in consequence, than human speech can
express — he, when he begins to tell you of it, is commonly
simply incoherent. He boasts on occasion, and with equal earnestness, of the piety and of the viciousness, of the gaiety and
of the seriousness, of the brutality and of the peacefulness of
the early days. Any chance number of an early newspaper
would tell you more about the pioneer community than he will
tell in a month.

The prevalence of overexcitement, then, is perfectly evident.
And the dissipations of the town were, in a large part of their
extravagances and bad consequences, the obvious result and
expression of this purely physical nervous overstrain. Just how
many previously respectable and sober men went to the devil
in the gambling-halls or with the help of the fast women can
never be known. They were undoubtedly far too numerous.
The universal demoralization of which the authors of the
Annals dream is, however, just as undoubted an absurdity. No
such thing took place. The dissipation was, of course, always
showy; it burned much midnight oil; and in a city that had
no street-lamps and few police, it was free to make itself very
visible in the darkness of every night. And when someone supposed to have been at home a clergyman, or when a locally
well-known lawyer or a prominent merchant, joined the young
fools about a gaming-table and also went to the devil, one may

be sure that the most drunken eyes saw the fact and that the most delirious memory preserved it, to the exclusion of many less exciting and more important social truths. The undoubted recklessness of the society as a whole lay, however, not in the fact that everybody openly gambled or did worse; for not everybody was dissipated; but the true sin of the community did consist in its tolerance of the open vices of those who chose to be vicious. Truly respectable men, whether clergymen or not, did not elbow their way to the gaming-tables; but public opinion, for reasons that have often ere this appeared in these pages, was not stern enough towards social offenses, but believed in a sort of irreligious liberty that considered every man's vices, however offensive and aggressive they might be (short of crime), as a private concern between his own soul and Satan. Here was the trouble, and in this respect only was the whole San Franciscan community alike responsible both for the early dissipations and for their inevitable consequences.

As to the actual extent of this mischief among individuals, the numbers of those engaged in the wilder dissipations cannot be estimated; yet it may well be doubted whether they at any time formed more than a comparatively small fraction of the American inhabitants. We are, after all, a persistently serious people in the matter of social amusements. And in San Francisco we had a great deal of business to do; and we did it. It took up nearly all of our time. The nervous overstrain of this business showed itself in many other forms besides the tendency to be dissipated, and the fast men and women were, as even the annalists once or twice admit, after all but the froth on the turbid current.

III. *Conservatism, Churches, and Families*

BUT now for some of the more conservative forces. These one finds in three ways very well-known and commonplace forms: namely, in the family, in the school, and in the church, all of which soon appear in San Francisco in their ordinary American dress, though just a trifle altered by the social disturbances of the place and the time.

The not very trustworthy state census of 1852 showed a population in the whole state of 264,435. Of these, to judge from the very rough estimates made, very nearly four fifths were American citizens, and of those again the great majority were, of course, by birth Americans. About one ninth or one tenth of the whole were women, and about one tenth children.[23] San Francisco, like all the other towns of the state, was subject to great fluctuations of population, but may be supposed in the early years to have contained, on the average, about one eighth of the population of the state, which again, between 1852 and 1856, may have increased from fifty to eighty per cent. The proportion of women and children in the city was always greater than the proportion in the state at large, in case the southern portion is left out of account.

On May 2, 1853, at a May Day celebration, there was in San Francisco a procession of school children to celebrate the occasion.[24] About one thousand children were in the train. Each one carried flowers; and the sight was a pleasant one for San Franciscans, although it was by no means the first time that homeless men had been reminded of the presence of happy homes in their midst. There had been, as we remember, families and children even in Yerba Buena, and the gold excitement had not killed them. A certain pioneer absurdity, formerly frequently repeated, which tells how, at a time during the early golden days, there was just One Lady in San Francisco, and she a newcomer, who was reverently, silently, and sentimentally worshipped by the vast, rude, and drunken throngs about her, must, of course, be dismissed to oblivion, along with that other scandalous assertion that in the early days there were *no* ladies in San Francisco at all. In fact, there were several good women at the outset, and many later.

---

[23] Compare Tuthill, p. 357; *Annals,* p. 505; and the official summary of the census, reported by the secretary of state to the Governor, in January 1853. With this summary of the census of 1852 that published as an appendix to the United States census returns of the Seventh National Census does not quite agree, and the details are plainly much confused in the returns.

[24] See *Annals,* p. 447. May 1 came that year on Sunday.

These good women and children needed churches and schools, while good husbands and fathers joined in the wish. In September 1849, when the street-preacher, the strong-hearted "Father" Taylor, entered the harbor on board a crowded vessel from the Atlantic coast, he heard, indeed, from a man who came out to the ship before they landed, strange and boastful stories about the jolly degeneracy of the place. But he failed, on landing, to verify in all respects these tales. The informant declared the gamblers to be the aristocracy [25] of San Francisco. As for religion, there had indeed been a church, but that had been turned into a jail, he believed; at all events he knew of only one preacher of recent standing in town; but that one was now a gambler.[26] The good Taylor found, however, upon landing, that what he humorously calls this informant's "ecclesiastical history" was, on the whole, false. The old schoolhouse on the Plaza, once used for religious meetings, was indeed now a jail; but there were other places of worship. Taylor had, indeed, a little trouble in finding Methodists. He at last found that "Brother White," who lived "in the woods" (that is, among the dwarf oaks and the shrubbery), on Washington Street near Powell, had a little cloth and board house where he held Methodist "class-meetings" and "prayer-meetings" on Sundays, with a "class" of twenty. Taylor himself set to work busily to prepare a church for his denomination. Resolutely he crossed the bay, toiled in the redwoods behind San Antonio Creek, cut and hewed his own lumber, and then, carrying it to San Francisco, helped build his own place of worship. It was ready by October 8, 1849.

---

[25] William Taylor's *California Life Illustrated* (New York, 1858), p. 16.

[26] With such stories the early Californians of a certain sort amused themselves continually. Little dependence can be placed in any such gossip, whether about San Francisco or about any other place. The *New York Evening Post* correspondent, above cited, had heard of a Methodist parson who was now a bar-tender. As a fact, the early California clergymen were on the whole very remarkably faithful, intelligent, laborious, and devout. One would have suffered sadly without them.

But this remarkably energetic fashion of preparing the way of the Lord, and of laying the axe at the root of the tree, did not, after all, result in building the first San Francisco church. That first one was Rev. O. C. Wheeler's Baptist church, built in the summer of 1849, before Taylor's arrival. And already in that summer and autumn there existed several other church organizations in San Francisco: [27] namely, Rev. T. Dwight Hunt's pioneer union organization, formed in 1848, Rev. Albert Williams's "First Presbyterian Church," which for some time dwelt in tents, and Rev. Dr. Ver Mehr's Episcopal organization, which had its beginnings in this first autumn. The Mission church had to suffice for Catholic communicants until 1851, when the first Catholic church appeared in the town proper.

The early relations of the Protestant pioneer pastors with one another were of the most cordial character. And their little groups of communicants were both earnest and active. Out of this pastoral fellowship and this devotion of the laymen sprang the numerous early church charities that the annalists mention.[28] As for the place that these churches occupied in the community, there can be no doubt that, however the numbers in the early churches might compare with those in the gambling-saloons, the spirit of the new community was at least as well represented by the former as by the latter. For if the saloons represented its diseases, these stood for its health. "Father" Taylor delights to tell how the most aggressive of his street-preaching undertakings always received, if not active support, then at least quietly friendly sufferance from the gamblers whom he was attacking. There was from the first the characteristic American feeling prevalent that churches were a good and sober element in the social order, and that one wanted them to prosper, whether one took a private and personal interest in any of them or not. The religious coldness of a large number who at home would have seemed to be devout did not make the progress of the churches in California less sure, nor

---

[27] See more details in the records given in the *Annals*, p. 687 ff.

[28] See also Rev. Albert Williams: *Pioneer Pastorate and Times* (San Francisco, 1879), p. 63 f.

their value as socially conservative forces less generally recognized.

Rev. Albert Williams mentions, in a passage of the book just cited,[29] the delight of being able to address the vigorous young men of early San Francisco. The San Franciscans, when they went to church at all, were, he declares, uncommonly inspiring audiences, because they were so manly, attentive, and intelligent. In the manuscript that I have previously cited as furnished to me from diary and recollection by my mother, I find, amid numerous other reflections on the early social conditions (reflections that have throughout much influenced my comments), an account of the first time when she herself attended church in San Francisco, in the early months of 1850. The journey across the "plains" and a few troubled months in the mines and at Sacramento had led my father, after the great flood at the latter place, to come with my mother and her child to the bay. The building where she thus first attended church services she found larger than she had expected, and well filled, although she saw but six or eight women present. What especially aroused her interest in the audience was this splendid group of ardent, young, thoughtful, and manly faces, all so full of deep and reverent attention to the services. The thing was no commonplace affair to them. It meant homelike and religious associations, aroused thus afresh in their minds in the midst of a sordid and weary land. She saw in their countenances an "intensity of earnestness" that made her involuntarily "thank God for making so grand a being as man." It seems worth while thus to add to the possibly biased statement of the pioneer preacher this impression that was received at her first church-attendance in San Francisco by my mother, as a mere listener and a stranger.

This use of my mother's manuscript leads me to pass from the topic of the churches to record a few of her impressions of the early social and family life of San Francisco, as seen from the point of view of a dweller within doors. She passed a considerable time in 1850 in a little circle of San Francisco fami-

[29] Page 141.

lies that were held together mainly by those ties of social and religious sympathy which might be supposed most effective at such a moment, and in the midst of such exciting conditions. Of the outer world she had, of course, to see and to hear a great deal; and her account of this is much what one might expect from what one otherwise knows, save that she had occasion to hear of some particular instances of great business undertakings, speculations, and failures that it might be amusing to recount in these pages if there were only enough space left. But one must pass to social life proper.

Everyone has heard how, in early San Francisco life, the family ties seemed sometimes almost as weak as the families were rare. Divorces were in proportion far too numerous and easy. Some men seemed to prize their wives the less because of the very fact that there were in the country so few wives to prize. Of all this the early papers make frequent complaint, and the early travelers frequent mention, although the facts are also often much exaggerated. The causes, however, of this too general disrespect for the most significant relations of life, my mother seemed to see as rather deep-lying. In the new land, namely, to speak of the matter first from the side of the women concerned themselves, one's acquaintances could not always be strictly chosen, nor one's conduct absolutely determined by arbitrary rules. One had to adapt oneself to many people, to tolerate, in some people with whom one was thrown, many oddities, and much independence, so long as the essentials of good behavior and good purposes remained. The difficulty, however, for certain well-meaning but foolish among the younger women who found themselves in the midst of all this new life was to sacrifice some of the nonessentials of social intercourse, as they knew them, without sacrificing anything either of their own personal dignity or of their true delicacy of feeling. Many such women failed to solve the problem. Little by little they sacrificed this or that petty prejudice which dignity would have counseled them to observe; and so erelong they were socially more or less distinctly and disastrously careless, both as to behavior and as to companionship. But such mild degeneration is not an element of strength in the union of a

family. Men often prized their wives less because the wives
grew thus foolishly lighthearted and were, on the whole, less
to be prized. Nor was there a lack of fault on the other
side. If women fell into these unguarded habits, such as
the custom of letting men who chanced to be their friends,
and chanced to be lucky, give them, with careless Californian
generosity, expensive presents on every occasion when these
friends had made some new success in business, and if such
"Californian" ways, however innocent in their beginning, led
to misunderstandings in the end: still, on the other hand, husbands who found themselves absorbed in business rivalry with
a community of irresponsible bachelors, and who accordingly
lamented the hostages that they themselves had long since
given to fortune, often neglected without reason their families
and so in time lost the affection that they had ceased to deserve.
In short, as my mother (who, in the course of a few years, had
occasion to hear of or to see a number of these broken California families) judged the too general trouble, it was one that
might be said to lie in the lonesomeness of the families of a new
land. The family grows best in a garden with its kind. Where
family life does not involve healthy friendship with other families, it is apt to be injured by unhealthy if well-meaning friendships with wanderers. The lonesome man, far away from home,
seeking in all innocence of heart the kindly and elevating
companionship of some good woman, the good-humored young
woman, enjoying in all her innocence also the flattery and the
exaggerated respect of a community of bachelors, the foolish
husband, feeling his wife more or less a burden, in a country
where so few of his friends and of his rivals have such burdens
to hamper them; such are the too familiar figures of social life
in a new land. From their relationships spring the curious un-
happiness that at length come to mar the lives of so many good,
easy souls. Add to the picture the figure of the bachelor friend
aforesaid, venturing not only to flatter, but, in his rudely courteous or in his more gently diffident manner, to comfort the neglected wife, with honest words and with kindly services; and
one sees how much in danger, under such circumstances, may
be the true interests of all family life. If one wants a high aver-

age of domestic peace and of moral health, one must not look
for it too hopefully in the domestic lives of the most among
those who ought to prize one another highest: namely, wedded
companions, in very few ·countries. These people may indeed
be wise and find all that you could wish for in the way of true
happiness; but too many of them will be seen to be blind to the
worth of their privileges, just because these happen, at that
place and time, to be so rare. Such, then, was my mother's general observation. But she saw many cases indeed of people who
were sensible enough to know when they were happy and to
live in the best of domestic relations. Such families were, in
their place, the salvation of this restless and suffering social
order. For about them clustered the hopes for the future of
society. In them were reared the better-trained children. In
them careless wanderers saw the constant reminders of the old
home. To increase their numbers, to quiet their fears, to satisfy
their demands, men were willing to make vast sacrifices. It was
indeed largely in the hope of seeing erelong many such families
flocking to the state that those men who felt their own interests
in the country to be fairly permanent were willing to toil for
order in the arduous fashions exemplified by the great vigilance
committees.

IV. *Popular Justice in February 1851*

Not the same judgment, by any means, can be passed upon
the San Francisco vigilance committees of 1851 and 1856
as we have already passed upon the popular justice of the miners. In some respects, to be sure, there is an unfortunate likeness. Both in the mines and in San Francisco carelessness had
led to a destructive general license of mischief-makers. In both
places the men of sense were forced at last to attend to their
social duties. But in the mines there was, for a while, a far too
general, a very absurd and wicked trust in lynch law as the best
expression, under the circumstances, of the popular hatred of
crime. San Francisco, as a community, never went so far as
this. In that city lynch law was, both in 1851 and in 1856, the
expression of a pressing desire so to reform the social order that

lynch law should no longer be necessary. What the success of these efforts was we have to see from the facts.

The condition of society that so well expressed itself in the fire of May 4, 1851 had, nearly three months earlier, led to the first of the greater outbursts of popular indignation at crime,[30] that of February 1851. On the 19th of February a merchant named Jansen was assaulted and robbed in his own shop by two men, who came in the evening, pretending to be customers. The crime, though not the first or the worst of its sort, seemed especially atrocious to the community, which chanced to be in a sensitive mood. The *Alta*, usually in those days a very sober and sensible paper, became for the moment a trifle overexcited. Nobody, says the editor a day or two later, is secure, even in his own dwelling. And the ruffians, if arrested at all, are never punished. "How many murders have been committed in this city within a year! And who has been hung or punished for the crime? Nobody. How many men shot and stabbed, knocked down and bruised; and who has been punished for it? How many thefts and arsons, robberies, and crimes of a less note; and where are the perpetrators? Gentlemen at large, citizens, free to reënact their outrages." Under these circumstances, however, who is to blame? The *Alta* with an amusing unwisdom, proceeds to make the lawyers who defend criminals the first persons responsible for the trouble. Such a lawyer is a "father to the thief and robber, aye, to the mur-

---

[30] The affair of the "Hounds," in 1849, generally mentioned as the first important case of popular justice in San Francisco, is a typical illustration of the short and easy methods of the early golden days, but it is otherwise comparatively insignificant. A company of young rascals, having paraded the streets on a number of occasions, under the name of the "Hounds" and under the pretense of being a society for mutual protection, made at last their long tolerated disorderly behavior intolerable. They began violent assaults on the Chilians present in the town and were promptly suppressed. Their leaders were tried and convicted by a popular court, wherein two judges (of whom Gwin, then just arrived, was one) were appointed by the people "to assist the alcalde." The prisoners were then sentenced to long terms of imprisonment, which, of course, were never inflicted upon them. See *Annals*, p. 552 ff.

derer, even." "We cannot see how any honest man, knowing or
having reason to believe another guilty, can ransack heaven and
earth for arguments for shielding him from punishment." Next
to the lawyers, the courts and the police are most to blame.
"The city would be infinitely better off without them. They are
no terror to evil-doers." And so, finally: "We deprecate lynch
law, but the outraged public," etc., etc.

Under these circumstances the news that two men had been
arrested as the perpetrators of this assault aroused the people
to riotous indignation and to eloquence. One of these two men
was soon said to be a certain rogue named Stuart, notorious in
the mines. On the 21st the two men arrested were confronted
with the wounded Jansen. The supposed Stuart he was said to
have recognized at once as one of his assailants, and he had
only a little doubt about the other prisoner. Accordingly when
on Saturday, the 22nd, the two were to be brought up before
the court in the city hall for preliminary examination, the people [31] collected, grew more and more excited, read copies of a
well-written and rather foolish handbill (which called upon all
good citizens to assemble on Sunday, at two o'clock, on the
Plaza, for the sake of somehow ridding the community of its
robbers and murderers), and so at last, with a shout: *"Now's
the time,"* rushed towards and into the recorder's courtroom,
in order to seize the prisoners. [32] But a company of militia, the
"Washington Guards," which had been called out and was now
on parade, ready to defend the officers of the law, entered the
courtroom just after the first of the mob had rushed in, cleared
the room with fixed bayonets, and so saved the prisoners, who
were then imprisoned in the not very secure basement of the
city hall. The guards thus earned many hoots and hisses, in so
much that the wayward and still wholly disorganized crowd
followed them home to their armory, challenged them to a
fight, and were with difficulty persuaded at last to disperse.
About dusk that evening a more sensible and dignified public
meeting took place near the city hall and was addressed by

---

[31] "The *people,* in the highest sense of the term," declare the
authors of the *Annals* (p. 315), and "not a mob."

[32] *Weekly Alta* for March 1, 1851.

several speakers, among them Mr. Sam Brannan, the lion-hearted, a man always in love with shedding the blood of the wicked. A committee of prominent citizens, of whom he was one, was appointed by the public meeting to consider the situation and also to assist the police in guarding the accused overnight; and this committee's proceedings, after the greater meeting had adjourned, were also reported in the *Alta* of the next day. Mr. Brannan begged his fellow members to take the chance now so kindly given them by fortune and to try the prisoners themselves forthwith. He was tired of the law. He was "much surprised to hear people talk about grand juries, or recorders or mayors." He was "opposed to any farce in this business." Mr. Brannan's less enthusiastic fellows on the committee overruled him as to these somewhat immoral proposals; but they too were not free from excitement. Even the moderate and cautious Mr. Macondray, a prominent merchant, and one of the committee, declared that no court would dare to discharge these men; no lawyer would dare to plead their cause. But he very sensibly pointed out that a committee appointed by the sovereign people to guard prisoners could not well turn itself into a jury and try them.

Now, however, one serious defect and danger about all this ardent and sincere popular indignation against the two prisoners lay in the fact that the supposed Stuart was really quite an innocent man, whose name was Burdue. He had been mistaken for the true assailant by poor Jansen, who was lying very seriously hurt with a concussion of the brain. The resemblance of the accused to the real criminal Stuart was indeed remarkable; but there were people in San Francisco who could on occasion identify the accused as an innocent man, unless indeed the popular indignation at crime should forbid for the moment all defense of any supposed criminals.

Fortunately, however, the general sentiment of the wiser men of San Francisco favored giving the two accused a fair chance. And therefore, when on the next day the people assembled once more, a no less stern but much more sensible spirit prevailed than on the previous morning. Mr. William T. Coleman, later so noted in connection with both the great vigilance committees, came forward with a motion to appoint a committee to agree upon a plan of action, and this committee, having been chosen, reported that a judge and jury should be named, who should try the criminals at two o'clock the same day. This plan was submitted to the people and adopted.[33] The jury was appointed by popular consent. Great difficulty was found in getting a popular judge to serve; but at last one Mr. J. F. Spence was chosen, and two assistant judges were appointed. The chief actors in the subsequent trial were thus the result of some genuine reflection and of a careful choice, and the trial was therefore saved from becoming what the mob wished it to be — a disorderly mock trial.

At two o'clock the popular court was complete master of the situation, and met in the district courtroom. Without any resistance from the officials this time, the prisoners were considered as subject to the jurisdiction of the new tribunal, although they were not removed from their cells. Two lawyers, prominent through many later years in California as attorneys, consented to defend the prisoners — Judge Shattuck appearing for the supposed Stuart, Mr. Hall McAllister for the other; but counsel for the people was harder to find, regular attorneys declining, very naturally, to serve. Mr. Coleman at length undertook the work. The jury were known men; and to Mr. R. S. Watson, their foreman, now of Milton, Massachusetts, I am indebted for a very interesting oral account of the scene. Mr. Watson himself did not sympathize in any degree with the extravagances of the mob, and, as we shall see, his influence was

---

[33] Not, however, until a wicked attempt had been made, by four members of the committee of the night before (i. e., of the guard appointed for watching the prisoner), to arouse the mob to immediate action by means of an incendiary handbill, signed by these four. The handbill pretended to "report" how these four knew that there was no question of the guilt of the prisoners. The paper was apparently the work of Mr. Sam Brannan, whose name was first signed to it, the other names being Wm. H. Jones, E. A. King, and J. B. Huie. One sees thus how near the San Franciscans were led to committing a brutal crime, by reason of the noisiness of hotheaded and officious men.

ultimately used, with that of others, to save the prisoners. But the moment was one when the advice of cautious men was especially needed, and one may be glad that such were willing to serve.

The trial of the supposed Stuart took precedence and, as we shall see, was the only act of the tribunal. The testimony, as the *Alta* shows, was of two sorts. Some of the witnesses declared themselves able to identify this man as one Stuart, somewhat notorious at Sacramento and in the mines as a most dangerous character, and several times proved guilty of theft and, they said, of worse. The other witnesses knew only that Jansen, who we remember was suffering ever since the assault from concussion of the brain, had said that this man looked so much like his own assailant that there could be little doubt about the identity. Judge Shattuck ably insisted upon the fact that, as the defense was the denial of this man's identity with the notorious Stuart, as well as with the assailant of Jansen, the cause of justice would demand some scrutiny of the prisoner's antecedents and life. Time was needed for this. And Judge Shattuck "had had no time to consult with the accused, to ascertain who were his friends and acquaintances, or to inquire in the case." [34] Under these circumstances, with a savage crowd in the court-room occasionally interrupting and demanding the death of the prisoner, Judge Shattuck felt that his defense was somewhat hampered, and he begged the jury to remember the terrible responsibility of their position. He made some effort to get testimony to clear the prisoner, but the time allowed him was too short, and, as later appeared, the prisoner's few acquaintances, who, after all, were not exactly prominent citizens, were afraid to risk facing the popular tribunal and the mob, and were not easy to find that evening. Time wore away in wrangling about the case; the mob grew more and more impatient, and the counsel for the defense was frequently interrupted and once or twice insulted. As Mr. Watson tells me, he himself was one of those on the jury most anxious to consider carefully the worth of Mr. Jansen's evidence, and he did not find it satisfying. For

---

[34] *Alta* of February 24, in the weekly of March 1, as cited.

the injured man, lying in a stupor, had only been with difficulty aroused to view the prisoners. In the room had been, besides these prisoners, only poor Jansen's own friends. What thing more natural than that, under such circumstances, the man should reply: "Yes," when asked if these strangers were the men who had hurt him? When the jury at last retired, this doubtfulness, and in fact actual worthlessness, of the testimony in question was strongly insisted upon by the foreman and two others, and although nine of the jury were ready to convict, these three held out firmly, through a long deliberation and after many ballotings. Much tumult, meanwhile, raged outside the court-room, and to some extent in it. The better class of citizens were urging the crowd to be patient; while the crowd were weary and disgusted to think that, now the beautifully simple machinery of popular justice was once set up, it somehow would not run smoothly, but was subject even to delays. During this time it was, and after ten o'clock at night, that Mr. E. S. Osgood [35] learned that two men were accessible, and living down on "Long Wharf" (Commercial Street wharf), who could swear to the true identity of the prisoner and to his whereabouts on the night of the assault. Before making an effort to go down in the thick darkness to the not very safe regions of Long Wharf, Mr. Osgood came forward in the courtroom, announced his purpose, and begged the court to be willing to wait for the new evidence and to admit it when it should come. Someone present, as Mr. Osgood has told me, called out, asking him who he was; another thereupon shouted that this newcomer in court was well known to certain present as one Osgood, a responsible person; a third shouted: "No, I know who he is, one of these scoundrels that are trying to get their accomplice here off free" — and hereupon some angry discussion followed. Mr. Osgood gave his name and his business, but, as the *Alta* says, "the crowd refused to hear any further testi-

---

[35] Now a resident of Cambridge, Mass. I have heard from him his own account also of the following scene, which, with his name mentioned, is described more briefly in the *Alta* report, as cited. The two accounts agree so far as they refer to the same occurrences at all.

mony." Yet Mr. Osgood set off in the darkness to find his witnesses, and after some gloomy wanderings he was successful. With some trouble he persuaded them to come with him to the court from their lodgings on Long Wharf. But before the return of the three, the case was for the time ended.

At nearly midnight, namely, the jury had returned to court, and the foreman had reported that they could not agree. Mr. Watson remembers well the unpleasant scene presented to himself and his fellow jurymen, with the weary and angry crowd all about, who began to call for the names of the disagreeing jurors and to shout: *"Hang them too."* But the scene was not to last long. The good citizens present were firm, the mob had diminished by reason of the lateness of the hour, the leaders insisted that the sovereign people, having referred the case to a jury, must abide by its decision, and the people were at last induced to disperse. One device to pacify them seems to have been a resort to that great medicine wherewith the American rids himself of his dangerous social passions, just as the Aristotelian spectator of tragedy purges himself of his "pity and fear." This *katharsis*, namely, is, with the American, political agitation. When Mr. Osgood returned with his witnesses, he found some of the recent heroes of popular justice loudly shouting: *"Hurrah for Weller."* An impromptu political meeting had in fact just been taking place, and all the good citizens who were still out of bed were so interested in this new matter that Mr. Osgood with difficulty learned from them what had become of the prisoner. At last he heard that the popular tribunal had adjourned *sine die*, and that the prisoners had been left with the authorities for trial. And thus happily ended an affair in which the citizens of San Francisco had shown some of their worst as well as some of their best traits. A volunteer night patrol, organized by the merchants, thenceforth for a time aided the police force of the city, which was all this time small, poorly trained, generally neglected, and ill-paid, getting its wages in depreciated city script.

But the great year of the popular tribunals was as yet only begun. The newspapers might hope that the city would escape the curse of popular justice, but the temper of the public made such escape impossible. One thing, however, was secured by the February outbreak: the public would be sure in time to learn from it the proper lesson as to the dangers of mere mob law. The supposed Stuart was some months later shown to be a rather weak, but, as to legal offenses, an innocent man. For the moment he escaped from San Francisco, only to fall a little later once more into trouble, in the interior, by reason of his singular resemblance to the redoubtable Stuart. From this trouble also he was released through evidence produced by the very San Franciscans who had been so near hanging him in February. The other prisoner accused of the assault on Jansen was later convicted, and sentenced to the penitentiary, by a regular court. But he also was still later shown to be innocent, and was finally released. For the time, however, the mass of the citizens could not know how criminal might have proven the hasty methods of the 22nd and the 23rd of February. When the committee of June was formed, with such men as the late foreman of the jury of February 23 in prominent places upon it, there was, however, a very decided effort made from the first to avoid every appearance of disorder. That the committee was needed at all resulted, as said, from the temper of the public mind, which, without some serious lesson in the troublesome work of popular justice, could not have been induced to forsake in any wise its over-confidence and its carelessness.

V. *The First Vigilance Committee*

WE study, in this book, the incidents that exhibit the popular character and the play of social forces, rather than those that have only an adventurous interest. The first Vigilance Committee is rich in dramatic situations, but, after its first formation, its history shows little further that is novel in the way of socially important undertakings. Upon its early moments alone we shall dwell. Absolutely necessary, in order to distinguish it from the more disorderly and transient committees of the mines, would be, of course, a careful and sober organization. This it got, at the outset of its work, in June. What followed vindicated the good sense of the organization, but throws little new light on the ethics of popular justice.

The fire of May 4 had rendered the public more sensitive, discontented, and suspicious than ever; but a genuine popular reform had not yet taken place. Reforms must have something to date from, and two or three minor popular excitements, produced by attempts at arson or by other crimes, were not sufficient for the purpose. On Sunday, June 8, a very able letter appeared in the *Alta* proposing the immediate formation of a committee of safety and suggesting a plan for its operations. The plan as stated was admitted to be somewhat undigested, but was probably so strongly expressed chiefly for the sake of arousing popular attention. The usual complaints were made as to the social condition. The committee of safety was to improve matters by boarding in time the vessels that arrived from Australia and by refusing to let any doubtful characters land from them; while, as to the ruffians now in the city, ward committees of vigilance were arbitrarily to single them out and to warn them to leave the city within five days on pain of a "war of extermination" to be prosecuted against them. "Let us set about the work at once. It may be well to call a public meeting in the square, to organize and carry out these views. Without this, or some other similar plan, the evil cannot be remedied; and if there is not spirit enough amongst us to do it, why then in God's name let the city be burned, and our streets flow with the blood of murdered men." The letter was throughout very well written. It is remarkable as not referring directly and openly to any one case before the public and as not getting its inspiration from any one popular excitement or mob, and also as coming from one of the most cautious and conscientious of the jury at the recent trial of the false Stuart.[36] Some of the writer's friends guessed at the authorship of the letter, and at breakfast at his restaurant, Sunday morning, he was accosted

---

[36] Namely, from the pen of Mr. R. S. Watson, who on seeing the *Alta* of that date in the file that I have used, now feels able to identify with absolute certainty this letter as the one that he remembers having written at that time to the press.

by several of them and asked about the matter. The *Alta* itself noticed the letter approvingly; and Mr. Watson had, as he says, "touched a train already laid." Others were on the point of a similar movement.

A few editorial and inspired articles in the *Alta* on Monday and Tuesday are the only public indications during those days that anything of importance was going on among the citizens interested in the new movement. The *Alta* of Wednesday, June 11, brings sufficient evidence, however, both of the movement and of its first consequences. The editor remarks, that morning, that mobs are indeed of no service in suppressing crime. But "the next affair of the kind will be of a different character, if we are correctly informed in regard to certain organizations of our citizens, which are now and have for several days been progressing. We understand that quite a large party banded themselves together at the California Engine House on Monday night, for the purpose of punishing incendiaries and other criminals." The organization of the committee had indeed been already provisionally perfected. Mr. Sam Brannan, with his wonted zeal, had offered them a room, and his offer had been accepted. Two taps on the engine-house bell were to call the committee together. The promptness of the work of organization showed how many besides the anonymous correspondent of the Alta had had the thoughts to which he gave such vigorous expression. Prominent on the committee, besides the two already mentioned, were Mr. William T. Coleman, Mr. Stephen Payran,[37] Mr. S. E. Woodworth, and many others.

---

[37] Although Mr. W. T. Coleman is by popular reputation the most prominent among the executive leaders of the first committee, Mr. W. W. Carpenter, writing from Petaluma, under date of March 25, 1874, to the *Oakland Transcript,* and professing to give something of the "secret history" of the committee, makes Mr. Payran its "chairman" throughout, as well as its greatest hero. The organization of the committee, with a comparatively few leaders and a large rank and file, makes such questions about the division of honors very frequent in the reminiscences of various pioneers. There was, however, as to personal credit, no true first hero in this very honest and active company of intelligent and able leaders.

But, as this same *Alta* of Wednesday learned even as it was going to press, the committee had no sooner organized than it had undertaken work. A thief, one Jenkins, a common ruffian of a very low type, had been detected Tuesday evening in the very act of burglary on Long Wharf and, attempting to escape in a boat, was caught and brought back. At ten o'clock Tuesday night the members of the committee were called to their first appointed headquarters [38] (near the corner of Sansome and Bush streets). For two hours the committee were engaged in examining the case, and at midnight Mr. Sam Brannan announced their verdict to the crowd assembled outside the rooms. The criminal, he said, was to be hanged in an hour or two on the Plaza. The execution took place at two. An attempt was made by the police on the Plaza to get Jenkins away from the committee, but the effort was hopeless, and the "old adobe," now so near its doom, did almost its last public service, before the June fire burned it down, in serving, through one of its projecting beams, as a gallows to hang Jenkins.[39]

A time of feverish public excitement followed. The coroner's inquest implicated certain people as connected with the execution of Jenkins; but the committee, in a very dignified publication, declared all their members, of whom a complete list was given, equally implicated, and announced their firm intention to work for the purification of the city. This plain statement relieved the public mind. The committee was no merely secret organization; and its members were among the best-known men of the city. It plainly expressed the general sentiment. The question why, then, could not this honest general sentiment have expressed itself before, in the selection of good and efficient officers, now came too late. Once for all, only a

---

[38] In the *Annals*, p. 570, erroneously put at the corner of Pine and Battery streets, on this occasion.

[39] Mr. Watson has given me a very interesting account of this whole night, for which I wish that I had more space. The weather, as appears both from the *Alta* and from his account, was unusually clear for a June night in San Francisco, and the moon was very brilliant. The popular excitement all night was of the greatest, but of course the general feeling fully supported the committee.

glimpse of the terrible scenes of lynch law could make this public serious. And so the committee was indeed a necessity. Here, in fact, is one of the heretofore frequently mentioned cases where popular justice was not in itself sin, but was the confession of the past sin of the whole community.

The work during June, July, and August was both impressive and important. That it frightened the rogues, sent many of them away, and hanged three more besides Jenkins is, as the reader now sees, the least of its merits. More important was the manifest sobriety and justice of the methods. The committee caught, tried, and hanged the true Stuart, who made at the last a full but untrustworthy confession. But by doing this piece of work the committee accomplished an act of justice to the poor fellow who had been mistaken for Stuart in February. He, namely, was now in jail in the interior, under sentence of death, all because of another consequence of his resemblance to Stuart. And the committee, when the truth had once become known, made every effort to save him and to set him free, and succeeded. Not mere vengeance, then, but justice was the obvious motive of its acts. In August the committee came nearly to an open collision with the authorities, who, at an unguarded moment, rescued from the rooms of the committee two of its condemned criminals, Whittaker and McKenzie. The committee, however, some days later, by a skillful and effective surprise, recaptured these two and hanged them at once, all without more than the mere show of violence towards the police. Successfully, then, the risk of an open fight with officers of the law was overcome. But the lesson of this was a serious one. Popular justice in San Francisco would, it was plain, involve fearful risks of an open collision between the officers and the people and would be a great waste of social energy. Why not gain in future, through devotion to the duties of citizenship, what one thus in the end would have to struggle for in some way, perchance at the expense of much blood?

When the committee at last ceased its activity, this lesson was in everybody's mind. That the lesson was not more permanently taken to heart by San Franciscans is indeed unfortunate. Too many of the citizens still felt themselves wanderers on the face of the earth. But at all events a good beginning had been made in righteousness.

VI. *Social Corruption and Commercial Disaster*

THE years 1852 and 1853, and especially the latter, were in San Francisco years of rapid growth and of great general prosperity. The year 1854, however, marks an important era in San Francisco social evolution. It was the year in which began the first great financial depression of California. Individual fortunes had suffered in all sorts of ways, but the general solvency of the mercantile community had persisted. At last, however, continuous overconfidence in the rapid development of the wealth of the country led to the natural result. The production of the mines began to fall off, immigration decreased, many people left the land, the consumption of food diminished, interest and rents declined in San Francisco, and thirty per cent of the warehouses were left empty.[40] This second stage of commercial life is universal in new countries, only the swiftness and the particular conditions of the calamity varying from place to place. And one who has grown up in new communities always listens with amusement to the enthusiasm of sanguine investors in the enterprises of some just settled portion of our territory, when they declare that the first stage of the life of the newly prosperous region is demonstrably only a faint indication of the continuous and unceasing future growth of its wealth. For, as the lifelong dweller in new countries knows, the enthusiasm of these early investors is as ruinous to them as it is valuable for the new country. Their ideas are indeed, in one sense, well founded. What they hope for is certain to come in time, only for others, and not in general for them. The evolution of the new land will not be what they think, a steady growth in wealth. The first great commercial crisis of its history will be, in proportion to its wealth, the worst of all; and these sanguine investors will be destroyed like flies in autumn. The second period of its growth, the winter-time of this great de-

[40] J. S. Hittell's *History of San Francisco*, p. 217.

pression, when all but the very strongest of those early investors have become poor as church mice, is the true time for a cautious, hard-working, and shrewd man to make his appearance in the land. He will be wiser than his predecessors and far less·extravagant. He will buy at low prices their half-abandoned property, and in later years they will bitterly reproach him, instead of themselves, for the wrong that gave him a chance to reap what they had sown. This law of the almost universal failure of the pioneers of a new country was well exemplified in San Francisco.

The law is a beneficent one; for the interests of pioneers are at first much narrower than the true and historical interests of the country that they seek to subject to their private schemes. "Something of the decay of business in the city," well observes Mr. J. S. Hittell,[41] "must be attributed to the growth of agriculture. Many of the immigrants of 1852 had gone to farming, and they were joined by thousands of farmers in the next year, so that there was a large increase in the production of grain and vegetables, and a correspondent decline in the quantity of flour imported, in the number of ships needed, and in the profit of consignees, warehousemen, jobbers, and draymen in the city." But all this, of course, meant the final advantage of the whole country, San Francisco included.

The immediate consequence of the crisis was the revelation of much social corruption that had been growing, but that had been previously hidden. People had boasted of the wild dissipations of 1849 and 1850, forgetting that all these dissipations had seemed so noteworthy just because they were *not* characteristic of the real temperament of the people and were a transient and inflamed symptom of the unnatural excitements to which the more weak and foolish of the young men yielded. But now this wilder dissipation had passed into the background of popular attention. Nobody any longer called the gambling-halls respectable.[42] The boastful sinners of the earlier

---

[41] Ibid.

[42] Gambling continued to be licensed in San Francisco until 1855, but long before that time met with steadily increasing condemnation. The *San Francisco Herald* of April 7, 1852 shows the

days had become willing to behave in a more commonplace fashion. But the sins that men boast of are never their worst. What San Francisco had not boasted of being able to produce was sin such as was represented by the distinguished swindler and forger, Henry Meiggs, whose business undertakings, begun early in the city's history, culminated in his crimes and in his flight in the autumn of 1854. Californians had been supposed, above all things, before those days of 1854, to discourage and despise underhand dealings and duplicity of every sort. The annalists boasted in their book of the commercial integrity of the city in even its wildest days; and, indeed, the average integrity of the early merchants was high. But pioneer recklessness has as its correlate an extravagant tendency to hero-worship. The good fellow is easily adored in a new city — all the more easily because one has had no means to judge of his weaknesses by means of a lifelong acquaintance. The same general carelessness that tends to corrupt the morally weaker members of pioneer society expresses itself by trusting extravagantly any clever man whose manners are pleasing. The trust gives him more than his share of power, and the lack of public spirit in the community gives him a chance to abuse his privileges. And so San Francisco produced Meiggs and was responsible for him and his tribe as much as for the gambling-halls; perhaps more still.

Meiggs was early a general favorite: a man shrewd, generous, and speculative. He was a lumber-merchant, who, as

view generally taken of these gambling-halls at that time. They still constitute a "prominent feature of life in San Francisco," but "public opinion in the main is opposed to their existence, and they are tolerated for no other reason, that we know of, than that they are charged heavily for licenses." They abound, continues the editor, all along Commercial Street, and on Long Wharf, at the foot of that street. Almost all of them are owned by foreigners. The business, however, is "not so extensively followed as it was last year." "Persons of respectability and standing seldom visit the saloons nowadays for play," although at one time many such persons used to do so. "The public are becoming more and more opposed" to the business "every day." By the end of 1855 the *Bulletin* condemns the gamblers as among the worst elements of society.

such, profited, of course, by the growth as well as by the occasional partial destruction of the early city. He became deeply
interested in developing the city in the direction of his own
wharf, at North Beach, where land was cheap and where land-
titles were comparatively unclouded. In connection with this
work he found a place in the city council, a body that in the
early days best represented the errors of the community, being wasteful and selfish where it was not dishonest. Meiggs
himself entered it with honest intentions, no doubt, and secured
the passage of numerous ordinances for the benefit of his part
of the city. But his undertakings grew on his hands, and his
debts increased as rapidly. He borrowed all that he could on
his own security, and then began a bold enterprise: namely,
borrowing on the city's security without authority. His method ·
of accomplishing this was as courageous as it was characteristic
of the place and time. The city, as we know, was then and for
years afterwards deeply in debt for many vast and usually
needless outlays. For its genuine expenses it required, meanwhile, much money and, in place of that, was pleased to increase its debt by paying its monthly bills in warrants, which
were worth in the market some fifty or sixty per cent of their
face value and which were, in fact, later mostly repudiated.
The warrants were prepared by filling out blanks supplied to
the controller in book form,[43] which were made valid by the
signatures of the mayor and controller. These warrants, according to the since current story, used, in a large number of
cases, to be signed in advance, in blank, for the convenience
of the officers, who could thus more rapidly fill out the blanks
for each new creditor. Now, Meiggs, as a city father, as a well-
known and responsible citizen, and as a man largely interested
in large city contracts, had frequent, easy, and unwatched access to the offices and books of the municipal corporation — a
freedom that, surely, nobody ought to regard with disapproval,
since Meiggs was such a good fellow. Therefore, when cautious investors hesitated to lend more on Meiggs's real estate,

---

[43] See, on this matter, the account of Meiggs's career, in J. S. Hittell, op. cit., pp. 218 ff., especially pp. 220 and 221. Hittell's account
is an excellent one and needs only a little to supplement it.

and when they began to reflect that a man so much involved as he would surely carry down all his endorsers with him in case he fell, the good Meiggs was now ready with a presumably trustworthy collateral security: namely, with numerous city warrants, valued at fifty per cent — warrants that he was understood to have received from the city in connection with the vast contracts in which he was interested. These securities had a foundation quite independent of Meiggs's solvency, and the cautious lenders joyously received them as collateral.[44] For months nobody thought of inquiring at the controller's office for proof of the value of these certificates, for they were of well-known appearance and were not interest-bearing; [45] and so, with the fall of real estate in 1854, Meiggs became more and more involved, and his use of city securities became more and more important to him. His courage was equal even to forging promissory notes, and detection then erelong became imminent. Accordingly, Meiggs quietly stocked a staunch little ship with provisions, took some of his friends and his brother aboard, and sailed, one day in October 1854, out of the Golden Gate and vanished. Then, of course, his failure and flight were at once announced. The more cautious creditors took their collateral to the city offices for examination and were overwhelmed to learn that their city paper was forged and worthless. The signatures might be genuine, but the certificates were not.

There were reasons why the public never learned just how much the energetic Meiggs had stolen. He never came back, and many people who lost by him felt henceforth a certain delicacy about explaining their relations with him. For the moment, however, Meiggs was regarded as an exemplary rascal, and men wondered how deep into the business life of San Francisco this sort of corruption had eaten. If Meiggs, people added, had only been content with cheating his bankers, one could have forgiven him; but, as report insisted, he had cheated his washerwoman. That, men declared, was too bad, even for

[44] See the humorous article in the *Pioneer* for January 1855, Vol. II, pp. 16 ff., where Meiggs's exploits are duly celebrated.

[45] Hittell, loc. cit.

California.[46] But, as they felt, he was, after all, only a remarkable instance of an evil that was far too common. For one thing, there were no sufficient public safeguards against such rascality. San Francisco was still without any very efficient police, and especially without any detective police.[47] If violence was no longer so common, the crimes of skill were directly encouraged by the whole condition of society. The just cited writer in the *Pioneer* says of the state of affairs, referring especially to frauds in commercial matters (Vol. II, p. 327): "Each day has its tale of depravity. We appeal . . . to the tale that is told from man to man, each day, in the public streets. . . . Is it not manifest to all that the cause of this continued flood of crime is the uncertainty of punishment, — nay, the almost certainty of escape?" And, on p. 330, the same writer, after discussing the apathy of prosecuting attorneys and of other public officials as one great evil of the times, goes on to enumerate some of the sorts of greater offenders from whom the community is suffering: "Such are those who influence the time, place, and manner of the acts of public officers, so as to reap a benefit therefrom; who get contracts with the State and city by corrupting legislation . . . misuse the public securities intrusted to their care . . . corrupt judges and juries. . . . These great crimes, which have so long prospered amongst us, leave us no security. Life, liberty, and property have no safety when the tribunals are corrupted, and the poor man hides his little store and flees with it to other lands." Thus opens the era of commercial ill-feeling and suspicion in San Francisco — an era that lasted until after the great Vigilance Committee. Its especial exponent in the newspaper press began to appear in 1855 as the *San Francisco Bulletin*. Not so much violence as corruption was now the enemy.

Of Meiggs it remains to be said here only that the rest of

---

[46] *Pioneer*, loc. cit., p. 17. J. S. Hittell, loc. cit., erroneously puts Meiggs's flight in September. See the *Pioneer*, Vol. II, p. 297.

[47] See, in the *Pioneer*, Vol. II, pp. 321 ff., an interesting article on "A Detective Police." Meiggs's crimes and escape are mentioned as a good example of the easy lot of a clever criminal in San Francisco.

his career showed, in a fresh way, how completely the life of new countries is sometimes given over to Satan, to vex the inhabitants thereof with diabolical miracles. Even the commonest laws of moral evolution seem, namely, occasionally suspended in such lands, so far as concerns, not the communities indeed, but certain individuals. And thus the weaklings are tempted by the sight of rogues who let the viper of wickedness sting them, but somehow do not fall down dead, as they ought. Capricious fortune saves some rogues, not merely from physical penalties, but apparently from the most inevitable of their well-earned moral penalties. Such a diabolical miracle was permitted to be wrought in the case of Meiggs. In his home of refuge in South America this wretch, namely, later became a distinguished and useful citizen, a great investor, a trustworthy financier, a man much prized by the government and people of Peru for his skill, for his amiability, and for his generosity. He took advantage of his success to satisfy in some fashion (according to Mr. Hittell, by buying up at reduced rates his old notes) the claims of his San Francisco creditors, who benevolently forgave him all in after years. The real mischief that he had wrought he could, of course, never make good; but it was granted him to die as an honored man — surely a most vile caprice of fortune, however much Meiggs's own fine energies may have contributed to the result. That he ever truly repented does in no wise appear. If he had repented, he would have come back to California and gone to jail, where he belonged.

By 1855 we see the fruits both of the aforesaid natural causes and of all this commercial and social corruption, in the great failures of February, and in the great business depression of the rest of the year. Page, Bacón & Co. and Adams & Co., two of the greatest of the city business houses, the one a banking-house, the other both a banking and an express company, failed and carried with them numerous lesser firms.[48] The financial

---

[48] The sequence of the events of the crisis appears in the *Pioneer's* "Monthly Summary," Vol. III, p. 238. Contemporary with the crisis was the excitement in San Francisco about the "Kern River Mines," a typical instance of the early California mining excitements. This one was especially ill founded and transient.

condition of the municipality was meanwhile growing worse
and worse. The message of the mayor, March 12, 1855,[49]
showed the liabilities of the city incurred since May 1, 1851, to
sum up as $1,959,000, the deficit for one year past being some
$840,000. The house of Page, Bacon & Co. resumed payment
March 29, only to close its doors anew and finally on May 2.
A long struggle over the assets of Adams & Co. began with the
failure of that house, and this was to last for years, involving,
and in the end destroying, the personal reputations of a good
many people. The city, later in the year, having been authorized by statute to examine through a commission its floating
debt, and to fund the properly incurred and legally valid portion thereof, managed to repudiate $1,737,000 of its warrants,
recognizing as its valid indebtedness only some $322,000. This
act, either an appalling confession of corruption or a most disgraceful repudiation (or more probably both), stands happily
alone of its kind in San Francisco history.[50] All these things,
however, were the work of the people at large, who had tolerated and encouraged sin so long and who now selfishly tried
to shirk its penalties.

VII. *The New Awakening of Conscience*

THE CONSCIENCE of San Francisco, however, began to speak
through the pages of the new paper, the *Bulletin,* in the
autumn of 1855. A perfectly clear or a very highly organized
conscience it was not yet, but it was stern, manly, cruel, and
unsparing towards its own past lapses, courageous, hopeful,
and ardent. The messenger who was inspired to speak its words
was in no old-fashioned sense a prophet, although fate was
pleased to make him a martyr. He was a very plain and pro-
saic man, who obviously learned from his new task, as he went
on, even more than he taught to others, and who, for the rest,
was not free from selfishness in the conduct of his mission;
since, as is plain, he not infrequently felt a good deal of personal spite against the public sinners that he assailed. His

---

[49] *Pioneer,* Vol. III, p. 368.
[50] J. S. Hittell, op. cit., p. 227. *Pioneer,* Vol. IV, p. 309.

weapons, moreover, were the dangerous ones of personal journalism. His methods forced him to be always ready with a fresh denunciation of somebody, and he was sure, therefore, to commit much injustice if he continued long upon his path. But for the time he quickly gained the support of the respectable classes, because the cause that he pleaded was so much above all his own personal weaknesses and errors, and because the need of plain speech was so pressing. James King, "of William," as he, following a practice occasionally found in new communities, called himself, by way of distinction from other Kings, had been engaged in banking and had been ruined by the late panic. The field of San Francisco newpapers was crowded, but still nobody had made a business of preaching concrete righteousness in short and readable paragraphs, with broad-faced type used for the headings, and with plenty of personal applications scattered all through the editorial columns. To do this was King's opportunity. He began his enterprise in October 1855, without at first any peculiarity of outer form to mark his journal, save its very small size. Three successive enlargements rapidly followed,[51] with his success, and by the opening of the new year one finds his style, his form of typography, and his plans of battle fully developed. King loved to gather around him a little cloud of correspondents, both friends and foes, to assign them a column or two at one side, and then to discourse to them in his manly and vigorous way in "leaders" and "notes." Plainly the one editor was nearly always speaking, and King's name stood at the head of the first editorial column, yet he persisted in his merely amusing editorial "we." His correspondents addressed him plainly by name and wrote approval, entreaty, expostulation, or objurgation as the spirit might move. King encouraged them very frequently to say just what they thought. Occasionally a gambler wrote to defend his profession, or an orthodox man, full of interest in this worthy, but plainly unregenerate editor, wrote to beg King to save his own

---

[51] The file that I have before me, that of Harvard College Library, opens with number 20, October 30, 1855, and is nearly continuous until late in 1856. I know of no enlargement of earlier date than October 30.

poor soul while the lamp still held out to burn. King enjoyed all such letters; and they all alike made his paper sell. He had a thoughtful and speculative vein in his mind also, and sometimes touched on deeper problems.

Meanwhile, it was his life to assail official, business, and social corruption of every sort, and that not impersonally. Duels he declined to enter upon, once for all; and the rights of the public to a plain denunciation of the rascals were his daily insistence. Yet this work, honestly undertaken, could not rest with personal quarrels. King had to assail the public apathy and carelessness that permitted this sort of thing. And that assault constitutes the permanently valuable element in his work. Nobody cares now how far King's personal hatreds were well founded. It was his denunciation of the whole social condition that was significant.

And serious was indeed the corruption that he talked of so plainly. In forsaking the wilder old dissipations the community had still kept the feeling that respectability was an affair of the heart for each individual. Public respectability, such for instance as demanded the banishing of disreputable houses from the principal dwelling-house streets of the city, was nobody's concern. But King made it somebody's concern.[52] He very plainly and by name assailed the city officials whose private and illegal connivance was especially and demonstrably to blame for these things, and promised to publish the names of the proprietors and lessors of every such house if the nuisance were not abated. "It's no use trying to dodge the 'Bulletin,' gentlemen," he added. And in fact his paper farther on, in treating of the same evil, did mention more names in a disagreeable way,[53] threatening always worse. The result, at least in part, of this plain speech, was action by the aldermen, and a committee report on the condition of the city, in respect of

[52] A correspondent, November 8, 1855, complains of a most noticeable and offensive establishment just about to be opened, "situated in the midst of respectable family residences, and on one of the most public thoroughfares." In connection with this letter King makes the threat noted in the text.

[53] See editorial, November 26, 1855.

the evil mentioned – a report that, as published in the *Bulletin* of November 28, is one of the saddest confessions ever made by the governing board of a municipality. There is no sort of privacy, the committee says, about the evils complained of. The best families of the town are daily and unavoidably insulted by the immediate neighborhood of impudent evil in its least bearable forms, all good women, all children, being alike subjected to this disgrace. The committee knows of no possible remedy that will not of necessity include a reorganization of the police force. In fact, as is plain, while there were numerous pure and happy homes in San Francisco, there was as yet no really clean, pure, and large neighborhood in the city to which respectable families could go for their dwelling-places and be safe. The struggle for a true and humane life was still a hand-to-hand fight in public with legions of loathsome little devils.

In another direction King had to fight against an equally widespread and even less curable form of popular infidelity: namely, the general toleration shown towards gamblers – a toleration that after all these years was still too prevalent. The gambler is King's pet villain, and especially towards the last of his work does the bold editor, constantly improving in his seriousness of speech, dwell upon the general social evils of the recent prevalence of gambling and upon the esteem shown by some to the most notorious gamblers. Public opinion in California has never, says King, really approved of gambling, but has only permitted it, at first for lack of law, then later by virtue of habit. But at all times, in California as everywhere, gambling has been a sin, and professional gamblers, whether licensed or not, have always been criminals. "A good citizen looks not to the laws of the state to guide him in ethics. 'As many as have sinned without the law shall perish without the law.'" In such fine fashion King seeks to exclude the professional gamblers once for all from the ranks of respectable and honest citizens, whether the laws have ever encouraged their business or not. The state, insists King, is just coming out of chaos into a normal condition, and the true and healthy public sentiment that has always existed is just finding a chance to express itself. Let no one try to resist it.

The discussion in the course of which occur these expressions, themselves taken from the *Bulletin* of April 28, 1856, is especially noteworthy. Gamblers had undertaken to reply to King's repeated denunciations. Why denounce, they had said, men who only gambled so long as the law permitted it and who now obey the law and do not follow public gambling as a profession any longer. After all, have not the professional gamblers usually been men of marked ability and fine minds, who were driven to gambling as a business by the narrowness of their daily lives and by a certain honorable pride? — The honorable man of business, replied King, is the man "who in all his cares for this life has not neglected to cultivate those higher feelings of the heart — a reverence to God, and a desire for the moral improvement of his race." [54]   It is in this connection that the very correspondent to whom these words of King are a reply, plainly one of the more good-humored of the gambling brotherhood, addresses King (in words that remind one of the well-known Turkish official's exhortation to Layard) and begs the able editor to give up this absurd care about the "public" good. I, he says, am one of "a large number who have long since ceased to worry their minds with schemes for the *public* welfare — a class, by the way, much more numerous than you imagine — who confidently look forward to the time when you will join their number, and rest from the thankless and unprofitable task which you have imposed upon yourself. You are pursuing a course that will certainly drive you to despair if persisted in."

VIII. *The Crisis of May 1856*

THE TIME of rest for King was indeed not far off. It was expedient just then that one man should die for the people, and King's services, although not nearly faultless, had been so excellent that the gods seem to have esteemed him worthy of an unspeakable honor, and they chose him as the man. He was shot down on the public streets, May 14, 1856, by one James

---

[54] *Bulletin*, April 21, 1856.

Casey, a recently elected supervisor, an editor of a lesser journal, a politician of the baser sort, and a former convict in the New York state penitentiary, a man whom King had denounced and exposed. King died six days later of his wound; but meanwhile the deed had aroused the greatest exhibition of popular excitement in the whole history of California. In lamenting and avenging the fate of this sturdy champion of a manly public spirit, the entire community experienced a new outpouring of that spirit, and King's death did far more than his life could possibly have done to regenerate the social order. That the immediate expression of the new life was the greatest of the vigilance committees is, after all, to my mind, the least important of the great facts of the situation. Such an expression, in view of Californian habits and feelings as they were at that time already formed, was indeed inevitable, but it was not the really essential social fact, which was that, upon King's death, there followed for many a really new life. This crisis was a revelation to them, which they never forgot.[55]

Why just the death of King, rather than many far worse evils then patent to any observer in San Francisco, aroused so fearfully the popular attention is a question of social psychology that one can more easily pretend to answer by a reference to well-known facts than really put to rest by genuine explanations. A popular hero is always needed before the people can be converted from their sins; and King, as we see, had some really heroic stuff in him. He seemed for the moment a martyr pure and simple. Wherefore had he fallen? Because he had

[55] Concerning Casey himself and the details of his quarrel with King, all the accounts of the great committee have repeated the well-known statements for which the contemporary newspapers are of course the source. See especially Tuthill, p. 432, J. S. Hittell, p. 244. On the whole career of the committee, Tuthill's account is the fullest so far published in book form, although I had no access to the personal reminiscences that have since been made public from time to time. My space and purpose, after I have described the opening scenes, will limit me in great part to a discussion of the social bearings rather than of the external events of this best-known and most frequently described scene of our story.

served the people and had spoken fearlessly against evil. Who
was now safe? Surely no honest and plain-spoken man. Who
could now prosper here, in such an unpurified community?
Only the rogues. And the so much needed families — would
they now crowd to this land of promise? Certainly not, so long
as the blood of this husband and father, dead in his city's cause,
cried to heaven in vain for vengeance. Would the courts suffice
at such a crisis? Nay, one's executive officers of the law were
not trustworthy. Judges indeed might mean well and do well.
But the sheriffs, and the deputies, and the police, not to mention the prosecuting attorneys — who had confidence in them?
What but a revolution could deliver the community from the
body of this death? Such thoughts were in many minds and
were embodied in most of the newspaper comments. The
Herald, whose editor the *Bulletin* had often sharply denounced,
now, in return, spoke of the shooting of King as an "affray";
but it was almost alone in failing to share the popular feeling.
Most people had forgotten King's failings in their sense of the
public calamity of his death. In this one fact they saw a con-
densed expression of the whole corrupt state of society. In
such a state of popular feeling a mob was imminent. The business men therefore chose to calm the spirits of more excitable
people and to enlist their active service in the cause of good
order, by choosing the only alternative. They avoided mob law,
pure and simple, only by organizing the most remarkable of
all the popular tribunals, whereby was effected that unique
historical occurrence, a Business Man's Revolution. For such
was the Second Vigilance Committee of San Francisco.

On Wednesday afternoon, May 14, had appeared the denunciation of Casey by King that led to the shooting. The same
afternoon it was that King was shot. The next day's *Bulletin*
appeared with a blank column in place of the usual editorial
and published in full the official documents from New York
upon which King had founded his denunciation of Casey as a
convict. The morning press had freely commented on the occurrence, and the public excitement had been great. Calls for
the Vigilance Committee were already in print, and in secret
the new organization was already under way. The *Bulletin* of

Friday contained very little news, but was crowded with furious letters from correspondents, with denunciations of the *Herald's* course in opposing the formation of a vigilance committee and with other like expressions of excitement and rage. The announcement was made that the new committee was progressing finely with its organization, several thousand names being now supposed to be enrolled, to obey the orders of the executive committee, whose meetings were of course private.

Both the excitement and the formation of the committee continued during the next few days. Saturday's *Bulletin* contained an item bearing on an important incident of the organization, an incident since much discussed: namely, the visit of Governor Johnson to the rooms of the Vigilance Committee. Mayor Van Ness, feeling the dangers of the situation, with Casey confined in a not very secure jail, with newspapers so violently calling for vengeance, with a vigilance committee in process of formation, under the direction of the most prominent merchants, with King lying at death's door, had sent for the Governor to come down to the aid of the law. This Know-Nothing Governor, however, was not the ablest of California's statesmen, and the situation at San Francisco was far beyond his power to understand or to improve. As is now known,[56] Governor Johnson, on his arrival in the city Friday afternoon, called privately upon Mr. Coleman, who was already understood to be at the head of the executive committee, and, according to Mr. Coleman himself, seemed to appreciate the feelings of the San Francisco people, and gave the impression that he was willing to let them act as they saw fit, so long as they were careful to act as a body and in an orderly way.[57] But late in the

---

[56] Through Mr. William T. Coleman's statements, especially his elaborate one in B. MS.

[57] Mr. Coleman, in this interview, reminded the Governor, as an old Californian, of what had passed under similar circumstances before in the state, and then said (as Mr. Coleman now words it) "that I did not want him to feel that we were taking any advantage of his position; but I honestly expressed to him my convictions of the necessities of the hour, and of what we wanted to do, and would do, as a body." "We" meant of course the executive committee.

evening, the Governor, in company with several other persons, visited the already well-guarded rooms of the committee [58] and in a somewhat more official tone sought to make his hostility to the purposes of the committee evident. He first sent word in to the committee rooms that he desired speech with Mr. Coleman. The members of the executive committee, within doors, urged Mr. Coleman, as he went out, not to commit them to anything, to leave their freedom of action quite unimpaired, and to make no useless promises to the Governor.[59] Mr. Coleman was of the same mind. The visitors stood at first in the anteroom, waiting for their interview, and when Mr. Coleman came out, all together met in a bar-room to the right of the entrance. Mr. Coleman seemed to General Sherman "pale and agitated," a fact that the former seems not to have remembered, if it was real at all. But, at all events, the Governor, "just as if he had not asked the same questions a few hours before, in our former interview" (as Mr. Coleman indignantly remarks), began to ask afresh about the purposes of the committee. Mr. Coleman responded that the people were determined, now at last, to see justice done in the city. This organization was no mob, but it meant to see that Casey should not escape, and that San Francisco should not be left to her present sort of legal officers to prevent that escape.

Hereupon Johnson made a proposal, whose nature and reception form the great topic of interest and of controversy concerning this interview. According to Johnson's own view, and to General Sherman's recollection of the matter, Johnson proposed that "if Coleman and associates would use their influence to support the law, he (the Governor) would undertake" that Casey's legal trial should be as speedy and effective as possible, under the law. He even offered "to be personally

---

[58] The visitors included General Sherman, just before that time appointed by the Governor major-general of the state militia. His well-known account of the interview is found in his *Memoirs*, Vol. I, pp. 121 ff. The committee were now meeting in the Turnverein Hall on Bush Street.

[59] So much I have orally from Mr. E. S. Osgood of Cambridge (already cited above), who was present within doors at the moment.

responsible for Casey's safe-keeping until his trial, or until his execution in case he should be convicted. Mr. Coleman, according to the same account,[60] "admitted that the proposition of the governor was fair, and all he or any one should ask," and retired to submit it to the executive committee. After consultation, says this same account, Mr. Coleman reappeared, with a number of other men, representatives of the committee; "the whole conversation was gone over again, and the governor's proposition was positively agreed to, with this further condition, that the Vigilance Committee should send into the jail a small force of their own men, to make certain that Casey should not be carried off or allowed to escape."

This account, however, which makes Mr. Coleman and his companions surrender at once to the Governor, and so undertake to leave Casey's trial to the regular courts at the very moment when all San Francisco was moved to instant vengeance, is antecedently absurd. No California committee ever at such a moment abandoned its work. Had the Governor offered or been able to offer his co-operation in a joint action of the popular body and of the officers of the law, such a joint action, for instance, as had been possible in the Hounds' affair in 1849, the committee might have yielded something of its own claims. But no such offer was now even remotely possible. And the Governor meanwhile was not able to speak to the committee with any force behind him. His authority was unsupported. The militia companies of the city were already enrolling themselves in a body on the committee lists, and the arms in the city were already in large part in the committee's possession. The militia force of the state at large was powerless; and public opinion everywhere favored immediate justice upon the murderer of King. A committee formed at such a crisis would have felt itself to be merely trifling with its enrolled thousands of members had it entertained for a moment such a proposition from an actually impotent governor and had it suspended at the very outset its deliberate purposes.

And, in fact, not only antecedent probability, but sound testi-

---

[60] See General Sherman's *Memoirs*, Vol. I, p. 122.

mony, is against General Sherman's memory, a memory that, for the rest, was hardly meant by the Creator for purely historical purposes, genial and amusing though its productions may be. In this case the vigilance members directly concerned very plainly contradict General Sherman's account. Mr. Coleman heard the Governor's proposition, indeed, just as General Sherman reports it, but he did not assent to it. He first declined to make any compromise without consulting his associates. "I then," he declares (B. MS. as cited), "went back to the executive room, and reported the conversation briefly; and Governor Johnson's proposition met with prompt resistance; every voice was raised against any halting, any hesitation, any parley, any concession short of prompt action." The committee of members, sent back with Mr. Coleman to continue the discussion with the Governor, accordingly explained to the latter this decision of the executive committee and made but one concession: namely, that no action should be taken by the executive committee to remove Casey from the jail until Governor Johnson had received an hour's written notice of such intended action. Meanwhile it was agreed that a guard of committee members should enter and be allowed to remain in the jail for the time, to see that the prisoners were safe, but not to supersede or interfere with the lawful officers. In case this should be permitted, the representatives of the committee promised the Governor, as Mr. Coleman says, "That we would remain quiet for the present; and they might rely upon our making no demonstration . . . until we gave formal notice of any change we wanted to make. And furthermore, if we changed our status, if we wished to withdraw from the contract," it was promised "that we would withdraw our forces from the jail, and leave it in their possession." All this, as Mr. Coleman insists, "was agreed to on our part in the most perfect good faith." The Governor, he continues, misunderstood this action, interpreting it as an armistice, and the committee felt much aggrieved when they found out the fact the next day.

With this account of Mr. Coleman's the memory of Mr. Osgood, as expressed to me recently in conversation, fully agrees.

Mr. Osgood was one of the committee members who accompanied Mr. Coleman on his return from the executive rooms to the bar-room, where the Governor was waiting. There can therefore be little doubt as to the understanding of the affair at the moment from the side of the very cool-headed and able members of the committee.[61] The spectacle of the Governor of the state here blundering into a worthless agreement with a body of men whom he could neither awe by any show of official force nor thus privately approach with any sense of his official dignity was not edifying, and the affair ruined him politically with both of the chief parties concerned in San Francisco affairs at that moment. The committee men despised him thenceforth, but no more than did the "Law and Order" men. Governor Johnson, it is plain, had not even the good sense to get his agreement with the committee, such as it was, into a written form.

During these busy days the "Law and Order" men themselves voiced their opinions in the *Herald,* but they were powerless to resist the general popular sentiment. They were generally either politicians or lawyers. What they had to say was itself often sound enough. Its application to this diseased community was, however, the real difficulty. A reformation was needed, this moment of popular excitement was the proper one to begin it; and yet no beginning was possible just here and now that did not take the too familiar and yet so dangerous form of a popular tribunal. To resist the committee was only to throw the city the more certainly into the hands of a furious mob. The popular passion existed and was for the time irresistible. The committee's possible service would lie in directing

---

[61] As to the carrying out of his agreement in the sequel, there can also be no doubt that the Governor was notified by the committee of their intended action before they took Casey out of the jail, and that before this action itself they early endeavored to correct Johnson's misunderstanding of the result of the interview; see Sherman, op. cit., Vol. I, p. 123. "Treachery," then, there was none, only distinct refusal to submit to the Governor's· wishes, coupled with a willingness not to act too hastily.

and controlling this passion, which no "Law and Order" sentiment could now quell. So serious are the situations that long-
indulged social crimes produce!

On Sunday the first great act of the new organization was
carried out. The committee went to the jail and took therefrom
Casey himself, conveying him safely to their own rooms. Nor
did their action stop here. Another now notorious criminal was
confined in the jail, one Cora by name, who had some months
previously shocked the community by shooting a United States
marshal, General Richardson, for showing public disapproval
of Cora's mistress, herself also a person of no doubtful notoriety. The committee, in the carrying out of the popular will of
the moment, felt itself justified in seizing Cora also, whose legal
punishment was not very imminent.

The seizure of these two was made an imposing spectacle.
The executive committee called out twenty-four companies,
of a nominal force of one hundred each. All the men had received a brief drill since the organization of the committee.
Many were old soldiers themselves; all were used to arms; and
a large number of Frenchmen who had joined the organization
were especially noteworthy for their fine appearance as soldiers. The movements of this body were skillfully directed, all
the detachments into which the force was divided converging
to the vicinity of the jail on Broadway, without any mistakes
or confusion. About an hour was spent by the committee at the
jail, where the leading members of the executive committee
made their demands of the officers and finally gained, through
their quiet show of irresistible force, the peaceable surrender
of both the prisoners, Casey being first given up, and then
Cora. Houses all about were covered with spectators, and the
streets in the rear of the committee's force were thronged. The
vast majority of those present as spectators warmly, although
very quietly, approved of what was going on, and this first
deed of popular justice, as executed by the great committee,
was the most orderly and impressive of its sort so far in the
history of California.[62]

---

[62] I have before me the accounts given by the *Bulletin* for Monday, May 19, and the *Alta* of the same date (as repeated in the

IX. *Popular Vengeance and the New Movement*

THE MORAL effect of this scene was very great, but it was only the first of a series. May 20, at half past one, King died. The news was on public bulletin-boards at once, and the whole community was in mourning. The *Bulletin* appeared that afternoon without any comments on the death of its editor, time permitting only a four-line notice of the fact before the number was printed. The public excitement was tremendous. All the church bells were tolled; the prominent business houses were closed, their doors being draped in black; the flags on the numerous ships in the bay were run up at half-mast; vast crowds gathered in the streets near the committee rooms. No such disorder, however, was manifest now in the crowd about the committee rooms as had shown itself in 1851, on one similar occasion, when an immediate execution was expected. When the announcement was made that the members of the executive committee were trying Casey, and that all should be done decently and in order, the citizens quietly dispersed. The regular police of the city had meanwhile little to do. The committee did not try to supersede them as yet in other respects and gave over into their hands one or two petty offenders whom citizens arrested and brought to the rooms that evening. But the public mood appalled for the moment all offenders, great and small. The men popularly accused of being Casey's "conspirators," in the imagined "plot" that rumor made responsible for King's death, were in hiding-places.

Chief among these supposed "conspirators" was Mr. Edward

---

steamer extra edition of May 21). The *Alta* account makes the number of companies present twenty-six. See, further, Tuthill, p. 439; J. S. Hittell, p. 249; Sherman, Vol. I, p. 124. Sherman makes the blunder of remembering this Sunday as the day of King's funeral. King was not yet dead. One has only to compare the remarkable good order displayed on this occasion with the tumultuous scenes of the early affairs of 1851, and with their hurrying and excited crowds of spectators, with their quarrels and their dangerous uncertainty of action, to see how well the arts of lynch law had now been learned.

McGowan, whose *Narrative of the Author's Adventures and Perils while persecuted by the San Francisco Vigilance Committee of 1856* (published by the author at San Francisco in 1857) is a book as entertaining as it is characteristic and unprincipled. Mr. McGowan (who still survives) had for some time been a personal friend of Casey's, had fully sympathized with the latter's indignation at King's cruel reference to certain youthful indiscretions of Casey's in New York State, had known also, on that fatal afternoon, of Casey's intention to "fight" King, and had even "embraced" the convict hero before the combat, bidding him an affectionate farewell (see the *Narrative,* pp. 14 and 15). Mr. McGowan had intended to follow Casey to this field of honor and see what the *Herald* next day called the "affray." King, of course, would be armed, it was supposed, and "like almost all old Californians," Mr. McGowan "was accustomed to such sights; and, naturally enough, when I knew that a fight was about to take place, curiosity prompted me to witness it." Under these circumstances Mr. McGowan was indeed exposed to cruel suspicions of sharing in a conspiracy to kill King. It was within the next few days reported, falsely, he affirms, that he had lent Casey his own pistol for the occasion, and Mr. McGowan soon found it necessary first to hide, and then, by the help of his many friends, to fly. He was, in the sequel, pursued by members of the committee, far into the southern country, but finally escaped, and later returned to the city. I take Mr. McGowan's naïve statement of his connection with King's death in perfectly good faith, since it is unnecessary to judge his character more severely than his own confession forces one to do. Good citizens do not behave in just this way, but Mr. McGowan was only in this sense a "conspirator."

A "plot," then, "to assassinate" King had probably existed only in the sense that a number of those who, like Casey, had grievances against the plain-spoken editor had frequently talked over their feelings and their wrongs and had become more and more resolved to call him to account in their own way. This way, however, was not one that could be much furthered by a "conspiracy to assassinate," because their moral code implied, as a matter of so-called "honor," something like a single combat in every such case. Any aggrieved person, namely, might shoot King on sight, since King once for all refused to fight regular duels, but "honor" would imply that every such assassin should take some apparent chance of being shot in return and so should go alone to accost King. How much chance should be given to King to defend himself would, of course, depend, according to the well-known and amusing code of frontier street-fights, upon the taste of the individual assassin. Casey's taste preferred, as is also known, an immediate sequence of shot upon meeting, in such wise as to give King the least possible chance to return his fire. And, of course, all who knew beforehand of Casey's intent, were alike accessories to the murder. But an effective conspiracy to *unite* in a murderous assault upon King would have been quite repugnant to all the gentlemanly instincts of these fellows.

While the citizens mourned for King, the executive committee tried his assassin, as well as Cora. No jury was used in this case, the executive committee sitting as court,[63] but every opportunity is said to have been given to both men to offer any defense that they had. Both were, however, guilty of murder, and so much is clear. Both, moreover, had committed murder to avenge "insults," and both the "insults" were of a sort somewhat unavoidable in a world where spades are, after all, sooner or later, sure to be called spades by somebody, and that especially where the spades are already public property. One thing only the committee could yet do for its prisoners. It would not hang them too hastily. It would give them a little time to think and would let them see spiritual advisers, if they desired, before the execution. This last privilege, I regret to say, is amusingly described by a prominent member of the committee (in a statement that has been among the several that I have had the good fortune to read) as an act "giving the prisoners the *benefit of clergy.*" It is to be hoped that the "benefit" was appreciated, even if it was not precisely the same as the thing formerly called by that name.

---

[63] See Mr. Coleman's statement, B. MS.

May 22 was set for King's funeral. The executive committee is said (by Mr. Osgood in his oral statements to me) to have been moved to appoint that day for the execution of Casey by reason of their fear that a rescue, similar to that of Whittaker and McKenzie in 1851, would early be attempted. At all events, just as the funeral procession was following King to Lone Mountain, after a service at the Unitarian Church, in which several clergymen had joined to honor the martyr editor, the committee took its opportunity and publicly executed both Casey and Cora, in front of its rooms, at a moment when the vast crowds in the neighborhood were slightly lessened by the departure of so many to witness the burial. The solemnity and good order of the execution are well known. Both the prisoners had been warned of their doom the day before. Both, as Catholics, had received the sacrament from ministers of their faith, and Cora was, before his execution, and by the order of his confessor, married to the mistress on whose behalf he had slain Richardson. Cora himself met death very coolly and without complaint. Casey, from the improvised platform in front of the rooms, made a brief and slightly incoherent and agitated dying speech, wherein he denied that he was a murderer. His now aged and still living mother, he averred, had taught him to avenge insults. He had acted upon the teachings of his childhood, and what he had done was no murder. Let no one publish to the world and to his mother that it was murder. Might God forgive him his many sins and receive his spirit. And so the wretch died.

With this act, thought many, and General Sherman among the rest,[64] the committee would have done its work, and would disband. Had it, however, done so, there would be hardly any place for the committee in history. The incidents thus far were but the beginning of the new movement, and their own significance lay elsewhere than in the hanging of one or two rogues. Not the execution of King's murderer, but the prosecution of King's work was the mission of the people of San Francisco at the time. And the Vigilance Committee, with all its defects, represented this mission.

---

[64] *Memoirs*, Vol. I, p. 124.

The great task, of course, was to purify municipal politics. Directly the committee could do nothing to this end, save to terrify and to banish a few notorious ballot-box stuffers. But indirectly much could be done, by so popular a body, to organize public opinion and to prepare it for the coming municipal elections of the autumn. The problem, of course, lay in the choice of the activity to which the committee should devote itself to gain this end. So powerful a body must be tempted, of course, to misuse its power, and unless it did so, the committee would soon be in danger of losing hold on the now overexcited public. A vigilance committee is once for all an evil presence in a city; and its tendency to spread abroad disease is as sure, even in the best of cases, as its tendency to cure disease. The great committee was productive of more good than evil only because in the sequel it was not left to its natural tendencies, but was constantly guided by cautious and conscientious men, whose acts were not always wise, but whose purposes were honest and rational. Now that they had begun, they felt it a sin to abandon their task until they saw more fruit than the death of two scoundrels. But in order to finish their voyage safely they must steer clear of numerous and dangerously near rocks.

X. *Perils and Triumphs of the Great Committee*

THE *Bulletin* of May 29 I choose at random among the numbers published during the early weeks of the committee's life as illustrating the dangers to which the committee was now subject from the side of its friends. The editor (by this time Thomas S. King, the brother of James) writes on "What the People expect of the Vigilance Committee." "The people," says the editor, "look to them for reform — a radical reorganization in spirit if not in fact — of our city government." The remaining persons suspected of conspiracy against James King must, he continues, be caught, tried, and, if found guilty, hanged. But the committee must not stop there. It must purify the ballot-box. And how? "If we would have order hereafter, an example must now be made of the ballot-box stuffers. If there is any one in the custody of the committee on whom ballot-box stuffing can be clearly proved, his punishment should be exemplary. We are not ignorant of the weight of the words we utter. Tampering with elections is, in fact, the most heinous of crimes. It is worse than treason. . . . We do not mean . . . to make suggestions to the committee. But it appears to us that to insure the future purity of elections, an *example* should be made. . . . It may be that there are other means, but if not, let the men who have insulted our community, disgraced our State, and sown the seeds of which we have been lately reaping the fruits, meet their due fate, DEATH BY HANGING — the words must be spoken — not in revenge for the past, but as a warning to all who might be inclined to emulate their example in the future. Hang one ballot-box stuffer, and we shall have no more of them."

This loose talk is echoed by one or two correspondents whose letters appear in the same number (one H. B. G. in particular). So fatally blind is the righteously indignant citizen, at such moments, to the fact that the punishment of a wretch is after all of no more importance than is the wretch himself, save in so far as such punishment conduces to good order. Good order, however, is destroyed once for all by mere caprice. Inevitable are such outbursts as the one that led to the hanging of Jenkins and of Stuart in 1851, or of Casey in 1856; inevitable, namely, when the reaction in favor of good order involves strong passions and bitter repentance at once. But after such a passion has cooled a little, to deify its instrument, the Vigilance Committee, or to glorify its law — namely, caprice — this is not inevitable and is criminal. Yet just this was what these unwise friends of the committee desired when they wanted the Vigilance Committee to undertake all God's work of vengeance in San Francisco, and to make "examples," without regard to the law or to the current sense of humanity. Ballot-box stuffing could not be cured by hanging this or that man; but it could be cured by effective popular agitation. And the committee could and did agitate, partly by investigating and exposing past crimes of ballot-box stuffing, and partly by undertaking to banish, with threats that were only intended for momentary effect, a few of the guilty men. The indirect good it did in these ways is certain, for thus the public was instructed in the seriousness of the evils.

Yet not only in this matter was the committee tempted by its friends to go beyond bounds. A great popular movement, controlling so much power and organized so well, suggested to foolish and ambitious persons numberless political schemes. There were the old grievances of California against the general government: the aforetime long-delayed payment of the Frémont war claims, the still pending slow and uncertain efforts to settle the Spanish land-titles, the imperfect mail service, the burdensome tariff. And all these things some men were now disposed to bring up, and such men would suggest that, with some more independent flag, even with a Bear Flag, a vigilance committee might look well. Secession had occasionally been talked of. Why not make this a movement to gain, by at least a bare threat of secession, concessions of some sort from Washington authorities? If such concessions should be refused, why, then, let the government take the consequences.

That such nonsense was actually heard in some men's talk in those days is undoubted. The leaders of the committee were themselves far from every such influence, but the rank and file were numerous, and the foreigners among these, the Frenchmen for instance, together with some of the native Californians themselves, took delight in such ideas, all of which were dangerous in the highest degree to the good order of the whole movement. Nor were all the Americans concerned by any means guiltless in this matter.[65]

Not only such wildcat politics (as one may venture not too

---

[65] The frequent letters of "Caxton" in the *Bulletin* had sometimes taken openly a disunion tone before the coming on of the crisis. So, in particular, his letter published April 9, 1856, a monument of the wordy unwisdom of this since so well-known California political and literary author. Mr. Coleman, in his B. MS. statement, speaks of the disunion propositions privately made to the committee leaders, and promptly rejected. Mr. Osgood speaks to the same effect in his oral account to me. The prevalence of disunion sentiments among certain classes of the California pioneers in the years before the war would form an interesting topic for a special research.

disrespectfully to name the opinions of the men who talked in those days of a Pacific Republic), but also many less immoral absurdities vexed the committee with calls for attention. In the course of its career, so Mr. Coleman tells us, the committee was much flattered and troubled by invitations to act as high court of justice to settle disputes arising in the interior of the state, or elsewhere: — "Not only criminals from distant parts of the State, but all kinds of acts occurring at sea were brought before us, or we were asked to undertake their trial and punishment, to redress wrongs, personal disagreements, moral misdemeanors, social irregularities . . . cases of fraud in money matters . . . family strifes . . . divorces." The committee could easily have spent many months or years upon such matters; but such were not within its province.

More serious difficulties beset the committee in the direct prosecution of its chosen tasks of purification. First of all, in order to have even the most moderate efficiency, the committee had to arrest and confine in its own quarters certain suspected persons, and to investigate in secret session the charges of election frauds or of other offenses made against them. This undertaking involved many risks and made for the committee many new enemies. One of the most notorious of the earlier prisoners was "Yankee Sullivan," who is said to have known a great deal about the conduct of recent elections in certain wards, and who was pressed by the committee for some days with questions concerning ballot-box stuffers. The poor wretch was overcome with terror at his position, fancied that he was to be hanged, and on the morning of May 31 committed suicide in his room, cutting his arm with a case knife and bleeding to death. While no suspicion of foul play rested on the committee itself in connection with this affair, one could not help seeing that such an occurrence indicated much sternness on the part of the committee towards its prisoners, either in questioning or in threatening them or in both. The enemies of the committee used Sullivan's name thenceforth freely in speaking of the arbitrary acts of the body.[66] And the aforesaid loose talk of the friends of the

---

[66] Sullivan's suicide has been attributed, by certain of the committee members, to something resembling delirium tremens: see

committee gave the "Law and Order" people some just cause for alarm. The public could not know as yet how conscientious and cautious the leaders of the executive committee for the most part were, nor how little they were disposed to shed the blood of any save murderers. In ignorance of this fact, however, the "Law and Order" men felt more and more disposed to lead a reaction against the committee. On June 2, in the afternoon, a mass meeting of the opponents of the committee was called to meet on the Plaza; but the friends of the committee came also, and the affair was both disorderly and ineffective, although no worse missiles than hard words were interchanged. The speakers at the meeting were all lawyers, Colonel Baker being prominent among them. The crowd constantly interrupted the proceedings and called for new speakers or denounced the enemies of the committee. It was evident where the confidence of the public was still placed, and in San Francisco the "Law and Order" party could accomplish nothing.

Once more, then, the Governor was called upon to interfere, and he was quite willing, although by no means ready. He had appointed General Sherman commander of the second division of the state militia, and he now appealed to General Wool, United States commander in the department, for the necessary arms and ammunition. For, as the committee had at their control nearly all the arms in San Francisco, the state had no force with which to begin operations against the rebels. But the United States authorities were not disposed to take part in the domestic troubles of California without definite instructions from Washington. With Commodore Farragut, commanding the navy yard at Mare Island, the committee had in fact already begun a comparatively friendly correspondence, to assure themselves that the United States war vessel then lying in the harbor should not be used, unless by direct orders from a superior authority, to threaten or to suppress them. With General Wool they also sought to remain on good terms. He, however, seems to have been personally opposed to the committee, and

J. S. Hittell, p. 252. On the effect of this and other occurrences of the moment upon the "Law and Order" party, see Sherman, Vol. I, p. 124; cf. Tuthill, pp. 449, 450.

in conversation on May 31 with Governor Johnson and other
state officials he used expressions that were interpreted by the
latter as a definite promise to lend arms and ammunition for
the suppression of the "insurrection." But upon further consideration, Wool felt that he could do nothing without orders from
Washington, and said so, in writing, to the great disgust of the
"Law and Order" men, and of the Governor himself.[67] The
Governor accordingly dispatched to the President at Washington a request for help.

Meanwhile, however, Johnson was not idle at home. On June
3 he issued a proclamation declaring the county of San Francisco in a state of insurrection and directing "all persons subject to military duty within said county to report themselves
for duty immediately to Major-General William T. Sherman,"
to serve under the general's orders until disbanded. His proclamation also ordered the Vigilance Committee to disperse. A
writ of the state supreme court, commanding the committee to
give up the body of one of its prisoners, was at nearly the same
time evaded by the executive committee, who concealed for
the time their prisoner when the officer came with his writ. An
open collision with the state authorities seemed now imminent.
It was prevented only by the impotence of the state authorities.
Few men responded to the Governor's call, or appeared to obey
Sherman's orders, and after a few days Sherman himself met
the Governor once more at Benicia and reported his failure to
raise a force. At the same time a "conciliation committee" of
certain San Francisco citizens who were not members of the
committee came to meet the Governor at the same place, seeking to arrange some sort of truce between the hostile parties.
The Governor himself was now much under the influence of
Chief Justice Terry of the state supreme court, the most active

---

[67] For facts and opinions about the controversy on Wool's supposed promise, see Sherman, Vol. I, pp. 125, 126; and the correspondence between Wool and Johnson as published in the Sen.
Ex. Doc. 43, 3rd Sess. 43rd Congress. For Wool's interpretation of
his own rather unguarded words used in conversation with the Governor, see p. 7 of this correspondence; for Johnson's interpretation,
see ibid., p. 24.

of all the foes of the committee. This gentleman, later notorious as the slayer of Broderick, and already prominent as a representative of the ultra-Southern element in California political life, was outspoken in favor of open war against the rebels, whom, according to Sherman, he neatly described on this occasion as "damned pork-merchants," thereby not ineffectively indicating, after all, both the true character of this movement as a Business Man's Revolution and his own true character as a despiser of mere business men. The private interview of the officials after they had seen the "conciliation committee" was not fruitful of practical devices. General Sherman, despairing of success under the present conditions, resigned his commission, and returned to his daily business in San Francisco. The Governor thereafter appointed Volney E. Howard major-general in the place of Sherman, and the efforts to raise a militia force went on. To the very end, however, they were ineffective.

The committee, meanwhile, was not idle. It had for some time begun to prepare itself for a collision with the state authorities in case such should be forced upon it. In front of the rooms on Sacramento Street the members of the executive committee had caused to be made a strong barricade of sand-bags (the "Fort Gunnybags" of all the traditions since current concerning the affair). This they had armed with numerous cannon. Their small arms were kept within doors, their guard was always strong and vigilant, their new bell, now ready on top of the building, could summon at any moment their thousands of subordinate members. The meetings of this always small but energetic and authoritative executive committee were held within the rooms and in secret. The thousands of the members of the general committee had, of course, their natural influence upon the conduct of the executive committee; but they could not determine its action, and they were pledged to obey its orders.

The life of San Francisco during the following weeks of June and July was a very curious one. Ordinary business, indeed, went on much as usual, save in so far as its undertakings were a little delayed by the distrust of capitalists, or by the engrossing social duties that so many of its most active representatives now had to perform. The courts sat and enforced their processes as usual, save that they might not interfere with the committee itself. The respectable enemies of the committee went about openly, working and talking against it; but they were not able to accomplish anything. Those rogues who feared the committee had for the most part disappeared. Order prevailed in the city. But meanwhile the grim cannon of Fort Gunnybags, the ceaseless and secret activity of the executive committee within doors, the sensitiveness of the public to every hint of danger, and the occasional events or rumors of a startling sort showed the community how near they all the time were to terrible events. No wonder that the resolve constantly grew to prevent in future, by every honest means, the coming of another such crisis. If outward quiet was nearly always maintained, distrust of the future, doubt, and anxiety were always present.

Later in June the committee caught what Mr. Coleman, in his statement, calls its "white elephant": namely, Judge Terry himself. The courageous and violent supreme judge could not bear to see the law set at naught. He came to San Francisco to do what he could towards resisting the committee. On June 21 he did actually interfere with an attempted arrest that some of the committee "police" were making, and his interference led to a personal encounter between him and one of these police, Hopkins by name. In the scuffle Judge Terry drew a knife and stabbed Hopkins. The alarm-bell was forthwith sounded, the whole general committee was called out, and Judge Terry was arrested and taken to the fortress on Sacramento Street, amid tremendous popular excitement. Some arms that had still remained in the possession of "Law and Order" men were on this occasion seized, a large number of that party were arrested, and the day closed with the authority of the committee more undoubted than ever. Hopkins, meanwhile, lay seriously but, as the event proved, not fatally wounded.[68]

The arrest of Judge Terry furnished the committee a new reason for remaining in power some time longer. But it also

---

[68] See *Bulletin* of June 23.

put them in a very difficult position. If Hopkins should die, one could only with great difficulty avoid hanging Judge Terry, unless, indeed, one was willing to abdicate, and leave the mob to hang him itself. But to hang by popular judgment a supreme judge is an act involving certain obviously embarrassing responsibilities. And if, as later actually proved to be the case, Hopkins should not die, then a supreme judge whom one could not effectively banish nor yet imprison long, whom one must not hang, and whom one could not gracefully release without any punishment, would indeed be a "white elephant."

In the sequel the committee passed anxious weeks discussing the case, waiting for Hopkins to be out of danger, and reasoning with the undaunted prisoner, who was quite as certainly a good fighter as he was a bad supreme judge. It is probable that Judge Terry highly enjoyed his really very advantageous position. He refused to make any terms with the executive committee, which was finally forced to release him, without any other punishment than was involved in his disagreeable detention in Fort Gunnybags for the seven weeks of waiting for a verdict.[69] And thus the greatest danger of the committee's existence was happily passed.

The other acts of the committee, its only further executions, those of Brace and Hetherington, both murderers,[70] its curious

---

[69] "His release," says Mr. J. S. Hittell, p. 256, "was regarded by some persons as giving power to the most formidable enemy of the reform movement." The first bitter disappointment of the hotheaded friends of the committee is vented in the *Bulletin* for August 8, 1856, as soon as the release is announced. The blindness of these hotheaded friends was often something marvelous.

[70] Brace had committed a murder two years before. Hetherington killed one Dr. Randall in a quarrel, July 24. Both were publicly hanged July 29, after a fair trial before the executive committee. Only four lives were thus taken by this committee, all of known murderers. The only other punishment inflicted was banishment, imposed upon several notoriously bad characters and upon a few convicted ballot-box stuffers. And, as we see, the rest of the effective activity of the committee consisted only in making arrests, in detaining prisoners for examination, in investigating the topics that it

and hardly warranted interference in the investigation of the
city land questions, its successful avoidance of all open con-
tests with Federal authorities, and its final parade and retirement from activity on August 18 — these are things of which I
need not speak further in detail. The first real test of the success of the committee in its one true work, which was to agitate
for a reform in municipal society and politics, came at the
autumn elections, when the people sustained the whole movement by electing city officers to carry on in a legal way the reform that had been begun without the law. And thenceforth,
for years, San Francisco was one of the best-governed munici-
palities in the United States.

The reader will hardly ask, after all I have said, for any
lengthy final view of the rights and wrongs of this greatest of
the popular movements in California history. Under the circumstances, as we have seen, it was inevitable. What had made it
inevitable was a long-continued career of social apathy, of treasonable public carelessness. What it represented was not so
much the dignity of the sovereign people as the depth and bitterness of popular repentance for the past. What it accomplished was not the direct destruction of a criminal class, but the
conversion of honest men to a sensible and devout local patriotism. What it teaches to us now, both in California and elsewhere, is the sacredness of a true public spirit, and the great
law that the people who forget the divine order of things have
to learn thereof anew some day, in anxiety and in pain.

With the improvement of municipal business the moral and
intellectual progress of society did not altogether keep pace. If
one learned the importance of public spirit, one did not learn
for many years to devote enough time to the higher human interests. But at all events the essentials of civilization had been
fought for and gained; and the San Franciscan was thenceforth free to serve God as his own conscience dictated.

---

took under consideration, and in protecting itself against threatened
assaults.

Chapter VI

LAND-TITLES AND POLITICS

$\mathbf{I}$N treating of the period that followed the constitutional convention, I have thus far dealt mainly with the local occurrences of the golden days and have said little of the general problems of the state at large. The struggle for order, in the mines, in San Francisco, and in all the lesser commercial towns, rapidly developed the character of the new California population, and so produced everywhere alike that much enduring, often rash, always toilsome race of the pioneers, with their well-known overconfidence in short and easy social methods, with their not less noteworthy shrewdness in controlling their own social excesses, and with their remarkable power of organizing quickly for the purpose either of defending the established authorities, if these should meet their approval, or of setting the authorities aside, if these should seem to them dangerously inefficient. But if this character grew rapidly under the various local influences, the future of the state at large must be affected very greatly by the further conditions that determined not so much the character as the fortunes of the population of the whole country. Of these conditions the first was the state of the land tenure in all the most promising agricultural regions of the new state.

I. *Early Land Troubles*

$\mathbf{T}$HE UNCERTAINTY of the land-titles at the time of the conquest and during the interregnum we have already, in some fashion, studied. How significant all this must be for the future of the state is evident at a glance. The future California must needs be an agricultural province, whatever the gold excitement might for the time make the country seem. And that its land-titles should soon be settled, and in an honest way, was an essential of all true progress. How the people came to a consciousness of this fact, and how this consciousness entered into certain deeds of the struggle for order, I can only sketch in this connection. The wild schemes of the early interregnum had passed away with time, but the newcomers of the gold period were subject to somewhat similar illusions and dangers. If things had appeared as they did to the comparatively small group of Americans in the dawn of our life here, even before the gold-discovery, how long should this complex spider-web of land-titles, wherewith a California custom or caprice had covered a great part of the territory, outlast the trampling of the busy immigrants? Who should resist these strange men? The slowly moving processes of the court — how could they, in time, check the rapacity of American settlers, before the mischief should once for all be done, and the memory of these land-titles buried under an almost universal predatory disregard of them, which would make the recovery of the land by its legal owners too expensive an undertaking to be even thought of? The answer to this question suggests at once how, amid the injustice of our treatment of Californian landowners, our whole history has illustrated the enormous vitality of formally lawful ownership in land. This delicate web, which our strength could seemingly so easily have trampled out of existence at once, became soon an iron net. The more we struggled with it, the more we became involved in its meshes. Infinitely more have we suffered in trying to escape from it than we should have suffered had we never made a struggle. Infinitely more sorrow, not to speak of blood, has it cost us to try to get rid of our old obligations to the Californian landowners than it would have cost us to grant them all their original demands, just and unjust, at once. Doubt, insecurity, retarded progress, litigation without end, hatred, destruction of property, bloodshed — all these have resulted for us from the fact that we tried as much as we did to defraud these Californians of the rights that we guaranteed to them at the moment of the conquest. And in the end, with all our toil, we escaped not from the net, and it binds our land-seekers still.

At all events, however, the critical character of the situation of California landowners at the moment of the coming of the gold-seekers appears plain. That all the rights of the Californians should ultimately be respected was, indeed, in view of our rapacious Anglo-Saxon land-hunger, and of our national bigotry in dealing with Spanish Americans, impossible. But there were still two courses that our population might take with regard to the land. One would be the just-mentioned simple plan of a universal squatters' conspiracy. Had we agreed to disregard the land-titles by a sort of popular fiat, then, ere the courts could be appealed to and the method of settling the land-titles ordained by Congress, the disregard of the claims of the natives might have gone so far in many places as to render any general restitution too expensive a luxury to be profitable. This procedure would have been analogous to that fashion of dealing with Indian reservations which our honest settlers have frequently resorted to. Atrociously wicked as such a conspiracy would have been, we ourselves, as has been suggested above, should have been in the long run the greatest sufferers, because the conspiracy could not have been successful enough to preserve us from fearful confusion of titles, from litigation and warfare without end. Yet this course, as we shall see, was practically the course proposed by the Sacramento squatters of 1850, and for a time the balance hesitated between the choice of this and of the other course. The other course we actually adopted, and it was indeed the one peculiarly fitted to express just our natural meanness and love of good order in one. This was the plan of legal recognition and equally legal spoliation of the Californians — a plan for which, indeed, no one man was responsible, since the co-operation of the community at large was needed, and obtained, to make the Land Act of 1851 an instrument for evil and not for good. The devil's instrument it actually proved to be, by our friendly co-operation, and we have got our full share of the devil's wages for our use of it. But bad as this second course was, it was far better than the first, as in general the meanness and good order of an Anglo-Saxon community of money-seekers produce better results than the bolder rapacity and less legal brutality of certain other conquering and overbearing races.

In the winter of 1849 and in the spring of 1850 our rapacity first became noticeable under the new conditions. As it happened, the city of Sacramento grew up on land near Sutter's

Fort, and, of course, within the boundaries of Sutter's own grant of land, which he had received from Governor Alvarado in 1841. In the first months of the town's life numerous lots of land were sold under this title, and those who acquired the new property profited, of course, very greatly by the rapid growth of the place. But by the winter of 1849 there were enough landless, idle, and disappointed wanderers present in Sacramento to make the existence of landownership thereabouts appear to these persons as an intolerable burden, placed upon the necks of the poor by rapacious land speculators. Such reflections are, of course, the well-known expressions of human avarice and disappointment everywhere in the world. Here they assumed, however, a new and dangerous form. One asked: How comes it that there is any ownership of land in this golden country at all? Is this not a free land? Is it not our land? Is not the public domain free to all American citizens? The very simple answer was, of course, that this land was not public domain, but Sutter's former land, sold by him, in the free exercise of his rights, to the founders of Sacramento. And this answer was, moreover, especially significant in this particular case. For Sutter's ownership of "New Helvetia" was by this time a matter, so to speak, of world-wide notoriety. The young Captain Frémont's Report, which, in various shapes and editions, had years before become so popular a book and which the gold-fever made more popular than ever, had distinctly described Sutter as the notorious and indisputable owner of this tract of land in 1844. If occupancy without any rival for a term of years could make the matter clear to a newcomer, Sutter's title to his "establishment" seemed beyond shadow. Moreover, the title-papers of the Alvarado grant were on record. Governor Alvarado's authority to grant eleven leagues to Sutter was indubitable, and none the less clear seemed the wording of the grant, when it gave certain outer boundaries within which the tract granted was to be sought, and then defined the grant so as to include the "establishment at New Helvetia." Surely, one would say, no newcomer could attack Sutter's right, save by means of some purely agrarian contention. A settler might demand that all unused land in California should be free to every settler, and that Mexican landownership should be once for all done away with. But unless a man did this, what could he say against Sutter's title to New Helvetia?

The complaining idlers in Sacramento were, however, quite equal to the task of overthrowing this argument. What, after all, was a Mexican title worth beside the rights of an American citizen? This grant of Sutter's might indeed be a test case, but then so much the more must the test determine the worthlessness of all Mexican pretensions. The big Mexican grant was to this new party of agitators, who already delighted to call themselves "squatters," an obviously un-American institution, a creation of a benighted people. What was the good of the conquest if it did not make our enlightened American ideas paramount in the country? Unless, then, Congress, by some freak, should restore to these rapacious speculators, the heirs of a justly conquered and dispossessed race, their old benighted legal status, they would have no land. Meanwhile, of course, the settlers were to be as well off as the others. So their thoughts ran.

Intelligent men could hold this view only in case they had already deliberately determined that the new-coming population, as such, ought to have the chief legal rights in the country. This view was, after all, a very obvious one. Providence, you see, and manifest destiny were understood in those days to be on our side, and absolutely opposed to the base Mexican. Providence, again, is known to be opposed to every form of oppression; and grabbing eleven leagues of land is a great oppression. And so the worthlessness of Mexican land-titles is evident.

Of course the squatters would have disclaimed very generally so naked a statement as this of their position. But when we read in one squatter's card [1] that "surely Sutter's grant does not entitle to a monopoly of all the lands in California, which were purchased by the treasure of the whole nation, and by no small amount of the best blood that ever coursed or ran

---

[1] Published during a later stage of the controversy, in the *Sacramento Transcript* for June 21, 1850.

through American veins," the same writer's formal assurance that Sutter ought to have his eleven leagues whenever they can be found and duly surveyed cannot blind us to the true spirit of the argument. What has this "best blood" to do with the Sutter grant? The connection in the writer's mind is only too obvious. He means that the "best blood" won for us a right to harass great landowners. In another of these expressions of squatter opinion I have found the assertion that the land speculators stand on a supposed old Mexican legal right of such as themselves to take up the whole territory of California, in sections of eleven leagues each, by some sort of Mexican pre-emption. If a squatter persists in understanding the landowners' position in this way, his contempt for it is as natural as his willful determination to make game of all native Californian claims is obvious.

The squatter party, as it appeared in the winter of 1849 in Sacramento, was encouraged to develop its ideas by reason of the unsettled condition of the country. It was easy for men to feel that in this land, where no very definite government yet existed, where even the new state, before its admission, must seem of doubtfully legal character, every man might do what seemed right to himself and every new party might propose any view, however subversive of good government. A request for the old Californian order of things was not yet developed; a newcomer was often hardly conscious that there ever had been an old order. And when one heard about it from the men of the interregnum, one also heard the cruelly false tale, begotten of the era of our conquest, about the injustice, the treachery, and the wickedness of the old government and people. One felt, therefore, well justified in wishing a new and American order of things to replace every relic of Mexican wretchedness. And, just because such conquest as this of California was a new experience in our short national history, one was often wholly unmindful of the simple and obvious principles according to which the conqueror of a country does not, by virtue of his conquest, either dispossess private landowners, or deprive the inhabitants of any other of their private rights. One was, in fact, so accustomed to our atrocious fashion of conquering, dispossessing, and then exterminating Indian tribes that one was too much disposed, *a priori*, to think of our conquest of California as exemplifying the same cruel process.

The first scenes of the land agitation at Sacramento in the winter of 1849–50 have been but imperfectly described for us. Bayard Taylor mentions them briefly, and so does a later correspondent of the *New York Tribune*.[2] A recent article of my own on the topic[3] has, since its publication, called out some very interesting contemporary letters that a pioneer, now living in Oakland, California, has preserved, which bring the scenes of the early agitation well before us. I make one extract from them here. They were published in a late number of the *San Francisco Bulletin*:

"I will endeavor," says the writer of the letter, himself a newcomer in Sacramento, who is addressing an Eastern friend, "to give you some idea of life in Sacramento, by relating some events that occurred this evening: It is rather a dark one, and walking along the levee requires some care to avoid falling over the numerous obstructions, but it was a political meeting that I stumbled into as I passed up R Street. That you may understand the state of things, I will explain a little; the question of land-titles and squatter's rights is just now greatly agitating the public mind. In several instances where men have squatted upon land without the precincts of the city, others have pretended to own it and ordered them off, and in one case the city authorities, on a man's refusal to vamose, sent a force and pulled down his shanty.

"Last Saturday evening a meeting of squatters was held outdoors. I was not present, but hear that much opposition was expressed to the measures adopted by the city officers, some

---

[2] See the number of May 22, 1850.

[3] Published in the *Overland Monthly* for September 1885 and originally intended as a chapter of the present volume. The subject, however, quite outgrew the limits of this book, and while I have made one or two extracts from the article in my text here, I am obliged, for the most part, merely to refer the reader to this somewhat detailed study of the events that led up to the "squatter riot of 1850 in Sacramento."

of whom were present, and replied in no very courteous terms. The meeting this evening was intended as an opposition to the other, and styled 'Law and Order.' The speaker's stand was on some boxes piled up against the 'Gem,' a bowling, drinking, and gambling saloon. A board nailed against it, about even with the speakers' heads, supported a row of candles, which burned without a flicker, so still was the air. A large and democratic crowd were assembled. A committee was appointed to draw up resolutions, which were read. In the preamble the squatters were spoken of as having acted lawlessly and in contempt of the authorities. The substance of the resolutions was that the city council should be sustained at all events; that a committee should be appointed to proceed to Monterey and obtain a copy of J. A. Sutter's title to the land claimed by him, attested to by the governor of California.

"This land comprises most of the territory on which the city is built. They were read with much interruption, and on the question being put, indignantly rejected.

"At this juncture, another speaker arose, and commenced, but was interrupted with cries of 'Your name?' 'My name is Zabriskie,' he replied. In a respectful manner he avowed his determination to speak his sentiments, and beginning with the hand-bills which had been printed, calling a meeting to sustain 'law and order' in the community, he considered it an insult to the people to suppose that any were otherwise inclined. Then, in regard to the preamble, which spoke contemptuously of 'squatters,' in an eloquent speech he asked who carried the 'Stars and Stripes,' the institutions and laws of our land into the far West, and have now borne them even to the shores of the far-off Pacific? Then arose from the crowd the reply, '*Squatters.*'

"He then moved that this preamble be rejected, and the motion was carried without a dissenting voice. So he went on with each resolution, speechifying and moving that some be rejected, some adopted, and some amended, most of his motions being carried unanimously, making altogether a different set of resolutions than the projectors had calculated upon. He went strongly for sustaining the authorities in carrying out such just laws as they should enact. On the resolution which so read, he experienced much opposition, the sovereign people being extremely jealous that laws should be made, which, however just in the eyes of their makers, would be otherwise in *their* view. He contended that a man might squat where he pleased, and leave for nobody who could not show a better title than himself; that when a judiciary was appointed over the State was the time to decide the validity of titles, until which time, society would be benefited, the squatter would be benefited, the land, and consequently, the owner, whoever he was, would be benefited by its being brought under cultivation."

After the river flood of January 1850 had passed over the town of Sacramento, the quarrel was temporarily suspended, especially by the prosperous opening of the spring of 1850, which sent many of the malcontents early to the mines. But persistent spring floods forced many of these to return afresh to the now once more prosperous city. The discontent broke out again, and the title-papers of Sutter's grant, when once found and published, were soon made the subject of very bitter and unfair quibbles and quasi-legal objections. By the beginning of summer the squatter movement had become formidable in Sacramento and in the adjacent country. Its followers had organized an association, had begun a regular system of squatting on all vacant lots in and near the town, and were already planning every even remotely feasible sort of resistance to the real owners who held under the Sutter title. As Congress had still done nothing to settle titles in California, and as the state had not yet been admitted, the squatters had the affrontery to pretend in their public utterances that there was no legal support actually in existence for the California grants. They declared that even the legislature, which had already once met, had had no business to pass laws bearing on the subject of land. Still less, they said, had the so-called city of Sacramento, in its corporate capacity, any right to interfere with squatters. And as for the processes of state courts, if worst came to worst, these must be defied. Breathing out such threatenings, the squatters met frequently during the summer, in a more or less public fashion. They excited the attention of many in other parts of the state, and the alarm of all wiser men who appreciated their purposes. They were ably led. Among others, Dr. Charles Robinson, of Fitchburg, Massachusetts, later so prominent as Governor of Kansas, was especially noteworthy as a squatter leader. His conscientious motives in supporting the squatter doctrine, his sagacity in conducting the movement, and his personal courage in forcing it to an issue are all obvious. Obvious also is his wicked and dangerous use in this connection of the then current abstractions about the absolute rights of man and the higher will of God, together with his diabolical activity in resisting the true will of God, which was of course at that time and place simply the good order of California. Every moral force, every force, namely, that worked for the real future prosperity of the new commonwealth, was *ipso facto* against these lawless squatters. The "land speculators," whom they directly attacked, were indeed as greedy for gold as anybody in California and were as such no more worthy of esteem than their even Christians. But these speculators chanced, in just that case, to represent both the old Californian order of things, which we were bound in sacred honor to respect, and the majesty of the newborn state as well, to which every citizen owed the most devout allegiance so long as he should dwell within its borders. To these two great obligations the squatters were traitors, and their movement was unfortunately the father of much more treason, which showed the same turpitude, if not the same frankness.

But, for the time, they were unable to do more than to bring about a riot and a consequent reaction of popular feeling against themselves — a reaction which ended the possibility of any general predatory conspiracy throughout the state against the old land-titles, and which therefore introduced the squatter movement to the second stage of its sinful life, so that it became thenceforth no longer an open public enemy, but a treacherous corrupter of legislation and a persistent pettifogger in the courts of justice. The cause of the riot was this: in August 1850 the squatters were deeply disappointed at an adverse decision in a suit of some importance brought against one of their number. Angry and defiant, they were disposed to take the advice of Dr. Robinson and to appear in force and armed in the streets of Sacramento and to resist by violence and forthwith all court processes served upon any of them. A stormy Saturday-night mass meeting was devoted to threats of this sort. Only about forty, however, were finally bold enough to follow Dr. Robinson to battle on August 14. The landowners, encouraged by the vigorous orders of the mayor, improvised a posse on the streets, at the sight of the armed rioters; and a collision took place in the effort to disperse the squatter party. Shots were exchanged, three men were killed, one of them a squatter leader and one the city assessor, and five persons (including Dr. Robinson) were wounded. The city was thrown into the wildest excitement, popular indignation was aroused to a white heat, and no squatter was for the time safe within the limits of the town; for the large neutral floating population, no less than the people dependent for their business life upon the regular landowners, were now alike determined to put an end to the disturbance. News of the affair traveled quickly through the state; militia hastened to Sacramento from San Francisco, an exaggerated alarm spread through the country for a few days, and the agitation of the summer of 1850 was for the time quickly put down.[4]

The public dread of the squatters, also, of course died away as quickly, and with it much of the momentary popular indignation. Nobody had time in California to reflect on the true significance of such movements, and although the riot had once for all made open and widespread violence an impossible device, there was still a chance for the squatters, in the second stage of their movement, to form a so-called Settlers' Party and to agitate in a less violent way for state or national legislation in their favor. At Sacramento they remained, by dint of liti-

---

[4] In the article above referred to, the fatal encounter of the day after the riot, an encounter in which the sheriff of the county was killed, together with two or three of the opposing party, is also described; and the scenes of the crisis are in general recounted in a detailed manner not here possible. Dr. Robinson himself recovered from his wounds, escaped any effective prosecution, was elected to the legislature of 1851, and left the state in the following summer.

gious persistence and of political agitation, a serious practical vexation for many years, until the Sutter title was finally confirmed, the grant surveyed, and a government patent given for the land.

II. *The Native Population, and the Later Struggle for the Land*

From direct and general assault by violence the Mexican grants as a body were thus erelong safe, however numerous might be the affrays that from time to time would take place over one or another of them. But many were the troubles through which they were yet to pass, and we in California ourselves with them.

Three roughly defined classes may be named into which the land claims of the Californians might be distinguished. There were, first, the claims that were obviously and notoriously valid. Such were the claims of individuals or of families who had for many years lived on their estates, in undisputed ownership, their titles being also recorded in the archives. Against such claims no merely technical objections ought to have received a moment's hearing. The sole problem in such cases, in itself often difficult enough indeed, was to distinguish by a just survey the boundaries of these claims from the surrounding public lands. For in the old days it had been customary to grant land in parcels of eleven leagues or less, but without any exact definition of the boundaries. Outside boundaries were named, within which the tract granted was to be found; and questions might often arise concerning the proper position of the grant within these boundaries. Only in such cases as Sutter's, where an "establishment," or an existent dwelling, was mentioned in the grant as already existent and as included in the tract granted, could the situation of the grant, at least in part, be forthwith determined. In other cases the problems of the survey might have all degrees of vagueness. Still, concerning the actual right of the grantee to the amount of land described in his grant and, under any survey, to that portion of his claim which immediately surrounded and included both his own dwelling and the lands that he had long and without question occupied under his grant; concerning all this right there could be no shadow of doubt. Such rights should have been simply and promptly confirmed.

A second class of cases involved problems of more or less obscurity. The more recent grants, even when held in good faith, might be subject to very proper question. Conflicting grants might also be found to exist and might need careful examination before settlement. The nature of certain pretensions might be very doubtful, and the highest legal authority might have to study them with great care. Such, for example, were the cases of the Mission property, where the question whether the church had properly either any complete title or any equitable right in the extensive old Mission estates was one that could not be settled at a glance.[5] And such a problem as whether San Francisco was or was not a pueblo, and so entitled to its four square leagues of land, demanded the most elaborate and scholarly study; and the highest authorities long differed concerning it. For the examination of such matters as these a competent tribunal was indeed needed and should have been provided without delay.

The third class of claims were the simply fraudulent ones, and these proved in the end unfortunately too numerous. The worst possible way of dealing with them was, of course, to delay examining them. Any time wasted in wrangling over predatory objections offered to the undoubtedly genuine and traditionally recognized rights of the older landowners was so much time and inducement given to the rascals to invent either false new claims or false evidence for these claims. Novel and suspicious claims, such as that of Limantour to a great part of the city of San Francisco, a claim not heard of before 1851, should have been, as soon as presented, among the first subjects of rigid judicial investigation. And the appointed tribunals should therefore have been free to devote time to these, instead of be-

---

[5] An impression remained in fact long prevalent that the church was at least in equity the owner of the Mission estates, and certain writers have been at great pains to keep this erroneous impression before the public mind.

ing long detained over an examination of every possible quasi-legal objection that could be offered to the well-known and well-established claims of the older landowners.

These principles were perfectly obvious, and there can be no doubt of at least one often mentioned device by which the true ends of justice could have been furthered. The Californian archives were, save for a few inevitable losses, in our possession. Mr. William Carey Jones, as United States commissioner, in 1849, for the examination of the land question in California, spent much time in preparing his lengthy and able report upon the land claims, as shown by these archives. It would, therefore, have been the natural and just course on the part of Congress to confirm, by a simple act, all those recorded and undisputed land grants whose owners had been in actual and quiet possession for a term of from five to ten years before the conquest. This act could have been executed by commissioners, as the first step towards the judicial settlement of the land problem in California. Then either the same commissioners or other tribunals could have been appointed to consider the settlement of the doubtful matters as a second step towards the final goal.

So obvious was this method that from 1850 to the present day there have not been wanting those who have praised it as the sole proper device. Such at first advised it; and later they with many others lamented that it had not been chosen. But we were too selfish to be wise. What we did was far less just, and also far less clever.

The Land Act of 1851 was the work of Senator Gwin, the same who had led captive the poor native Californians in the constitutional convention. Gwin protested, against Senator Benton and others who, on the floor of the Senate at Washington, very justly and wisely opposed his scheme, that he desired nothing so much as to be fair to the Californians. In fact, his bill, as presented at the session of 1851, was not in appearance so black as at heart it was. Commissioners were to be appointed to examine all California land claims. These claims were, within a stated period, to be presented before the board by the claimants, the grantee appearing for those who held under his grant, and a Californian pueblo appearing for its citizens. Claims not presented within the stated period were to be no longer regarded, but the lands in question were then to be considered as having been reincorporated in the public domain. All claimants must appear before the board as suitors against the United States, which, as represented by its attorneys, was formally to resist their claims in every case. The board's decision, however, was not to be regarded as final. On behalf of either party appeal would lie, from this decision, to the United States district court, and thence to the United States Supreme Court itself. And if the United States attorneys should see fit, they might thus force the claimant, even in the clearest possible case, to fight for his own long universally recognized property in three successive courts, at an enormous expense. For, as is seen, all claims were to be treated alike. All, whether actually disputed by private individuals or not, were to be regarded as called in question by the United States, which, of course, would sue to have them restored to the public domain. In this shape, substantially, the act was passed.

The true spirit of the act was made plain at the next session of Congress, when Gwin introduced his infamous supplementary land bill, which failed to pass. The act of 1851 had been a device for delaying the just recognition of all land claims in California and for putting all honest Californian landowners in the position of presumably fraudulent claimants, whose right to their own was to be considered as doubtful until proved by positive evidence, in possibly as many as three courts. The supplementary bill, if it had passed, was meant to encourage whoever had no rights in the land to steal from those who had rights, so long as these rights were thus unjustly held in abeyance under the act of 1851. If, said the bill, anyone "in good faith" had settled on land "believing it to be public land," and if, later, this land was found to be within the limits of a confirmed Mexican grant, then the well-meaning squatter in question should be permitted – to retain his stolen tract of one hundred and sixty acres, while the Californian landowner was to be "compensated" by receiving a "floating title" to an equivalent number of acres, which he might choose where he could, from the public lands in the state. When we remember that the principal American objection to the Mexican grants was that they took up so much of the "finest agricultural lands of the State," the significance of the supplementary bill becomes plain. One ought to add that Senator Gwin never grew ashamed of this abortive attempt at predatory legislation, and mentions it with a certain pride in that manuscript statement of his career which he prepared for the use of Mr. Bancroft's library. Some of the California newspapers very vigorously condemned the unhappy bill at the time when it was first presented,[6] and it was undoubtedly too advanced for the current public opinion of the state, however much it might fall short of the original purposes of the squatters.

Into the complex and difficult history of the greater California land cases there is here no space to enter. The Land Act of 1851 made everything for a while doubtful. Case after case was appealed to the district and then to the supreme courts; numerous and very able lawyers were employed for many years, and the estates of the Californians were, for these years, in jeopardy. The effects may readily be imagined. The poor Californians, no business men to begin with, were thus forced into the most wearisome sort of business. They must, as it were, gamble for their own property, under the rules of an alien game, which they found largely unintelligible. Their property was meanwhile rendered hard to sell, and taxation fell upon them more heavily than upon the wandering and irresponsible mining population. Their lawyers they could pay only with the land itself. With squatters they had continually to wrangle. The government had put them before the country in the position of presumably fraudulent claimants; and they must therefore meet with an only too general suspicion that the best of them were actually such. Their position was demoralizing and disheartening. The southern part of the state, where the most and the wealthiest of them lived, was, from Monterey downward, sadly neglected by early state legislation. For years it reaped little advantage from the gold-discovery, and much injury from

---

[6] See *San Francisco Herald* of May 29, 1852 for a letter on this topic — a letter that the editor fully approves.

the presence of the gold-seekers in the north. Its natural and, from its own point of view, justifiable efforts to escape from its unhappy position by means of a division of the state were easily defeated by the healthy and yet merciless determination of the bulk of the Americans of the north to permit no chance for slavery to gain a foothold on the coast. This determination forbade any successful effort to free the southern half of the state from the control of the existing constitution.[7] Not long before the outbreak of the Civil War, further efforts were making towards the same end, but this time with a more pronounced political purpose. Yet, both first and last, all these efforts were doomed to fail, and for the poor natives, whom the general government thus so shamefully harassed, there was no deliverance from the neglect and taxation of the financially ill-managed state government. It is not to be wondered at that, under these circumstances, the Californians — who had never been exactly moral heroes — rapidly tended towards the utter degradation in which we had always meanly declared them to have been placed by nature.

But as for us, who thus sought to despoil by legal means those

---

[7] The division of the state was a subject of agitation in the south, among the native Californians and others, during 1851, and often later. There can be no doubt that the native Californians concerned in the matter desired in good faith to be relieved from the unequal and serious burdens of the existing state government, and little doubt, also, that Southern politicians expected advantages to the cause of slavery from such a division, and therefore labored for it. See in the *Alta* (steamer edition), September 15, 1851, the call from citizens of San Diego for a convention to consider the division of the state; and on October 1, 1851 a further call from citizens of Los Angeles County, together with the report of a state division meeting at Los Angeles, and an *Alta* editorial, expressing very calmly the first natural northern sentiment on the matter. See, further, *Alta* (steamer edition) for October 15, containing further editorial and news, both bearing on the topic; and November 1, containing a full report of the convention at Santa Barbara in favor of division. The movement, as here represented, proved to be seriously disunited, and hence was ineffective. The *Alta*, while never growing violent in condemnation, still, of course, disapproved.

whom we were too orderly to rob on any grand scale by violence, we could not altogether escape from the demoralization that we tried to inflict. "Woe unto thee, O land," it might very truly be said, "when thy landholders are a dangerous class." But just such a class were for years, in some counties, our own lesser landholders of American stock, and all because the claims that they had usurped were of uncertain legal validity, their undertakings consequently of doubtful profit, their business, as landholders, resisting the Mexican grants a sort of gambling, while their views of law, of duty, and of life were darkened by a dim consciousness of their own injustice and by a strong consciousness of their own insecurity. While our state courts, with a noble severity, thanks to the general learning and good character of our lawyers, usually undertook rigidly to guard the vested rights of the Californian landowners during the long years that must elapse before the general government could be ready to confirm the doubtful grants, and while these courts were nearly always ready to eject naked trespassers, to give the unconfirmed but *prima facie* valid Mexican claim the benefit of the doubt, and to interpret liberally the terms of the often rudely expressed grants, still it could not always be profitable or even possible for a Californian landowner, or for his legal successors, to resist all squatters. Sometimes, as in the notorious and infamous case of the first foundation of the now so fine and progressive city of Oakland, a great tract of land would be lost to its owners by the deeds of some crowd of deliberate and unprincipled trespassers,[8] who would not even undertake to justify themselves by any such theory of predatory morality as had been preached in the gospel of the Sacramento squatters. Oftener, when smaller parcels had been seized here or there by squatters, the native land-claimant, or those who held under him, found it possible and convenient, perhaps after years of bickering and litigation, to compromise with the settler for a small sum and so to give him a clear title. But during all these intervening years how unhappy

[8] See the *Centennial History of Alameda County*, chapter xxix, for an account of this affair.

the position of the squatter himself! He was raising his crops on land that he professed to regard as a portion of the public domain, to be acquired by him through pre-emption. In fact, however, he was using a large part of his income in resisting the various suits brought against him by the claimant under the old grant. His pretended "quarter-section" of public land was hardly a salable possession. A fellow settler who might have chosen to buy a title to some other bit of land from the original claimant might be his next neighbor and might even some day buy the Mexican title to his own tract. Then would arise bitterness of the worst sort, not now between American and Californian, but between the American fellow settlers. Quarrels that would soon lead to threats and that might at any moment lead to assaults, and so to murder, were such a settler's daily bread for year after year. Until the Supreme Court at Washington should reach the case and decide it — nay, until the official survey of the tract, if the grant was confirmed to the Californian claimant, should be completed and again approved (perchance once more, after further appeals on the survey to the Supreme Court) — until all this should be ended, there was often no relief to the quarrelsome life of the persistent squatter, unless indeed his neighbor's shotgun should some day cut short his litigious misery. And this was the life of thousands of petty landholders in California during the years when land litigation was most serious. No wonder that, under such circumstances, two great evils were brought upon the state, whose effects we have not yet had quite time to outgrow: the one a negative evil, the long and lamentable obstruction of the material prosperity of the state by the discouragement of agricultural enterprise; the other a positive evil, the moral mischief done to the country by the encouragement offered to thriftless and disorderly squatters and by the exclusion of a great number of the best sort of farmers' families, who left the state early, or never came to it at all, because of the uncertainty of land-titles and because of their fear of the quarrels and disorders of this long transition period.

If one adds to this picture that of those numerous degraded

Spanish or half-breed outlaws, the creatures of our own injustice, the sons sometimes or the former servants of the great
landowners whom we had robbed, if one remembers how they
infested country roads, harassed lonely farms, assaulted the
mail-coaches, and plundered the miners through all these
weary years, one sees at length in full how our injustice
avenged itself upon us and by what misery we paid for having deliberately set at naught fundamental conditions of social existence. From the first moment of the conquest until the
end of these early days we showed how we were come to this
land to get ourselves our own private enjoyments; but we also
showed how we thereby did get for ourselves nothing so much
as public calamities. To this continual petty disorder there was
indeed at last a relief. The greater claims being decided, the
more serious quarrels ended, the state was at length free, in
the years since 1870, to develop far more rapidly her material
and moral resources, to attract a large new population, and
to cultivate the arts of civilization. Yet even today one hears
occasionally of the old sort of land quarrel, with its brutal
and sometimes bloody consequences. And meanwhile, if one
complains of the unfortunate concentration of the land in a
comparatively few hands, of the lack of small proprietors in
certain parts of the state, and of the evils attendant upon such
a state of things, one has to remember that these evils also are
in great part a result of the policy that, instead of encouraging the old Californians to sell their grants in small tracts to
newcomers, forced them at length to part with their lands in
vast tracts to their lawyers or to scheming speculators, so that
these profited by the misfortunes of the Californians, to the
lasting injury of the whole state. — "You will not fail," Buchanan had said in the secret dispatch to Larkin, "prudently
to warn the government and people of California," and "to
arouse in their bosoms that love of liberty and independence
so natural to the American continent." "If the people should
desire to unite their destinies with ours, they would be received as brethren," Buchanan had added, thus assuring the
Californians of "the cordial sympathy and friendship of the
president." Such were our sacred promises to these people in

1845, promises none the less sacred because they were part of an intrigue. And such is the wretched tale of how we kept faith with our victims.

III. *Early Political Conflicts*

WE must now glance, in conclusion, at the causes determining the purely partisan political life in California during the period with which we deal.

The somewhat diminished enthusiasm of the Americans in California for their own national government, which had, from the outset, neglected them, was still equal to the task of taking sides, with some bitterness, in the great national political questions. The skill of Southern politicians present in California, and the irresistible course of events in the political world at that moment, at once gave the Democratic Party the upper hand in the state and favored, on the whole, the Southern wing of that party. Very evil seems, from one point of view, this partisan influence in state politics. For the early political life of this region, upon whose destiny the great national questions themselves could for the moment have little immediate influence, was thus directed by party men, whose actual objects must of course be, under such circumstances, little save office and patronage. In largely academic discussions of national questions that, vastly significant in themselves, were here, for some years, used chiefly as pretenses, and in quarrels and bargains concerning the distribution of offices, time was, therefore, spent that ought to have been devoted to the inner political growth of the new state. The "great heroes" of those days generally quarreled over purely personal ambitions and grew great because they were skillful in managing corrupt political organizations. But all this evil had another side. When the American lets the corrupt party managers rule him, he does so with an immoral but still often clever submissiveness, because party wrangles not only are in themselves amusing, but also are an excellent preventive of any elaborately dangerous and revolutionary legislation. Early California was full of social problems. It is characteristic of the people that in deal-

ing with these problems their legislators were generally forced
to restrict themselves to very conservative enactments. The
politicians might, indeed, squander public money, or sell offices
for votes; but, in general, they might not try, nor even propose,
any revolutionary social schemes. This conservatism used as its
instrument, very frequently, the corrupt party organizations
themselves.

The later history of the squatter agitation is in point as illustrating this tendency. The Settlers' Party failed from the outset to accomplish anywhere nearly as much as it desired in the
way of getting various state laws passed for harassing or for
indirectly despoiling, by any plausible device, the Californian
landowners during the pendency of the great land litigation.
For this party had again and again to submit itself to the despotism of the greater party organizations. The main object of
the Democratic or other leaders was to get a senatorship, or
to control patronage, or to do some like thing. To this end,
one took sides in national politics; one abused, for instance, all
supposed abolitionists; one talked of Jeffersonian principles;
one appeared as the champion of the people; or, above all,
one manipulated party conventions. These activities led towards one's goal. Not so, however, could one succeed if one
offended everybody else to please the squatters. Yet, to satisfy
the Settlers' Party, one would have had to do this. This party, indeed, formed an influential faction in state politics for years
and toiled to get various sorts of statutes passed for harassing
the Californian grant-holders. The schemes proposed were
often ingenious, and tried to avoid obvious constitutional objections. Once, in 1856, the squatters did succeed in getting
passed a very dangerous statute, which was ultimately declared unconstitutional. But they failed, in the end, to get a
constitutionally valid and legally effective statute into the state
lawbooks to carry out any of their direct or indirect designs.
Since we as a body hated the Californian land-claimants so
bitterly, our general although not perfect forbearance in the
matter of our legal enactments concerning them must be attributed partly to our instinctive good sense, and partly to the

strictness of that aforementioned corrupt party discipline itself, which, by demanding the submission of all individual interests to the ends of the party, kept in the background people who, like the squatters, were disposed to assert their
independence and to disorganize the political parties for their
own purposes.

In the first legislature, which was held at San Jose, much
important business was done under great physical difficulties
and with the disadvantage of the presence of too many careless and disorderly members in the body. By the end of 1850
the political parties were in a fair way to be organized, and
the legislature of 1851 was largely spent in a struggle over the
election of the United States Senator to replace Colonel Frémont, whose "short term" was soon to expire. The election,
after many ballotings, had to be postponed for a year; and
during 1851 the Democratic Party first clearly showed its supremacy in the state and elected Mr. John Bigler to the state
governorship. This official served two terms — a popular and
unprincipled politician, whose influence was in no wise for
good.[9] In 1852 the United States Senator was elected, Colonel
John B. Weller getting the position. But at this point began in
earnest the struggle between the two heroes of early California politics: Broderick, who fully intended to get the rank
of senator when the next vacancy should occur, and Gwin,
who had been one of the first pair of senators elected, and who
now confidently looked forward to re-election in 1855. The
remarkably dramatic struggle of several subsequent years, between the Southerner and the Irishman,[10] we are not concerned to follow in this book, the more so as its most important scenes lie outside our chosen period. The reader may be

---

[9] It was during Bigler's administration that the first agitation
against the Chinese in California took place, although the question
at that time had a very different appearance from the one that it has
since assumed.

[10] David Broderick, although born in America, was the son of an
Irish stone-cutter and grew up amid Irish surroundings. He learned
the political art in New York, under Tammany influences.

referred, if he will, to the able, interesting, and not unamusing
book of Mr. James O'Meara,[11] where the whole story is told
with a worshipful admiration of the heroic deeds that took
place during the warfare. A characteristic event in the struggle
was the effort of Broderick to get the legislature, in 1854, to
elect him to the senatorship one year in advance of the regular
time. A bill to authorize such an election was introduced in
Broderick's interest, the idea being that, as Broderick had a
majority in the joint vote of the two houses of this legislature,
no opportunity ought to be given to his fellow Democrats to
destroy this majority before the next legislature should meet.
The bill was defeated only after a long struggle, in which brib-
ery, liquor, threatened violence, and even actually attempted
violence were not lacking on both sides. Before the next legislature met, Broderick was in a very small minority in his own
party; but the crisis of the Kansas controversies enabled him
erelong to come to the front in politics as an opponent of the
ultra-Southern wing of his party and as a champion of freedom. He alone could cope with the influence of Gwin, whom
he outdid in the management of primary elections and of conventions, as Gwin, in turn, had the advantage of him in political experience, in social position, in oratorical skill, and, for
some years, in the actual possession of power. But Broderick
was the better loved by his friends. He was generous and
warmhearted, he hated the Southern aristocracy, he represented
the pride of the born freeman and of the laborer's son; and although political and other principles never meant much to him
in comparison with personal success, and although he, like
most of his opponents, looked upon the state as an oyster, to
be opened as one might, he nevertheless managed, in the sequel, to seem a sort of leader in the struggle against the extension of slavery, and so as a representative of the good cause
on the Pacific coast. With his later career, with his election to
the Senate in 1857, with his disgraceful bargains over the second senatorship on that occasion, with his brief career at
Washington, and with the tragedy that first full made him a

---

[11] *Broderick and Gwin* (San Francisco, 1881).

popular hero in 1859, when he was killed by Judge Terry in a duel, the limits of my task forbid me to deal. Broderick's name has ever since been, for many, a name to conjure with, although one asks in vain what legislative work of importance he can be said to have accomplished. Legislative work, however, is the last thing that one may demand of a man of Broderick's position and popular reputation.

An episode in this struggle and in the political history of the state was the brief and quite fruitless success of the Know-Nothing Party in 1855. Many had looked to this party for the salvation of the state from corrupt influences. Its actual success, however, resulted from its alliance at this election with the ultra-Southern Democrats, whose only desire, at the moment, was to defeat Broderick. A victory so won meant nothing, and led to nothing, save the choice of an incompetent Governor — Neely Johnson — and a new disappointment for many of the better citizens of California. The Know-Nothing movement hereupon quickly came to an end, and the Democrats assumed once more their natural position at the head of affairs, which they kept until the outbreak of the war. On the whole, the early years of California state politics furnish a decidedly unsatisfactory picture so long as one looks at the positive results. Some very good legislation was, indeed, accomplished for San Francisco interests, but it was marred by some decidedly bad work relating to the same city. Some serious mistakes, such as the first foreign miners' tax, were promptly corrected, and some problems of the new social order were well dealt with; but as to the whole, rather on the negative side, rather in the dangers avoided than in the positive legislative work done, must the value of the early political activity be placed. The conflicting interests present in the young state urged often to very hasty legislative action, and, despite political corruption — yes, often because of such corruption — such hasty and dangerous action was again and again avoided.

The lesson of the legislative work of these early years is one very common in American history. As we find everywhere in our land, the danger of popular sovereignty, at least in times of peace, is not so much its hastiness as its slothfulness, its corrupt love of ease, its delight in old and now meaningless phrases, and in the men who use these phrases. Such men do not destroy the existing social order, but while preserving it from sudden injury, they fatten themselves upon the slow decay that goes on in its less vigorous parts. The people do not permit these parasites to do much positive mischief; and the party organizations are, on the whole, conservative forces. But what the people permit the party managers to do is to stand in the way of true and healthy progress, and to cause public needs to grow dangerously great before the selfish political squabbles can be subordinated to the satisfaction of these needs. In a very new part of the country, however, where the social order is a tender plant and is capable of a rapid and healthy growth of its own, while it is very easily endangered by any injurious external assaults, this tendency of ours to tolerate political corruption rather than political officiousness is certainly far more prudent than the reverse tendency would be. While we condemn the immorality of such toleration of corrupt men, let us then not forget the relatively good effects of this very tolerance in many new lands, and in California in particular. A people with less political skill than our own would have suffered far more from earnest but visionary schemers than we in California suffered from the whole crew of selfish politicians. While we submitted to these latter we still actually used their own partisan phrases and their personal ambitions as the instruments for impeding the course of dangerous legislation, and so we saved ourselves, sometimes, not indeed from the just penalties of our political sin, but from the consequences of sins that we were happily able to avoid committing.

One word here in anticipation of later events. During the Civil War, California, which really could not have been led out of the Union by the most skillful party of managers, still, having seemed at the outset a trifle in danger, gained by the consent of the government an exemption from the direct burden of the war, for which it probably well repaid by the assistance that its treasure gave to the government during the long financial difficulties. Many of its citizens did indeed take personal part on one side or the other. But they left the state to do so, and at home all remained tranquil. The prevailing sentiment of the state was unmistakably loyal. The close of the war found the new land rapidly and steadily progressing. The coming of the great railroad introduced, a few years later, a new life, with fresh responsibilities and trials, so that thenceforth the golden California of the early days fades farther and farther into the background, and a great agricultural and horticultural country today works, in its way, upon the problems of its social life, while it is still under the influence of the traditions of that golden past.

IV. *Conclusion*

THE RACE that has since grown up in California as the outcome of these early struggles is characterized by very marked qualities of strength and weakness, some of which, perchance, even a native Californian like myself, who neither can nor would outgrow his healthy local traits, may still be able to note and confess. A general sense of social irresponsibility is, even today, the average Californian's easiest failing. Like his father, he is probably a born wanderer, who will feel as restless in his farm life, or in his own town, as his father felt in his. He will have little or no sense of social or of material barriers, he will perchance hunt for himself a new home somewhere else in the world, or in the old home will long for some speculative business that promises easy wealth, or again, on the other hand, he will undertake some great material labor that attracts him by its imposing difficulty. His training at home gives him a curious union of provincial prejudice with a varied, if not very exact, knowledge of the sorts of things that there are in the world. For his surroundings from infancy have been in one sense of a cosmopolitan character, while much of his training has been rigidly or even narrowly American. He is apt to lack a little, moreover, complete devotion to the life within the household, because, as people so often have pointed out, the fireside, an essential institution of our English race, is of such small significance in the climate of California. In short, the

Californian has too often come to love mere fullness of life and
to lack reverence for the relations of life.

And yet, as we have seen, the whole lesson of his early history, rightly read, is a lesson in reverence for the relations
of life. It was by despising or at least by forgetting them that
the early community entered into the valley of the shadow of
death; and there was salvation for the community in those days
only by virtue of its final and hard-learned submission to what
it had despised and forgotten. This lesson, I confess, has come
home to me personally, as I have studied this early history,
with a quite unexpected force. I had always thought of the old
days as times of fine and rough labors, amusements, and crimes,
but not as a very rational historical process. I have learned, as
I have toiled for a while over the sources, to see in these days
a process of divinely moral significance. And as a Californian
I am glad to be able to suggest what I have found, plain and
simple as it is, to any fellow Californian who may perchance
note in himself the faults of which I make confession. Here in
the early history are these faults, writ large, with their penalties, and the only possible salvation from them.

After all, however, our lesson is an old and simple one. It is
the State, the Social Order, that is divine. We are all but dust,
save as this social order gives us life. When we think it our
instrument, our plaything, and make our private fortunes the
one object, then this social order rapidly becomes vile to us;
we call it sordid, degraded, corrupt, unspiritual, and ask how
we may escape from it forever. But if we turn again and serve
the social order, and not merely ourselves, we soon find that
what we are serving is simply our own highest spiritual destiny
in bodily form. It is never truly sordid or corrupt or unspiritual; it is only we that are so when we neglect our duty.

Index

i

A NOTE ON THE TYPE

The text of this book is set in Caledonia, a Linotype face designed by W. A. Dwiggins. Caledonia belongs to the family of printing types called "modern face" by printers — a term used to mark the change in style of type-letters that occurred about 1800. Caledonia borders on the general design of Scotch Modern, but is more freely drawn than that letter.

Mr. Dwiggins planned the typographic scheme and designed the binding. The book was composed, printed, and bound by The Plimpton Press, Norwood, Massachusetts.